House of God...Gateway to Heaven

A Centennial History of the
Greek Orthodox Cathedral of the Annunciation

To Tina and Marty,
with best wishes,

Nicholas M. Prevas
November 3, 2013

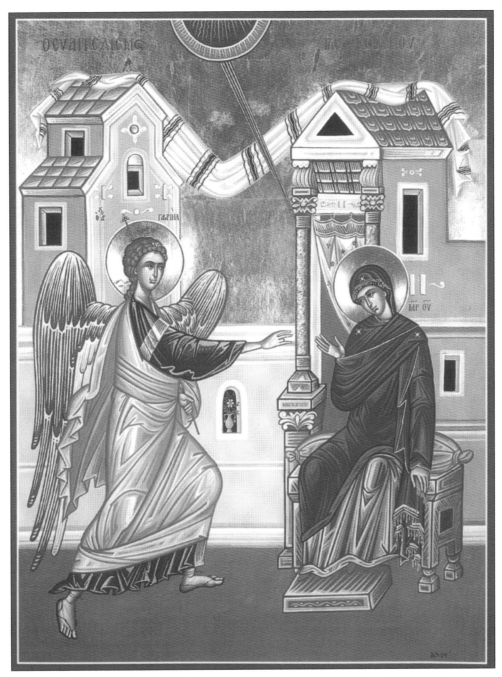

Archangel Gabriel announcing the imminent birth of the Christ Child to the Virgin Mary.

Apolytikion (Hymn) of the Annunciation

Σήμερον της Σωτηρίας ημών το Κεφάλαιον

Σήμερον της σωτηρίας ημών το κεφάλαιον, και του απ᾽αιώνος Μυστηρίου η φανέρωσις. Ο Υιός του Θεού, Υιός της Παρθένου γίνεται, και Γαβριήλ την χάριν Ευαγγελίζεται. Διό και ημείς συν αυτώ, τη Θεοτόκω βοήσωμεν: Χαίρε Κεχαριτωμένη, ο Κύριος μετά σου.

Today is the Beginning of our Salvation

Today is the beginning of our salvation and the manifestation of the mystery that is from eternity. The Son of God becomes the Son of the Virgin, and Gabriel announces the good tidings of grace. Therefore, let us also join him and cry aloud to the Theotokos: Hail, thou who art full of grace, the Lord is with thee.

The Associate Congregational Church at the corner of Maryland Avenue and Preston Street as it appeared in 1910. The Romanesque-style edifice was designed by the famous Architect Charles E. Cassell and was originally built in 1889 for the Associate Reformed Church. Vacated by the Protestant congregation in 1934, the Annunciation Greek Orthodox community purchased this magnificent church in 1937 and began a new era of progress and expansion.

Courtesy of the Maryland Historical Society

Section of a 1906 map showing the Associate Congregational Church and its surrounding neighborhood as it appeared at the beginning of the 20th century. From the *Atlas of the City of Baltimore, Maryland*, compiled from Actual Surveys and Official Plans by George W. and Walter S. Bromley, Civil Engineers. The historic volume of maps was published by G. W. Bromley and Company, Philadelphia, Pennsylvania, in 1906.

Courtesy of the University of Baltimore, Special Collections

House of God...Gateway to Heaven

A Centennial History of the
Greek Orthodox Cathedral of the Annunciation

Baltimore, Maryland

Nicholas M. Prevas
Parish Historian

Published by the
Greek Orthodox Cathedral of the Annunciation
24 West Preston Street
Baltimore, Maryland 21201

ISBN-13: 978-0-9790235-0-7
ISBN-10: 0-9790235-0-5

Library of Congress Control Number: 2007937244

Printed in the United States of America

Dedication

*To those early Greek immigrants
whose struggles and sacrifices laid the foundation
for the Annunciation Cathedral community of today.*

————————————

*With great pride, I present this volume in loving memory
of Father Constantine M. Monios who led the congregation for
over a quarter-century. His passion for the preservation of our
rich history inspired me throughout many years of research as
I documented the story of our beloved Cathedral, the
House of God…Gateway to Heaven.*

Main entrance to the Greek Orthodox Cathedral of the Annunciation.
The inscription above the portico translates as *House of God…Gateway to Heaven.*

Photograph courtesy of J. Brough Schamp © 2005

Table of Contents

Foreword

Twenty-five years ago, The Reverend Constantine Monios commented upon the importance of preserving the history of Baltimore's Greek Orthodox community. In his introductory remarks to the 75-year history of the parish published in 1982, Father Monios stated: "One cannot isolate the reality of today nor the promise of the future from the study of the past. What we are or what hope to be is, in large measure, based upon what we were and what we experienced." His eloquent words were inspiring to many, especially to our parish historian, Nicholas Michael Prevas.

As the Annunciation Cathedral proudly reflects upon its first century of progress, Mr. Prevas has completed a magnificent centennial history. Many of the early segments of our fascinating story, which could easily have been lost in obscurity, are now carefully preserved in a well-documented narrative complemented by an outstanding selection of rare photographs. The author's detailed research work and unique writing style have resulted in a stellar publication for the Greek Orthodox Archdiocese of America.

Readers will have the opportunity to learn the details surrounding the establishment of the Annunciation community, the hardships faced by the immigrant congregation, and how the parish overcame many obstacles during the early decades of the 20th century. The story is filled with the dedication and perseverance of that remarkable immigrant generation. Among its many themes, the book touches upon the entrepreneurial spirit of the Greeks, their desire to preserve the Orthodox faith and traditions, and how the politics of Greece impacted the immigrants in America during the post World War I era. In Baltimore, for instance, the parish divided into rival factions, worshipping from two different church locations during the 1920's until a reconciliation was reached.

The book also explains how the urgent need for expansion led parish leaders to ultimately acquire the magnificent edifice on Preston Street, thus saving the historic church from demolition. Another elusive fact is that the original congregation that worshipped on Preston Street back in the 1890's was a Protestant denomination known as the Associate Reformed Church. The building adapted beautifully to the Orthodox faith when the Greek Orthodox community purchased the church nearly fifty years later in 1937.

These are just a few of the many intriguing aspects of parish history that Mr. Prevas has brought forth in greater detail in his third book. With a unique introduction about the Greek immigrant experience, the story is divided into decades culminating with the parish's Centennial in March of 2006. As an added feature, the section entitled Special Historical Collections provides supplemental information on various topics of interest. The book also includes a comprehensive Name Index for easy reference. I am confident that Nicholas Michael Prevas and his superb historical writing, *House of God…Gateway to Heaven*, will be remembered for years to come. This book will undoubtedly be used as a primary reference source by future generations of parishioners, as well as researchers and scholars, anxious to learn about the fascinating story of Baltimore's Cathedral of the Annunciation.

The Very Reverend Constantine Moralis, *Dean*　　　　*Feast Day of the Annunciation*
Greek Orthodox Cathedral of the Annunciation　　　　March 25, 2007

Author's Acknowledgements

I extend my sincerest gratitude to the following people for their assistance in helping me to present this 100-year history of the Greek Orthodox Cathedral of the Annunciation. The Very Reverend Constantine Moralis encouraged the concept of a definitive history book as the parish's centennial celebration approached. Despite his busy schedule as Dean of the Cathedral, he enthusiastically offered valuable suggestions and carefully proofread various drafts of the manuscript for clarity and content of religious matters. My aunt, Olga Markulis Matsos, who assisted in editing my first book published in 1982, agreed to serve as the proof-reader for this project. Her insightful view of parish history, coupled with her knowledge of the English language, especially grammar and punctuation skills, enhanced the presentation of this story. Using her expertise, she spent countless hours working with me over the last three years. I will forever be indebted to her for the tremendous assistance and loving support she provided throughout this work.

At the design firm of Plum Creative Associates, Ruth Schmuff served as project coordinator and proved to be a valuable consultant. She displayed a cooperative spirit and was most helpful as the parish history transformed over the course of three years into a magnificent book design. Her professional layout of the text and images, refining of the captions, and creative suggestions on how to best present the book's content, all contributed to the success of this endeavor. She worked closely with her husband, Karl Egenberger, who scanned hundreds of images and offered his artistic talents in retouching photographs and, in some cases, recreating portions of images from damaged original prints. To Ruth and Karl, I express my utmost measure of appreciation.

A heartfelt note of thanks goes to James Keefe, a professional photographer and friend, who graciously donated his time and talent. He visited the Cathedral and parish cemeteries on numerous occasions capturing the right lighting for photographs to ensure the best possible reproduction in the book. Photographer Michael J. Frangos graciously loaned me images from the vast collection of photos he had taken at parish events throughout the 1980's and 1990's. The Towson Copy Center, under the management of Jimmie Stewart, was another source of great assistance. Jimmie, along with his able staff of Curtis Mason and Brian Smith, copied countless documents, photographs, and chapters of the book throughout various stages of the process. Also, a special thank you is extended to Colleen J. Dugan from Severn Graphics. As the workflow necessitated, she scanned numerous images and provided her expertise in the restoration of various photographs and documents.

From the Annunciation Cathedral, I wish to acknowledge the kind assistance of Lucy Hagopian, Cathedral Business Administrator. She provided me with a variety of sources as needed and offered valuable editorial suggestions and insight based upon her four decades of service to the parish. I also wish to thank Christos Motsiopoulos who served as the primary translator of various Greek language documents, newspaper articles, letters, and parish council minutes. With enthusiasm, he promptly responded to my requests for these translations. During the 1980's, Dimitra K. Poulos and Chrysoula and Efthymios Ponticas had provided translations of the 1922-1929 parish council minutes and other documents. Their efforts proved most helpful to me in writing about that time period. Betty Jean Alevizatos, Cathedral Archivist, understood the scope of this work and the need to constantly access materials from the parish archives. She cooperated fully with requests and assisted in locating material from the collection.

Appreciation is also extended to Thomas L. Hollowak, Head of Special Collections at the University of Baltimore, who provided steamship photographs and information, postcard images, maps of Baltimore City, and access to rare editions of the Baltimore City Directories. At the Maryland Historical Society, David Prencipe, Associate Director of the Prints and Photographs Collection, coordinated the reproduction of special images used in the book. Peter G. Pitsakis, President of the Greek-American Historical Society of Philadelphia, provided information from his files concerning some of the early Greek Orthodox priests who traveled to Baltimore. Jacques Kelly from *The Baltimore Sun*, a well-known author and expert on Baltimore history, provided valuable suggestions and inspired me to compile the Name Index for the book. He graciously allowed me access to his collection of unique photographs that led to the creation of "A Pictorial History of the Annunciation Cathedral Building" which is included in this volume.

Countless parishioners shared stories relating to the parish history, prompting additional research and the discovery of long-forgotten documents at the Maryland State Archives. To all those who assisted with information, I extend my sincerest gratitude. Many people also loaned or donated photographs relevant to the parish's history. The donors of the images that were acquired over the years and used in this book are gratefully acknowledged in the section entitled Photo Credits. A special thank you goes to Olympia "Bebe" Paul, the niece of The Very Rev. Joakim Papachristou. She graciously donated rare photographs and documents that inspired the creation of his memorial tribute in the Special Historical Collections.

And finally, this book could not have been completed without the patience and support of my dear mother, Zinovia M. Prevas. The need to focus on research and writing became a top priority and took precedence over many other activities associated with daily life. Her steadfast understanding of the importance of this work allowed me to devote thousands of hours of my creative energy into this production. The project also evoked many fond memories of my beloved father, Michael N. Prevas, who fell asleep in the Lord on December 29, 1998. He was my research partner during the course of countless family history and church-related projects. His discipline, perseverance, and focus were undoubtedly with me during the detailed writing of this book. I will always treasure the assistance offered by my parents over the years. Their love and support greatly influenced the outcome of this writing endeavor.

Nicholas M. Prevas, *Parish Historian*
Greek Orthodox Cathedral of the Annunciation
Baltimore, Maryland

Sponsors

The Annunciation Cathedral wishes to acknowledge the generous financial contributions of the following sponsors toward the publication of *House of God…Gateway to Heaven.*

David and Matina Psoras Bonnen – *in loving memory of her aunt, Eftihia Paxenos*

Evan and Ceres Alevizatos Chriss – *in loving memory of their parents,*
    Christ and Chrissie Alevizatos and Andrew and Sophia Rogokos

Arthur S. and Tina A. Constantinides – *in honor of her mother, Nota Alexander,*
    in loving memory of her father, Alexander J. Alexander, and in loving
    memory of his parents, Louis J. and Mary J. Constantinides

Mary A. Craten – *in loving memory of her husband George J. Craten, her son Frank Craten,*
    her brother Thomas "Sam" Aleck, her sisters Catherine Aleck and Angeline Tricoglou
    Duklewski, and parents Kay and Theodore Aleck and Smaro and John Craten

Lucy Hagopian – *in loving memory of George, Evelyn and Janice Hagopian*

Dr. Avraam, Vasi Lea, Costa, Demetri, and Nicholas Karas – *in honor of her mother,*
    Maria Minadakis, in loving memory of her father, James Andrew, and in loving memory
    of her grandparents, Louis and Kyriaki Minadakis and Evangelos and Vasilia Andrew

Gus J. Karayinopulos – *in honor of his parents, James and Mary Karayinopulos*

The family of the late Louis John Kousouris

Julia F. Krometis – *in loving memory of her husband, Lt. Col. August A. Krometis*

The Laconian Association "Lycourgos-Taygete" of Baltimore –
    in loving memory of its founders and departed members

Stefany and JoEllen Laun – *in loving memory of their grandparents, Joseph P. Laun*
    and Stefanos and Loula Fantopoulos

Mary Hamilos Markakis, children, and grandchildren – *in loving memory of*
    James N. Markakis, and in loving memory of Christ and Angela Hamilos
    and Nicholas, Garifalia, and Emmanuel Markakis

Dr. Constantine G., Thalia L., George C. and Theodore C. Mesologites –
    in loving memory of their father and grandfather, George C. Mesologites

Presbytera Mary C. Monios, children, and grandchildren –
    in loving memory of The Reverend Constantine M. Monios

The Very Reverend Archimandrite Constantine Moralis –
in honor of his parents, Peter John and Sarah Vrachalus Moralis, and his family, John and Betty Lou Moralis and Angela Moralis and their families

Georgeann N. Morekas – *in loving memory of her grandparents, Georgia and George J. Karangelen and Ekaterina and Spiros Morekas*

John G. Noppinger, Jr. – *in honor of his mother, Dorothy Noppinger*

Gary T. and Donna Z. Padussis – *in loving memory of his father, Theodore G. Padussis*

George H. and Louise "Fi" Pappas – *in loving memory of their parents, Harry G. and Kalliope H. Pappas and Peter and Amalia Nicholson*

Harry P. and Anna Z. Pappas – *in loving memory of their parents, Kalliope H. and Harry G. Pappas and Angeline and Thomas Zambounis*

James N. and Nancy Pappas – *in loving memory of his father, Alexander H. Pappas, and in honor of his mother, Chrysanthe Alevizatos Pappas, and in loving memory of her mother, Helen Karas, and in honor of her father, Steve Karas*

John Paterakis, Sr. – *in loving memory of his parents, Isidoros and Kyriaki Paterakis*

Efthymios G. and Chrysoula C. Ponticas – *in loving memory of their grandson, Nicholas John Slifer*

Nicholas M. Prevas – *in loving memory of his grandparents, Nicholas and Eugenia Prevas and George and Athena Markulis*

The Estate of Peter Themistocles Prevas

Zinovia Markulis Prevas – *in loving memory of her husband, Michael N. Prevas*

Dennis J. and Demetra Psoras – *in loving memory of his parents, James and Penelope Psoras*

Loretta Prevas Siotka and family – *in loving memory of Peter John Prevas*

Charles and Carolyn Tsakalas – *in loving memory of their parents, Nicholas and Rodanthi Tsakalas and Iakovos and Helen K. Marmaras*

Irene K. and Louis P. Vlangas – *in loving memory and in honor of Vlangas, Germanakos, Karavas, Douvres, Orfanos, Skleres, and Koras family members*

Gloria Prevas Zarkos – *in loving memory of her parents, Themistocles and Mary Prevas*

Introductory Remarks

In presenting his third publication, Nicholas M. Prevas traces the progress and development of the Annunciation Cathedral over the course of ten decades concluding with the celebration of the parish's 100th Anniversary in 2006. Throughout this work, the author sometimes references historical accounts associated with specific individuals or families to illustrate a theme or story line. For every account included there are undoubtedly countless other similar stories. The purpose of this book is to capture the essence of significant events in the history while offering the reader a flavor of parish life as it existed during each decade. The material presented is based upon the author's extensive research over many years and his review of all pertinent records of the parish.

Compiling and highlighting the vast number of sources covering 100 years of history was a most challenging task. Great care was exercised when interpreting the data and in the selection of the material included to ascertain the historical relevance to the overall scope of the project. This volume contains the author's best interpretation of the source materials available and represents his vision of the parish history. The Special Historical Collections provides detailed information and additional photographs on specific topics. The Bibliography is divided into categories listing the various source materials used in writing the book. The section entitled Photo Credits is sequenced in chapter order and includes a brief description of each image with its corresponding source. The Name Index allows the reader to find the pages where names are included in the story or appear in captioned photographs.

The perseverance required for the completion of *House of God…Gateway to Heaven* began over thirty years ago. In the correspondence file at the Woodlawn Cemetery office, a letter was discovered, dated August 24, 1972, written by the author when he was only 14 years of age. At that time, he was researching his family history and sought information about his father's siblings who were buried in the old Greek Section of that cemetery in the 1920's. Little did he realize that a historical journey was about to unfold as a result of that inquiry. By 1980, his genealogical projects had expanded and he found himself immersed in writing the church's 75-year history. His first book, *History of the Greek Orthodox Cathedral of the Annunciation*, was published in 1982 and received national acclaim. Over the years, he continued his research and uncovered additional documentation and photographs concerning the parish history. His second publication, *Gone But Not Forgotten* released in 2001, brought forth the fascinating story of Annunciation Cathedral's first burial grounds established in 1912.

A review of these publications appeared in the *National Herald*, a weekly Greek-American newspaper published in New York, in May of 2004. In an article entitled "Eternal Be Their Memory," Mr. Steve Frangos, a noted author and historian, praised Nick Prevas' works as "…critical for the development of our own self-understanding of Greek-American history…. Whether or not future researchers will be able to locate as detailed a record in their home communities as Mr. Prevas has in volume has yet to be seen. Mr. Prevas has without a doubt set the standard for all such future accounts…. Now both the living and the dead owe this man a debt that can never be repaid. There are so very few who write about the Greek-American experience and fewer still who do it well and with anything approaching grace. In the truest sense of the old Greek folk saying, Nicholas Prevas has given back more than he was ever given."

Balcony stained glass windows showing the Crucifixion of Christ (center) with the
the four Evangelists depicted from left to right: St. Luke, St. Mark, St. Matthew, and St. John.

Photograph courtesy of James Keefe © 2005

Historical Highlights of 100 Years

1890's	Greek immigrants begin to arrive and settle in Baltimore
1906	Formal establishment of the Greek Orthodox Church "Evangelismos"
1907	Arrival of Rev. Constantine Douropoulos as the first full-time priest
1909	Parish incorporated under Maryland State Law; Acquisition of the Homewood Avenue and Chase Street Church
1912	First Orthodox burial grounds purchased at Woodlawn Cemetery; Greek language school established for parish children
1915	Formation of the first youth group organization, Greek-American Athletic Association
1918	Formation of the first chartered affiliate of the parish, Greek-American Association "Progress"
1921	Establishment of the Greek Orthodox Archdiocese in New York
1922	Visit of the first Archbishop, Alexander of Rodostolou; Political turmoil between Royalists and Venizelists escalates
1923	Charter amendment supporting the new Archdiocese causes Royalists to form the Holy Trinity Church at Broadway and Monument Street; Greek community remained divided by politics for nearly seven years
1926	Establishment of *Enosis* (Union), first ladies' group
1929	Reunion of Baltimore's Greek Orthodox Community at the Homewood Avenue Church
1935	The Very Rev. Joakim Papachristou begins a fifteen-year pastorate
1936	Establishment of the *Philoptochos* (Friends of the Poor) Society
1937	Purchase of the Preston Street Church for future expansion; Historic procession from Homewood Avenue to Preston Street; Professor Athanasios Theodorides employed as choir director
1938	Consecration of the Preston Street Church by Archbishop Athenagoras
1940-1945	War Years are marked by Greek War Relief efforts and countless displays of American patriotism by the Greek community
1942	Purchase of the Greek Center (Cathedral and Preston Streets)
1943	Establishment of the Greek Orthodox Cemetery on Windsor Mill Road
1946	Fortieth Anniversary Year Celebration; Establishment of EONA (youth organization)
1948	Ordination of American-born Deacon Soterios Gouvellis as the new Assistant Priest
1950	Controversial dismissal of both Father Gouvellis and Father Papachristou; The Very Rev. Philotheos Ahladas begins his four-year tenure

1951	Choir groups reorganized with Georgia Topal as director; Organization of GOYA (Greek Orthodox Youth of America)
1952	Establishment of the St. Nicholas Greek Orthodox community
1954	The Rev. George P. Gallos, the first full-time American-born priest, begins his eleven-year pastorate
1955	Establishment of the Ladies' Tea Guild (later renamed Women's Guild)
1956	Fiftieth Anniversary Celebration; Presbytera Anna Gallos becomes music director
1958	Parish Assembly votes for Annunciation to remain at Preston Street
1959	Groundbreaking for new Education Building adjacent to the church
1960	Opening of the Education Building
1961	Dedication of the Education Building officiated by Archbishop Iakovos
1965	Donation of new *iconostasion* to complement extensive interior renovations; The Rev. Emmanuel E. Bouyoucas begins his ten-year pastorate; Georgia Tangires becomes music director
1966	Church name officially changes from "Evangelismos" to "Annunciation"
1967	Testimonial honoring Lawrence Cardinal Shehan and Archbishop Iakovos; Lucy Hagopian begins her career in the Annunciation Church office
1970	Establishment of the St. Demetrios Greek Orthodox community
1971	First Athenian Agora Festival
1975	Parish is elevated to Cathedral status with Bishop Silas officiating; The Rev. Elias Velonis begins as Assistant Priest for a four-year period; The Rev. Constantine M. Monios becomes the new Dean of the Cathedral
1979	Ordination to the priesthood of Deacon Mark B. Arey who served until 1982
1980	Interior renovations in the Byzantine style approved by parish assembly
1981	75th Anniversary Celebration spans an eight-month period; Opening of the Chapel of the Holy Wisdom within the Education Building
1982	Opening of the Cathedral Parking Garage on Maryland Avenue; Opening of the Chapel of the Holy Resurrection at the parish cemetery; The Rev. Louis Noplos becomes Assistant Priest through 1996
1984	Establishment of the Annunciation Orthodox Center following the purchase and renovation of five historic town houses
1985	First pilgrimage to the Holy Land
1986	First woman elected as Parish Council President (Loretta S. Prevas)
1987	Annunciation parish marks 50 years at the Preston Street Church

1989	Cathedral Building marks 100 years of existence as a house of worship
1990	Ecumenical Patriarch Dimitrios I visits Washington, D.C.
1992	Cathedral receives historic designation by the Commission on Historic and Architectural Preservation
1994	Acquisition of additional Preston Street town houses for future expansion
1995	First Adult Bible Study Retreat
1996	90th Anniversary Doxology celebrated at Annunciation Cathedral; Ordination of Deacon Constantine Moralis to the Holy Priesthood; Rev. Louis Noplos assigned to the St. Demetrios Greek Orthodox Church
1997	Visit of Ecumenical Partriarch Bartholomew to Annunciation Cathedral
1998	Extensive interior renovations are completed
1999	Elevation of Metropolitan Demetrios of Vresthena as the new Archbishop of America
2000	Tri-Parish Millennium Celebration on New Year's Day; Completion of the Cathedral Elevator and dedication ceremonies; Father Monios observes 25 years as Dean of the Cathedral
2001	Rededication of the Mentis Room established in 1975; First Winter Bible Camp program held at the Annunciation Cathedral
2002	The Very Rev. Constantine Monios fell asleep in the Lord; The Rev. Constantine Moralis elevated to the status of Archimandrite and installed as Dean of the Annunciation Cathedral
2003	Enthronement of Metropolitan Evangelos as spiritual leader of the Metropolis of New Jersey
2004	Father Dean Moralis Bookstore opens in the Education Building
2005	Ordination of Deacon Peter J. Thornberg to the Holy Priesthood
2005-2006	Centennial Celebration begins with Salutations to the Virgin Mary followed by a yearlong itinerary of historic, religious, and social events culminating with the 100th Anniversary Hierarchical Divine Liturgy and Centennial Grand Banquet

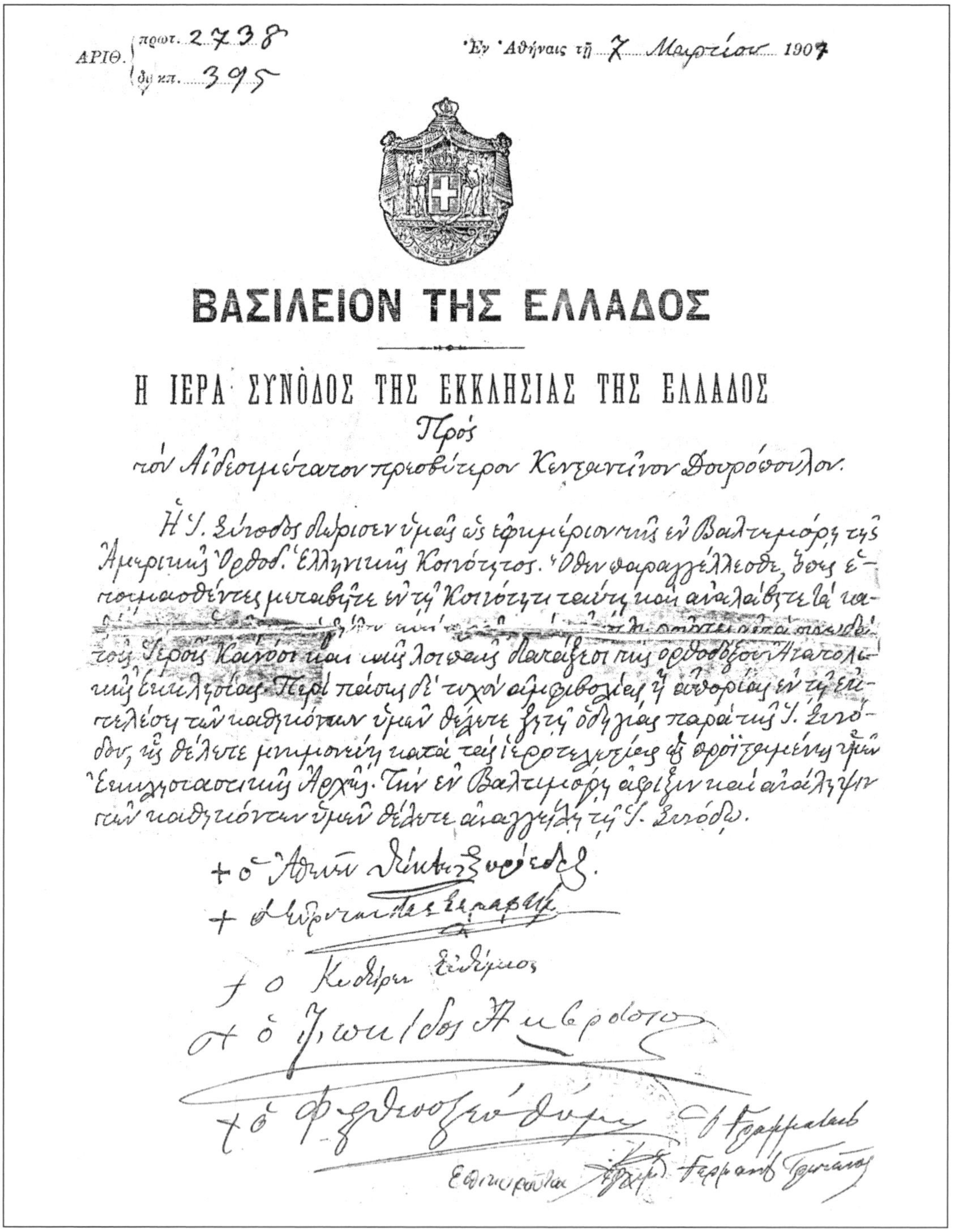

Ἐν Ἀθήναις τῇ 7 Μαρτίου 1907

ΒΑΣΙΛΕΙΟΝ ΤΗΣ ΕΛΛΑΔΟΣ

Η ΙΕΡΑ ΣΥΝΟΔΟΣ ΤΗΣ ΕΚΚΛΗΣΙΑΣ ΤΗΣ ΕΛΛΑΔΟΣ

Πρὸς

τὸν Αἰδεσιμώτατον πρεσβύτερον Κωνσταντῖνον Δουρόπουλον.

[handwritten body of letter]

[signatures of the Holy Synod members]

The Holy Synod of the Church of Greece appointed The Reverend Constantine Douropoulos
as the first full-time priest of Baltimore's Greek Orthodox community on March 7, 1907.

Opposite Page: The *S.S. Sofia Hohenberg* was launched in 1905 and accommodated 30 first-class, 50 second-class,
and 1,500 third-class passengers. Its last voyage under the Austro-Americana Line occurred in June 1907.

Introduction

Ellis Island...the *S.S. Sofia Hohenberg*, a passenger ship of the Austro-Americana Line, steamed into the bustling New York harbor on May 10, 1907. In the early years of the 20th century, a boat filled with Southern European immigrants arriving in New York was a typical scene. For the immigrants aboard these steamships, passing through the gates at Ellis Island would be the first step of their unique odyssey in America. For most, the journey across the Atlantic was motivated by the desire for economic betterment.

However, among the hundreds of Greeks that came through Ellis Island that day, one particular immigrant bringing his entire family was far from typical. In fact, their arrival in America was of historic significance to an entire Greek Orthodox community that anxiously awaited them. Making the two-week journey from Patras, Greece, was The Reverend Constantine Douropoulos, age 45, accompanied by his wife, Alexandra, age 38, and five of their children ranging in ages from five to thirteen. The ship's manifest listed them with $50, and the destination of Father Douropoulos was written simply as "Greek Orthodox Priest at Baltimore."

The Great Hall at Ellis Island, 1909.

Passenger list of the *S.S. Sofia Hohenberg* shows the
Douropoulos family arriving in New York on May 10, 1907.

The Reverend Constantine Douropoulos

The "Evangelismos" (Annunciation) Greek
Orthodox Church, one year after its founding, had
acquired its first full-time priest. Parish members
anticipated with great excitement the imminent
arrival of Father Douropoulos and his family. This
event added a sense of stability to their new
community. Greek Orthodox worship services,
following the centuries-old traditions of the Eastern
Orthodox faith, would now be conducted on a
regular basis in Baltimore, Maryland. The *Greek-
American Guide*, published later in 1907, listed
Baltimore as one of the first 20 Orthodox parishes
to be established in the United States.

How the Baltimore Greek community got to
this point illustrates its unwavering determination.
First, it should be noted that the official establishment of the "Evangelismos" Church in 1906
probably went unnoticed by most of Baltimore
City. Events of that era provide insight. The Greeks
were among the later-arriving immigrant groups
and spoke a strikingly different language. Anti-
foreign sentiment was everywhere and most
apparent to any immigrants with strange sounding
names, customs, and traditions, like those of the
Greeks. Two years earlier, in February of 1904, the
disastrous Great Fire had wiped out the heart of
Baltimore's business district and the city, with a
population of over 500,000 people, was busy
rebuilding itself from the rubble and ashes.
Therefore, in March of 1906, a gathering of obscure
Greek immigrants attending church services was
far from newsworthy.

Scene from the Great Fire of Baltimore
February 7-8, 1904.

From a religious perspective, however, the first Divine Liturgy of the "Evangelismos" Church was of tremendous significance. Sunday, March 18, 1906, marked the official beginning of Orthodoxy as an established religion in the State of Maryland. The chronicle of parish history over the last one hundred years is impressive. It illustrates how a small religious community, initially comprised of dedicated immigrants, would mature and evolve into Baltimore's Cathedral of the Annunciation, one of the largest and most progressive Greek Orthodox parishes in the United States.

The fascinating story of the Cathedral of the Annunciation, however, begins prior to that historic gathering that occurred one hundred years ago. To better understand, we must first look back to the late 19th century and the difficult economic times confronting Eastern Europe. The Kingdom of Greece, for instance, was largely agricultural and unable to sustain the needs of its people. With stony fields throughout many regions, the country's population was rural and poor. Rumors of the great opportunities in America spread even to the distant provinces and financially-depressed villages where steamship company agents, anxious for passenger revenues, boasted of great wealth and gold in the streets. With the promise of a new and better life in America, the mass exodus began.

Between 1890 and 1910, nearly 200,000 Greeks, or one-tenth of the population of Greece, made the journey across the Atlantic and began settling throughout the United States. Initially, most intended to work a short time, earn their small fortunes and return home. After a while, however, many decided to make the land of opportunity their permanent home. From the beginning, most Greek immigrants were city dwellers. Farming had no appeal to these people because they equated farming with poverty. The transition from peasant life to an urban setting was, in fact, difficult for many.

The reality of city living was in sharp contrast to the hillsides, mountainous regions, and islands of Greece to which they were accustomed. Not everyone was able to adapt and some were homesick from

Immigrating to America in 1894, Gregorios Prevas (far right) posed with relatives on a return visit to Greece in 1900.

The peak year for immigration was 1907 when over 45,000 Greeks came to the United States.

the onset. Many were forced to live in cramped quarters such as boarding houses where contagious diseases spread easily under less than sanitary conditions. Illness was everywhere and death came frequently. The average life span was no more than 40-50 years. Unfamiliarity with the English language was, needless to say, a formidable obstacle. Hostility from many people, including other immigrant groups, was often very common.

However, despite the hardships the pioneer Greeks faced, the fact remains that almost all were able to raise their standard of living much more than would have been possible had they remained in Greece. Economic independence was their dream and many chose to invest their first dollars in some type of business endeavor. The Greek immigrant, as an entrepreneur, first appeared on the streets of New York as a peddler, often selling a variety of candy and fruit from a tray hanging around his neck. This was the humble beginning of the confectionery—a business soon to be associated with being Greek.

By 1870, the first Greek confectionery in America was established in New York, furnishing employment opportunities for immigrants anxious to learn the trade. Less than a decade after the establishment of this historic first candy-making business in America, the first Greek confectioners appeared in Baltimore City, marking the beginning of what would soon be a colony of Greek candy makers. The 1877 city directory listed Eleftherios Chryssophoudy, age 29, a wholesale and retail confectioner at 135 Lexington Street. By 1879, his 21-year-old brother, Panayiotis, had joined him as a clerk in the store. Both were recorded in the 1880 Federal Census. By 1885, only a handful of Greeks were listed among the city's residents…a saloonkeeper, a fruit dealer, and a few confectioners.

In terms of the actual development of a Greek community in the city, however, the arrival of a significant number of Greeks did not occur until the 1890's. These initial immigrants who settled in Baltimore were primarily from the mainland province of Laconia, Greece. Many settled in close

Many of the early Greek immigrants operated businesses at market houses throughout the City of Baltimore. This was a typical scene at the Lexington Market, 1910.

proximity to the eleven market houses throughout the city. Within a few years, enterprising Greeks could be found at Lexington, Fells Point, Cross Street, Belair, and other markets where they often worked grueling 16-hour days. With perseverance, the early pioneers not only survived, they excelled in their endeavors. They rented or purchased properties and established themselves in either candy-making, fruit and vegetable sales, or peanut vending. In the Baltimore Business Directory for 1902-1903, over two dozen Greeks were listed under the heading of "Confectioners."

Examining the listings of Greek immigrants, one immediately notes the absence of women. Only a small handful of Greek women traveled to America during those early years. Census and passenger records document a few examples. Anna Stavrakos journeyed to America in 1896. She joined her husband, Epaminondas, a well-respected businessman at the Hanover Market who later served on the first parish council. Constantina Nifakos with her four-year-old daughter, Efrosini, immigrated in 1901, joining her husband, Sotirios, known as Charles Nemphos. He was successful in many business pursuits and later became a charter member of the parish. These early women were pioneers in their own right. By 1910, however, passenger arrival records show that one of every five Greeks passing through Ellis Island was a woman. News from America and the anticipation of a better life here no doubt prompted this changing trend.

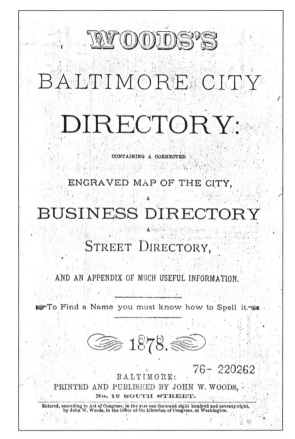

Baltimore City Directories provided the addresses and occupations of city residents.

Constantina and Sotirios Nifakos (Charles Nemphos)

Greek immigrants rented market stalls and horse carts using these 19th century license documents.

Professor Aristo Soho

education. Soho then taught at St. John's College in Annapolis during the 1890's and received his Ph.D. in 1898 from The Johns Hopkins University. By 1902, he became a professor of Romance Languages at Baltimore City College. One source described Professor Soho as "bearded, muscular, and even more temperamental than most scholars." His education and business acumen would no doubt be a great asset to his compatriots. Soho later played an active role in organizing the Greek community.

During these years, a Greek by the name of Aristogeiton Soho arrived—not fitting the description of the typical immigrant seeking profitable business ventures. After graduating in 1880 from the Royal Gymnasium in Lyra, Greece, he taught Greek for seven years in his native country. By 1887, he had arrived in Baltimore to further his

Until this time, except for a brief attempt by Russian Orthodox clergy, there was little activity to meet the spiritual needs of the early Orthodox Greeks. In fact, history even tells of questionable individuals, without credentials, acting as priests in isolated colonies, ministering without authority wherever financial gains were the highest. Only New York and Chicago had established churches in the early 1890's, offering the opportunity for Greeks to attend worship services. In Baltimore, the first meaningful attempt to fill the religious void came in or about 1895. The first Greek Orthodox place of worship was established at Bond and Gough Streets through the financial support of Christos Tsembelis (Sempeles) and his five brothers, George, Nicholas, Peter, Sarantos, and Theodore, who were

Sempeles Brothers Confectionery at the Belair Market with Peter Sempeles (left) and George Giovannis (right).

Christos Sempeles, one of the early organizers of Baltimore's Greek Orthodox community.

prospering confectioners at 427 Colvin Street near the Belair Market. One of the brothers, George Sempeles, would later have the distinction of being elected the first parish council president.

This event was consistent with the fact that the Greek Orthodox Church in America originated from the actions of the immigrants themselves, and not by the directive of the church authorities in Athens or Constantinople—the latter being the world center of Orthodoxy. Living in a new land, religion played an important factor in uniting the Greek immigrants. A missionary priest, Reverend Theodoros Papaconstantinou, was brought to Baltimore to conduct services, and for the first time Greek Orthodox chanting was heard in the city. Unfortunately, the timing of the venture was not right. The small number of Greeks, unable to keep up with the expense of maintaining a house of worship, soon abandoned this attempt. It would be another decade before regular church services would be conducted in Baltimore.

The late 1890's saw a period of growth in the number of Greeks emigrating from their homeland. Much of this was attributed to unsettled economic and political conditions resulting from the Greco-Turkish War of 1897. The only attempt to curtail departures were government-issued circulars warning people of the "many dangers and privations" they could expect in foreign lands. Though no permission was needed to leave Greece, the government was able to demand military service of the emigrant after his return from abroad. For instance, Epaminondas (Peter) Asimakes, upon visiting the homeland, completed his Greek military service during these years and proudly posed in uniform for the camera. Later returning to Baltimore, he became a staunch supporter of the Greek community.

Though the initial Greek colony of Baltimore was largely comprised of Laconians, people from other regions and islands of Greece also began to arrive and enjoy prosperity. One notable example is Anastasios Coroneos who holds the distinction of being the first immigrant from the Island of Kythera to settle in Baltimore. Arriving in 1897, the city directory soon listed him as a confectioner at 1919 Orleans Street. Hard work led to financial success, and he sent for his wife, Margarita, and children to join him in Baltimore. Within a short time, he boasted a chain of confectioneries and was able to help other relatives and friends from Kythera establish themselves in this city. Anastasios Coroneos was one of numerous Greek businessmen who would later provide assistance in organizing a Greek Orthodox church.

Epaminondas (Peter) Asimakes, 1899
and his Greek military discharge dated 1906.

Anastasios Coroneos

With pride and determination, the early immigrants overcame many obstacles. The story of Evangelos Vasilakos illustrates the persevering spirit of that era. After working for others, he saved enough money to venture out on his own—selling candies with a pushcart. Soon, he rented property only to have his business destroyed in the Great Fire that swept through the city in the winter of 1904. Forced to completely start over, he moved to South Baltimore to pursue his economic independence. A down payment toward the purchase of a storefront property in the 600 block of East Fort Avenue was his next achievement. Within a few years, Vasilakos owned a thriving confectionery, sent for a bride from Greece, and established a family.

Despite the challenges they faced, some quickly made the decision that America would be their permanent home. Peter J. Conits, residing at 203 Jasper Street, has the distinction of being among the first in the Greek colony to receive American citizenship in Baltimore. Naturalization records show this 21-year-old immigrant officially renounced "all allegiance and fidelity" to the King of Greece on May 16, 1898, in the Superior Court of Baltimore City. He had accompanied his father, Dimitrios, to the United States in 1891, seeking a better way of life. Like so many others, they did not realize that soon their entire family would bid farewell to the homeland and set sail for America.

Evangelos Vasilakos

Many of the early Greeks in Baltimore made the voyage to America on the *S.S. Amsterdam* of the Holland-American Line.

Annie Martens
and John L. Voulgaris

The financial gains made by these pioneering Greeks led to the arrival of brothers, sisters, cousins, wives and children. Some, who were single, also took brides of non-Greek heritage. For instance, records from the Court of Common Pleas show eight Greeks marrying non-Greek women between 1892-1902 in non-Orthodox ceremonies. One was John L. Voulgaris, an adventurous 26-year-old entrepreneur from the Island of Andros. He married Annie Martens, age 24, on July 16, 1901, with Rev. F. A. Conradi officiating. Their wedding took place at the First German United Evangelical Lutheran Church located at 1728 Eastern Avenue. The Voulgaris couple ran the first Greek-owned boarding house at 1722 Thames Street in the Fells Point district of the city for over a decade.

Some of the Greek men, desiring to marry and establish families, requested brides who were sent from the villages. Often these Greek girls would leave with merely a photograph of the man they would marry upon crossing the Atlantic. Other immigrants traveled back to their homeland and returned within a few months with a bride. The story of George Konstantopoulos (Konstant) is a superb example. As an established confectioner with his brother, Antonios, at the Lexington Market since 1895, he returned to Greece and married Evanthia Sourtzis from their village of Paleopanayia in the province of Laconia.

In the spring of 1899, the newlyweds returned to America, aboard the *S.S. Amsterdam*, anticipating a prosperous new life…one that never materialized. Sadly, within two weeks of arrival, Evanthia Konstant, age 25, died from kidney disease on May 23, 1899, at 400 Clay Street, their residence near Lexington Market. The undertakers, Jacob Ahrens & Company at 754 Eutaw Street, handled the final arrangements. The obscure death certificate was recorded under a misspelled name, "Avinthia Sourgn," with the birthplace listed as Europe—further distancing her from her Greek heritage. Two days later, a small group of compatriots gathered on a remote hillside within the New Cathedral (Catholic) Cemetery in West Baltimore to witness her burial. Evanthia S. Konstant has the tragic distinction of being the first death of a Greek immigrant to occur in Baltimore.

George and Georgia Konstant (the earliest known Orthodox wedding in Baltimore) posed in 1905 with their first two of ten children: James, age 4, and infant John.

This curious saga, however, continues the following year. By the spring of 1900, Dimitrios Koniditsiotis (Conits), who also was a confectioner at the Lexington Market, wrote to Greece for his young daughter, Georgia, to come to America to be the new bride of recent widower George Konstant. Within two weeks of her arrival on May 25, 1900, Georgia Conits, age 16, and George Konstant, age 25, were united in marriage and took their place in history as the first Greek Orthodox wedding to occur in the City of Baltimore. Shortly after, the 12th Federal Census of the United States was conducted on June 8, 1900. The newlyweds were listed in the census at 400 Clay Street with Georgia Konstant's length of residence in America recorded as "1/12" of a year.

At the beginning of the 20th century, the small Greek colony again expressed an interest to establish a church. Their efforts, however, were hampered primarily by a shortage of priests. At one point, they numbered only ten throughout America, attempting to serve the Greek communities by traveling from city to city. In Baltimore, periodic religious services, as well as sacraments, were performed by these early pioneering priests.

Evanthia Sourtzis Konstant was the first death among the early Greek immigrants. For reasons unclear, she was buried under her maiden name on May 25, 1899.

The 1897 birth certificate of Katherine E. Stavrakos shows the common misspelling of immigrant names. She was the first child of Greek descent born in Baltimore.

The Rev. Theodoros Prousianos was in Chicago as early as 1895. He later served the Philadelphia area and visited Baltimore in 1904.

The Very Rev. Nathanael Sideris arrived in New York on August 1, 1899. His earliest known visit to Baltimore was in the spring of 1902.

The first baptism was celebrated for Katherine Stavrakos, the seventh child of Epaminondas and Anna Stavrakos. Her birth took place at 143 East Camden Street on July 2, 1897. Notably, she was the first child of Greek descent born in Baltimore to be baptized in the Orthodox Christian tradition.

Archival documents also reveal that a few children of early immigrants were born in area hospitals—an indication of the rising prosperity of some Greek families. On June 1, 1901, George and Georgia Konstant welcomed their first son, James, who was most likely the first male child of Greek parents born in this city. Then, after arriving in Baltimore as newlyweds in the spring of 1901, Gregorios and Kaliroi Prevas celebrated the birth of their first son, James, on April 20, 1902. Both infants were born at the prestigious Johns Hopkins Hospital and visiting priests were required once again to perform baptismal sacraments.

City records also confirm that visiting priests were in Baltimore regularly between 1902 and 1904 performing Orthodox marriage ceremonies. For instance, on May 11, 1902, The Very Rev. Nathanael Sideris officiated at the wedding of Amalia Stavrakos, age 21, to Costas G. Doukas, age 26. Then, on October 16, 1904, The Rev. Theodoros Prousianos performed the wedding of Pota Conits, age 19, to an enterprising 26-year-old named Theodore Doukas. Both clergymen served during these years at the Annunciation Greek Orthodox Community of Philadelphia, founded in 1901, and traveled to Maryland upon request to conduct sacraments.

The presence of these visiting priests in Baltimore illustrates how the Greeks attempted to preserve those things paramount in their lives—the Orthodox faith, Greek language, and their native customs. The influx of Greeks continued steadily from the years 1900 to 1905, bringing the total Greek colony to over one hundred in number. These immigrants believed that, in addition to their financial success, becoming part of the American dream required the establishment of a church. The Orthodox Church was an integral part of their lives in Greece and was now definitely needed here in America—an exciting yet foreign land so different from their prior surroundings.

Early parish histories concur that by 1905, itinerant priests were conducting services and ceremonies in various locations throughout Baltimore City. First in the home of the Konstantopoulos Brothers (George and Antonios) at 628 W. Lexington Street, then at a hall at Baltimore and Paca Streets, and still later at Gay and High Streets. Serious discussion among a small group of prosperous Greek businessmen was soon taking place. The timing was right to plant the seed of Orthodoxy in Baltimore…a formal church community was on the horizon.

Margarita A. Coroneos with her grandchildren left to right: Andrew, Anastasios (Tase) and Catherine T. Cavacos, circa 1912.

Greek immigrants from cities across the United States were prominently featured in a 275-page book entitled *The Greeks in America*, published in Chicago by Spyridon A. Kotakis in 1908. One of the eight pages devoted to Baltimore shows Menas Tzortzopoulos (George) and John Mentis.

NEW YORK—March 22, 1906, Edition No. 1187

ΑΤΛΑΝΤΙΣ

"ATLANTIS" NATIONAL DAILY GREEK NEWSPAPER

Ἡ Ἑλληνικὴ παροικία Βαλτιμόρης.

Καθ' ἃ γράφουσιν ἡμῖν ἐκ Βαλτιμόρης ἡ λειτουργία τῆς παρελθούσης Κυριακῆς, εἰς ἣν παρέστησαν περὶ τοὺς 150 ὁμογενεῖς, ἦτο ἐπιβλητικωτάτη.

Ἐπίσης ἡ συνεδρίασις ἐστέφθη ὑπὸ μεγάλης ἐπιτυχίας, ἐγγραφέντων τῶν πλείστων συνδρομητῶν τῆς ἐκκλησίας. Εἰσεπράχθησαν δὲ ἐκ δικαιωμάτων ἐγγραφῆς, ποικιλλόντων ἀπὸ $1 ἕως $25, ἐν ὅλω $216.50. Ἐκ μηνιαίων συνδρομῶν, προπληρωθεισῶν διὰ 3 ἕως 12 μῆνας $153. Ἐξ εἰσπράξεων κηροῦ καὶ δίσκου $37.65 ἤτοι ἐν ὅλω $407,15.

Μετὰ τὴν ἐγγραφὴν ἔλαβε χώραν ἡ ἐκλογὴ τῶν μελῶν τῆς ἐπιτροπῆς, ἐξελέγησαν δὲ παμψηφεὶ οἱ ἑξῆς: Κωνστ. Διαμαντόπουλος, ταμίας, Γεώρ. Κοσκέτος, γραμματεύς, σύμβουλοι δὲ οἱ κ.κ. Γεώρ. Κωνσταντόπουλος, Ἠλίας Καραγγελές, Θ. Καβάκος, Θ. Δούκας, Γ. Τσεμπελῆς. Ἐθεωρήθη περιττὴ ἐκλογὴ Προέδρου πρὸς ἀποφυγὴν πάσης τυχὸν ἐκ κακῶς ννουμένης φιλοδοξίας διενέξεως καὶ χά-

ριν ἰσότητος μεταξύ των. Αἱ ἐγγραφαὶ ἐξακολουθοῦσιν ἀθρόαι, χάρις εἰς τὴν δραστηριότητα τῆς ἐπιτροπῆς καὶ εἰς τὴν ἐκτίμησιν, ἣν τρέφουν οἱ ἐκεῖ ὁμογενεῖς πρὸς τὰ μέλη τῆς ἐπιτροπῆς.

Τῇ αὐτῇ ἡμέρα ἀπεφάσισεν ἡ ἐπιτροπὴ ὅπως προσφέρῃ εἰς τὴν Ἑλληνικὴν Κοινότητα τῆς Βασιγκτῶνος τὸ ποσὸν ἑκατὸν δολλαρίων προπληρωτέων διὰ μίαν ἑξαμηνίαν, ἵνα ὁ ἐν Βασιγκτῶνι ἐφημέριος ἱερουργῇ ἐν Βαλτιμόρῃ ἑκάστην τετάρτην Κυριακὴν, ἤτοι σχεδὸν ἅπαξ τοῦ μηνός. Ἐλπίζεται ὅτι ἡ Ἑλληνικὴ Κοινότης Βασιγκτῶνος, εἰς ἣν διεβιβάσθη γραπτῶς ἡ τοιαύτη ἀπόφασις τῆς ἐπιτροπῆς διὰ τοῦ ἀντιπροέδρου καὶ ταμίου τῆς ἀνωτέρω κοινότητος, οἵτινες παρευρέθησαν ἐν Βαλτιμόρῃ καθ' ὅλην τὴν τελετὴν τῆς ἡμέρας ὡς θεαταί, θὰ λάβωσιν ὑπ' ὄψει τὴν τοιαύτην αἴτησιν, προκειμένου περὶ τοσούτου θεαρέστου καὶ ἐθνωφελοῦς σκοποῦ.

In the spring of 1906, the *Atlantis* newspaper documented the formal establishment of the Greek Orthodox Church in Baltimore, Maryland. The large sum of money collected from those in attendance that day was $216.50 for membership fees, ranging from $1.00 to $25.00; monthly dues, prepaid for three to twelve months totaling $153.00; and $37.65 from candles and the tray collection.

Opposite Page: Baltimore City Hall decorated for the Jubilee and Homecoming Week, September 9-16, 1906. City residents celebrated the reconstruction work accomplished in the two years since the Great Fire.

1906-1915

On March 22, 1906, the *Atlantis*, a national daily Greek newspaper published in New York, described the historic events that took place in the State of Maryland. "As they write to us from Baltimore, the Divine Liturgy of last Sunday, attended by 150 fellow countrymen, was most impressive." Following the church services, an organizational and fundraising meeting was held, members were enrolled, and a church committee was formed. Over $400 was collected that day—a notable amount for that time. The formal establishment of the Greek Orthodox Community "Evangelismos" (Annunciation) had taken place on Sunday, March 18, 1906, at the Union Hall at 500 East Fayette Street, near City Hall Plaza. Officiating at this historic Divine Liturgy was the visiting priest from the nation's capital, The Very Rev. Joakim Alexopoulos.

That day, the St. Sophia Greek Orthodox Community of Washington, D.C., was offered the amount of $100, prepaid for six months, so their priest could conduct church services in Baltimore every fourth Sunday. The Washington parish, established two years earlier in 1904, graciously agreed. Soon, Father Joakim Alexopoulos began traveling to Baltimore once a month to officiate at the Divine Liturgy. He also performed sacraments during his tenure as visiting priest. For instance, marriage records for Baltimore City document that Father Alexopoulos

The Very Rev. Joakim Alexopoulos

Olga and Peter Skalchunes with their
infant son Nicholas and daughter Mary, 1909.

During the early 1900's, the organization and supervision of all Greek Orthodox churches in America were ill-defined. The act of raising funds, for instance, signaled a departure from the way finances were handled in the old country. In Greece, Orthodoxy was the official state religion and the government paid the salaries of priests. The people's financial obligation to the church was very limited. In contrast, the immigrants would now have to administer the money themselves for church operations. This added responsibility also led to a sense of empowerment.

Individual groups organized their communities as independent bodies, owned property, and found priests to conduct religious services. Some secured their clergy from the Holy Synod in Athens and others from the Patriarchate in Constantinople. The Greek community of Baltimore turned to the Holy Synod for guidance and requested that a priest be assigned to their new church. By the spring of 1907, the Metropolitan of Athens appointed the Rev. Constantine A. Douropoulos to the Annunciation community of Baltimore. The entire Douropoulos family said goodbye to their ancestral village of Zatouna, nestled within the mountains in the province of Arcadia, and began the next chapter of their own history.

united at least three Orthodox couples in Holy Matrimony: Panayiotis (Peter) Skalchunes and Olga K. Doukas on July 15, 1906; Konstantinos Vlahos and Georgia Vlangas on December 30, 1906; and Michael Doukas and Demetra Karangelen on January 20, 1907. Father Alexopoulos later became Bishop of the Boston Diocese (1923-1930).

In reference to the organized parish, the *Atlantis* newspaper also mentioned that "the election of a president was considered unnecessary" in order to avoid disputes arising from misunderstood ambitions and "for the sake of equality" among all members of the church committee. Apparently, the initial decision not to have officers was reconsidered. Later in 1906, the following were elected to serve as the first Board of Directors of the Annunciation Church: George Sempeles, President; George Konstantopoulos, Vice President; George Giovannis, Secretary; Constantine Diamantopoulos (Diamond), Treasurer; and Theodore A. Cavacos, Theodore J. Doukas, Leonidas A. Dezes, Anastasios Gavaris, Elias Karangelen, Panayiotis (Peter) Skalchunes, Nicholas Skevas, and Epaminondas Stavrakos.

Patriarch Joakim III of Constantinople, 1908.

On Sunday, May 12, 1907, a mere two days after arriving in America, Father Douropoulos was in Baltimore and conducted his first sacrament, the marriage of Constantina Doukas to George Antonakos. The Orthodox people of this city now had a full-time priest who took up residence with his family at 2511 E. Fairmount Avenue. A rare book by Spyridon Kotakis entitled *The Greeks in America*, published in 1908, described this well-educated priest as an ideal clergyman who enjoyed "great respect and appreciation" due to his humility and goodness. Like other priests who were sent to the United States, Father Douropoulos now found himself employed by a parish council instead of his ecclesiastical superiors.

The Rev. Constantine A. Douropoulos posed for this photograph at the Selby Studio on West Lexington Street in Baltimore, 1908.

The immigrant communities were initially under the jurisdiction of the Ecumencial Patriarch in Constantinople, Turkey, who in theory took responsibility for all Orthodox missions. By 1908, Patriarch Joakim III transferred this authority to the Holy Synod in Athens. Following this historic decision, many assumed the Church of Greece would then assign a bishop to America. It would be ten years, however, before any bishop would arrive

and attempt to govern the Orthodox churches. In the interim, the Greek immigrants were able to make progress in preserving their faith and heritage.

One of the few documents existing from this first decade of parish history provides an insight into the challenges faced by the Baltimore congregation. At a meeting of the parish council, held on December 10, 1908, the oldest known roster of dues-paying church members was compiled. It lists 68 church supporters whose names were recorded that day for posterity. Census statistics for that year, however, show Baltimore had a population of 400 Greeks. The parish council, led by President Constantine Diamantopoulos (Diamond), authorized Mr. Nicholas Gounaris to visit members of the Greek community to raise funds on behalf of the church. Educating new immigrants to financially support the church was crucial to its success.

One of the major events in the early history of the church occurred in 1909, when the Trustees of the Greek community applied for and received a Certificate of Incorporation under the laws of the State of Maryland. Their religious society would be known as "The Greek Orthodox Church Evangelism [sic] of Baltimore City." The signers of the charter document, dated June 4, 1909, included: Constantine Diamond, Theodore Doukas, Nicholas Gounaris, Charles Nemphos, Peter George, Peter Skalchunes, George Konstant, Theodore Cavacos, Anastasios Gavaris, Peter Karangelen, and Leonidas Dezes. At the time of incorporation, it was noted that all charter members, with the exception of Mr. Gavaris and Mr. Dezes, had already become American citizens.

Then, nearly four months later, on September 26, 1909, by charter amendment, the parish curiously inverted its name to "The Orthodox Greek Church Evangelism [sic] of Baltimore City." The congregation's name, "Evangelismos," the Greek word for Annunciation, projected the bright future. It refers to the good tidings brought to the Virgin Mary by Archangel Gabriel announcing the imminent birth of the Christ Child. To the Greeks of Baltimore, it symbolized the good news of the Orthodox faith in their new country. While securing a charter, the "os" was left off the title "Evangelismos." The Americanization of the name as "Evangelism" was often used and boldly printed on church letterhead through the late 1920's...an interesting footnote in parish history.

ΙΣΤΟΡΙΚΑ ΣΗΜΕΙΩΜΑΤΑ

Ἐκ τοῦ σημειωματαρίου τοῦ ἀξιοτίμου κ. Νικολάου Γούναρη, συμβούλου τῆς
Ἐκκλησιαστικῆς Ἐπιτροπῆς κατὰ τὸ 1908.

●

ΠΡΑΚΤΙΚΟΝ: — Κατ' ἀπόφασιν τῆς Ἑλληνικῆς Ἐκκλησιαστικῆς Ἐπιτροπῆς Βάλ-
τιμώρης, ἐπιτρέπεται εἰς τὸν κ. Νικόλαον Γούναρην, σύμβουλον νὰ εἰσπράτ-
τῃ χρήματα ὑπὲρ τῆς Ἑλληνικῆς Ἐκκλησίας Βαλτιμώρης, "Ο ΕΥΑΓ-
ΓΕΛΙΣΜΟΣ".

Ἐν Βαλτιμώρῃ, 10 Δεκεμβρίου 1908.

Κωνσταντῖνος Διαμαντόπουλος, Πρόεδρος　　　Ἀν. Γάβαρης, Γραμματεύς

Κατάλογος Μελῶν τῆς Κοινότητος κατὰ τὸ ἔτος 1908

◆

1. Ἀγριανιάτης, Παν.	24. Καβάκος, Θεόδ.	47. Παναγιωτόπουλος, Ἠλ.
2. Ἀλικάκος, Παν.	25. Καβάκος, Παν.	48. Πετρόχειλος, Στυλ.
3. Ἀνδριώτης, Στ.	26 Καλοπαΐδης, Γεώρ.	49. Πορφύρης, Δημήτ.
4. Ἀραχωβίτης, Χρ.	27. Καλογερίδης, Μ.	50. Πρέβας, Ἰωάν.
5. Ἀσημάκης, Ἐπαμ.	28. Καλυβήρας, Ἰωάν	51 Σοφός, Νικόλ
6. Βούλγαρης, Ἰωάν.	29. Κακαρούκας, Παναγ.	52 Σαπουνᾶς, Ἐμμ.
7. Βασιλάκος, Εὐάγγ.	30. Κορωναῖος, Ἀναστ	53. Σάμιος, Νικ
8. Βλάχος, Γεώρ.	31. Κορωναῖος, Θεόδ.	54. Σγουπάκος, Παναγ.
9. Γάβαρης, Εὐστρ.	32. Κορωναῖος, Μιχ.	55. Σιάχος, Ἀντ.
10. Γούναρης, Νικ.	33. Κωστοπλίας, Γρηγ	56. Σκαλτσούνης, Παναγ.
11. Γάβαρης, Ἀναστ.	34. Κωνσταντόπουλος, Γεώργ.	57. Σκεύης, Δημ.
12. Γαβριήλ, Σπύρ.	35. Κωνσταντόπουλος, Ἀντ.	58. Σκεύης, Α. Παναγ.
13. Διαμαντόπουλος, Κων.	36. Λέος, Γεώρ.	59. Σκεύης, Δ. Παναγ.
14. Διζές, Νικ.	37. Μαγουλᾶς, Παν.	60. Σόμπος, Χρ.
15. Διζές, Λεων.	38. Ματθαῖος, Θρασ	61. Σκορδαλῆς, Ἰωάν.
16. Δούκας, Γ. Α.	39. Μέντης, Ἰωάν	62. Σουρῆς, Ἰωάν.
17. Δούκας, Μ.	40 Μαριναῖος, Χριστ.	63. Σουρτζῆς, Ἀντ.
18. Δούκας, Θεόδ.	41 Ναστόπουλος, Εὐστρ.	64. Σταυρόπουλος
19. Εἰκοσπένταρχος, Χαρ.	42 Νικολετσέας, Ἀναστ.	65. Σορόκας, Νικόλ.
20. Ἡλιόπουλος, Λεων.	43 Νιφάκος, Σωτ.	66. Σταυράκος, Ἐπαμ.
21. Κοσπέτου, Ἀδελφοί	44 Παππαδογιαννόπουλος	67. Τζωρτζόπουλος Θεόδ.
22. Καραγκιουλές, Δημ.	45. Παππαδάκος, Σταυρ.	68. Τζωρτζόπουλος, Μινᾶς
23. Καραγκιουλές, Ἠλ.	46. Παπαζήσογλου, Χαράλ.	

ΔΙΟΙΚΗΤΙΚΟΝ ΣΥΜΒΟΥΛΙΟΝ ΤΗΣ ΚΟΙΝΟΤΗΤΟΣ ΚΑΤΑ ΤΟ ΕΤΟΣ 1908

Κων. Διαμαντόπουλος, Πρόεδρος　　Α. Γάβαρης, Γραμμ.　　Γ. Κωνσταντόπουλος, Ταμ.
Θεόδ. Δούκας, Νικ. Σορόκος, Δ. Καραγκιουλές, Λεων. Διζές, Ἐπαμ Σταυράκος,
Νικ. Γούναρης, Θεόδ. Καβάκος, Σωτ. Νιφάκος, καὶ Παν. Σκαλτσούνης, Σύμβουλοι.

Historical Memorandum dated December 10, 1908

By resolution, Nicholas Gounaris was authorized to collect donations on behalf of the parish.
Members in good standing were listed in alphabetical order. The Board of Trustees for 1908 included:
Constantine Diamond, President; Anastasios Gavaris, Secretary; George Konstant, Treasurer; Theodore
Doukas, Nicholas Sorokos, James Karangelen, Leonidas Dezes, Epaminondas Stavrakos,
Nicholas Gounaris, Theodore Cavacaos, Sotirios Nifakos, and Peter Skalchunes.

George Tsembelis (Sempeles) along with his five brothers ran a thriving confectionery business at the Belair Market. Constantine Diamantopoulos (Diamond) operated a candy-making shop at 105 West Lexington Street near Liberty Street. Early businessmen like Sempeles and Diamond were sometimes called the "Mayflower Greeks." The hard work and determination of these pioneering immigrants provided the impetus to begin a formal church community in Baltimore.

The first president of the Board of Trustees was George Sempeles who served in 1906 and 1907. During his tenure, the parish was successful in obtaining the services of a full-time priest from church authorities in Greece. Constantine Diamond was elected parish council president in 1908. Under his leadership, a search committee was successful in finding a church building for the Greek Orthodox congregation.

George Sempeles,
First Parish Council President

Constantine Diamond,
Second Parish Council President

Elias Karangelen and his wife, Anastasia, posed with their children (standing left to right):
Nicholas, William, and Demetra. In 1907, Demetra Karangelen married Michael Doukas (far right).
The 1908 roster of church members, shown on the opposite page, listed both Michael Doukas (no. 17)
and Elias Karangelen (no. 23). They were among the earliest Greek families to settle in South Baltimore.

Leonidas Dezes

Constantine Diamond

Theodore Doukas

Peter Karangelen

Certificate of Incorporation and Signers
of the Historic Charter dated June 4, 1909

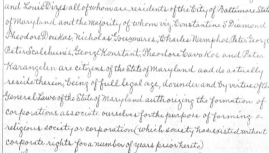

Nicholas Gounaris

Charles Nemphos

Theodore Cavacos

George Konstant

Peter Skalchunes

Peter George

The Beginning of Wisdom is the Fear of the Lord (Book of Proverbs 1:7) is the translation of the Greek phrase on the stained glass window originally installed at the Homewood Avenue Church.

During Father Douropoulos' tenure, the community witnessed the transition from a rented church hall to the acquisition of a permanent house of worship. An advisory committee to the Board of Trustees, composed of Charles Nemphos, Antonios Konstant, Nicholas Gounaris, and Menas George, was assigned the task of finding a suitable location. To secure the transaction, Theodore Cavacos, a charter member, mortgaged his Roland Avenue property and provided the church with a $4,000 cash down payment.

Land Records show that on October 5, 1909, the Greenmount Avenue Methodist Episcopal Church, located at 1100-1104 Homewood Avenue, at the corner of Chase Street in East Baltimore, was acquired for $12,000. The Cavacos funds were applied to the purchase and the remaining balance of $8,000 was secured by a mortgage to the Provident Savings Bank. Within ten years, in January of 1919, the mortgage was paid in full.

The legal documents to acquire the church were officially signed by "Rev. Constantine A. Douropoulos, President" of the "Orthodox Greek Church Evangelism"—most unusual during an era when laymen were in unquestioned control of church administration. In the month prior to the acquisition, the charter was amended to include the priest as an elected member of the Board of Trustees. Without other records from that time, the reason for inverting the church's name and electing the priest as council president remains a mystery. Regardless, purchasing the Homewood Avenue Church helped solidify the community.

The Greek immigrants now owned their own building, a House of God, one they could adapt to the Orthodox tradition. A stained glass transom installed in the entrance foyer would greet parishioners for the next two and a half decades. Illuminated in brilliant red-colored glass lettering were four words in the Greek language: *Arhi Sofias Fovos Kyriou* (The Beginning of Wisdom is the Fear of the Lord). The first floor area contained a large hall that was soon used for meetings and for teaching classes. Two winding staircases, comprised of twenty wooden steps on each side of the main entrance, led parishioners to the main sanctuary on the upper level. The acquisition of a church building ushered in a new era of progress. Continuing this positive trend, the well-respected Professor Aristo Soho was elected president of the parish council in 1910.

Church activities began to flourish, as did the sacramental life of Baltimore's Orthodox Christians. The Greek population continued to grow as immigrants married and started families. This is evident from the Greek households listed in the U.S. Federal Census. Of note to this parish is the census conducted in April of 1910. At 1106 Homewood Avenue, the parish house adjacent to the church, Father Constantine and Presbytera Alexandra Douropoulos were listed with all eight of their children, two cousins, and a servant. The two youngest children, Athanasios and Helen, were born in Baltimore. Their oldest son, Dionysios, was studying at The Johns Hopkins School of Medicine to become a doctor. Dionysios Douropoulos also assisted his father in teaching the parish children to read and write Greek.

Presbytera Alexandra Douropoulos with Athanasios and Helen, her two youngest children who were born in Baltimore.

The Very Rev. Parthenios A. Rodopoulos

Title page of the oldest parish registry book written by Father Parthenios Rodopoulos, 1911.

During the early part of 1911, a "reorganization" of the parish took place. Two historic publications clearly indicate that following the departure of Father Douropoulos, the "Greek community was reorganized" and afterward continued to make "great progress." The exact cause of this reorganization remains unknown. Adding further to the mystery is the absence of any registry of sacraments during the four-year tenure of the learned and scholarly Reverend Constantine Douropoulos, one of the most prominent Greek Orthodox priests in America at that time.

City records, however, document he was still in Baltimore as late as May 7, 1911, performing a wedding ceremony while the parish council, under the leadership of Theodore J. Doukas, prepared to welcome his replacement. Whether or not there was dissension over his level of authority can only be speculated. One fact, however, remains clear. Father Douropoulos is the only priest in 100 years of parish history to ever serve as president. After he departed for Pittsburgh, the role of the priest was redefined and kept separate from the Board of Trustees—which is believed to be the essence of the parish reorganization of 1911.

As his successor, the community welcomed The Very Rev. Parthenios A. Rodopoulos who arrived from Pittsburgh during the spring of 1911. In eloquent penmanship, this 39-year-old clergyman, with a Doctorate in Theology, inscribed the title page of the oldest existing ecclesiastical records of the parish. The "Book of Registry of the Eastern Orthodox Greek Community Evangelismos of the Theotokos" was dated May 12, 1911. As the second full-time priest in Baltimore, Father Rodopoulos began keeping organized records of the sacraments he performed. These and subsequent ledger book entries of countless baptisms, weddings, and funerals, chronicle the joys and sorrows of parishioners from a bygone era.

Anastasios Eliopoulos and Stamatiki Karangelen (seated) were married on September 15, 1912. Standing *l to r* : George Eliopoulos, Gus Kargas, Bestman Antonios Sourtzis, Peter Eliopoulos, Dimitra E. Carellas and George Carellas. Children *l to r* : Mary and Athena Carellas.

Diamando (Jenny) Karukas married Anastasios Routzounis (Ernest Rose) on November 24, 1912. The Rose family ran the first Greek-owned bakery in Baltimore called the Sparta Baking Company.

Dimitrios Pavleros and Yiannoula Spanakos (seated center) were united in Holy Matrimony on January 21, 1912. Left to right: Epaminondas and Mary Asimakes holding daughter Jenny, Peter and Stavroula Spanakos, Bestman George Lericos, John Pavleros, George and Stavroula Lericos with their children, William and Julia. An unidentified gentleman posed on the *flokati* rug.

The Vlangas Family, 1908. Standing left to right: Elias Vlangas (in traditional *foustanella*), Peter Christakos, William E. Vlangas, Nicholas Sorokos and Theodore G. Vlangas. Seated left to right: Peter E. Vlangas, Georgia Vlangas Vlahos holding infant Sophia, Konstantinos Vlahos and George E. Vlangas.

The Baltimore County Confectionery and Ice Cream Parlor, 525 York Road in Towson, Maryland, with Proprietor James T. George (right), 1912.

Broadway Market, Broadway and Fleet Street in the Fells Point district, circa 1915. The Prevas confectionery and soda fountain business (lower left) was established here in 1899 shortly after John P. Prevas (inset) arrived in Baltimore. He was listed in the oldest known roster of church members dated 1908 and served as a *psalti* (cantor) during the early years.

The immigrant parish's sense of unity and strength in these early years is evident by the many activities that began to unfold. Once established in a house of worship, they turned their attention to the challenge of preserving the ancestral language for their children. The first Greek language school was established at the church hall in 1912 with Mr. S. Karras as the first instructor. Subjects included reading and writing of the Greek language as well as religion and Greek history. In addition, the school children presented plays and commemorated ethnic holidays such as the observance of Greek Independence Day. The immigrants demanded long hours of study from their children. The first generation absorbed the language and culture of America from the public schools and all things affiliated with their heritage from the Greek school. A diverse education was viewed as a necessity for their success.

The desire to learn more about the heritage of their newly-adopted country was wonderfully demonstrated during this period. A small group of parish children attended the National Star-Spangled Banner Centennial Celebration held at Fort McHenry in September of 1914. The children learned the origin of the American national anthem, composed during the famous Battle of Baltimore in 1814, and were photographed with their chaperone, Kaliroi (Kate) Prevas, who assisted the Greek school instructor during those years.

The oldest known Greek School diploma, dated July 8, 1916, documents the graduation of 14-year-old James G. Prevas.

Program Booklet for the Star-Spangled Banner Centennial Celebration held in September of 1914.

Kaliroi Prevas (center) and a group of parish children visited Fort McHenry for the Star-Spangled Banner festivities in 1914.

Parish leaders also realized that in addition to the common bond offered by church life, a sense of community was also needed when a death occurred. In Greece, the dead were not embalmed, but rather buried on church grounds and, after a few years, their sacred bones were unearthed, cleansed, and preserved. By contrast, in America the dead were buried in cemeteries and not disinterred. During the period from 1900-1910, the Greeks who died in Baltimore were interred in cemeteries scattered throughout the city. This evoked a sense of isolation that led to serious discussion among parish leaders for the establishment of a cemetery.

Under the leadership of Antonios D. Konstant, the goal of securing burial grounds was realized in 1912, only three years after the church became incorporated. In what would be the first of four distinct purchases in the North Avon section at Woodlawn Cemetery, a 1,000-square-foot parcel of land in the shape of a circle was acquired for $500. Church Secretary Peter Nicolopoulos (Nicholson) finalized the business details. Arranged in five rows, it contained nearly 50 grave plots and was named the "Greek Circle." On January 18, 1912, a group of mourners attended the first Orthodox funeral at Woodlawn. That day, Father Rodopoulos conducted the burial of Epaminondas Vasilakos, the two-year-old son of Evangelos and Angeliki Vasilakos from South Baltimore.

Parish Council President Antonios Konstant and his wife, Katherine, circa 1912.

The "Greek Circle" was founded in 1912. It is located within Baltimore's historic Woodlawn Cemetery near Gwynn Oak Avenue. Church Secretary Peter Nicholson (inset) established the business relationship with cemetery officials.

Dimitrios Koniditsiotis, a confectioner at the
Hollins Market, was murdered in the fall of 1912.

GREEK FIGHTS POLICE

George Saradoupolos, Accused Of Murder, Resists Two Sergeants.

THREE MEN ROLL IN STREET

After Attempting To Use Pistol And Hatchet, The Prisoner Is Subdued With Blow Of Night Stick.

Battling for their lives with a man wanted for murder, Sergeants Carberry and Hughes, of the Southwestern district, fought George Saradoupolos, a Greek, for 15 minutes on Hollins street, near Carey, shortly after 10 o'clock last night. The policemen succeeded in overpowering the man only after they had stunned him with their night sticks.

Saradoupolos is alleged to have murdered a fellow-countryman, James Conitsiotis, 1108 Hollins street, on the morning of October 27, when Conitsiotis caught his slayer in the act of robbing his home.

The arrest last night was due to the sharp wits of Mrs. Kate Prevas, who is living in the house where Conitsiotis was killed. She knew both the dead man and the accused. She was walking on Baltimore street, near Carey, shortly before 10 o'clock, when she saw Saradoupolos a few paces ahead.

Woman Warns Police.

Meeting Sergeants Carberry and Hughes a minute later, she called in an excited voice, "There goes Conits' man." The Sergeants did not catch the meaning of her words, and she repeated them, adding, "policemen steps and m to go le three the in ake the Market ition. prisoner doupolos

WIDOW ACCUSES GREEK

Declares Saradoupolos Is Man Who Killed Conilsiotis.

PRAYED FOR HIS PUNISHMENT

He Hid His Him In fied As St

Identifying session of G charged with as one that widow of th fronted the Police Static

Conitsiotis he grappled his home. was dying a

SLAYER DIES IN ASYLUM

George Saradoupolis Confessed To Killing James Conitsiotes.

Death probably cheated the gallows yesterday when it claimed George Saradoupolis, who confessed a month ago to Detective Porter that he had stabbed James Conitsiotes last October. Saradoupolis died at the Springfield Asylum for the Insane, where he was taken a week ago from the jail, where he was being held pending trial in the Criminal Court on the charge of murdering Conitsiotes.

A day after his arrival at the asylum the Greek made an attempt to end his life. The physicians say he was a raving maniac. He refused food and fought the physicians. According to Dr. Charles J. Carey, the cause of the man's death was pneumonia, due to his weakened condition.

The Conits murder story was highly publicized in the newspapers during January and February of 1913.

Another interesting story regarding the Greek Circle illustrates how the immigrants clung together through hardships. In West Baltimore, Dimitrios Koniditsiotis (James Conits), age 60, was murdered on October 27, 1912, while attempting to subdue an intruder he caught robbing his Hollins Street home. It was a sensational crime story for that era and no less than ten articles appeared in the newspapers. *The Baltimore Sun* reported how members of the Greek colony "joined with the police in searching the city" for the killer as a "steady stream of visitors" called upon his widow, Eleni, to offer sympathy.

The killer turned out to be a Greek named George Saradopoulos who was described as "the only Greek loafer in Baltimore, because he would not work, while the rest of his fellow countrymen are a thrifty lot." Saradopoulos evaded authorities for over two months before his violent apprehension, legal proceedings in criminal court, and ultimate death after spending just four days at the Springfield Asylum. The murder of James Conits, patriarch of one of the earliest Greek families to settle in Baltimore, was a tremendous shock to the parish. His tombstone is the oldest original monument in the historic Greek Circle—the first Orthodox burial ground in the State of Maryland.

The following year, the first financial institution of the Greek community was organized. Charter records reveal that on December 23, 1913, the Greek-American Building and Savings

Association of Baltimore City was incorporated and managed by twelve directors: Professor Aristo M. Soho, President; Stylianos Petrohilos, Vice President; Peter N. Nicholson, Secretary; Stephen Monocrusos, Treasurer; and Anastasios Coroneos, Antonios D. Konstant, Leonidas A. Dezes, Theodore S. Agnew, Michael Doukas, Theodore Angeletopoulos, John P. Lauber and George F. Lang. With its office initially at 307 N. Paca Street, the association assisted compatriots in securing loans and purchasing properties. Helping its members meet their financial needs would, in turn, solidify and strengthen the community.

The church progressed during its first decade due to the devoted energies of numerous individuals and successful businessmen. One such entrepreneur was Stylianos Petrohilos who was born in Smyrna, Asia Minor, and raised on the Island of Kythera. He was involved in numerous organizations such as the Masonic Order, the Greek-American Building Association and the Pan-Hellenic Union. His untimely death on November 17, 1914, at the young age of 39, resulted in the first large bequest to the Annunciation community. According to his last will and testament, nearly $2,300 was disbursed to the Greek Orthodox Church—an outstanding amount for that era. Stylianos Petrohilos, the first great benefactor of the parish, was laid to rest in the Greek Circle at Woodlawn and special memorial services were held annually in his honor for over two decades.

Emmanuel Cavacos, Nicholas Coroneos, Stylianos Petrohilos, 1909.

Church Secretary
Stephen Monocrusos

Stylianos Petrohilos (far right) became the first great benefactor of the Annunciation Church.
He posed with business partner Harry G. Pappas (far left) and two employees in their unique store
that had entrances from 109 Park Avenue (confectionery) and 108 N. Liberty Street (cigars), circa 1912.

Interior view of a typical Greek confectionery store, 849 North Gay Street near Ashland Avenue.
Left to right: John Asimakes, Jenny Asimakes (toddler), Epaminondas and Mary Stavropoulos Asimakes, 1912.

For many Greeks, the financial success of their businesses and establishment of a church indicated their future was to be found in the United States. This does not imply they broke ties with their mother country. Many immigrants routinely sent portions of their earnings to families who remained in Greece. The outbreak of the Balkan Wars of 1912-1913 also released a flood of patriotism among the immigrants in America who recalled Greece's long and enduring history of struggle against the Ottoman Empire. In New York, the Pan-Hellenic Union had great success in its efforts to mobilize volunteers.

It was estimated that throughout the United States over 40,000 immigrants departed to join the army in Greece which was allied with Serbia and Bulgaria in the military conflict against Turkey. Among them were Constantine Cavacos, Peter Chrisikos, Leonidas Christakos, George Conits, Nicholas A. Coroneos, Agesilaos Doukas, James Doukas, James George, Thomas George, Nicholas Karangelen, William Karangelen, George Katsaros, Nicholas Mandrapilias, Spiros Morakeas (Morekas), Athanasios Panos, Nicholas Panos, George Sempeles, John Stamatakos, Stavros Vlahoyiannis, George Vlangas, and others.

Upon conclusion of military hostilities, they returned to their adopted country and resumed American life. Many, who decided to make America their permanent home, brought even more relatives and friends to the land of opportunity. By this time, steamships of the National Greek Line, such as the *S.S. Patris*, were in full operation bringing immigrants directly to America from seaports such as Gytheon, Kalamata, Patras, and Piraeus. The arrival of additional Greek immigrants during this period is chronicled in the Baltimore City Directories. New immigration to the city continued steadily during the first decade after the establishment of the church.

The *S.S. Patris* brought thousands of immigrants to America for over a decade (1909-1920).

Nicholas A. Coroneos   George Koniditsiotis (Conits)   Agesilaos Doukas

ΕΛΛΗΝΟΤΟΥΡΚΙΚΟΣ ΠΟΛΕΜΟΣ 1912 Ἀνίχνευσις ὑπὸ τοῦ ἱππικοῦ ἐν Ἠπείρῳ.

Actual battle scenes from the Balkan Wars (1912-1913) were photographed and distributed
through postcards. The Greek immigrants in America were extremely proud to serve their homeland.

The substantial growth of the Greek communities in America, however, did not produce organizational stability. Without the supervision and guidance of a hierarch, the churches were run as self-contained, independent organizations. Within parishes, there were disputes over administrative matters. The parish priest, hired by laymen to attend to spiritual needs and administer sacraments, was often regarded merely as an employee. In his book entitled *Greeks in America*, published in 1913, Thomas Burgess commented on the dismal situation: "The only solution seems to be a resident bishop for America; may his advent be soon!" Five more years would pass before church officials from the homeland would visit to set the groundwork for an archdiocese.

The history of Baltimore's Greek community during the period after the Balkan Wars is quite sketchy. Parish council minutes, which could provide more insight into this era of organizational growth, are non-existent. (Note: The oldest record book of Cathedral parish council minutes begins with the year 1922.) Fortunately, information about the priests of the community, with reference to the

The Very Rev. Chrysanthos Kaplanis

time period they served the parish, can be found in the books of baptisms, weddings, and funerals. An examination of these church documents reveals that after a two-year tenure, Father Rodopoulos left Baltimore sometime in May or June of 1913.

Shortly after, by June 25, 1913, The Very Rev. Chrysanthos Kaplanis, age 37, was welcomed as the third full-time priest. Father Kaplanis, from the city of Megara near Athens, had immigrated to America in the fall of 1912 and was first assigned to the Greek community in Philadelphia. The only information about his six-month tenure in Baltimore concerns the number of sacraments he performed—sixteen baptisms, four weddings, and five funerals. Various sources, however, reveal his final week at Annunciation was marked by tragedy. On January 10, 1914, Petros K. Doukas, a young stock clerk, was crushed to death in a freight elevator. Six days later, Dimitrios Zafirakis succumbed to pneumonia and was survived by his 18-year-old widow, the former Katherine Stavrakos. Following these funerals, all handwritten records kept by Father Kaplanis end abruptly in January of 1914, strongly indicating his departure from Baltimore.

Petros K. Doukas (left) along with his sister Katherine and brother Dimitrios K. Doukas settled in Baltimore by 1910.

Furthermore, the total absence of any recorded sacraments for the remainder of 1914 suggests no full-time priest had been assigned to the parish that year. Two historic documents substantiate this theory. The first is the Baltimore City marriage record of Harry G. Pappas, age 29, to Kalliope Pistolas, age 18, on March 1, 1914, who were wed by Father Joakim Alexopoulos, the visiting priest from the St. Sophia Church in Washington. Eight months later, the administration account for the late Stylianos Petrohilos listed the payment of $27 to bring a "Greek Minister" from Philadelphia to perform his funeral services on November 19, 1914. The priest was Father Christos Angelopoulos who would be assigned to Baltimore on two separate occasions in the upcoming decade.

Even without a priest during 1914, the parish carried out its responsibilities in a systematic manner. For instance, for each burial in the Greek Circle, the church sent a formal letter of authorization to the Woodlawn Cemetery office. These historic letters, written by the early Greek immigrants, are preserved within the cemetery archives and document the names and titles of church leaders during an era in which no parish council minutes exist. Early parish secretaries, such as Peter Nicholson, Stephen Monocrusos, Basil Constant, and George Stavropoulos, managed church affairs as they operated their own successful business endeavors—stabilizing the Annunciation parish as it matured and evolved into a viable religious organization.

The Very Rev. Joakim Alexopoulos performed the wedding of Kalliope Pistolas to Harry G. Pappas at the Lehmann Hall on Howard Street on March 1, 1914. The bride (wearing a veil) and groom are standing in the center of the photograph. Bestman Stylianos Petrohilos (seated) would pass away later that same year.

The Very Rev. Iakovos Leloudas

The marriage certificate of George Stavropoulos and Sophia Karangelen was signed by Father Leloudas, October 10, 1915.

for five continuous years and activities progressed. For example, the first youth organization was established in 1915 and named the "Greek-American Athletic Association." The first officers were James Kamites, President; Nicholas Laskaris, Vice President; Niketas A. Konstant, Secretary; and Elias Kyriakos, Treasurer. Eight young men served as directors for this historic first youth group. They included Nicholas L. Dezes, George Karangelen, Spiros Katsaros, James G. Konstant, Louis Lambros, Nicholas Papadopoulos, George Sapounas, and Peter Vlangas. When the youth association later dissolved, its treasury was turned over to the Annunciation Church.

During this time, the first major social event in the community was presented—a drama depicting the exploits and tragic death of Athanasios Diakos, a national hero in Greece's 1821 war for independence from Turkish occupation. George Konstant donated the cost of all required scenery and a stage was built in the church hall. The main theatrical roles were played by the following: Lena Hadjecosta, Constantine Chambers, Spiros Katsaros, Niketas A. Konstant, John Mavromihalis, and Peter Nicholson. Directing and acting in the performance was Elias Mavromihalis. Well-educated in Greek and quite the eloquent speaker, his role as organizer and director of the play was appropriate. Elias Mavromihalis would be recognized for decades as an outstanding poet laureate of the Greek community, even delivering sermons on ethnic holidays and other special occasions.

The Greek community received its next priest through the efforts of parishioner Nicholas Sakelos who was acquainted with The Very Rev. Iakovos Leloudas. Father Leloudas, age 53, originated from Sakelos' hometown of Nafpaktos. After arriving in America in 1907, Father Leloudas was assigned to the parish in Springfield, Massachusetts, and by 1914 was transferred to nearby Holyoke. Upon receiving Sakelos' letter of invitation, he accepted the offer to become the fourth full-time priest in Baltimore with a clearly-defined job assignment— a $50-monthly salary which included the duties of church maintenance. Within a year, his salary was increased to $75 per month.

With the arrival of Father Leloudas in January of 1915, the listings of sacraments again began to be recorded quite regularly. He served Baltimore

Left to right: Elias Mavromihalis, Niketas A. Konstant and Panayiotis Paraskevakos in a classic studio pose, circa 1915.

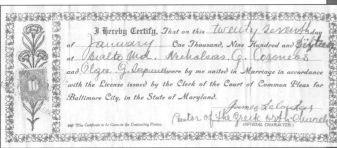

Father Leloudas often used James or Jacob for his first name as shown on the Coroneos-Sapounas marriage certificate, 1916.

Olga Sapounas and Nicholas G. Coroneos posed in this romantic fashion on their wedding day, January 27, 1916.

The first decade also brought acclaim to a parishioner who had devoted himself to artistic studies. Emmanuel A. Cavacos, from the Island of Kythera, had established himself in Baltimore after living briefly in Egypt. His brother, Theodore, was a well-known confectioner in the Hampden district and encouraged his schooling in the arts. While enrolled at the Maryland Institute to study painting, the director of the Rinehart School of Sculpture was greatly impressed by his talent and strongly advised him to focus on sculpture. In 1911, Emmanuel Cavacos was awarded the prestigious Rinehart Scholarship which enabled him to pursue his studies at the Beaux Arts School in Paris.

Two years later, his work entitled "Aspiration" was awarded honorable mention at the *Salon des Artistes Francais*. Another of his unique creations was known as the "Weeping Widow." This landmark monument within the Woodlawn Cemetery depicted his sister-in-law, Mary, mourning the death of his brother, Theodore. Emmanuel Cavacos became a renowned figure in the art world and his award-winning sculptures were soon featured at exhibitions in Paris, New York, Chicago and other cities including Baltimore. (*See p. 90.*)

Emmanuel A. Cavacos and a postcard of his famous sculpture "Aspiration," which was awarded honorable mention in Paris, 1913.

Petros D. Nifakos (Peter Nemphos), Poet

Another noteworthy achievement of that era was in the field of literature. The earliest known member of the parish to have his writing published was Petros D. Nifakos (Nemphos). In May of 1917, the Cosmos Printing Company of New York distributed the poignant poetry of this scholarly immigrant in a 16-page booklet entitled *O Ponos Mou Pros Tin Filtatin Patrida* (My Pain for the Beloved Homeland). His poems covered a variety of themes including the struggles faced by compatriots as they adjusted to the American way of life. The literary work of Petros Nifakos, whose father was a highly-respected priest in the village of Milea in the province of Laconia, received wide circulation and brought a great sense of pride to the Baltimore congregation.

The parish was also fortunate to have laymen who were gifted with fine singing voices and the knowledge of Orthodox Church hymns. They were called *psaltes* (cantors). In the years before the advent of choirs, these men chanted the liturgical hymns and responses to the priest during worship services. One of these early cantors was Stavros Vlahoyiannis. He was involved in many aspects of church life and proudly witnessed Father Leloudas perform the baptism of his children. Like most

Ο ΚΑ·Υ·ΜΟΣ ΜΟΥ ΑΠΟ ΤΗΝ ΞΕΝΗΤΕΙΑ

Ἔχω καρδιὰ στὰ στήθη μου θλιμμένη
  δὲν ἀντέχει τοῦ ἔρωτος λαλιά,
εἶναι γεμάτη λύπαις, πικραμένη,
  σὲ ἀτελείωτη θανάτου ἀγκαλιά.

Στῆς ξενητειᾶς τὰ δίκτυα μπλεγένη
  δὲν ἔχει πειὰ παρηγοριά.
Γιὰ νὰ παρηγορήσω τὴν καρδιά μου
  πρέπει νὰ λάβῃ ὅ,τι ποθεῖ.

Πρέπει νὰ λάβῃ ὅ,τι ἔχει χάσει,
  τῆς μάννας μου τὴν τελευταία εὐχή.
Φωνὴ ἄχ τὶ οὐράνια ποῦ σὰν ἀντικρύζω
  τῆς πατρίδος φωνὴ τρομερὴ

Ποῦ φωνάζει τὰ παιδιά της νὰ ἔλθουν
  καὶ στὸ Μὰρς αὐτὴ τὰ καλεῖ.
Νὰ τῆς δώσουν τῆς δόλειας βοήθεια,
  ποῦ τὴν πλήττει ὁ ἐχθρός,
  τὴν πονοῦνε τὰ στήθεια.

Τὰ παιδιά της στὰ ξένα θλιμμένα
  δὲν θὰ μποροῦναι νὰ φθάσουν ἐκεῖ
ἐκεῖ ποῦ ἡ πατρὶς ἡ γλυκειὰ τὰ καλεῖ
  καὶ τρέχουν τριγύρω θλιμμένα.

Τῶν βουνῶν ἡ πολύοσμος αὔρα
  ἐκχυλίζουσα τ' ἄνθη φυσᾷ,
καὶ ἡ αὐγὴ χρωματίζει χρυσᾶ
  τῆς πατρίδος στὰ ξένα τὴν λαύραν.

Nifakos' poem, entitled "My Sorrow from a Foreign Land," recounts the loneliness of the immigrant generation.

Stavros and Vasiliki Vlahoyiannis with their children: Ekaterini, Dimitrios and Eleni, 1918.

Greeks of that era, the Vlahoyiannis family never imagined that political storm clouds gathering in the homeland, thousands of miles away, would soon affect them in the United States.

In the meantime, the desire of the immigrants to perpetuate the many aspects of Hellenism in America led to the first officially chartered organization affiliated with Baltimore's Greek Orthodox community. It was named the Greek-American Association "Progress" and existed for over a decade promoting "social, literary, dramatic, fraternal, and musical" endeavors. Organized on December 6, 1918, by George Stavropoulos, Charles Nemphos, and John Prevas, this group was the first to sponsor an *Artoclasia* (ceremonial blessing of holy bread) and later held social functions raising money to benefit the parish. The oldest existing photograph of an event sponsored by the association shows a well-attended dance held in 1921 complete with patriotic décor.

By the end of the first decade, emigration from the homeland had gained in momentum. Statistics for 1914 alone show that approximately 14,000 Greeks departed from ports in the greater Athens area. The number swelled to 18,000 in 1915. Letters sent to relatives and friends in Greece recounted many wonderful aspects of the American way of life including the lure of financial independence. Some who arrived at Ellis Island made the journey by train to Baltimore, Maryland. For almost ten years, the Greek population of this city had been afforded the opportunity to participate regularly in worship services of the Eastern Orthodox faith.

The Greek-American Association "Progress" sponsored a dance at the Lehmann Hall, 852 N. Howard Street, in February of 1921. "Progress" was the first chartered club within the Greek community of Baltimore. It would be followed in later years by regional and philanthropic organizations.

Newlyweds George Sempeles, age 38, and his wife, Vasiliki, age 24, arrived in New York on August 24, 1915.

Church membership had grown substantially and there was reassurance that the Annunciation community was progressing in a positive direction. Within a short time after acquisition, the former Methodist Episcopal Church at the corner of Homewood Avenue and Chase Street had been transformed into the first Greek Orthodox Church in the State of Maryland. It was the focal point for all events associated with Greek culture. The parish council, as early as 1915, was even discussing a possible relocation to larger quarters—an event that would not occur for two more decades. What was not realized in Baltimore, or elsewhere, was that new problems and deep divisions within the Greek community were about to unfold. Even though the church was the center of activities, Greek ethnicity and politics sometimes took precedence over religious matters. As a result, the upcoming decade of parish history would be remembered as one of unrest and instability.

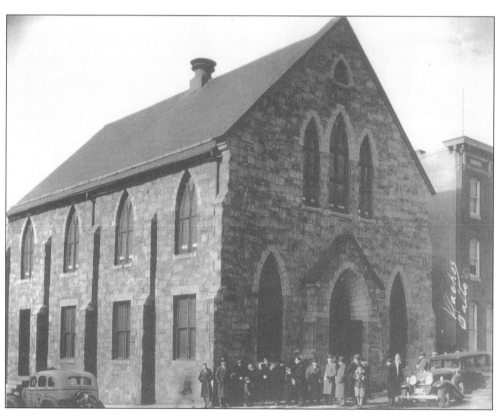

The Greek Orthodox Church of the "Evangelismos" (Annunciation) stood at the corner of Homewood Avenue and Chase Street. Purchased in 1909, this location served the community for nearly three decades. The adjacent row house, 1106 Homewood Avenue, was the parish rectory.

Opposite Page: Wedding of Erifili A. Coroneos and George Vaggi, Polish Home Hall on South Broadway, January 24, 1918.

1916-1925

During the spring of 1916—the Tenth Anniversary of Annunciation—the main topic of parish business was the community's burial grounds. Four years after its purchase, the "Greek Circle" at Woodlawn was nearly filled and the church was negotiating to acquire a larger section. The Woodlawn Cemetery had offered 6,000 square feet for $4,500…a price tag beyond the means of the Greek community. Apparently church leaders were persistent negotiators. Records show an agreement was finally reached after five months of discussion. In explaining the discounted price, Woodlawn officials wrote, "The Greek Church is an old customer of our Cemetery and its members are generally of moderate means." Therefore, they were "willing to make more than reasonable concessions in this one instance." By the summer of 1916, the expansion of the burial grounds was accomplished.

The agreement for the purchase of the "Greek Plot" was signed on August 16, 1916, by Leonidas A. Dezes, Parish Council President; Antonios Konstant, Treasurer; and Basil D. Constant, Secretary. The total cost of only $2,100 was paid to the cemetery in five installments over the next three years. By April of 1919, Church Secretary George Stavropoulos issued the final payment of $600 with a letter of appreciation to the cemetery office. Later that year, Past President Leonidas Dezes, who was instrumental in acquiring this section, died at the age of 50. Hundreds of respectful mourners were in attendance on November 22, 1919, as he was laid to rest in the first row of the parish cemetery.

The decision to purchase this second section in 1916, which allowed for nearly 325 burials, could not have been timed better. Within two years, the tuberculosis and influenza epidemics that swept across America also

The "Greek Plot" consists of nearly 325 single graves arranged in thirteen rows. It is located in the picturesque North Avon section of the Woodlawn Cemetery.

THE WOODLAWN CEMETERY COMPANY

August 16, 1916.

THE ORTHODOX GREEK CHURCH EVANGELISM, of Baltimore, Maryland, hereby agree to purchase from THE WOODLAWN CEMETERY COMPANY a piece of ground as part of GREEK CIRCLE, as shown on diagram hereto attached, for the sum of Twenty-one hundred dollars, ($2,100.). And I agree to pay for the same as follows: Three hundred dollars cash, Two hundred dollars January 1, 1917, Five hundred dollars May 1, 1917, the balance, of Eleven hundred dollars, to be paid within twelve months from May 1, 1917. Should the Eleven hundred dollars not be paid within the time above stated, Six per cent will be charged on the said Eleven hundred dollars from May 1, 1917,

Under the presidency of Leonidas (Louis) A. Dezes, the parish acquired additional cemetery property in 1916 known as the "Greek Plot."

Widower John Kousouris stood in solemn vigil over the casket of his wife, Maria, on March 12, 1919.

affected many of the Greeks in Baltimore. The contagious nature of these illnesses often forced the afflicted into isolation within the confines of hospital institutions. As burials became more frequent, names of victims like Anastasia Theodorides, Diamando Routzounis (Rose), and Marigo Prevas were added to the memorial hymns chanted at Annunciation. Records show that during the period from 1916 to 1919, Father Iakovos Leloudas performed over 60 funerals, as one family after another made the somber procession up the winding path to the Greek Plot.

The Coroneos family provides one example of these tragic times. Compatriots who celebrated the wedding of Erifili Coroneos to George Vaggi on January 24, 1918, gathered nine months later to attend funeral services for this bride. She died from influenza at the age of 26 and was laid to rest on October 17, 1918—one of three Greeks who were buried that same day at Woodlawn. History also documents a number of parish women died during childbirth. For instance, John Kousouris mourned the death of his 32-year-old wife, Maria, while welcoming the birth of a daughter, Christina, in March of 1919. The emotions must have been overwhelming. With faith and resolve, these pioneering Greeks resumed their lives. The events of that era were difficult, to say the least, and no doubt took a toll on record-keeping and church administration.

Leonidas and Stavroula Dezes (seated) with their children: Nicholas (far left); Alex (center); Tassea (far right); Vasilios (front left); and Olga (front right), circa 1913.

During this second decade, attention was also placed on the church building. With membership increasing, the idea was proposed to relocate. The St. John the Baptist Roman Catholic Church at the northwest corner of Paca and Saratoga Streets seemed most suitable, but the price of $70,000 was not feasible. It is interesting to note that even up to May of 1925, the St. John's Church was still being considered for purchase by the parish general assembly but no decision was reached. While searching for larger quarters, the idea of renovating the Homewood Avenue church gained popularity, at least among a minority group led by Parish Council President George Katsaros.

Documents from September of 1918, however, show the legality of the parish council's decision—to hire G. Walter Tovell, a contractor, to renovate the Homewood Avenue Church—was challenged in Circuit Court. The bill of complaint filed by Basil D. Constant, Leonidas A. Dezes, and Stephen Monocrusos claimed the majority of the parish was opposed to the alteration of the church and that the council had failed to secure the necessary majority vote, as required by parish regulations, to spend $10,000 on a renovation—a large sum for that era. Opponents were also concerned about financial stability, claiming the parish only had a cash reserve of $1,000.

Shocked by the legal action brought against them, church leaders George Katsaros, George Stavropoulos, and Nicholas Sorokos diplomatically retreated from the renovation project and ended the dispute in a most interesting manner. Within a month, in an effort to restore harmony, a new president, George Poulitsas, assumed leadership of the parish council in October of 1918. Considering America's recent involvement in World War I, a "Greek Church Resolution," preserved only in court records, was issued by outgoing President George Katsaros, on September 20, 1918, which stated in part: "Whereas the War Industries Board at Washington, D.C., in view of the shortage of

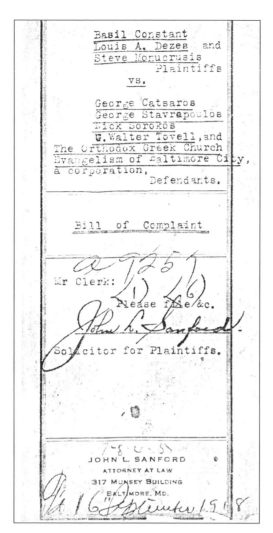

Basil Constant
Louis A. Dezes and
Steve Monucrusis
            Plaintiffs

vs.

George Catsaros
George Stavrapoulos
Nick Dorokos
G. Walter Tovell, and
The Orthodox Greek Church
Evangelism of Baltimore City,
a corporation,
            Defendants.

Bill of Complaint

Mr Clerk:

Please file &c.

Solicitor for Plaintiffs.

JOHN L. SANFORD
ATTORNEY AT LAW
317 MUNSEY BUILDING
BALTIMORE, MD.

Circuit Court records dated September 16, 1918,
show that parish leaders were involved in a legal dispute
over the validity of a church renovation project.

George Poulitsas (Politz), Parish Council President,
later served as church secretary from 1920-1921.

George Katsaros, Parish Council President,
also served as a cantor during the early years.

labor, material, and for other reasons relative to the present war, asks that this work be postponed until after this war shall have been won: now, therefore, be it Resolved by the Trustees of the Greek Orthodox Church Evangelism [sic] of Baltimore City, recognizing and considering the pure patriotism of the Greeks…as citizens and residents of their adopted country, the great United States of America, and having evidenced their loyalty by sending many of their people to the battle front…that we do hereby order all work on said Church stopped…and we do hereby solemnly pledge ourselves to stand behind our President, the Honorable Woodrow Wilson, Commander-in-Chief of the Army and Navy of the United States of America, in every way to help win this war."

The avid patriotism shown by the Greeks in America during the time of the First World War was evident not just through church resolutions but by the large numbers who enlisted in the armed forces. Once the Selective Service Act was passed in 1917, Greek-Americans enthusiastically responded to the call for volunteers. After the Armistice was signed in November of 1918, grand celebrations were held in cities everywhere. The Greeks, proud of their new country, joined in the revelry. The war was over, but another type of conflict had already begun.

Louis Matthews

Louis Chios

James J. Doukas

George A. Markulis

Clockwise from top: George B. Conits, George J. Karangelen, Nicholas Maniatis and James G. Konstant, circa 1920.

Though attempting to assimilate into American society, the Greek immigrants were still immensely tied to their native culture, traditions, and politics. As opposing political parties in Greece formed during World War I, Greek communities across America also began dividing along political lines. The key players in the ensuing drama were King Constantine I and Prime Minister Eleftherios Venizelos. The two statesmen first split on the issue of Greece's intervention in the Great War. King Constantine felt the Axis powers were invincible and that his small nation should remain neutral. Venizelos strongly favored his country's support of the Allies and accused the King of pro-Germanism. The opposing parties became known as "Royalists" and "Venizelists."

In the fall of 1916, Venizelos went to Thessaloniki and established a revolutionary government resulting in the dethronement and exile of King Constantine. As a state-run church, Orthodox hierarchs were immediately drawn into the controversy. Archbishop Theocletos, the royalist hierarch of Athens, vigorously denounced Venizelos and discredited him in the eyes of the people. Liberal priests supporting Prime Minister Venizelos refused to acknowledge the King and his

Eleftherios Venizelos (1864-1936)
Prime Minister of Greece

Constantine I (1868-1923)
King of the Hellenes

The steamship *S.S. Espagne* brought Orthodox Church leaders from Greece to the United States in 1918. Their historic mission ultimately led to the establishment of the Greek Orthodox Archdiocese in New York by the fall of 1921.

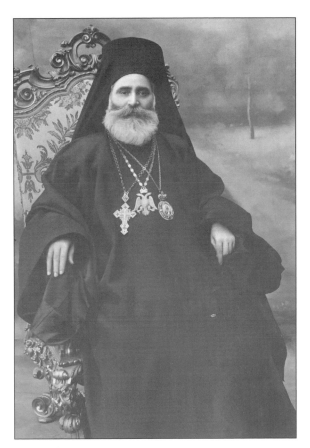

Meletios Metaxakis, Archbishop of Athens, who later became the Ecumenical Patriarch of Constantinople.

family during church services. Soon after, a special council of bishops appointed by Venizelos publicly defrocked the royalist Archbishop and replaced him with Meletios Metaxakis who was regarded as a Venizelist. The reaction in both Greece and the United States was violent.

Throughout America, church communities divided into volatile factions and trouble awaited any priest whose political views were contrary to the majority of board members. Without a central authority, the transfer of priests from one parish to another only worsened with the injection of politics. The first attempt to centralize the churches came in the summer of 1918 when Meletios Metaxakis, Archbishop of Athens, came to the United States to set the groundwork for an organization. Passenger arrival records provide interesting documentation on this historic visit that would soon impact the Orthodox parishes in America.

On August 22, 1918, the *S.S. Espagne*, a steamship of the French Line sailing from Bordeaux, France, arrived in New York. Among the passengers was 46-year-old Metropolitan Meletios Metaxakis. A Greek bishop named Alexander of Rodostolou, age 43, accompanied him. Six people were part of their "diplomatic" entourage which included a deacon, a secretary, and a teacher. Their trip to America was recorded as an "ecclesiastical Greek mission" with the final destination as the Greek Consulate in Washington, D.C. Many hoped their arrival would bring peace and order. Unfortunately, the visit also triggered the emotions of the royalists and aggravated the factional strife.

Bishop Alexander of Rodostolou, who later became the first Archbishop of the Greek Orthodox Archdiocese.

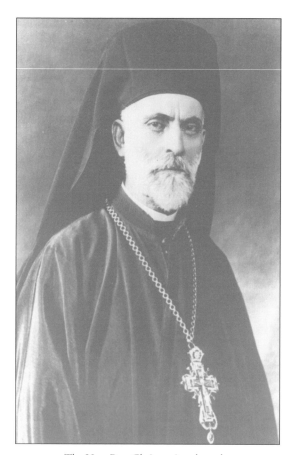

The Very Rev. Christos Angelopoulos

The Very Rev. Polykarpos Marinakis

In the fall of 1918, trouble began when Metaxakis installed Bishop Alexander of Rodostolou as the Synodical Exarch to administer to the Greek Orthodox churches in America. Alexander faced difficulties and was quickly labeled a Venizelist. His political leanings were clear when he sent a decree to all parishes ordering them to cease commemorating the king's name during religious services and instead commemorate the Greek nation and army. In Baltimore, the royalist clergyman, Father Iakovos (Jacob) Leloudas, refused to follow these instructions and news of his insubordination quickly got back to the Bishop.

The idea of replacing Father Leloudas was being discussed by the summer of 1920, as a brief telegram sent to the church on Homewood Avenue by Bishop Alexander clearly indicates. After five years of service, Father Leloudas was dismissed. Two pro-Venizelist successors were to follow. The Very Rev. Christos Angelopoulos, a native of Argos, Greece, assumed duties by September 1920 and, for reasons unknown, only stayed two months. Then, as a replacement, The Very Rev. Polykarpos Marinakis, who originated from Smyrna, Asia Minor, was assigned to the parish on November 4,

1920. His tenure was also short-lived. After the royalist party triumphed in the elections later that month, Father Marinakis refused to recognize King Constantine's return to the Greek throne and soon faced repercussions.

By the spring of 1921, the parish council, under the leadership of pro-monarchist George Stavropoulos, invited Father Leloudas back to Baltimore. Dismayed by the situation, Father Marinakis pleaded his case to Bishop Alexander in a telegram dated April 6, 1921. Apparently, the council was about to discharge him for failure to recognize the Holy Synod. From his message, we also learn that some of Baltimore's Venizelists suggested for Father Marinakis to establish a new church. The confused clergyman wrote, "Let me know what to do. Must I stay here or not." The Bishop decided it was best not to split the community and instead transferred him to another church. After five months of service, a disheartened Father Marinakis vacated the parish house at Homewood Avenue and Chase Street.

To the delight of the royalists, The Very Rev. Iakovos Leloudas was welcomed back to serve in

George Stavropoulos, Parish Council President (1919-1921).

Stylianos Pamfilis, Parish Council President (1922-1923).

Baltimore. Meanwhile, after deposing Metaxakis in Athens, the Holy Synod dispatched Germanos of Troyanos as the new royalist bishop for the United States. The strong feeling aroused by this political feud is documented on the passenger list for Bishop Germanos Troyanos, who arrived in New York aboard the *S.S. King Alexander* on July 2, 1921. He listed himself as Archbishop for the Orthodox Church of America. A telegram from the Holy Synod to the Greek Legation in Washington reinforced this position forbidding Archbishop Meletios Metaxakis and Bishop Alexander "all interference with the affairs of the Greek Churches in America. Please communicate the above to all priests." No doubt frustrated by these developments, the Venizelists would be revitalized by upcoming events.

Unswayed by the royalist Greek Legation, Archbishop Meletios Metaxakis invited clergy and church leaders to a meeting in New York during the summer of 1921 to incorporate the parishes under one central authority. It would be the first Clergy-Laity Congress—a meeting that evoked resentment from those who feared that the efforts of the self-governed churches, built with the hard-earned monies of the immigrants, would soon be undermined. In the midst of much chaos, a constitution was agreed upon and the newly-formed Greek Orthodox Archdiocese, at that time labeled as a political arm of Prime Minister Venizelos, was officially incorporated during the fall of 1921.

Another event that helped the cause of the Venizelists occurred in November 1921 when Meletios Metaxakis was elected as the new Ecumenical Patriarch of Constantinople. He departed for the homeland following a powerful farewell speech calling for parish unity. As a result, the tide of support in America began shifting back toward Bishop Alexander. In Baltimore, Venizelist support was evident at the parish council election held in February 1922. Stylianos M. Pamfilis was elected President along with a new Board of Directors. The oldest existing parish council minutes begin with this administration and were diligently kept by Peter Vlahopoulos, parish secretary. Within a few months, however, these church leaders would find themselves involved in a civil suit against the church. It was a most unusual scenario that unfolded in the following manner.

By the spring of 1922, Mr. Pamfilis received important news and announced it to the parishioners. By decree, the new Patriarch Metaxakis reinstated the Greek Orthodox communities in America under the jurisdiction of the Ecumenical Patriarchate—ending their dependence on the pro-royalist bishops of the Holy Synod in Athens, Greece. This change in authority gave the Venizelist cause added strength. Royalists were outraged by the decree and Father Leloudas realized his position was once again in jeopardy.

The minutes from the parish council meeting held on March 21, 1922, state clearly the council's desire to replace the current royalist priest. After church leaders consulted with Bishop Alexander in New York, Father Leloudas received his termination via "registered letter" shortly after the celebration of Holy *Pascha* (Easter). Filled with bitterness, the clergyman found himself dismissed from Annunciation for a second time. Records show by May 5, 1922, The Very Rev. Christos Angelopoulos, a known supporter of Venizelos, was enthusiastically welcomed back for a second term. Baltimore, like many other Greek communities, seemed hopelessly divided.

A major step toward unity occurred on May 17, 1922, when Patriarch Metaxakis issued a Synodical Tome that formally announced the establishment of the American Archdiocese and named Bishop Alexander as the first Greek Orthodox Archbishop in the United States. In this historic document sent from the Patriarchate in Constantinople, all churches were advised to "willingly cooperate with him in everything regarding the good administration of the ecclesiastic affairs of the Archdiocese" in order for them to "secure the appreciation and benediction of the Mother Church and the blessings of God."

This rare interior view of the Greek Orthodox Church on Homewood Avenue shows The Very Rev. Iakovos Leloudas conducting the services of the *Apokathelosis* (Lowering of the Body of Christ from the Cross) on Holy Friday, April 14, 1922. Father Leloudas, assisted by an acolyte, posed for this photograph a few weeks before his replacement was named.

The historic first visit of Archbishop Alexander to Baltimore's Greek community took place on
Sunday, May 21, 1922. The Archbishop (wearing glasses) posed outside the Homewood Avenue Church
with parishioners and the newly-hired priest, Father Christos Angelopoulos (standing beside him).

A banquet in honor of Archbishop Alexander (far left) was held at the Liberty Hotel, 1439 N. Charles Street,
owned by Christos Alevizatos (seated fifth from left). The priest, parish council, and members of the congregation
dined with the first Archbishop and his Archdeacon Germanos Polyzoides (seated to his right), May 21, 1922.

Four days later, on Sunday, May 21, 1922, Archbishop Alexander visited Baltimore, accompanied by his Archdeacon Germanos Polyzoides, and celebrated the parish's first Hierarchical Divine Liturgy. Afterward, a banquet was held at the Liberty Hotel on Charles Street owned by Christos Alevizatos, a member of the parish council and avid supporter of the new Archbishop. That day historically came to symbolize the beginning of a working relationship between the parish and the new Archdiocese. In 1922, however, the Archpastoral visit evoked unfavorable response from the royalists who wanted Father Leloudas reinstated. The battle lines had now been drawn.

The following month, records from the Circuit Court of Baltimore City show that the royalists filed a civil suit against Father Angelopoulos and the parish council in an attempt to regain Father Leloudas' position as official parish priest. Emotions were at a fevered pitch. On June 29, 1922, *The Baltimore Sun* ran an explosive article, "Greek Priest Fight Renewed in Court – Basis of Trouble is Division of Opinion as to Central Head of Orthodox Church." The royalists claimed the Holy Synod, not the Ecumenical Patriarch, was in charge of the transfer of priests and therefore the dismissal of Father Leloudas was illegal.

Father Angelopoulos (left) and Father Leloudas (right) were at the center of the political controversy. On June 28, 1922, the royalist supporters of Father Leloudas took legal action. The following day, *The Baltimore Sun* published this unique story.

GREEK PRIEST FIGHT RENEWED IN COURT

Rev. Jacob Louloudas Makes Another Effort to Oust Incumbent Pastor.
PETITIONS FOR INJUNCTION

Basis Of Trouble Is Division Of Opinion As To Central Head Of Orthodox Church

Fight for control of the Greek Orthodox Church, Homewood avenue and Chase street, has been renewed. Legal action was taken again yesterday to remove the Rev. Christos Angelopulos as pastor and to reinstall the Rev. Jacob Louloudas, who was pastor before the installation of the Rev. Mr. Angelopulos last month.

The Rev. Mr. Louloudas and some of his followers, through James [T.] O'Neill, attorney, filed a bill in the Circuit Court, asking that the Rev. Mr. Angelopulos be enjoined from acting as priest of the church, and that he and the officers of the church be prohibited from interfering with the Rev. Mr. Louloudas in the discharge of his duties as priest.

To Show Cause By July 18.

An order was signed by Judge Carroll T. Bond, requiring the Rev. Mr. Angelopulos and the officers of the church to show cause before July 18 why the injunction should not be issued.

Charges were made in the petition that the Rev. Mr. Angelopulos has no authority to act as priest of the church while that office is filled by the Rev. Mr. Louloudas.

Authority In Dispute.

It is contended in the petition that the authority of the Rev. Mr. Angelopulos is not derived from the Holy Synod of Greece.

This is the basis of the dispute which has split the congregation. The members cannot agree on the identity of the head of the Greek Orthodox Church. The supporters of the Rev. Mr. Louloudas declare the Holy Synod is the true head of the church, while the supporters of the new priest claim the Patriarch of Constantinople as the head.

That the new priest has no power to perform the sacraments of marriage and baptism and that a marriage performed by him would be open to question in the courts of Greece are maintained in the petition.

The Prevas Brothers were key organizers of the royalist movement within Baltimore's Greek community. Left to right: John Prevas and his wife, Katherine, with sons Nicholas and Peter; Themistocles Prevas and his wife, Mary; Nicholas Prevas and his wife, Eugenia, with children Marie, Peter and Charles, 1923.

The unusual court proceedings, which included a lengthy deposition of Archbishop Alexander, took much energy and consumed the parish agenda throughout 1922. Some monarchist families adamantly refused to partake of sacraments at Annunciation. For instance, as Father Leloudas awaited the outcome of the court case, he performed the marriage ceremony for Themistocles Prevas and Mary Petkovitis on January 28, 1923, at the Polish Home Hall on South Broadway. At one point, Father Leloudas even filed a complaint that he was deprived access to his room at the parish house by the family of his rival, Father Angelopoulos, and was "compelled to procure sleeping quarters" at a nearby hotel. In the end, the royalists' attempt to oust Father Angelopoulos failed. The court case was dismissed on February 15, 1923, and Father Leloudas left Baltimore, never to return.

The departure of Father Leloudas, however, did not symbolize the end of Baltimore's royalist movement. In fact, in the early months of 1923, political hostility worsened. Following the news

of King Constantine's death, the royalists requested a memorial service be conducted. Father Angelopoulos and the parish council refused. Then, at the general assembly meeting held on May 13, 1923, the parish voted to officially recognize the Greek Orthodox Archdiocese in New York as its "superior ecclesiastical authority." This charter amendment was signed by Stylianos Pamfilis, Nicholas G. Coroneos, George Katsaros, Nicholas Gounaris, Christos Alevizatos, Peter Vlahopoulos and Vasilios Andreadis. From the royalists' perspective, Annunciation was now a "Venizelist" church.

During the spring of 1923, the royalist movement in Baltimore gained momentum under the leadership of John P. Prevas who, like the majority of royalists, originated from the province of Laconia. They desired to form an independent church and advertised for a priest in the *Atlantis*, a national daily Greek newspaper. The Rev. John Magoulias traveled from Ohio, was interviewed, and became their clergyman. The building at 701-703 North Broadway at the corner of Monument Street was rented and converted quickly for

The Rev. John Magoulias,
Holy Trinity Greek Orthodox Church

The business card of Father Magoulias was
preserved in the files at Woodlawn Cemetery.

Orthodox worship services. Soon, a parish house was established at 2105 Jefferson Street where Father Magoulias and his family resided throughout the decade of the 1920's.

Royalist leaders chose the name "Holy Trinity" for their church and even secured donations, icons, and support for their new venture from the Holy Trinity Russian Orthodox congregation located a few blocks away on Fairmount Avenue at Jackson Square. After weeks of intense preparation, the first Divine Liturgy of the Holy Trinity Greek Orthodox Church was conducted on Sunday, July 1, 1923, with Father Magoulias officiating. Substantial donations were made to the new parish and to further distance themselves from Annunciation, the royalists followed the Julian Calendar rather than the more progressive Gregorian Calendar used by the Venizelists.

Many Greeks expressed concern over the split of the community into two rival churches and Annunciation leaders paid close attention. Families such as Asimakes, Karavedas, Karukas, Mavromihalis, Prevas, Stavropoulos, Thiamengos, and Vlahoyiannis, who once supported the Homewood Avenue Church, were now aligned with the church on Broadway. An election of officers was held and John Coliviras was named first president. The Holy Trinity Church also started offering classes in religious studies and a Greek language school for the children. Two churches were now seeking support and membership from Baltimore's Greek population. Parish council minutes from August through October 1923 allude to discussions about reuniting the community…yet nothing materialized.

The year 1924 began with a visit from Archbishop Alexander who came from New York to officiate at Annunciation's Divine Liturgy on New Year's Day. He arrived in Baltimore to find the Greek community had now followed the trend of other Orthodox congregations in America—divided along political lines into rival churches. In the meantime, the royalist Metropolitan Germanos had been recalled to Greece. As his successor, an even more impassioned leader named Metropolitan Vasilios Kombopoulos was sent to continue promoting the royalist fervor in America.

An example of the feelings aroused by the separation of Annunciation and Holy Trinity can be illustrated by the difficulty that arose regarding the use of the burial grounds. As Holy Trinity parishioners passed away, Woodlawn Cemetery opened graves in the Greek Plot as they had done for years after receiving authorization from the Greek Church. It appears that Holy Trinity leaders

Harry G. Pappas served as Council President of the Annunciation Church in 1924 and wrote to Woodlawn about the conflict over the use of the parish cemetery.

The Greek Orthodox Church,
EVANGELISM
Corner Chase Street and Homewood Avenue

Baltimore, Md., October 18th 1924

Woodlawn Cemetery.
Woodlawn.
Maryland.

ATTENTION OF MR. GREEN.

Dear Sir:

I understand that there has been several burials made in the lot belonging to the above church, for which no were permits for opening the grave/issued. I desire to notify you herewith that no graves must be opened, unless you obtain a written permit from the Greek Orthodox Church "EVANGELISM", signed by the President Harry G. Pappas of the Greek Community of the above Church. If there should be a burial made without this permit, we shall be compelled to charge you, the necessary amount, which should have been paid by the relatives of the deceased. Namely $20.00 for members and $50.00 for non-members.

I also would like to have you furnish me with a list of the burials made for the years 1923 and 1924 with the names, ages and addresses of the deceased.

Thanking you for this information, and knowing that you will assist us in the above, I am,

Yours truly

Harry G. Pappas
President.

attempted to hide their status as an independent parish from cemetery officials. Needless to say, Annunciation was not pleased to learn that Holy Trinity was using its cemetery.

In a letter dated October 18, 1924, Harry G. Pappas, president of the parish council, alerted Woodlawn officials about this disturbing matter and warned that no graves were to be opened without a written permit from Annunciation. In addition, Mr. Pappas requested a list of the Greek burials for 1923 and 1924. Whether or not Annunciation collected fees from those families is a matter of speculation. For cemetery officials, the message was clear. They would be charged a fee if they continued to allow Holy Trinity members to use the Greek Plot.

Within two weeks, the royalists were forced to secure their own burial grounds. Records show that on November 7, 1924, the "Holy Trinity" section at Woodlawn was acquired for $1,200. It consisted of 90 graves, arranged in three rows, directly in back of the "Greek Plot" owned by Annunciation. The signer for the purchase was Elias Mavromihalis, President of Holy Trinity. The adversarial relationship between the two churches had now divided the sacred burial grounds into separate sections.

Elias Mavromihalis was Council President of the Holy Trinity Church from 1924-1926.

The Rev. Athanasios Avlonitis

The 1920's proved to be a turbulent era in the history of Baltimore's Greek community. Schism led to anger and confusion, dissolved business partnerships, and created hard feelings among compatriots. Internally, Annunciation even experienced turmoil affecting the Greek school, church administration and clergy assignments. For instance, parish council minutes from June of 1922 show the termination of the Greek teacher, Natalie Lazarides, who was hired in 1920. A committee also concurred with the teacher's own complaint that "it was impossible to conduct school while the children's parents do not show the faintest interest in the regular attendance of their children." The instructor, a graduate from a prominent college in Athens, even threatened legal action upon her dismissal. Fortunately the matter was settled and a new teacher, Peter Kargakos, was able to turn around the parental apathy.

In the midst of stabilizing the Greek school, the need suddenly arose for a new clergyman. For reasons unclear, Father Angelopoulos, who was nearing 60 years of age, tendered his resignation and departed in early August 1923. As his replacement, the Archdiocese assigned The Reverend Athanasios Avlonitis, the priest in Norfolk, who did not arrive in Baltimore until September 1923. Throughout these difficult times, the parish moved on with its business and planned activities.

For example, following the atrocities inflicted on the Greeks in Asia Minor by Turkish nationalists in 1922, Annunciation sponsored fundraising drives and sent donations to the Near East Relief organization headquartered in New York. With the expansion of church facilities unresolved, the parish council investigated and declined another property…a spacious Protestant sanctuary located at Maryland Avenue and Preston Street. In the booming economy of the early 1920's,

ΕΛΛΗΝΙΚΗ ΟΡΘΟΔΟΞΟΣ ΑΝΑΤΟΛΙΚΗ ΕΚΚΛΗΣΙΑ
Ο ΕΥΑΓΓΕΛΙΣΜΟΣ ΤΗΣ ΘΕΟΤΟΚΟΥ

however, the cost of $80,000 was beyond the means of the parish. Some fifteen years later, the Greek community would in fact purchase this impressive church building.

Many successful social functions were also recorded. For instance, following the Feast Day observance of the *Kimisis Tis Theotokou* (Dormition of the Virgin Mary), Annunciation sponsored a grand community picnic on August 28, 1923. It was held at Arion Park, featuring a Greek musical ensemble, perhaps in an effort to draw support from the Greek population at large. This earliest known picnic took place one month after the royalists officially withdrew from the parish. The following year, in November 1924, a special committee of two dozen parishioners, under the chairmanship of Harry G. Pappas and Nicholas D. Couzantino, was appointed to organize an elegant dance with a distinctive American flavor. This event was held on February 5, 1925, at the Lehmann Hall. That evening, Farson's Gywnn Oak Orchestra, under the direction of noted bandleader Gilbert W. Smith, was hired to entertain the Greek community.

However, even with the royalists gone from Homewood Avenue, church affairs remained unsettled. Priests continued to arrive and depart from Annunciation with alarming frequency. On February 7, 1924, Archbishop Alexander received this by-now-familiar request from Baltimore: "Father Avlonitis leaves community. Important you send Father Symeon at once." After serving for only five months, Father Avlonitis apparently returned to Norfolk. By early March 1924, The Rev. Symeon Emmanuel became the next full-time priest. Sixteen months later, the parish council accepted Father Emmanuel's letter of resignation. His service to Annunciation concluded on July 1, 1925, and the Archdiocese was again asked to find a suitable replacement. Records show that two letters of complaint from parishioners triggered the entire matter.

The Rev. Symeon Emmanuel

Members of the Annunciation Greek Orthodox Church gathered for a picnic outing at Arion Park on August 28, 1923.
Some of the families in attendance (left to right) included: Paxenos, Coroneos, Panos, Tzortzopoulos (George), Magulas, Conomos, Vlahopoulos, Carman, Matthews, Pappas, Stergiou, Sapounas, Mentis, Souris, Lericos, Panos, Pavleros, Pamfilis, Psomas and Gounaris.

ΕΛΛΗΝΙΚΗ ΟΡΘΟΔΟΞΟΣ ΕΚΚΛΗΣΙΑ
"Η ΑΓΙΑ ΤΡΙΑΣ"

Royalists attended a memorial service for King Constantine at the Holy Trinity Greek Orthodox Church,
Broadway and Monument Street, on Sunday, June 15, 1924. A sequel photograph from the event shows the church
interior (see next page). Uniformed representatives from the Greek Legation in Washington, D.C. were also in attendance.

This interior view of the Holy Trinity Greek Orthodox Church shows the elaborate
funeral bier created as a memorial tribute to King Constantine I of Greece who died in 1923.

At the Holy Trinity picnic, Father John Magoulias posed with the parish children,
a few parishioners, and the musicians who entertained the group at Arion Park, 1926.

The Very Rev. Constantinos Statheros

BOY, 7, DROWNS ON OUTING AT ROCK CREEK

Hamilton's children in the neighborhood of Berwick avenue poured into the home of Nicholas C. Coroneos today to view the body of his son George, seven, who was drowned yesterday when he fell into 10 feet of water in Rock creek where many of the congregation of the Greek Orthodox Church went for an outing.

Just how the little fellow was led into the accident has not been determined, although he did not seem to be dead when his body was drawn from the water. Rescuers worked over the body for a prolonged period before the coroner from Glenburnie pronounced death.

Young Coroneos was one of the favorites of his Sunday-school, which he attended regularly. He was in a gathering of several hundred when they started in buses for the shore, where there were church services prior to the entertainment features.

The tragic death of George N. Coroneos at the Annunciation Church picnic was reported in *The Baltimore News*, September 7, 1925.

Resignations were the order of the day. Even a few cantors left in dissatisfaction and, on more than one occasion, replacements had to be found in haste. Feelings of malcontent ran so high during the summer of 1925 that the parish council decided to postpone the community picnic until church affairs ran a smoother course. The event was finally rescheduled for Sunday, September 6, 1925…but the cloud over Annunciation only seemed to darken. What began as an afternoon of fellowship ended in great sorrow. The son of Nicholas and Olga Coroneos accidentally drowned at the parish picnic held at Myer's Shore at Rock Creek near Pasadena, Maryland. A letter sent from the church office authorized cemetery officials to prepare for the burial: "This is to advise you of the death of Master George Coroneos, age seven years." The Greek community, steadfast in its faith and traditions, comforted the grief-stricken family. A new clergyman, who arrived in Baltimore a few days prior to the ill-fated event, would conduct the funeral services.

Records show that by September 5, 1925, the parish council under the leadership of Peter Lambropoulos (Lambert) welcomed The Very Rev. Constantinos Statheros as the next priest. Father Statheros, age 36, originated from Dardanelles, Turkey, and immigrated to America in November of 1922, a year after the Archdiocese was formed. The passenger manifest of the *S.S. Saxonia* sailing from Cherbourg, France, listed his destination as New York and his sponsor was Archdeacon Germanos Polyzoides, the assistant to Archbishop Alexander. Following his assignment to Baltimore, Father Statheros also began instructing the students of the Greek language school. For his various services to the parish, he was paid a total monthly salary of $200. The Annunciation community's hope for stability, after receiving its ninth clergyman, would again be short-lived.

By the following summer, the parish council relieved Father Statheros of his duties as the Greek schoolteacher, eliminated his teaching stipend, and reduced his monthly salary to $150. To fill the position, Athanasios Angelidis was hired as the new teacher. Not surprisingly, after one year of service, Father Statheros departed from Baltimore for another church assignment. Parishioner complaints against priests who often demanded more rights and higher salaries led to administrative tension. Records show that salary issues dominated the agenda and likely triggered the many changes in clergy during this period.

It was fortunate that numerous Greek societies would start to emerge in Baltimore throughout the 1920's, assisting the churches in overcoming administrative and financial difficulties. In fact, many social functions held by these organizations served to unify church members during a time when political differences were pulling them apart. The founders of Annunciation could not have imagined that nearly twenty years after organizing, the parish would be overshadowed by such deep internal strife. How could two rival churches survive in Baltimore? One of several meetings to reconcile differences was held in the spring of 1927 at the Broadway Methodist Episcopal Church—a decidedly neutral location. Once again, proud participants on both sides of the political issue rejected attempts to reunite. Thankfully, a resolution to the conflict was only a few years away.

The Very Rev. Constantinos Statheros performed the burial rites for Gabriel H. Gabrielides on June 2, 1926.
This solemn gathering at Woodlawn Cemetery is the only known photograph showing Father Statheros in Baltimore.

Opposite Page: Laconian Association Officers, 1926. Seated left to right: Constantine Stamatakos, George Zarafonetis, Vice President; Niketas A. Konstant, President; George J. Karangelen, Treasurer; Dimitrios Karambatos, Secretary. Standing left to right: Louis Chios, George C. Konstant, Peter Rois, John Christopoulos, Constantine Kourniotis (Kanaras), James P. Karukas, Aristotelis Athanasopoulos (Harry Athas).

1926-1935

By the time the Annunciation Church reached its Twentieth Anniversary year, modest expansion of the church facility had begun. Parish council minutes show that electricity had been installed in the parish house, a furnished office was in place, and a "hot air system" was added for the comfort of worshippers. Land Records also show that the property at 720-722 East Chase Street, adjacent to the rear of the church building, was acquired on February 12, 1926. Shortly after, the council obtained a loan for $5,000 to pay for renovations. Though the specific nature of the expansion remains unclear, it is apparent that the parish was outgrowing its space as membership increased throughout the 1920's.

In fact, it was during this era that some of the largest organizations affiliated with Baltimore's Greek community were established and quickly gained popularity. On October 5, 1923, the Worthington Chapter No. 30 of the Order of AHEPA (American Hellenic Educational Progressive Association) was organized in Baltimore. First officers included: Stylianos M. Pamfilis, President; Victor Pappas, Vice President; Peter N. Nicholson, Secretary; Harry G. Pappas, Treasurer; Peter Vlahos, Warden; Nicholas G. Coroneos, Chaplain; Stephen Monocrusos, Captain of the Guard; and Peter Kargakos, Inside Sentinel. The Baltimore group was one of hundreds of chapters that ultimately formed across America still existing to this day.

The initial and primary objective of AHEPA, established in 1922 by Greek businessmen in Atlanta, Georgia, was to promote "pure and undefiled Americanism" among the Greeks—a proactive way to combat the prevalence of anti-foreign sentiment during that era fueled by the notorious agenda of the Ku Klux Klan. At the Annunciation Church in Baltimore, a most interesting example of American patriotism was displayed.

A memorial service was held for the late Warren Harding, President of the United States. Following his death on August 2, 1923, the parish council, composed of numerous members of AHEPA, approved up to $50 for a memorial wreath to mark the solemn occasion. In its fraternal form, the AHEPA also hoped to stay removed from the Greek political issues facing its compatriots.

Soon, however, the AHEPA found itself tangled in a unique form of rivalry. Those who opposed the AHEPA's mission, feeling it symbolized a doctrine of total de-Hellenization, organized to preserve the language, culture, and heritage of Greece. This group was named GAPA (Greek-American Progressive Association). Three years after GAPA was founded in Pittsburgh, Pennsylvania, the "Koraes" Chapter No. 14 was established in Baltimore in November 1926 with John Ressis, President; Achilles Hondroulis, Vice President; Nicholas Mallis, Secretary; and Vasilios Klosterides, Treasurer. The board of directors included Constantine Mesologites, Constantine Minadakis, Stylianos Sfekas, Michael Solomonides, and Sotirios Kouridis. Though GAPA and AHEPA were rivals, both organizations were products of immigrants attempting to adjust to American society. Their main difference was over the issue of language. AHEPA used English as its official language; GAPA

AHEPA "Worthington" Chapter Officers, 1926. Seated left to right: Stylianos Pamfilis, Past President; Constantine Cavacos, Treasurer; Victor Pappas, President; Peter Nicholson, Vice President; Andrew Alexander, Secretary. Middle row left to right: Anthony Raptis, Kostas Paxenos, Theodore Agnew, Harry Arhos, Harry Delaportis. Back row left to right: Angelo Schiadaressi, Nicholas Gounaris, and Athan Zissimos.

GAPA "Koraes" Chapter Officers, 1926. Seated left to right: Vasilios Klosterides, Treasurer; Achilles Hondroulis, Vice President; John Ressis, President; and Nicholas Mallis, Secretary. Standing left to right: Constantine Minadakis, Michael Solomonides, Sotirios Kouridis, Constantine Mesologites, and Stylianos Sfekas, Board of Directors.

promoted the use of Greek. For decades, both groups co-existed and flourished in Baltimore. The success of their social and philanthropic events would greatly benefit and solidify the congregation.

Other fraternal organizations also emerged during this period. These were the *topika somatia* (regional societies) comprised of immigrants who came from specific provinces or islands of Greece. These clubs originated to provide financial and philanthropic aid to their villages or regions, to perpetuate the traditions and customs of the homeland, and to strengthen the bond between fellow members. In Baltimore, one of the earliest organizations of this type was established by a later-arriving group of immigrants from the Island of Rhodes. They sought to assist their island in the Dodecanese which was under Italian occupation during that era. On March 25, 1924, the Pan-Rhodian Society "Apollon" of America, Lodge No. 4, was organized in Baltimore with Savas Kambouris as its first president. By the spring of 1927, a ladies auxiliary was founded with Stergoula Karpathiou as president and Athena G. Markulis as vice president. These women were among the first from their ancestral island to settle in Baltimore.

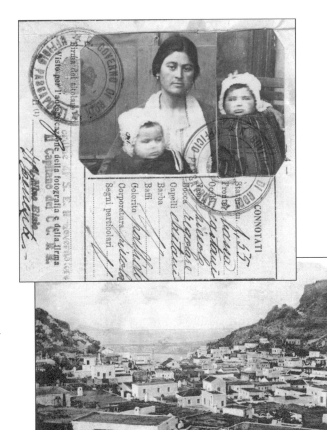

Passport photograph of the first Rhodian woman to arrive in Baltimore. Athena G. Markulis, with twin daughters Zinovia (left) and Panayiota (right), emigrated in March 1924 from the village of Lindos (shown above in postcard c. 1920's).

In the fall of 1925, a second Greek regional society, comprised of immigrants from the province of Laconia, was organized at the Holy Trinity Church. Records show the signers of the Laconian Association "Lycourgos" charter dated September 18, 1925, were Leonidas Christakos, Charles Panayiotopoulos, Charles Chambers, Peter G. Karangelen, Nicholas P. Prevas, and Elias Mavromihalis. The first president of the group was the distinguished Leonidas Christakos and other first officers were: George Kalogerakos, Vice President; Dimitrios Karambatos, Secretary; Niketas A. Konstant, Treasurer; and Directors George J. Karangelen, Constantine Kourniotis, Peter Bougadis, Dimitrios Plainos, George Panagakos, John Panos, and Peter Spanakos.

With a yearly commemoration to its patron saint, *Ayios Nikon*, the society provided financial assistance to the churches and villages throughout Laconia as well as donations to the Baltimore parish. The Laconian Society, as well as many of the other clubs that would later organize, followed a similar pattern of expansion. Soon after a chapter was established in Baltimore, auxiliary branches for the women, boys, and girls would be formed. Through social events, financial contributions, and participation in litanies of *Artoclasia* (blessing of the holy bread) to honor patron saints, the decade of the 1930's would show the *topika somatia* playing a prominent role in the life of Baltimore's Greek Orthodox Christians.

It was also during the mid-1920's that clubs with specific philanthropic goals within the church emerged. In September of 1926, *Enosis* (Union)

Charter of the Elpis Ladies' Society, 1929.

became the first Greek Ladies' Society established at Annunciation with Mary T. Cavacos elected as first president. Its purpose was to serve the church, the Greek school, and the needy. At the Holy Trinity Church, a similar ladies' society, *Elpis* (Hope), was organized in January 1929 with Jenny P. Asimakes serving as its first president. These clubs were the forerunners of the present day *Philoptochos* (Friends of the Poor) Society.

The Greek immigrants who had served in the United States military during World War I were also successful in organizing a club. The George Dilboy Post No. 12 of the American Legion took root in Baltimore on April 10, 1929. The first commander of this all-Greek American Legion Post was James

Greek School of Highlandtown students and their teacher, Stylianos Koufopandelis (far left), 1928.

Latgis. The American Legion was proud to have a "nationality post" comprised of "comrades whose forefathers were from Greece." The Honor Guard of Post No. 12 would soon take part in numerous distinguished ceremonies representing the community. The stability of many Greek societies and clubs, such as these, helped the Orthodox Church weather the political storm between the Royalists and Venizelists.

Throughout these troublesome times, Annunciation's parish council was able to continue looking to the future needs of the community. By the mid-1920's, choirs and organs accompanied the Divine Liturgies—a departure from customs in the homeland where this type of music was considered a "western innovation" and not typically used. Historically, up to this point, only the *psaltes* (cantors) sang the responses to the priest during religious services. In April 1923, however, records show $50 was paid to host a Greek church choir from Washington, D.C. Their performance must have been impressive.

Soon after, the spring 1923 general assembly approved the "installation of European music" with organ accompaniment and hired Spyridon Safridis as the first music director. Within a few months, a small choir was singing liturgical hymns for the first time in the church on Homewood Avenue. The community was slowly adapting to American culture though not without objections. The following year, after many debates, parishioners voted at the general assembly meeting on March 9, 1924, as to whether or not this type of music should be kept in the church. The music remained and by the mid-1930's a vibrant choir of voices complemented liturgical services at Annunciation.

Also, during this time, there was an increase in the number of Greeks, many from the islands of Chios and Rhodes, settling in the Highlandtown section of the city. Soon, the need for a Greek school in that area began to be discussed. On August 3, 1926, a formal proposal for a school was presented and approved at the council meeting. A Greek School of Highlandtown Committee was formed with Stylianos Sfekas, Nicholas Cianos, and Michael Parris. They hired the first teacher, Stylianos Koufopandelis, and enrolled students for classes that began in the fall of 1926 in a building at the southwest corner of Eastern Avenue and Oldham Street.

Greek Independence Day (March 25th) often included commemorative plays. Students of the Greek School posed in costume with their instructor Maria Nikoludis (seated center) following a presentation, circa 1930.

In reference to the Greek school on Homewood Avenue, an era of new stability began in 1927. Following a number of interim teachers throughout the decade, including priests assisting as instructors, the parish was fortunate to acquire the services of Maria Nikoludis who was among the earliest women from the Island of Chios to settle in Baltimore. She was hired in July 1927 at a monthly salary of $90. In addition to her talents and dedication as the Greek school instructor, she was soon acclaimed as a dramatics coach and theatrical director. Under her guidance, the language program was revitalized and Greek culture was nurtured during her tenure of over two decades.

The social life of Baltimore's Greeks flourished throughout the 1920's. Records show the sponsorship of ethnic holiday celebrations and Greek school programs that were popular and well-attended. One noteworthy event, however, remains a mystery. Evidence exists in the form of an ornate lapel ribbon dated September 27, 1926. The ribbon, with an inscribed medallion, clearly indicates that the "Greek Orthodox Ecclesiastical Christian Fraternity Evangelismos" held a commemorative event that day. Perhaps it was a celebration of the church's Twentieth Anniversary. With no reference to the event in parish council minutes, this elusive eighty-year-old ribbon remains a unique artifact of early parish activities.

Oi Dio Lohoi, 1926. Front children: Peter Sfekas and Mary Perentesis. Seated left to right: John Panos, Elias Mavromihalis, Katherine Mavromihalis, Irene Perentesis, Niketas Konstant and Anthony Pagonis. Standing left to right: James Petkovitis, George Zarafonetis, George Karukas, Euclid, Gregory, and John Perentesis, Leonidas Christakos, Dimitrios Karambatos.

Iphigenia en Avlidi, Keith's Garden Theatre, Lexington Street, circa 1930. Front row left to right: Katherine Kosmides, Amalia Nicholson, Irene Perentesis, Fi Nicholson, Evdokia Rados, Maria Nikoludis, Voula Rois, Mary Katsaros, Praxythea N. Coroneos, Patricia T. Panos. Back row left to right: Antigone Sakelos, Mary Perentesis, Josephine Constantine, Ann Papathomaides, Bertha Lericos, Lillie George, unknown, Mary J. George.

During this decade, some members of the community also started organizing their theatrical talents that led to the production of numerous plays. Among the first presentations were *Oi Dio Lohoi* (The Two Sergeants), *Horos tou Zalogou* (Dance of Zalogou) and *Nix Eleimosinis* (The Night of Charity) given by the Laconian Society. Later, Annunciation sponsored successful productions such as *Iphigenia en Avlidi, I Golfo, I Sklava, Oi Dio Orphanoi, I Kassiani* and others. Many of these plays were presented at the Lehmann Hall located at 852 North Howard Street.

These dramatic productions, along with many community events, have been preserved in fascinating photographs, offering a look at the customs, styles, and traditions of bygone times. The Greeks were proud of their heritage and often hired professional photographers for joyous as well as solemn occasions. Newlywed couples posed following wedding celebrations and mourners often had their picture taken with deceased loved ones as a lasting memorial tribute. These striking images, portraying the life of the immigrants, are one of the most treasured aspects of parish history.

Jenny P. Asimakes and Anthony Synodinos at their wedding reception, circa 1931.

The Rev. Philimon Sevastiades

Other firsts also occurred during this time. Annual church dances began in 1922 and were well-attended. A church bazaar was first held November 22-23, 1926, at the Lithuanian Hall located in the 800 block of Hollins Street in West Baltimore. An admission fee of fifty cents was charged. The official blessing to begin this first parish festival was conducted by the next clergyman assigned to Annunciation, The Rev. Philimon Sevastiades who emigrated from the Island of Rhodes. Father Sevastiades along with his wife and family moved into the parish house at 1106 Homewood Avenue by early September of 1926. Though he served Baltimore for two years, a lengthy time compared to other clergymen, his tenure would be remembered as one of defiance.

By the fall of 1927, the council found itself discussing the priest's transfer due to his faults and differences with the parish, but no decision was reached. Finally, at the parish council meeting held on December 12, 1928, there was unanimous agreement "to request the priest to submit his resignation for the good of the community." Within a few days, Parish Council President John G. Anderson received instructions from Archbishop Alexander who communicated by telegram: "We have appointed Rev. Nikiforos Pavlou as priest of your community. Your former priest is transferred to Roanoke. He was ordered to leave at once. Settle your accounts with Rev. Sevastiades so that he may have no excuse for delay."

As his replacement, The Very Rev. Nikiforos Pavlou arrived in January of 1929 to find a most unusual situation had developed. The defiant Father Sevastiades disobeyed orders and instead organized his own church in the Highlandtown district, much to the dismay of Annunciation and the Archbishop. Records from the Archdiocese show that by December 24, 1928, the Greek

Members of the Greek community posed at this Fourth of July gathering, circa 1928.

The Very Rev. Nikiforos Pavlou

Orthodox Church of St. Markella had been established at 521 South Ponca Street with Philimon Papaioannou, President; and Philimon Karavasilis, Secretary. Reverend Sevastiades' compatriots, however, began withdrawing their support; soon the St. Markella Church was forced to close its doors and Father Sevastiades left the city. As a result, in the early months of 1929, there were actually three Greek Orthodox Churches in Baltimore—something not seen again until forty years later and under much calmer conditions.

These turbulent events within the parish occurred following another unsuccessful attempt to reunite the Annunciation and Holy Trinity congregations. A meeting in April of 1927 held great promise but quickly deteriorated. Subsequent parish council minutes indicate the royalists still refused to acknowledge the lawful existence of the Greek Orthodox Archdiocese in New York. Needless to say, a demoralizing spirit enveloped the Greek community. Further disagreement amongst the royalists even resulted in the termination of their own Father John Magoulias after six years of dedicated service. He was replaced by The Rev. Dimitrios Yiannakopoulos who had barely settled in the parish house on Jefferson Street when news of the stock market crash in October 1929 made headlines across the country. After a decade of relative prosperity, the Greek community soon began to feel the affects of the Great Depression.

At the same time, political hostilities in Greece had subsided and many people had grown weary of a Greek community split into rival factions. With the advent of the Depression, income levels of parishioners decreased having a direct negative impact on church finances. Supporting two churches and two schools was deemed impractical and a tone of reconciliation was evident from both groups. A meeting held on December 13, 1929, led to an agreement to reunite the community under

Picnic outings were popular and well-attended during the early decades of the 20th century.

Leonidas Christakos, Parish Council President
of the Holy Trinity Church, 1929

the following conditions: Holy Trinity's Church would be closed; Holy Trinity's priest would receive a three-month salary; and the possessions and property of Holy Trinity would be moved to Annunciation. In the months that followed, some furnishings from the royalist church were even sold to the Holy Trinity Greek Orthodox Community in Charlotte, North Carolina.

Those who represented the Annunciation parish at the historic reunion meeting were Constantine Cavacos, Stylianos Pamfilis, Nicholas Manos, Jordan Genetos, Harry Arhos, Peter Vlahopoulos, Nicholas Gounaris, Athanasios Panayiotopoulos, and Peter Constantinides. Representatives from Holy Trinity included Leonidas Christakos, Elias Mavromihalis, John Prevas, Konstantine Parthemos, Kostas Kalantzopoulos, Kosmas Ioannou, and Constantine Kourniotis (Kanaras). All who attended took an oath to protect the interests of the Greek community. Father Nikiforos Pavlou, the priest of the reunited parish, led the singing of the liturgical hymn of the Annunciation, *Simeron tis Sotirias Imon to Kefaleon* (Today is the Beginning of our Salvation).

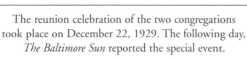

Baltimore Greeks Bury Ax That Caused Political Strife
12·23·29

Differences Engendered In Homeland Are Forgotten As Six Groups Join To Further Aims And Establish School For Children

Differences among Greeks of Baltimore, arising from political strife in their native land ten years ago, ended at Lehmann Hall last night.

The members of two local fraternal societies, two auxiliary organizations, the congregations of two churches and a Baltimore chapter of a national body laid the foundation for a united Hellenic society.

Plan Political Moves

Among the aims of the union of the 6,500 Baltimore Greeks under the guidance of a central committee, will be the political furtherance of the ambitions of the 2,300 registered voters among them.

Included in the representatives at the meeting, which was attended by about 1,500 persons, were members of the Likourgos, Rodion, Prodos and Elpis societies, Ahepa, Chapter No. 30, and the congregations of Holy Trinity Orthodox Church and the Evangelical Orthodox Church.

School To Be Established

Dimetrius Govakos, George Pamfelis and Nicholas Medinos sponsored the movement which they hope eventually to result in the financing of a school for the Greek children of the city. In this school the Greek classics would be taught in addition to the regular curriculum for grade schools.

The election of a governing committee for the united group will be held by the officers of the various societies within several weeks, it was said.

The reunion celebration of the two congregations took place on December 22, 1929. The following day, *The Baltimore Sun* reported the special event.

Constantine A. Cavacos, Parish Council President
of the Annunciation Church, 1929

News of the reconciliation agreement received an enthusiastic response from the community and a reunion celebration was held on Sunday, December 22, 1929. *The Baltimore Sun* covered the event the following day in an article entitled "Baltimore Greeks Bury Ax That Caused Political Strife," which stated in part: "Differences among Greeks of Baltimore, arising from political strife in their native land ten years ago, ended at Lehmann Hall last night." It was reported that over 1,500 people attended the historic gathering. Constantine Cavacos representing the Annunciation Church and Leonidas Christakos of the Holy Trinity Church gave inspiring speeches that "laid the foundation for a united Hellenic Society."

For the Greeks in Baltimore, the arrival of the 1930's was symbolic of a new beginning. Telegrams were sent to Archbishop Alexander informing him of this momentous event. Two months later, on Sunday, February 23, 1930, he visited the reunited Annunciation community on Homewood Avenue to celebrate a Hierarchical Divine Liturgy in honor of the occasion. The reunion in Baltimore was significant and set the tone for other divided congregations to follow. Evidence of a renewed spirit of Christian fellowship was soon demonstrated and helped to ease any remaining tensions.

For instance, parishioners elected Leonidas Christakos, the former royalist president, as the new president of their reunited parish in 1930 and again in 1932. To avoid inconveniencing students in the midst of their studies, the Holy Trinity Greek School was kept open until classes ended in the summer of 1930. Their instructor, Irene Daskalakis, was then hired to assist Maria Nikoludis at Annunciation. A further indication of improved relations occurred when the remaining Holy Trinity grave plots at the Woodlawn Cemetery were incorporated into what became known as the "Greek Section."

Greek School Diploma of Alexandria H. Cardiges, June 1930.

Greek School graduation. Left to right: Mary J. George, Peter G. Stavropoulos, Harriet Papapvlos, Irene Daskalakis and Maria Nikoludis (instructors), Eleni Orfanoyianni, Theodore J. George and Alexandria H. Cardiges, circa 1932.

Eight months into the reunion, the Greek community mourned the death of one of its most prominent and respected leaders, Stylianos M. Pamfilis, age 43. During his tenure as parish council president in 1922, the Annunciation Church hosted America's first Archbishop and won the aforementioned political court case. (*See p. 48.*) In 1923, during his second term as president, the parish officially recognized the new Greek Orthodox Archdiocese of America. He was also instrumental in organizing Baltimore's Worthington Chapter No. 30 of the AHEPA and was elected as its first president in 1923. In the year preceding his death, Mr. Pamfilis was a key negotiator in reuniting a Greek community divided by politics.

It was no surprise that on August 6, 1930, the church was filled to capacity for his funeral which was conducted by The Very Rev. Nikiforos Pavlou. Compatriots and friends, along with former adversaries, gathered to pay their respects to Mr. Pamfilis who, like many others of that generation, died so very young. To honor his memory, a regal monument over six feet high was erected at the Woodlawn Cemetery. Ascending the path to the "Greek Section," the monument is clearly visible as a landmark and symbolizes the hard work and perseverance of that immigrant generation.

The spirit of reunification gained momentum the following year and each event seemed to outshine the previous one. The parish's Ninth Annual Ball was held on Wednesday, February 25, 1931, at the Lehmann Hall on Howard Street. A highlight of the evening's program was a "Grand March" in honor of Leonidas Christakos, President of the Greek community. Three months later brought citywide recognition to the Greeks. On Monday, June 15, 1931, the American-Greek Political Club, under the leadership of Nicholas H. Modinos, sponsored a lavish banquet in honor of Governor Albert C. Ritchie. The event was held at the prestigious Rennert Hotel located at the corner of Liberty and Saratoga Streets. The ultimate event that year, however, was still to come.

Widow Lemonia Pamfilis (seated and partially hidden) with her children (left to right), Virginia, Manuel and Ann, at the unique monument dedicated to Stylianos M. Pamfilis, Greek Section at Woodlawn Cemetery, 1931.

On Monday, September 30, 1931, the Greek flag was officially presented to the State of Maryland as a gift from the Premier of Greece, Eleftherios Venizelos. This program was conducted at the War Memorial Plaza, across from City Hall, under the auspices of the George Dilboy Post No. 12 of the American Legion. With Post Commander James Latgis presiding, the flag was solemnly presented with pride to Governor Ritchie. It symbolized Greece's appreciation for the Maryland flag that it received in 1930 during the 100th Anniversary celebration of Greek Independence. Members of the Greek Legation in Washington, state and city officials, and the Greek Ambassador to the United States, Charalambos Simopoulos, attended the event. *The Baltimore Sun* reported on the impressive ceremony attended by over "700 members of local and District of Columbia Greek fraternal organizations."

It should also be noted that with the advent of the Depression, the middle-class aspirations of the Greek immigrants, though shaken, were not dissolved. The affluence of the "roaring 20's" had actually brought many into solid ownership of their own business enterprises. Fruit peddlers had become grocers, market stall confectioners opened sweet and pastry shops, and Greeks as restaurateurs would become the norm in cities everywhere. For a large segment of the parish, self-employment often provided a buffer from the harsh economic times faced by the country's industrial workers. The repeal of Prohibition in 1933 also led to noteworthy Greek success stories in the bar and packaged liquor business. A superb example was George B. Conits and his popular establishment at 4 West Oliver Street known as George's Café. The entrepreneurial spirit of that generation is unequalled in the story of Greek America.

Various Greek organizations participated in the presentation of the Greek flag to the State of Maryland held at the War Memorial Plaza on September 30, 1931. In the foreground, members of the Elpis Ladies' Society display their banner along with the flags of America and Greece.

George's Café, corner of Oliver and Charles Streets, near the Pennsylvania Station. Behind counter left to right: Proprietor George B. Conits, Peter G. Thomas, and George Kyriakopoulos, circa 1934.

George's Candies was located at 2304 East Monument Street. Menas Tzortzopoulos (Charles M. George) was well-known for the manufacture of fine chocolates, especially the chocolate rabbits sold at Easter.

Even though the 1930's would show that the Greeks of Baltimore were undoubtedly concerned with the problems of the Great Depression, the education of their children, and the struggle to maintain their Hellenic culture in American society, it would also be a time of revitalization for the Orthodox Church. The political controversy, which had caused a schism in the community for seven years, was truly over and a new leadership, determined to move on, had emerged in Baltimore.

Nationwide, however, criticisms against Archbishop Alexander mounted. His tenure as first Archbishop of America was controversial, to say the least, and there was a call for change in order to bring peace to a troubled Archdiocese. The first step toward harmony occurred in May of 1930, when the new Ecumenical Patriarch, Photios II, sent Metropolitan Damaskinos of Corinth to the United States. As a representative of the Patriarchate, his job was to temporarily govern the churches and assess the situation in America. During that summer, Archbishop Alexander was dismissed without trial, feuding bishops were reassigned to Greece, and a new spiritual leader was recommended for the Greek Orthodox Archdiocese in America— Metropolitan Athenagoras of Corfu.

Overwhelming approval marked the arrival of Archbishop Athenagoras to New York in February 1931. His reputation as a charismatic leader with great dedication and vision had preceded him. To be successful, he had to diffuse ill feelings from the recent Royalist-Venizelist controversy that still hovered over many parishes. One of the Archbishop's primary objectives was to improve the working relationship between clergy, laity, and church authorities. Following his enthronement, he began visiting Greek communities across America evoking a spirit of reconstruction and unity among Orthodox Christians.

The winter of 1931 ushered in a new era of cooperation. Within months, Father Pavlou received word from the Archdiocese stating that Archbishop Athenagoras desired to visit Baltimore. The Archbishop humbly requested to lodge at the parish house rather than stay at a hotel, perhaps as a goodwill gesture to spare the church any expense. At the council meeting of May 7, 1931, concern was expressed whether or not the parish house was in proper condition for his visit. The new spiritual

Parish Council President George B. Petite
and wife, the former Fevronia Kosmides, 1932.

Newlyweds James and Penelope Psoras (left) and her brother
Fotis Paxenos (right) at the Acropolis in Athens, Greece.
The Psoras couple settled in Baltimore by March 1926.

Archbishop Athenagoras of North and South America
served as spiritual leader of the Archdiocese from 1931-1948.

leader of America, whom they regarded with the highest esteem, deserved more suitable accommodations, prompting modest restoration work to the aging rectory. Though invited to Baltimore, the new Archbishop did not visit during that time. With the Annunciation community already reunited, perhaps he decided to focus his initial attention on parishes still in discord.

By the fall of 1931, Archbishop Athenagoras invited all parishes to a Clergy-Laity Congress in New York City from November 16-20, 1931. Delegates from Baltimore, including Parish Council President George Petite, attended the meetings that called for a more structured administration. Discussions and debates focused on a heated issue, namely the authority of the priest in church affairs. Domination of laity in decision-making, coupled with recent politics in Greece, had resulted in the general exclusion of clergy from parish administration. Though the general delegation reluctantly adopted uniform parish bylaws, it would still be a difficult issue on the parish level. At Annunciation, it would be later in the decade before proposed changes were actually implemented.

Graduates of the Theological School of Halki, 1910. Deacon Aristoclis Spyrou is seated third from the left.
In 1923, he became Bishop of Corfu. Eight years later he was enthroned as Archbishop Athenagoras of America.

The following year saw the departure of Father Nikiforos Pavlou. He had served a notable three-year term adding a sense of stability to the parish. Church records show that by April 5, 1932, The Very Rev. Joakim Malahias, age 47, was welcomed as Annunciation's next priest. He was the twelfth clergyman assigned to the parish. Later that year, *The Baltimore Post* described the new spiritual leader as a "kindly man with a dark pointed beard and genial, yet dignified good humor; a tiny cross pinning his tie." Father Malahias, who originated from the Island of Ikaria, often preferred wearing a business suit rather than the traditional clerical collar.

Father Malahias conducted numerous sacraments during his brief eight-month tenure in Baltimore. One notable funeral he conducted was that of a fellow Orthodox clergyman, The Reverend Polymenis Ahladas. This retired priest, who lived to 85 years of age, was born in Thrace, Greece, in 1847. He was known as "Papa Pavlos," which soon became the family's surname. Father Papapavlos served as a *psalti* (cantor) and assisted during the late 1920's in performing liturgical duties and sacraments. With a large gathering for his funeral on May 4, 1932, Father Papapavlos is the only Orthodox priest buried in the Greek Section at Woodlawn Cemetery.

The Rev. Polymenis Ahladas (Papapavlos)

During the spring of 1932, the Annunciation community received news from the Archdiocese that stirred excitement. A special church bulletin announced with great pride the much-anticipated first visit of the Archbishop at the end of May. "Solacing event! For the first time since his arrival in the New World, His Eminence Archbishop Athenagoras will visit our parish. His visit will be an official one. He will bless us, he will proclaim the word of God to inspire us, he will converse with us, as a Father with his children, in order to give us his good advice and his prudent commands."

Parish council minutes outlined the agenda for the special weekend with Archbishop Athenagoras. On Saturday, May 28, 1932, a welcoming committee met the Archbishop who arrived by train at the Pennsylvania Station. They proceeded to the Homewood Avenue Church where Vesper services were held followed by a dinner with board members at the home of Parish Council President George B. Petite. The following day, Archbishop Athenagoras, assisted by Father Joakim Malahias, celebrated his first Hierarchical

The Very Rev. Joakim Malahias

Archbishop Athenagoras and a large group of parishioners gathered at the Greek Section in Woodlawn Cemetery on Sunday, May 29, 1932. That day, he blessed this sacred burial ground and chanted memorial prayers over the graves. The Archbishop (center) was assisted by Father Joakim Malahias (wearing glasses) who is standing to his left.

Divine Liturgy at Annunciation. The parish council also invited Charalambos Simopoulos, the Greek Ambassador from Washington, D.C., who attended the service. (*See p. 379.*)

With two distinguished leaders present that Sunday, the parish council's bulletin for the event encouraged all "Hellenes of the City of Baltimore and the Suburbs" to attend, proving that "the fire of the Orthodox faith and the love for the homeland is not extinguished, but burns brightly…." After a dinner given in honor of the visiting dignitaries, Archbishop Athenagoras and a large entourage of parishioners proceeded to the Greek Section at the Woodlawn Cemetery. It must have been quite emotional for parishioners as he blessed the sacred burial grounds in the Orthodox tradition and chanted memorial prayers. A photograph of this historic gathering on May 29, 1932, shows the dynamic presence of the distinguished Archbishop that day.

Three months later, Archbishop Athenagoras would find himself back at Annunciation, this time with the Greek community in the national spotlight. The Tenth National Convention of the Order of AHEPA convened in Baltimore with over 5,000 delegates and visitors. Since the Homewood Avenue Church was too small, special church services were held on Sunday, August 28, 1932, at the Emmanuel Protestant Episcopal Church at Read and Cathedral Streets in order to accommodate the overflowing crowds. The following day, Mayor Howard Jackson gave the welcoming remarks at the official opening of the convention at the Lord Baltimore Hotel.

One of the highlights was the Grand AHEPA Parade that marched from the Fifth Regiment Armory to City Hall Plaza on August 31, 1932. *The Baltimore Sun* contained a colorful account of "units garbed in striking blues and vivid reds, and the beat of drums and music of bands that moved through extreme summer heat along the streets of Baltimore with Greek and American flags waving." Another AHEPA group that flourished during those years was the AHEPA Patrol. Baltimore's group, led by Captain Constantine G. Thomas, consisted of over two dozen young men who competed in military precision drills with patrols from other cities.

Themes of the convention speeches reveal the interesting message AHEPA was conveying in its tenth year. "We are 100 percent American, now and forever, but we wish to blend Hellenism with Americanism." Recommendations that AHEPA chapters "boycott films, plays, theatres, and books that hold Greeks up to ridicule or insult" were even included in their annual report, clearly showing that ethnic groups were still combating anti-foreign sentiments in their quest to assimilate into society.

The success of the large AHEPA gathering that summer once again proved that the size of the Annunciation Church was inadequate to serve the reunited parish. The continued growth of Baltimore's Greek population was also a key factor. The cramped quarters at Homewood Avenue and Chase Street became glaringly apparent during many religious services and social gatherings. The possibility of enlarging the church or purchasing a new one began to be discussed but was not formally acted upon until 1936.

MAYOR JACKSON GIVES WELCOME AS AHEPA MEETS

Addresses 600 Delegates As National Convention Opens

GREEK ORTHO[
ARCHBISHO[

Number Atten[
Week Sessi[
At 5,00[

The Ahepa Fez attracted many charming young ladies

Scrapbook clippings from the AHEPA Convention, 1932.

Many Baltimore Greeks gathered at Pennsylvania Station to greet Archbishop Athenagoras on his arrival for the AHEPA Convention. This photograph along with an article was featured in *The Baltimore News* on August 29, 1932.

Dignitaries who reviewed the AHEPA Parade from City Hall included: Governor Albert Ritchie; Archbishop Athenagoras; Col. W. W. Taylor; Rev. Joakim Malahias (wearing tie); and Mayor Howard Jackson (far right).

Special church services were held at the Emmanuel Protestant Episcopal Church at Cathedral and Read Streets due to the large number of convention-goers from various AHEPA chapters across America, August 28, 1932.

The AHEPA Patrol of Baltimore's Worthington Chapter No. 30 was led by
Capt. Constantine G. Thomas (tenth from left) and Sgt. John G. Perentesis (sixth from left), August 1932.

Archbishop Athenagoras and The Very Rev. Joakim Papachristou (visiting priest from Detroit, Michigan), posed with
Parish Council President George B. Petite. Father Papachristou would be assigned to Baltimore three years later.

COSMOPOLITAN BALTIMORE

Children of Ancient Greece Keep Old Customs and Standards

Religion Plays Important Part in Lives of 5,000 Greeks Here

Among Baltimore's 800,000 inhabitants are many thousands who have not always made their homes here, who have come from the countries of the world to dwell in the Monumental City. Their contributions to the life of the city, their colorful customs, the societies they have formed and the daily life they live—these are set forth in a series of articles, of which this is the tenth—the story of cosmopolitan Baltimore.

Today's article deals with the life of the Greek people in Baltimore.

By MARY FISHER

In Baltimore, Greek boys and girls are married in the Evangelismos Church—the Church of the Good Angel—with wreaths and dancing and showers of confetti, money and flowers, as in the "old country."

They still give old plays, sing the old songs. Regret, ever so faintly, lights their eyes at mention of the Mediterranean, blue and burning under the same sun that gleamed on Trojan Helen.

Old customs, old standards. Marriage among the 5,000 Greek people here is most often for a lifetime, and is taken with corresponding seriousness. The girls "date" for shows, dances and dinners before marriage, but the engagement is solemnized by the priest and the couple must be married in the orthodox church.

Religion or practicality? A little, perhaps, of both. Inheritance of property in the old country, owned by Baltimore Greeks, is legally denied the offspring of a mere civil marriage.

Pastor of All Maryland

Rev. Joakim E. Malahias, the minister of the Orthodox Church on Homewood Ave. and Chase St., in whose parish is centered the greater part of the Greek population of the city, has all the Greeks of Maryland in his charge; he goes to Cumberland to perform a marriage ceremony, or to Hagerstown in the wake of death. A kindly man with a dark pointed beard and genial, yet dignified good humor; a tiny cross pinning his tie.

In his church, too, there is a school conducted by Mrs. Maria Micaoloudis and Miss Helen Bouniatsis, with an "extension" school in Highlandtown, where the teacher is ..... tes. There is also a private teacher, Mrs. Trepoussi.

There are three clubs, charitable organizations, headed by Mrs. Calliope Pappas, Miss Irene Daskalakis and Miss Annie Cosmides.

The largest Greek organization here, however, is the Baltimore branch of the Order of the Ahepa, the president of which is Angelo Schiadaressi. When the national convention of the order was held here recently, the Ahepans, in tasseled fezes and the short skirts of the Greek soldiers, like Scottish kilts, marched through the city

Chrysanthe Alerzatos in Greek national costume

during the eclipse of a punishing, brassy sun.

In Baltimore, near the waterfront there are several Greek boarding houses and cafes, so usual in the day and soaked at night in the strange atmosphere of the docks. The lights of upper Broadway stop abruptly; here is another region, the streets peopled with a few drifting passersby, whose faces are indistinct in the darkness and whose gait takes them past merchant freighters, flat scows, a maze of smaller

shipping from whence drifts half-audible, mysterious sounds.

Uptown, the Greek restaurants are plentiful; there are confection stores too, and many of the candy and peanut stalls in the markets are run by Greeks. Peppermints and pastries. Also, there are some Greek delicatessens and five or six bakeries, where bread and cakes bring money into cash registers not so well filled during the past three years.

Many Attend Hopkins

Amateur theatricals among Baltimore Hellenes are generally given under the auspices of the Greek Theater Guild of Baltimore, putting on most of the plays sponsored by various organizations. When the University Players staged "Electra" and "Lysistrata" last year, they were aided by members of the Guild. Living in Baltimore with her husband is Mme. Nitza Calevas, of the Odeon Conservatory in Athens,

The Rev. Joakim E. Malahias, pastor of the Greek Orthodox Church.

a soprano who has often sung over the radio.

The list of Greeks who have studied at Johns Hopkins University and the Medical School is large, and there are now six Greek boys at Annapolis, at the Naval Academy.

A Greek, historian state came with Columbus to America; and later, one of the Hellen family of Greeks married the niece of Dolly Madison and the wedding took place at the White House, with President Madison as host.

Perhaps the second Greeks to come to America settled in Maryland. This was the Hellen family from England, Nathaniel Hellen probably being the first to bear the name in Maryland, his name appearing in the 1672 records of the Land Office. In 1790, Capt. Jersey Hellen and Joseph Hallen (or Hellen) were heads of families here.

In 1822, an American brig brought 10 Greek boys here as refugees from the massacre of Chios. One of them, Mussulas Colvocoressess, later entered the navy and became captain. He was aboard the Merrimac during the Civil War.

But the dazzling, white fame that hung over Greece in the dawn of her glory, young Baltimore Hellenes know little more than their contemporaries, the American school children.

Aristides and Plato, Socrates and his hemlock cup, Sappho, Archimedes, Aristotle, lovely Helen with her "ruinous face."

Names, all of them, found only in history books covered with dust of ages. It is the older Greeks here who, sighing for that cloudless glory, dream and hope that their country will some day struggle back again into the sun.

Many aspects of Greek culture were detailed in a feature story written about the Greek Orthodox community in *The Baltimore Post* on October 28, 1932. The story included such topics as marriage traditions, the inheritance of property in Greece, a description of Rev. Joakim Malahias, charitable organizations of the church, Greek-owned businesses, the production of amateur theatricals, and the 1932 AHEPA Convention. Chrysanthe Alevizatos, one of the youngest marchers in the AHEPA Parade that year, is shown above in costume.

The first visit of Archbishop Athenagoras to the Annunciation Greek Orthodox Church of Baltimore.
A well-known photographer of that era, Gus Vlachos, was often called upon to preserve many of the special
events in parish history. Father Malahias (wearing necktie) is seated to the right of the Archbishop, May 29, 1932.

Ladies' Entertainment Committee of the AHEPA National Convention held in Baltimore, Maryland, August 1932.
Seated left to right: Evdokia Rados, Irene Daskalakis, Amalia Nicholson, Chairperson; Stavroula Spanakos, Catherine Capsanes.
Second row left to right: Kalliope H. Pappas, Ann Papathomaides, Julia Pappas, Anna Kosmides, Mary Constantine, Despina
Constantine, Kalliope K. Pappas. Back row left to right: Jenny A. Synodinos, Clara Genetos, Betty Pamfilis, Helen Papaliou.

By January 1933, The Reverend Michael G. Andreades, age 59, became the next full-time priest at Annunciation. Born in Asia Minor, he was educated in Crimea, Russia, as well as the Patriarchal school in Constantinople. Well-versed in Russian and Greek culture, he received his Doctor of Divinity degree and was ordained to the priesthood in 1905. He served the St. Spiridon Orthodox parish in Seattle, Washington, until 1915. During that time, Father Andreades was administrative head for all Orthodox parishes on the Pacific Coast and wrote a formal report to Russian Orthodox Church leaders on the status of the early Greek parishes in America. Later, he would continue playing a positive role in church affairs when he became a priest of the Greek Orthodox Archdiocese.

The Rev. Michael G. Andreades

In Baltimore, Father Andreades revitalized the parish music program and instituted a modest choir. Two months after his arrival, *The Baltimore News* ran a colorful story that captured attention. "The Greek colony…will celebrate the Independence Day of their fatherland tomorrow with their accustomed enthusiasm." On Sunday, March 26, 1933, the corner of Homewood Avenue and Chase Street was the scene of a splendid observance of Greek Independence Day. The newspaper story concluded it was fitting that "Americans should join the Greeks…in hailing the birthday commemoration of the Grecian Fourth of July." The Reverend Andreades presided over the festivities featuring many parishioners dressed in traditional costumes.

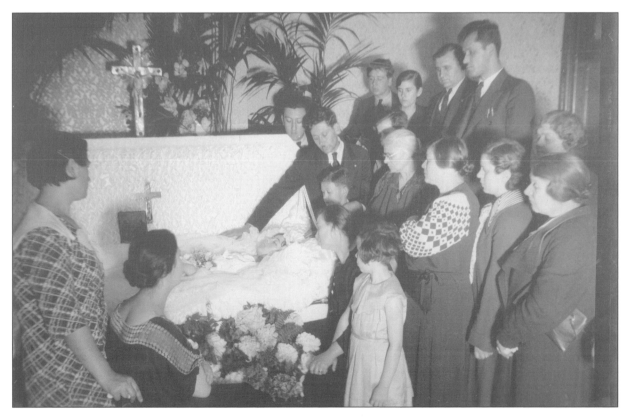

One of the last funerals conducted by Father Andreades during his tenure in Baltimore was for Anna Karavedas, the 13-year-old daughter of Dionysios and Vasiliki Karavedas, who died from typhoid fever. As was customary during that era, the young girl reposed in a bridal gown at her home, 13 South Fulton Avenue, June 10, 1935.

The Sons of Pericles, 1935. First row *l to r* : Jerry Vandora, George C. George, George Anderson, Vice President;
Peter Sfekas, President; George Mesologites, Secretary; Harry Anderson, Treasurer; Louis J. Constantinides. Second row *l to r* :
Theodore George, Alexander Pappas, William Zissimos, Basil Anargyros, Nick Kappiris, George Pappas, Spiro Agnew, James Sfekas.
Top row *l to r* : Peter Lericos, Theodore Constantine, Gus Poulase, Spiro Leanos, George Georgelakos and Gus Constantine.

The Daughters of Penelope (Ladies' Auxiliary of the AHEPA) organized a Baltimore chapter in 1935.
First officers shown in this elegant group photograph include Anna Kosmides, Vice President
(first row, fifth from left) and Amalia Nicholson, President (first row, sixth from left).

During the spring of 1933, the Annunciation Church was able to secure the services of James Venetos who had recently arrived in Baltimore and established his first residence in the parish house. Mr. Venetos served the church in numerous roles such as *psalti* (cantor), secretary, and Greek schoolteacher. Mr. Venetos also served as collector of church dues during the years before the stewardship program was established. He remained active in church administration for over two decades as the parish continued evolving into a more organized religious community.

Despite the economic problems of the Depression, various Greek clubs and societies continued to flourish. The early 1930's saw the formation of numerous additional groups. In February 1933, the Plato Chapter No. 80 of the Sons of Pericles (Junior Order of AHEPA) was organized with Harry J. Scaljon as its first president. By August 1933, the Original Greek-American Democratic Club was incorporated in order to promote the "political, civic, and educational welfare" of its members.

Another of the regional societies was also organized during this period. Immigrants from the Island of Kythera met at the home of John Mentis on January 7, 1934, and formed the *Panayia Myrtithiotissa* Chapter of the Kytherian Brotherhood. The first officers were James T. George, President; Peter Magulas, Vice President; Gregory Faros, Secretary; and Peter George, Treasurer. Sponsoring a yearly liturgical event, this group also divided its philanthropic work between the homeland and the local Greek community.

The influx of more Greeks to the Highlandtown region led to a growing enrollment of students at the Greek school annex. On October 2, 1934, the "Greek Community School of Highlandtown" was officially incorporated with George Boulles, Michael Pappas and John Sophocleus as its initial directors. Then, by a deed dated December 6, 1934, the Greek school acquired the property at the northwest corner of Ponca and Fleet Streets for an annual rent of $100 and classes soon expanded for the preservation of the ancestral language.

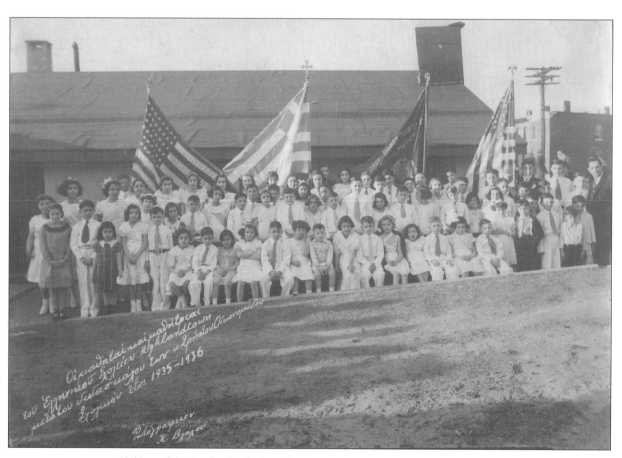

Children of the Greek School of Highlandtown gathered for a group photograph with
Christos Economides (far right), their instructor for the school year 1935-36. Flags of America, Greece,
and the George Dilboy Post No. 12 of the American Legion were proudly displayed in back of the students.

Parish Council, 1935-1936. Seated left to right: Menas George, Treasurer; Niketas A. Konstant, President; The Very Rev. Joakim Papachristou, Kostas Paxenos, Vice President; and Peter Spanakos. Standing left to right: Constantine Mesologites, George J. Karangelen, Anthony Synodinos, Secretary; and John Lambros.

Other groups to witness further expansion during the mid-1930's included the AHEPA and GAPA. In 1935, both fraternal organizations established women's clubs in Baltimore. On March 14, 1935, the "Alcmene" Chapter No. 27 of the Daughters of Penelope (Ladies' Auxiliary of the AHEPA) was organized with Amalia Nicholson as its first president. The following month, on April 21, 1935, the "Theano" Chapter No. 78 (Ladies' Auxiliary of the GAPA) was formed with Maria Nikoludis as its first president.

Soon after, members of the community who came from the western coast of Turkey, known as *Mikra Asia* (Asia Minor), also sought to form a regional society. Mass emigration from this region was prompted by the brutal Turkish massacres of the Greek people in 1922. One source, entitled *Near East Relief,* described in vivid detail the "...Smyrna disaster with the resultant evacuation of practically the entire Christian population from Turkish Nationalist territory."

Many who fled oppression came to America and some eventually settled in Baltimore. As a result of the city's growing population of Greeks from Asia Minor, it was decided to organize a regional society. On June 2, 1935, *Pronia*, later renamed the Pan-Karabournian Society of Karabourna, was established with Nicholas Andralis as its first president. The society's goals were to perpetuate its customs and traditions, commemorate its patron saint, *Ayios Eleftherios*, and provide charitable donations, not only to the homeland but also to the Baltimore parish through philanthropic deeds.

The establishment of these organizations reflects the rapid growth of Baltimore's Greek community. A corresponding increase in church membership at Annunciation, as well as other Greek communities, resulted in the need for changes in national church administration. Archbishop Athenagoras had proposed uniform parish bylaws that initially received mixed reviews at clergy-laity gatherings in the early 1930's. The suggested changes boosted the authority of Greek Orthodox clergymen whose power and prestige had diminished in the United States especially during the political turmoil of the 1920's.

Some parishes feared that sharing authority with the priest under the guidance of the Archbishop would bring an end to church administration to which they had become accustomed. Others realized a better-structured plan was needed to ensure stability of the churches in America. On Sunday, July 14, 1935, Niketas A. Konstant, president of the parish council, convened a special general assembly and welcomed Archbishop Athenagoras who came from New York to meet with the congregation and answer questions regarding the uniform parish bylaws.

It was a crucial meeting since the Baltimore parish was seen as a pacesetter within the Greek Orthodox Archdiocese. The Archbishop's eloquent message was well-received. Unanimously, the parish assembly voted in favor of the new constitution which established guidelines for the assignment and transfer of priests, rules and regulations regarding parish elections, and greater authority for the Archdiocese over church affairs. Two months later, the impact of these changes would be tested with positive results.

Under the new rules, following the resignation of Father Andreades, the Archdiocese assigned one of the most learned and highly-respected priests in the country to Annunciation. On October 1, 1935, a mere five months before the Thirtieth Anniversary of the parish, The Very Rev. Joakim Papachristou, age 47, assumed his duties as the new spiritual leader of Baltimore's Greek Orthodox Christians. His pastorate at Annunciation would last nearly fifteen years—a remarkable duration compared to his predecessors. A new era of stability and progress was about to begin.

The Very Rev. Joakim Papachristou

Opposite Page: The Associate Congregational Church at the corner of Maryland Avenue and Preston Street as it appeared in 1910. The Romanesque-style edifice was designed by Charles E. Cassell and originally built in 1889 for the Associate Reformed Church. Left vacant in 1934, the Greek Orthodox Community would purchase the building in 1937 and begin a new era of parish history.

1936-1945

The Greek Orthodox community was immediately impressed with its new clergyman. Father Papachristou was born in 1888 near Proussa, Asia Minor, and was baptized as Christos Papadopoulos. In 1914, he graduated from the famous Theological Academy of the Ecumenical Patriarchate in Halki, Turkey. As a deacon of the Orthodox Church, he took the ecclesiastical name, Joakim. During his years in Constantinople, he was a professor of Byzantine history at the French Hellenic University. By August of 1922, the Greco-Turkish War (1921-1922) had escalated and Turkish nationalists launched a final offensive against the Greek army with catastrophic results. Thousands of refugees were fleeing Thrace, Smyrna, and other regions throughout Asia Minor. In the midst of this upheaval, records show that on October 12, 1922, Deacon Joakim Papadopoulos secured second-class passage aboard the *S.S. Madonna* bound for America. Departing from Constantinople with $50, he arrived in New York on November 1, 1922. This historic passenger list also documented his ability to read and write French, a further indication of his advanced schooling and cultural refinement.

Within a month, Deacon Joakim Papadopoulos was ordained to the priesthood by Archbishop Alexander in Astoria, New York, and later changed his surname to Papachristou. He was first assigned to the Greek Orthodox community of Los Angeles, California, and would often travel far to minister to his parishioners. Following his departure from the West Coast in 1929, he served brief tenures at parishes in the following cities: New Castle, Pennsylvania (1929-1931); Detroit, Michigan (1931-1933); and Jamaica, New York (1933-1935). Father Papachristou, who had received a Doctor of Divinity degree, also took post-graduate courses at various American universities. His status as an Archimandrite (the title bestowed upon unmarried priests), along with his dignified manner and eloquent speech, brought an atmosphere of sophistication that would have a positive influence on the Annunciation Church.

In the fall of 1935, the Baltimore congregation cordially welcomed The Very Rev. Joakim Papachristou along with various family members who resided with him at 7702 Harford Road. They included his parents, Dimitrios and Maria; his brother, Themistocles; his widowed sister, Katherine Apostolides (Apostol); and her three children, Mary, Olympia and George. The detail-oriented nature of the new priest was demonstrated by one of his first major tasks. Father Papachristou did an exhaustive review of church records spanning nearly thirty years. To preserve the community's history, he organized and recopied various documents and listings into the parish registry books. Unlike some of the earlier clergymen, Father Joakim Papachristou carefully recorded all religious sacraments he performed, offering future generations of parishioners with a valuable source of genealogical information.

To enhance the Greek school program, Father Papachristou organized lessons for the study of religion once a week for each of the classes. During these years, the Greek school also maintained branches in Highlandtown and Sparrows Point and classes met every day for two hours after public school. The new clergyman was also instrumental in establishing a *Philoptochos* (Friends of the Poor) Society. The concept of forming a ladies' philanthropic organization began as a national movement in 1932 initiated by Archbishop Athenagoras. In Baltimore, at a meeting held on January 17, 1936, members from the two ladies' societies, *Elpis* and *Enosis,* merged to form the Baltimore chapter that was named the Greek Ladies' Philoptochos Society "Evangelismos."

At the parish council meeting on February 4, 1936, Father Papachristou announced the first officers of the new ladies' society. They included: Kalliope H. Pappas, President; Helen G. Perentesis, Vice President; Jenny A. Synodinos, Treasurer; Panayiotitsa N. Karangelen, Secretary; Theodora Cardiges, Assistant Secretary; along with Helen A. Dezes, Theodora N. Konstant, and Stavroula P. Spanakos as directors. The goals of the society were

Members of the Ladies' Philoptochos Society "Evangelismos," 1938. Directors seated left to right: Stavroula Spanakos, Georgia G. Karangelen, Theodora C. Pecunes, Assistant Secretary; Paraskevi N. Dezes, Vice President; Kalliope H. Pappas, President; Mary T. Prevas, Secretary; Thalia Hall, Treasurer; Maria P. Tsirigos, Stavroula G. Lericos, Helen A. Dezes, Theodora N. Konstant (second row, ninth from left). The two young girls in front are Peggy Andralis (left) and Margaret Cranidiotis (right). Note: Greek school instructor Vasilia Athanasopoulou (second row, far right).

Gathering of the GAPA (Greek-American Progressive Association). Members of this fraternal
group posed on the hill across the street from the Homewood Avenue Church on March 25, 1936.
The Greek Orthodox community often held Easter Resurrection services at this location.

to help the poor and needy families, visit the sick and elderly, and assist with various philanthropic causes. Initially focusing its efforts to aid the local parish, the scope of the society later expanded to serve numerous worthy causes encompassing the wider community.

Later that same year saw the establishment of yet another group. Students attending The Johns Hopkins University founded the Hellenic University Club on November 15, 1936. The club remained active until the outbreak of World War II. First officers included: George N. Harris (Pittsburgh, PA), President; John Alexander (Atlanta, GA), Vice President; Ramon Stewart (Springfield, MA), Secretary; and Baltimore-born Theodore J. George as Treasurer. Their objectives were to create fellowship, foster professional understanding, encourage education through the provision of scholarship aid to students, as well as to present lectures, social events, and cultural functions for the Greek community.

It should be noted that the community paused in 1936 to celebrate the anniversary of its founding. With the parish established in 1906, a 30th Anniversary observance was in order. Curiously, instead of celebrating the 30th Anniversary, a 25th Anniversary booklet was published that year. The booklet refers to the "Twenty-Fifth Anniversary of the Reorganization of the Greek Orthodox Community" and placed greater historical significance on the year 1911. This calculation also coincides with the oldest existing registry of sacraments dating back to May of 1911. All future anniversaries, however, would refer to 1906 as the year of the church's establishment.

Regardless, we do know that on February 16, 1936, a record number of Greeks gathered at the Lehmann Hall to attend a Twenty-Fifth Anniversary Ball organized under the chairmanship of John Lambros. Earlier that day, special church services were held followed by a banquet to celebrate the parish's "Silver Jubilee." Parish Council President

Niketas A. Konstant spoke of the proud record of achievements and commented on the future needs of an energetic parish that had outgrown its space. Father Papachristou also saw the need for a larger church and cooperated fully in exploring options for consideration. The pace of events would accelerate for the remainder of 1936.

There was also growing concern for additional burial grounds as the "Greek Section at Woodlawn" approached full capacity. In August of 1936, Annunciation was able to purchase adjacent grounds in the North Avon section. This fourth and final purchase, allowing for over 160 single interments, became known as the "New Greek Plot." In fact, the entire Greek Section consisted of single grave plots. This was the customary practice during those early years. The concept of acquiring family plots took form slowly because many Greeks of that era viewed the purchase of multiple grave plots in advance as a bad omen.

Prior to 1936, only two families had acquired family-owned lots directly from the Woodlawn Cemetery Company. Theodore A. Cavacos, who died in 1920, and his father-in-law, Anastasios Coroneos, who died in 1930, had been reinterred from the Greek Section into nearby family lots in

The impressive Cavacos monument at Woodlawn Cemetery was sculpted by Emmanuel A. Cavacos. This was the first family-owned lot in the North Avon Section.

the North Avon section marked by exquisite large monuments. It was not until the late 1930's that more parishioners began purchasing family lots in North and South Avon surrounding the Greek Section. The growing popularity of family lots would soon become a deciding factor leading to the establishment of independent church-owned burial grounds during the 1940's.

With the cemetery issue temporarily under control, all energy focused on the topic of church expansion. Throughout the summer and fall of 1936, numerous meetings were held to discuss whether or not to renovate the existing building at Homewood Avenue and Chase Street or to purchase a new church. The general assembly meeting of September 6, 1936, voted that a Building Fund Committee be "empowered to raise the sum of $25,000" for plans to enlarge the church building with additional halls and classrooms. That same day, over $5,000 was pledged by members anxious to assist with the expansion project.

However, by the January 1937 assembly meeting, it was realized that renovating the church would be more costly than $25,000 and other alternatives had to be considered. In the midst of this future planning, an exciting option materialized for the Greek community. A Protestant house of worship, formerly occupied by the Associate Congregational Church, was sitting vacant for three years at the corner of Maryland Avenue and Preston Street. This circular stone church was one of the most unusual architectural buildings in Baltimore. The famous architect, Charles E. Cassell, designed it in the Romanesque style with Byzantine touches. It was made of Port Deposit granite with Amherst stone trimmings. Eighteen polished granite columns supported the porch roof and carved foliage adorned the porch, windows, doors, and buttresses. Originally built for the Associate Reformed Church, it was constructed in 1889 at a cost of over $130,000. (*Note:* In 1900, the Associate Reformed Church and the First Congregational Church of Baltimore merged under the name of the Associate Congregational Church headquartered on Preston Street.)

This abandoned edifice, close to fifty years old, had tremendous potential with a price tag now within reach. It was spacious, centrally located, and architecturally reminiscent of Byzantine-style churches. Only one major obstacle existed. The

The Associate Congregational Church on Preston Street was left vacant in 1934. It was scheduled
for demolition to make way for a gasoline filling station before the Greek community purchased it in 1937.

Continental Oil Company had already slated the property for demolition to make way for a gasoline filling station. Building a gasoline station required a city council ordinance and though the ordinance had been passed on December 21, 1936, Mayor Howard Jackson had not yet signed the document. Only a small window of opportunity remained and the parish had to act quickly. Soon after, a delegation from the Greek community, led by Dr. Andrew T. Cavacos, visited City Hall and successfully appealed to the Mayor of Baltimore.

The turning point to secure the acquisition occurred on February 18, 1937, when Rev. Ross W. Sanderson, Executive Secretary for the Baltimore Federation of Churches, wrote directly to Mayor Howard Jackson. He conveyed the Federation's sentiments on four distinct issues. There was "no desperate need for a filling station" on that corner. The noble church building should be "preserved for ecclesiastical purposes." The Greek Orthodox Church had a cooperative relationship with the Protestant churches and "deserved every courtesy in its effort to serve its people in America." In

conclusion, Sanderson stated, "I speak the mind of many who would vastly prefer to see our Greek friends take over this property" rather than have it demolished and then commercialized.

Needless to say, the letter was persuasive. Within a week, the ordinance was rescinded and the magnificent edifice was saved from the wrecking ball. Throughout these events, church legal counsel John G. Schilpp played a key role as mediator between the numerous parties involved. A church committee, consisting of parish council members John Lambros, Harry G. Pappas, Nicholas G. Coroneos, and John Anderson, then worked with the Mayor to complete the transaction. Earlier that month, the parish had paid a refundable deposit of $12,000 hoping to stop the demolition of the historic church. The accomplishment of their ambitious endeavor was soon recorded in the Land Records of Baltimore City.

On February 26, 1937, the "Orthodox Greek Church Evangelism" represented by John Lambros, Parish Council President, purchased the vacant church and property at the northwest corner of

Maryland Avenue and Preston Street from the Mid-Atlantic Conference of Congregational Churches of New Jersey for a total cost of $40,500. To secure the transaction, the property was then mortgaged to the Calvert Bank for $25,000. Just five years later, in May of 1942, the mortgage would be paid in full and released. It was the beginning of a new era and parishioners were energized. Their new church was symbolic of the parish's future role as a prominent congregation within the city.

Renovations to facilitate Greek Orthodox worship and community activities began almost immediately, funded by generous donations from individuals and church-affiliated organizations. Everyone was focused on the 24 West Preston Street property—the new center of Greek Orthodox religious, cultural, and educational activity in Baltimore. In the months that followed, the exterior stone was cleaned, wrought iron fencing was added, and evergreens were planted on the front lawn. The altar was remodeled to conform to the requirements of the Orthodox faith and the *iconostasion* (altar screen) from the old church was modified and installed. The new church also had two aisles that made Annunciation unique from other Orthodox churches typically designed with one center aisle. Adjacent to the main sanctuary was a section of the building, known as the manse, with space for church offices, classrooms, and a hall for meetings and social gatherings.

In the Old World, Orthodox churches did not have pews. At Homewood Avenue, the congregation had followed this tradition with the men standing on one side and women standing on the other. Their new church, however, featured three sections of beautifully carved oak pews for seating up to 750 people during worship services and additional theatre-style seating for over 275 more in the balcony area. A pipe organ was also inherited from the prior owners and carefully restored. The interior of the sanctuary was cleaned and painted. Four magnificent Tiffany windows with original textured glass were preserved. The installation of additional stained glass windows and a variety of holy icons, donated in memory or in honor of parishioners, was soon underway and would continue well into the next decade.

With renovations in progress, the official move occurred just two days before the Palm Sunday services of 1937. A special procession and motorcade from the old Homewood Avenue Church to the new Preston Street Church took

The Annunciation Parish Council of 1937. First row *l to r*: Constantine Mesologites, The Very Rev. Joakim Papachristou, John Lambros, President; Niketas Konstant. Second row *l to r*: Stylianos Sfekas, Harry G. Pappas, Anthony Synodinos, Peter Spanakos. Third row *l to r*: John Mentis, George Karangelen, Kostas Paxenos, George Pappas. Back row *l to r*: James Constantinides, Nicholas G. Coroneos, John Anderson.

March 4th, 1937.

The Honorable Howard W. Jackson,
Mayor of Baltimore,
Baltimore, Maryland.

Dear Mr. Mayor:-

Today we have successfully consummated the purchase, on behalf of the Orthodox Greek Church Evangelism of Baltimore City, of the property formerly owned by the Associated Congregational Church of Baltimore, at the northwest corner of Maryland Avenue and Preston Street.

I thought it only fair to you to call attention of the newspapers of Baltimore to the splendid help you have given to the Greek Americans of Baltimore, generally, and to me personally, in this matter.

Yours very truly,

JGS-dfw
encl.

Church Attorney John G. Schilpp wrote a letter of thanks to Mayor Howard Jackson for his kind assistance to the Greek community, March 4, 1937.

Greek Congregation Moves Into New Home Of Worship

The Very Rev. Joakim Papachristou led the parish procession into the new church on Preston Street.
The Icon of the Annunciation was carried by Gus Karavedas (left) and Theodore Padussis (right), April 23, 1937.

place on Friday evening, April 23, 1937. This significant event in parish history included musical accompaniment of marching bands from the GAPA and AHEPA fraternal organizations. The following morning, *The Baltimore Sun* described the church's moving day: "The congregation first held a farewell service in the old church. After the service, the Rev. Joakim Papachristou, pastor, with the Rev. Thomas Daniels, of the Church of Saints Constantine and Helen, Washington, led a procession from the church, the priests carrying the bread and wine of the Communion....From the old church, the priests and members in the procession were taken in automobiles to the new location....The procession then moved into the new church....Before the altar, with its colorful sacred pictures, the pastor dedicated the edifice to the services of the Greek Orthodox Church, sprinkling the church and the congregation with holy water brought from the River Jordan...." Even a poignant farewell tribute to Homewood Avenue was written for the occasion. (*See* p. 381.)

Greek Orthodox Congregation Moves Into Its New Quarters

Solemn Ceremony Marks Occupation Of Edifice At Maryland Avenue And Preston Street—Palm Sunday Services Planned

Carrying three icons, one of which came from Mount Athos in Greece, members of the Greek Orthodox Church, Evangelismos, last night moved from their old house of worship at Chase and Homewood streets into the edifice purchased recently at Maryland avenue and Preston street.

The structure into which the Greeks moved formerly was occupied by the congregation of the Associate Congregational Church, now worshiping on Bolton street. The church at Maryland avenue and Preston street is being renovated. Repairs to date have cost $15,000 and it is estimated that $40,000 to $50,000 will be spent before the work will have been completed.

Farewell Service Held

The congregation first held a farewell service in the old church. After the service, the Rev. Joakim Papachristos, pastor, with the Rev. Daniel Thomas, of the Church of Sts. Constantine and Helen, Washington, led a procession from the church, the priests carrying the bread and wine of the Communion. Two boys, wearing blue and white uniforms, carried crosses, and two other boys, assisted by Kostas Paxenos, a member of the building committee, carried the icons. From the old church the priests and members in the procession were taken in automobiles to the new location.

Building Dedicated

The procession then moved into the new church. The bands of the Sons of Pericles Order of American Hellenic Educational Progressive Association and the patrol of the Junior Order of the Greek American Progressive Association played outside the church.

Before the altar, with its colorful sacred pictures, the pastor dedicated the edifice to the services of the Greek Orthodox Church, sprinkling the church and the congregation with holy water brought from the River Jordan.

To Mark Palm Sunday

At 10 A. M. tomorrow Palm Sunday, according to the calendar observed by the Greek Church, will be celebrated. Holy Week services will be held during the week.

On Friday night a picture of Christ in the sepulcher will be carried in a procession that will move outside the church while lamentations will be sung in a service symbolizing the burial of Christ. At midnight Saturday the congregation will assemble for celebration of Easter.

From *The Baltimore Sun*, Saturday, April 24, 1937.

Other newspaper accounts also gave the citizens of Baltimore a glimpse into Orthodox traditions. Article titles ranged from "Church Gets Site Slated for Gas Depot" to "Famous Old Church is Renovated by New Owners." The Holy Week services were no exception. For the first time, Greek Orthodox Easter became a newsworthy religious event as *The Baltimore Sun*, on Saturday, May 1, 1937, reported to its readers: "Following the Julian calendar, Good Friday was celebrated last night by the Greek Orthodox Church…with a service commemorating the burial of Christ. The procession circled the block with the priest and choir rendering Byzantine chants…followed by members of the congregation with lighted candles."

The article about Eastern Orthodox Holy Friday captured much attention and the next day city papers noted the Resurrection services in even greater detail: "At 1:00 a.m. today every light in the church was extinguished save that at the altar, from which the priest…lighted a candle and gave the invitation, 'Come ye and receive light from the unwaning light, then glorify Christ, who rose from the dead.' Young boys and girls of the church then came forward, lighted their candles from the priest, and passed through the congregation lighting the candles of the other worshippers. At last each person in the edifice stood with a lighted taper. After the service, the priest and congregation proceeded to the lawn of the church, where the services celebrating the Resurrection of Christ were continued, the priest chanting 'Christos Anesti' (Christ has risen from the dead) and the congregation repeating the chant. At the close, red dyed eggs, typifying new life and joy, were given to members of the congregation."

Following the transition to the new church, religious, cultural and social activities expanded at an even greater rate than before. According to the parish registry, the following were the first sacraments performed after the community's relocation: the baptism of Nicholas A. Christofilakis on May 2, 1937; the wedding of Anna N. Manos and William Stevenson, Jr., on May 9, 1937; and the funeral of Kaliroi Vandoros on April 28, 1937, in Havre de Grace, Maryland. Then, in June of 1937, the parish welcomed Professor Athanasios P. Theodorides to Baltimore. He served as Executive Secretary, Greek schoolteacher, *psalti* (cantor) and became musical director of an expanded Hellenic Byzantine Choir that was soon filled with the voices of young men and women of the parish. Professor Theodorides, a pioneer composer of liturgical music for the Orthodox churches in America, served the Annunciation community of Baltimore until his departure in August of 1948.

ΕΠΙ ΤΑΙΣ ΘΕΙΑΙΣ ΕΟΡΤΑΙΣ
ΤΩΝ ΠΑΘΩΝ ΚΑΙ ΤΗΣ ΑΝΑΣΤΑΣΕΩΣ
ΤΟΥ ΚΥΡΙΟΥ
Ο ΙΕΡΕΥΣ ΚΑΙ ΟΙ ΕΠΙΤΡΟΠΟΙ
ΕΥΧΟΝΤΑΙ ΥΜΙΝ
ΚΑΛΗΝ ΑΝΑΣΤΑΣΙΝ
καὶ
ΑΝΑΣΤΑΣΙΝ ΕΛΛΑΔΟΣ

ΩΡΟΛΟΓΙΟΝ
ΤΗΣ
ΜΕΓΑΛΗΣ ΕΒΔΟΜΑΔΟΣ
ΕΛΛΗΝΙΚΗ ΟΡΘΟΔΟΞΟΣ ΕΚΚΛΗΣΙΑ
«Ο ΕΥΑΓΓΕΛΙΣΜΟΣ»
Maryland Avenue & Preston Street
Baltimore, Md.

Holy Week Services brochure published by the Greek Orthodox Church "Evangelismos." The back cover of this wartime-era pamphlet dated April of 1943 stated: "On the holidays of the Passion and Resurrection of the Lord, the Priest and Parish Council wish you a good Resurrection celebration and the Resurrection of Greece."

Hellenic Byzantine Choir of the Annunciation Greek Orthodox Church of Baltimore, 1937.
Professor Athanasios Theodorides, Music Director (second row, fourth from left). Cantor James Venetos
(second row, fourth from right). Father Joakim Papachristou is standing in the center of the *iconostasion*.

During the years from 1935 to 1937, the GAPA (Greek-American Progressive Association) expanded with a number of youth-affiliated organizations. The group's objective was to encourage Greek youth to "perpetuate Hellenism and establish a fine code of ethics and good fellowship." Young men were able to join the GAPA Juniors (Sparta Chapter No. 47) which organized in November of 1935 with Michael Varipatis serving as first president. Soon after, the GAPA Patrol with James Georgakopoulos serving as commander was organized to conduct military precision drills. Adding further to their fraternal activities was the formation of a GAPA Band. This musical ensemble consisted of two dozen teenagers from the junior order with Constantine G. Konstant as their drum major.

In 1936, the GAPA Juniorettes (Chrysalis Chapter No. 38) was established for the young women under the guidance of Kalliope K. Pappas. A girls' musical group known as the *Mandolinata* also took form. These youth groups lasted until the early 1940's and helped to make the GAPA Ninth National Convention held in Baltimore from July 25-31, 1937, a most memorable occasion. The 1937 convention was the first major social event for the Greek community following its relocation from Homewood Avenue. Convention delegates and visitors from cities across America had the opportunity to see the splendid new church of the Annunciation community. A photographer's keystone lens captured the enormous gathering of conventioneers on Preston Street that summer.

The GAPA Band with one of its key organizers, Dionysios Karavedas (far right),
and its energetic young drum major, Constantine "Costaki" Konstant (far left), 1937.

GREEK-AMERICAN PROGRESSIVE ASSOCIATION

GAPA Juniorettes, Chrysalis Chapter No. 38, with group advisor, Kalliope Kleanthi Pappas, 1937.

The 1937 GAPA Convention was the first major social event following the parish's move to Preston Street.

The Kytherian Brotherhood with its president,
Gregory Faros (top row, far left), in 1938.

This *Baltimore Sun* article described the historic
consecration services held on Sunday, May 8, 1938.

The next event of historic significance took place a year after the church moved to its new home. Archbishop Athenagoras visited Baltimore on Sunday, May 8, 1938, and consecrated the historic sanctuary in the impressive Orthodox tradition. The dedication services began at dawn and lasted throughout the day. Part of the ceremony included the ancient tradition of sealing the relic of a saint within the center of the Holy Altar Table. For the consecration of the Annunciation Church, a relic from Saint Euthymia was chosen. Carroll Dulaney, a columnist for *The Baltimore News-Post*, recounted the event. "Holding aloft the golden platter with the Saint's remains," the Archbishop solemnly led a formal procession. "Everybody leaves the church, the doors are locked and the procession makes the circuit of the church grounds three times, halting in front of the main door each time to pray."

At this point, Archbishop Athenagoras proclaimed, "Raise the gates, O Ruler of ours, and let the King of Glory enter." The church doors were opened and the congregation entered the sanctuary. Later, the Archbishop placed the Saint's remains in the "Holy Sepulchre" of the altar where it was sealed. The mystical ceremony concluded with a Hierarchical Divine Liturgy. Another newspaper reporter colorfully described what he witnessed that afternoon: "There was a profusion of brocaded vestments, candles, flowers, and palms, and the choir sang Byzantine music in the liturgy of St. John Chrysostom." Little did parishioners realize that ten years later the same Archbishop would be elevated to the Ecumenical Throne in Constantinople as the world leader of Orthodoxy.

Later that evening, a Dedication Ball was held at the Alcazar Ballroom located at Cathedral and Madison Streets. The Executive Committee that planned the celebration consisted of George J. Karangelen, Chairman; Nicholas Coroneos, George Pappas, Constantine Paxenos, and Anthony Synodinos, Assistant Chairmen; and Niketas A. Konstant, Secretary. A *Dedication Memorial Book* was published to mark the momentous occasion and featured photographs of individuals and various organizations, as well as business advertisements. This impressive volume, with over one hundred pages, also contained the first synopsis of Annunciation's parish history written by Past Parish Council President Niketas A. Konstant.

The Karabournian Society with its president, John Tsolakakis (seated center), was photographed in 1938.

The Laconian Association under the presidency of Alexander Diacumakos (standing center with two youngsters), 1938.

Greek Orthodox Church "Evangelismos" (Annunciation), 24 West Preston Street
at the corner of Maryland Avenue, after purchase and renovations, circa 1939.

Father Joakim Papachristou with Peter J. Prevas (left)
and George C. Mesologites (right), Sunday, July 2, 1939.

The dream of establishing a larger church had become a reality. The first house of worship on Homewood Avenue, which had served the parish for nearly twenty-eight years, was now a fond memory—especially for those present at the first Divine Liturgy conducted there in 1909 by Father Constantine Douropoulos. It wasn't until four years after relocating to Preston Street that the old church officially became past history. The general assembly held on January 19, 1941, approved the sale of the property for $5,500 and the proceeds were applied to the deficit of the parish.

The memories from the old church, however, did not fade quickly. In fact, the concept for an entrance inscription, similar to the transom window at Homewood Avenue, was carried over to the new church. The suggested phrase, inspired by Father Joakim Papachristou, received overwhelming approval from church leaders. Within a few years, a profound inscription of four Greek words, *Oikos Theou...Pyli Ouranou* (House of God...Gateway to Heaven), would be carved into the stone above the main portico for posterity.

The Greek inscription over the main portico translates as *House of God...Gateway to Heaven.*

The Katsadoros family celebrated a double wedding on June 8, 1941. Georgette (left) married Stavros Katsikadakos. Her sister Stella (right) married Haralambos Mantakos.

By the close of the 1930's, additional social clubs were formed and met regularly at the new Preston Street location. On October 30, 1938, immigrants from the Island of Chios established the "Andreas Siggros" Chapter No. 8 of the United Chian Society in Baltimore. First officers included: Christopher Sfakianos, President; Constantine Pecunes, Vice President; James Venetos, Secretary; and Vasilios Klosterides, Treasurer. The organization sought to aid the welfare of the island's inhabitants, to commemorate its patron saint, *Ayia Markella*, to financially assist the many programs of the Annunciation parish, and would later sponsor scholarships for its needy students. By 1938, records also show that three distinct Greek-American Democratic Clubs had been established and were quite active as Greeks became more interested in civic matters and political affairs on the local, state and national level. Presiding over these clubs in the late 1930's and 1940's were successful businessmen such as John G. Panos, Constantine J. Pecunes, and Dr. Andrew T. Cavacos.

Then, in 1939, two more youth groups were formed. The Sons of Laconia "Leonidas" (Junior Order of the Laconian Society) was founded with Nicholas G. Stamatakos, President; Peter N. Karangelen, Vice President; Anthony N. Konstant, Secretary; and James K. Kargakos, Treasurer. Later, on December 10, 1939, the "Daphne Aphrodite" Chapter No. 49 of the Maids of Athena (Young Women's Auxiliary of the AHEPA) was established with Virginia S. Pamfilis, President; Evangeline N. Coroneos, Vice President; Georgia T. George, Secretary; and Ann S. Pamfilis, Treasurer.

Wrestling Champion Jim Londos (*The Golden Greek*) visited Annunciation on January 16, 1940, and posed with Father Papachristou and President George J. Karangelen (right).

Maids of Athena, "Daphne Aphrodite" Chapter No. 49, at the home of Mary Apostol (back row, fourth from left).
The club's four officers are seated center on the sofa (left to right): Ann S. Pamfilis, Treasurer; Evangeline N.
Coroneos, Vice President; Virginia S. Pamfilis, President; and Georgia T. George, Secretary, circa 1940.

Children of the Karabournian Society at an "Apokreatiko Glendi" (Pre-Lenten Party), circa 1943.
Standing left to right: Mary Hamilos, Helen Orfanos, Evangeline Karavasilis, Elizabeth Tsolakakis (Lakin),
Georgia Topaltzas (Topal), George Giavassis, James Hamilos, George Tsolakakis (Lakin) and George Kaludis.

Officers of the Philoptochos Society, 1940. Seated left to right: Cleopatra Behlivan, Treasurer; Penelope Georgelakos, President; Athena Pergantis, Vice President; Alexandria Cardiges, Secretary. Standing left to right: Theodora Pecunes, Vasiliki Apostolakos, Sophia Kanaras and Lemonia Pamfilis. (Note: The banner's wording invites both married and single women to join the philanthropic group.)

By the 1940's, many members of the first generation were attending professional schools and colleges in impressive numbers. No longer was the university graduate a rarity as was the case of Professor Aristo Soho, the parish council president of 1910, who received his Ph.D. from The Johns Hopkins University in 1898. It was a sign of the times, not just in Baltimore, but in Greek communities across America. Another sign of progress was the fact that xenophobic attitudes toward the Greek people had diminished, showing their integration into the mainstream of American society. Any doubts regarding the loyalty of the Greek-Americans to their new country were surely dispelled, as all energies were about to focus on the preservation of freedom in the fast-approaching World War.

The advent of World War II brought out the patriotic Americanism of the Greek community as shown by the enormous sums of money raised for war relief and the large number of those who answered the nation's call to arms. For the most part, the military build-up of Hitler's Germany during the 1930's was viewed as a distant issue across the Atlantic Ocean. The outbreak of war in 1939, coupled with Germany's alliance with Italy, fueled the flames of war across the European continent. A great turning point in Greek-American history occurred on October 28, 1940. The Italian dictator, Mussolini, tried to exercise his military might and force Greece to submit to his ultimatums. Instead, the Greek Prime Minister John Metaxas issued his emphatic *Oxi!* (No) to the demands, and Italy prepared to attack.

Skirted Greeks Hurled In Path Of Italians

Belgrade, Yugoslavia, dispatches reported today that skirted Greek troops such as these shown in ceremonial uniforms had hurled themselves across the path of Italian forces reported advancing through Albanian mountain passes into Greece. Rejection by Greek Premier-Dictator John Metaxas at 6 A. M. of Italian ultimatum demanding territorial concessions was signal for start of hostilities.

The heroic resistance of the Greek people to the Italian invasion that took place aroused the admiration of the world. Other European countries had succumbed to the Axis Powers. In the Mediterranean, however, the Greek people courageously subdued the invading Italian Army and provided a much-needed breathing spell for the Allies. In fact, Greece was one of the first nations to halt the aggressors, at least temporarily, since the war began. Suddenly, Greek-Americans were instilled with a new sense of confidence. Greek immigrants, once viewed by some as undesirable aliens, were elevated in status and dignity. Across America, prayers were offered in churches, and rallies and countless benefit programs were held in support of Greece.

In Baltimore, a special letter sent to parishioners from Father Joakim Papachristou and Parish Council President George Karangelen vividly describes the emotions of that era: "The horrible and bloody drama of Europe is now being staged in our beautiful Hellas. The Land of Light, the Root of Civilization, the Mother of Democracy—Immortal Greece—suffers the oppression of greedy and hateful dictators of Europe. The strong government of Greece, with her heroic children, answers in typical Grecian manner...We won't give in!" On Sunday, November 3, 1940, a large group solemnly gathered at the Annunciation Church to pray for the safety and guidance of Greece and the Allies. Delivering a passionate speech, Father Papachristou urged his congregation

Father Joakim Papachristou at the lectern, circa 1940.

George J. Karangelen, Parish Council President 1939-1940.

to immediately form a committee and begin raising money for the "relief of their stricken nation."

Soon after, the Maryland Greek War Relief was organized under the leadership of Parish Council President George J. Karangelen and thousands of dollars were raised within days. When the Greek War Relief Association (GWRA) was launched nationwide, the Maryland group became a viable member. Dr. Emil Malakis, a professor at The Johns Hopkins University, was named state chairman and worked with countless volunteers toward the ambitious national goal. The Greek War Relief Association wanted to raise ten million dollars across America to assist Greece in its plight. The Maryland chapter quickly took action. On December 14, 1940, *The Baltimore Sun* reported that "Greek-Americans in Baltimore and friends have contributed $15,000 to the homeland since it went to war with Italy." These fundraising efforts continued throughout the decade. As soon as the United States entered the war following the attack on Pearl Harbor on December 7, 1941, Greek communities across the nation also began vigorous drives for the aid of this country.

Collect Funds For Greece
Baltimoreans Active In Campaign For War Relief

In costumes of the native land of their ancestors, members of the Baltimore group working for Greek relief are shown in one of the mid-town hotels selling pins to aid their cause. Dr. David M. Robinson, center of attraction in the photograph, is chairman of the relief committee. Left to right are Katherine Konstant, Georgia Klosteridis, Dr. Robinson and Nicholas Anderson. Picture copyright, 1940, by The Baltimore News-Post. All rights reserved.

Greek War Relief efforts were well-publicized. This item appeared in *The Baltimore News-Post*, December 30, 1940.

$250,000 Pledged By Greeks Here To Buy Bomber

By ALDINE R. BIRD

Baltimore Greeks, descendants of a race that since Thermopylae has fearlessly purchased liberty with their very lives, today joined in the city-wide drive to avenge Pearl Harbor with bombers, and stand pledged to purchase $250,000 worth of defense stamps and bombs.

Miss Dorothy Lamour, Hollywood's sarong girl, coming to Baltimore today to boost the sale of defense stamps in industrial plants, will find the city's "stamps-for-bombers campaign" at a high-water mark.

CAMPAIGN SPEEDED

Yesterday the Advertising Club of Baltimore made history by setting a $1,000,000 goal for itself, and today fresh impetus was given the drive as Basil A. Thomas, central chairman of the nine United Greek

societies announced the drive for $250,000, adding:

"The Hellenic peoples who have always been steadfast in their loyalty and devotion to democratic principles and institutions, which they consider as a part of their heritage, feel privileged to do their part in helping rid the world of the enemies of democracy and in helping America 'bomb the daylights' out of those who by unscrupulous and das-

Continued on Page 2, Column 3.

The Greek community joined the citywide "Buy a Bomber" campaign publicized in *The Baltimore News-Post,* January 15, 1942.

Father Papachristou with his sister Katherine Apostol and her children *l to r* : Olympia (Bebe), George, and Mary, circa 1942.

Representatives of the United Greek Societies, February 1, 1942. Seated left to right: George Stavropoulos, James Apostolides, Michael Nicolaides, George Sideropoulos, Stylianos Sfekas, Father Joakim Papachristou, Peter Sfekas, George Konstant, Constantine Stamatakos, George Petite, George Mesologites, Menas George. Standing left to right: James Venetos, Michael Moskonas, Constantine Pecunes, Dr. Panos Morphopoulos, Steve Kaludis, Nicholas Brous, Dionysios Karavedas.

To assist the Greek War Relief efforts, parish women sponsored fundraising events and collected clothing for shipment to the destitute people of Greece. Volunteers posed with Father Papachristou in front of the building next to the church, 1941.

By January of 1942, nine "United Greek Societies" of Baltimore, under the chairmanship of Basil A. Thomas and Dr. Panos Morphopoulos, pledged to purchase $250,000 in defense stamps to help the war effort by joining the citywide "Buy a Bomber" Campaign. According to the newspapers, money collected would be earmarked for the "purchase of one or more bombers at the Martin plant in Baltimore." City residents were called upon to "strike a blow at a treacherous enemy" and avenge the attack on Pearl Harbor. *The Baltimore News-Post* applauded the campaign with articles and photographs that enhanced the public image of the Greek Orthodox community. Key organizers of the fundraising effort included: Constantine Pecunes, Parish Council President; Alexander Diacumakos, President of the Order of AHEPA; Dionysios Karavedas, President of the GAPA; and George Sideropoulos, President of the Greek School of Highlandtown.

Various leaders of the *topika somatia* (regional societies), quite prominent in Baltimore during those years, also joined the cause. Constantine Stamatakos of the Laconian Association, Menas George of the Kytherian Brotherhood, Argiros Poulos of the Pan-Chian Society, Philip Economides of the Pan-Rhodian Society, and Steve Kaludis of the Karabournian Society united their respective groups in working with the church to support the cause. On February 7, 1942, *The Baltimore News-Post* reported that the $250,000 goal of the Greek community had been surpassed! Another notable event that raised thousands of dollars toward the war effort was the "Charity Ball" sponsored by the United Greek Societies on January 31, 1943. That evening, the Alcazar Ballroom was filled to capacity, thanks to the widely circulated advertisement coordinated by the committee.

Mirroring the efforts of other churches and civic organizations throughout the city, the Annunciation parish also contributed to the Red Cross War Relief Fund. Successful fundraising drives were arranged under the chairmanship of Stylianos Sfekas in 1942, Constantine Pecunes in

Baltimore Greeks Cheer King's Arrival

Members of Baltimore's Greek community cheered when King George II., arriving by Pan-American Clipper, told them that American weapons are making it possible for the soldiers, sailors and airmen of Greece to carry on war against the Axis. The King is shown as he shook hands with a woman in the group who welcomed him and presented him with flowers.

1943, Nicholas L. Karangelen in 1944 and Peter Sfekas in 1945. The Greek community's war effort reflected American patriotism as well as ethnic pride. On Sunday, May 17, 1942, hundreds of young people from the Greek community marched in the "I Am An American Day" Parade in proud testimony of their citizenship. Parishioners also marched in subsequent parades during the 1940's wearing their colorful native costumes—a unified representation of Greek culture to the citizens of Baltimore City.

The following month, on June 10, 1942, the Greek community gave King George II of Greece an enthusiastic welcome on his arrival in Baltimore enroute to a meeting with President Franklin D. Roosevelt. *The Baltimore News-Post* contained the following account: "Several hundred representatives of Baltimore's Greek community were at the Pan-American base to welcome the Monarch,

including boys and girls in the traditional costumes of their homeland." In his speech, King George commented that American weapons were enabling the "soldiers, sailors, and airmen of Greece to carry on war against the Axis." Parishioners cheered the King of Greece with patriotic fervor.

Greek-Americans wanted to make their allegiance clear as thousands of sons and daughters of immigrants joined the United States armed forces. Most families had at least one member in uniform or engaged in an essential wartime occupation. It is estimated that nearly 700 young men and women represented Maryland's Greek community. Among those brave and courageous members of the first generation, twelve young men ultimately paid the supreme sacrifice: Gus A. Panos, George L. Chagouris, Angelo Kadamanos, Antonios Meligritis, Athan Papachristou, Basil Papathanou, Nicholas J. Prevas, John Printizis,

Parade marchers (back *l to r*): Beatrice Markulis, Bertha Prevas, Genevieve Markulis; (front *l to r*): Amalia Markulis, Gloria Prevas, May 20, 1945.

John P. Tsirigos in front of the manse, the original building adjoining the church, circa 1943.

Greek youth marched in the "I Am An American Day" Parade, Howard Street, circa 1944.

Daughters of Laconia with "Madame" Potula Horianopoulos, President (seated center), circa 1945.

Ladies Pan-Chian Society with Maria Nikoludis, President (front row center), February 2, 1946.

Evangelos K. Stratakis, Apostolos Theodorakos, John Vendelis, and Louis Xintas. As news of their deaths reached the Annunciation Church, parishioners gathered to comfort the grief-stricken families and memorial prayers were chanted.

Throughout the 1940's, the regional societies continued to play a major role in the war effort, providing financial and moral support to the many activities centered at the Annunciation Church. In fact, several new societies and chapters formed during the war years. Between the years 1943 and 1944, three women's auxiliaries of regional societies were formed: Daughters of Laconia "Taygete" with Potula Horianopoulos, President; the Ladies Pan-Chian Society with Maria Nikoludis, President; and the Daughters of Karabourna with Anthi Hondroulis, President. Greek immigrants from other islands also organized clubs. The Fraternal Order of Cypriots, "Stavrovouni," was founded in January 1942 with Elias Kyriakos as first president. In June 1946, the American Lerian Association, "Leros," was established with Kounia Kalandros as first president. Soon, a local chapter

of the Pan-Karpathian Educational Progressive Association was initiated. Peter Melissanos served as first president of the men's group and Frances Angelos was first president of the ladies' group.

Though most of the parish's energy and resources were poured into the war effort until 1945, the Greeks still found time to solve the everyday problems facing their growing church community. With membership on the rise, coupled with the concern once again for more space, a special general assembly meeting was held in March of 1942. Parishioners voted to purchase the building on the southeast corner of Cathedral and Preston Streets. Land Records of Baltimore City show the "Orthodox Greek Church Evangelism," represented by Constantine J. Pecunes, Parish Council President, and Theodore Papapavlos, Vice President, concluded the transaction on May 8, 1942, for $9,225. This building at 45 West Preston Street became known as the "Greek Center" and housed the church offices, Greek War Relief Association, and Greek school, with ample space for social and athletic activities.

Annunciation Parish Council, 1942. Seated *l to r* : Sam Malavazos, Father Joakim Papachristou, Constantine J. Pecunes, President; James Apostolides. Standing *l to r* : George B. Petite, Dionysios Karavedas, George Agnew, George Hagegeorge, Nicholas Karangelen and George Stavropoulos.

The "Greek Center" at Preston and Cathedral Streets was owned by the Annunciation parish from 1942-1950.

Archbishop Athenagoras and Father Papachristou led the parish procession to the Greek Center for the official blessing ceremony, September 6, 1942.

Four months later, the Greek community gathered to bless its new property. Parish council minutes show that on Sunday, September 6, 1942, Archbishop Athenagoras came to Baltimore and celebrated the Hierarchical Divine Liturgy with Father Papachristou. Afterwards, the Archbishop, carrying an Orthodox cross and *vasiliko* (basil flowers), led a formal procession across Preston Street for the official blessing of the parish's latest building acquisition—the Greek Center. The church choir, altar servers, the all-Greek American Legion post, fraternal organizations, and parishioners participated in this joyous and historic event. One of the first major social events at the Greek Center was the parish's Twentieth Annual Ball held on December 27, 1942, with a program booklet reflecting the patriotic theme of that era.

Later that year, the Highlandtown Greek School received financial assistance from the Annunciation congregation. A new modern school at the corner of Ponca and Fleet Streets was soon built at a cost of $10,000 to serve the increasing number of students. Within a decade, the need for a second Orthodox church to serve the Greek population in Highlandtown would also become a main topic of much discussion at Annunciation. Throughout these challenging years, Constantine J. Pecunes was elected as council president on six different occasions and served on the board of

Members of the GAPA and American Legion participated in the procession to the Greek Center.

Commander James Latgis (center) of the George Dilboy Post of the American Legion and members of the congregation gathered in the courtyard for the ceremony. Professor Theodorides led the choir in song for the procession across the street to the Greek Center, September 6, 1942.

directors for over a decade. His strong leadership and vision for the parish is documented in church records and greatly enhanced the progress of the community during that era.

Another problem that faced the community in 1942 concerned the Woodlawn Cemetery. With over 600 burials since 1912, the "Greek Section" was almost filled. Cemetery officials had offered the church additional burial grounds in close proximity to its present section. The proposal, however, only included single interment graves, not family lots. Negotiations with the Woodlawn Cemetery dominated the parish agenda throughout the rest of the year. At times, discussions on the matter were quite heated, as leaders of the Greek community remained steadfast in being able to sell family lots to parishioners.

By January 1943, the urgency of the cemetery issue was the main topic at the general assembly. A Cemetery Committee consisting of Niketas A. Konstant, Chairman; Dionysios Karavedas, Elias Kyriakos, George Agnew, James Karukas, C. G. Paris, and John Apostolakos was appointed to either purchase grounds at another well-known Baltimore cemetery or buy ground to be developed into a community cemetery. Shortly thereafter, a large

tract of land was put up for sale on Windsor Mill Road, adjacent to the Lorraine Park Cemetery, less than a mile from the Woodlawn Cemetery. With growing concern over space for interments, the committee proposed that Annunciation establish its own cemetery. This generated a fervor of interest and the plan began to unfold.

The general assembly of August 1943 directed the parish council to obtain a mortgage in order to secure and develop the cemetery property. Annunciation concluded its negotiations with the property owners at a price of $1,000 an acre. Land Records of Baltimore County show that two separate transactions completed the purchase. On October 13, 1943, the first six acres were acquired; on October 20, 1944, eight more adjacent acres were purchased from the same sellers for future expansion. The Annunciation community now owned a total of fourteen acres for burial grounds.

Considering the many events of that era—war relief efforts, paying off the purchase and renovation debts of the church building and Greek Center, and operating two Greek language schools—the decisive move into a cemetery project was impressive. It is noteworthy as very few Orthodox parishes in America can boast of such an

Constantine J. Pecunes served as Parish Council President for six different terms between 1941-1952.

endeavor. The cemetery committee then moved quickly, with the advice of outside expertise and legal counsel, in developing the burial grounds, establishing rules and regulations, and advertising pricing for the sale of family lots.

By the spring of 1944, the cemetery was ready for use and the Windsor Mill Road property was officially named the "Greek Orthodox Cemetery." The first burial was for Cosmas N. Lykos, age 49, on May 2, 1944. Two days later, Vasiliki G. Thomas, age 72, was laid to rest. During the first twelve months, nearly thirty Orthodox Christians were buried in the new parish cemetery. The dream of establishing a church-operated burial ground had become a reality. The hard work of the cemetery committee, parish council, and clergy was highly praised by the Annunciation congregation and the Greek Orthodox Archdiocese.

Later that summer, the interior of the sanctuary underwent a significant change in appearance. A new large icon, depicting the Virgin Mary being

Theatrical performance, Annunciation Greek School and Choir and Highlandtown Greek School, Alcazar Ballroom, June 24, 1945.
Front *l to r* : Marian Vardavas, Olga Markulis, Evangeline Marusiodis, Irene Carman. Middle *l to r* : Evelyn Mezardash, Athena Pistolas, Mary Markulis, Efrosene Brown, George Mihalos, Demetra Vlangas, Evelyn Venetos, unidentified, Zoe Clessuras.
Back *l to r* : Evangeline Maniatis, unidentified, Chrysoula Carman, Pat Papaminas, Julia Marusiodis, Helen Vardavas.

"Greek Orthodox Cemetery" on Windsor Mill Road in Baltimore County, Maryland.

Dionysios Karavedas played a key role in the acquisition of the Greek Orthodox Cemetery. He served as Council President from 1945-1946.

raised into heaven by fourteen angels, was created and installed on the rear wall of the Holy Altar. On August 23, 1944, in a special ceremony conducted by Archbishop Athenagoras and Father Papachristou, donors Constantine and Alexandria Maistros unveiled the magnificent wall-sized icon and received special blessings for their generosity. The Archbishop was pleased to attend this event and saw firsthand how the Baltimore congregation, even through the war years, had many initiatives on its agenda.

The Annunciation community responded to its recent investments with practical enthusiasm and launched a series of mortgage-burning drives. In May 1945, a Mortgage Burning Committee was formed under the chairmanship of C. G. Paris. Donations were divided into four categories (donor, large donor, benefactor, and great benefactor). Throughout the summer months, nearly twenty committee members diligently solicited funds on behalf of the parish. They included: Achilles Hondroulis, John Kousouris, Savas Kambouris,

Professor Athanasios P. Theodorides (center) with choir members left to right: Chrysanthy N. Pappas, Markella Mihalos, Cleopatra Athas, and Theodora N. Pappas, Easter 1945.

James Apostolides, John Apostolakos, Nicholas Gounaris, George Hondroulis, George Karangelen, Dionysios Karavedas, James Karukas, Niketas Konstant, Elias Kyriakos, Nicholas Manos, Constantine Mesologites, Nicholas Papadopoulos, George Petite, George Stavropoulos, and William Vlangas. Soon after, President Dionysios Karavedas reported on the impressive results of the campaign. Over $14,000 was collected and two mortgages were retired. The community celebrated with a mortgage-burning ceremony on August 18, 1945. Three years later, another fundraising drive was initiated to retire the remaining mortgage, and a "Last Mortgage Burning Drive" celebration was held at the Alcazar Ballroom on Cathedral Street. The future of the parish held great promise.

Internally, however, storm clouds were gathering over church administration. A special meeting of the parish council was held on September 5, 1945, attended by Archbishop Athenagoras who came to Baltimore to mediate a dispute regarding the priest. Though Father Joakim Papachristou was acknowledged as an excellent clergyman, certain council members openly expressed their concern over his authoritative leadership style. During the heated discussion, the priest emotionally tendered his resignation. The Archbishop, known for his skills in diplomacy, was able to reconcile the matter between the council members and their priest. The incident is note-worthy as it foreshadowed more difficulties ahead.

The year 1945 marked Father Papachristou's tenth year as priest at Annunciation. Strengthened relations with the Archdiocese, community-wide efforts focused on war relief, and responses to meet the needs of a rapidly changing congregation all contributed to a diverse roster of programs at Annunciation. The war was finally over, and those in the armed forces were coming home. Soon the parish would celebrate forty years in Baltimore. A church serving a handful of immigrants had evolved into hundreds of families from various regions of Greece. Significant changes were on the horizon. Old World customs were about to clash with new ideologies of a younger generation. It would soon be a time of transition.

A commemorative pin was issued for the celebration
of the "Last Mortgage Burning" in the fall of 1948.

Opposite Page: Members of EONA *(Elliniki Orthodoxos Neoleas Amerikis),* Greek Orthodox Youth of America,
took their first group photograph in 1946—the 40th Anniversary of the Annunciation parish.

1946-1955

The Annunciation community observed its Fortieth Anniversary in 1946. Although the war had ended a year earlier, this anniversary symbolized a crucial dividing point in parish history. It marked the official end of the wartime era and the emergence of new emphasis and new interests in the church. As a final salute to the Greek-American war effort, the community's veterans were honored on February 12, 1946, at a banquet organized under the chairmanship of Vice President James Latgis. Over 400 people attended the homecoming celebration held at the Emerson Hotel. Father Papachristou and Parish Council President Dionysios Karavedas were among the keynote speakers that evening. This notable occasion, covered by the local press, included a memorial tribute to the Greek-Americans who died serving their country.

The following month marked the official Fortieth Anniversary and special events were sponsored for the week of March 24-31, 1946, under the chairmanship of Louis N. Karangelen. An impressive 200-page *Fortieth Anniversary Celebration Book* was also published later that year. Hierarchical Divine Liturgies were conducted by His Eminence Archbishop Athenagoras; His Grace Panteleimon, Metropolitan of the Diocese of North Epirus; and The Very Rev. Joakim Papachristou. These were highly moving ceremonies, especially for honored guests George Sempeles and Constantine Diamond. They had served as the first two parish council presidents. George Sempeles, at the age of 29, had been elected shortly after the parish organized in the spring of 1906. Now, close to 70 years old, he was fortunate to witness this milestone celebration of his pioneering efforts. When Mr. Sempeles passed away the following year on April 24, 1947, he was regarded with such high esteem that the parish council of the Annunciation Church brought Archbishop Athenagoras from New York to conduct the funeral services.

The 40th Anniversary week also coincided with the church's name day on March 25th—the religious observance of the *Feast Day of the Annunciation.* Special programs and a grand celebration at the Alcazar Ballroom concluded the festivities. Some of the events were even attended by city and state officials, including Mayor Theodore R. McKeldin, further showing that Annunciation was making strides in its outreach to the larger community. In a congratulatory letter, Mayor McKeldin expressed best wishes to Father Papachristou that his continuing pastorate in Baltimore would be "blessed through holy offices and deeds of religious consolation, missions of mercy, and tokens of charity." Within a few years, however, the atmosphere at Annunciation would be quite the opposite.

The Greek community could look back proudly on many accomplishments. One of the most profound changes, as a result of the war, was its assimilation into American society. But the Annunciation parish of the 1940's, despite its energetic enthusiasm, still clung tenaciously to Old World traditions and beliefs. As young people began to question traditions, practices, and customs, the sharply different ideologies between the immigrant generation and first-generation churchgoers soon became apparent. For many Greek-American institutions, progress and innovation characterized the post-war era. Baltimore's Greek community, however, would experience a period of turmoil and unrest before ultimately evolving toward a positive course of growth.

An initial response to satisfy the evolving needs of the Greek youth occurred in January 1946, when a youth organization named EONA (*Elliniki Orthodoxos Neoleas Amerikis*) was established at Annunciation under the guidance of the church's talented choir director, Athanasios P. Theodorides. With his assistance, the young adults voted on a constitution and elected the following members as first officers: Mark Stanley Plakotaris, President;

Parish Council, 1946. First row left to right: Emmanuel Galanis, Nicholas G. Pulos, Secretary; Dionysios Karavedas, President; The Very Rev. Joakim Papachristou, James Latgis, Vice President; Frank Photiades, Treasurer; and John Mostakis. Second row left to right: George Stavropoulos, Louis N. Karangelen, Basil George, Nicholas Lambros, Andrew Mihalos, and George Agnew.

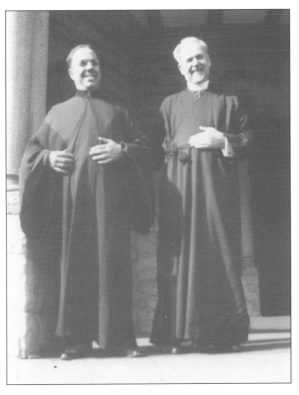

Father Philotheos Ahladas (left) served as the assistant priest to Father Joakim Papachristou (right) from 1946-1947.

Archbishop Athenagoras (left) and Father Ahladas (right) conducted the opening ceremonies of the AHEPA National Convention at the Lord Baltimore Hotel, August 23, 1946.

Tom Boulmetis, Vice President; Markella Mihalos, Secretary; Chrysanthy N. Pappas, Assistant Secretary; and Virginia Lambrow, Treasurer. EONA activities were divided into art, music, dramatic, and athletic committees and sought to promote fellowship among the youth of Greek descent.

The post-war boom was immediately evident as returning servicemen and women married and established homes and families. Annunciation experienced increases in church membership and in Greek school enrollment. The growing number of sacraments listed in the parish registry indicated the need for a second priest. In July 1946, the parish welcomed The Very Rev. Philotheos Ahladas who assisted Father Joakim Papachristou through December 1947 with his many pastoral responsibilities. In fact, Father Ahladas took charge of all ecclesiastical duties at Annunciation during the summer of 1946 after Father Papachristou suffered a heart attack requiring a four-month period of recuperation. One of Father Ahladas' first public events was to assist Archbishop Athenagoras at the opening ceremonies of the 20th National Convention of the Order of AHEPA that convened in Baltimore on August 23, 1946, under the chairmanship of Robert G. Contos.

Conventioneers on the steps of the Annunciation Church posed with Archbishop Athenagoras (center) after special church services conducted on Sunday, August 25, 1946.

The burial rites for war veteran Nicholas J. Prevas, age 26, were conducted by the assistant priest, Father Philotheos Ahladas, at the new Greek Orthodox Cemetery on Windsor Mill Road, November 5, 1946.

Acolytes posed with Father Joakim Papachristou, clockwise from top: Michael Mostakis, Nicholas Lykos, Steven Nichols, Theodore Capsanes, Anthony Kostopoulos, George Mezardash, Basil Koras, Tom Baglanis, Basil Kalandros, 1946.

There is a poignant story surrounding the Archbishop's visit to Baltimore that summer. Having heard the account of a young parishioner's medical condition brought on by serious war injuries, he went to visit him in the hospital. The heartfelt blessings given by the compassionate Orthodox Church leader deeply touched the family. Three months later, however, hopes were replaced by sorrow. On November 5, 1946, parishioners, war veterans, and the George Dilboy American Legion Post gathered at the Greek Orthodox Cemetery as Father Ahladas chanted burial rites over Nicholas J. Prevas, age 26, who was laid to rest with complete military honors.

By mid-November of 1946, church records show that Father Papachristou, now fully recovered, resumed his duties as the senior priest at Annunciation. During this period, the official parish name was changed to better reflect its growing strength and influence. Following approval by the parish assembly, the charter record was amended on December 5, 1946, with the official new name as "The Greek Orthodox Community of Baltimore, Evangelismos." A further example of the parish's commitment to education was also demonstrated during Father Ahladas' brief tenure as the assistant. Under his spiritual guidance, Dr. George Govatos and Dr. Michael Varipatis reorganized the Hellenic University Club which had been inactive since the outbreak of World War II. Dr. Varipatis was elected the first president of the revitalization effort which was successful as many first-generation members wished to further their education. By the following year, the Hellenic University Club, under the leadership of Peter J. Prevas and Father Ahladas, began preliminary planning of a formal Sunday school curriculum.

The tenth anniversary of the acquisition of the Preston Street Church was observed on Sunday, March 23, 1947. An inspiring message to parishioners was contained in the weekly bulletin. "It was an eventful decade, during which the world's map has been radically changed and the course of history has taken a new shape. During this transitional decade, we witnessed the greatest progress of our Community, commanding the praise of our Church Authority, the admiration of the other sister Greek Orthodox communities, and the esteem of our fellow American citizens."

The parish council of 1947, under the leadership of James P. Karukas, also designated that Sunday as "Greek-American Youth Day" with a special address delivered in English by George N. Pulos, a graduate of the Holy Cross Theological School and member of the Baltimore community. "Our achievements must and will be a challenge, for greater and better things, especially to our new generation, who inherit a noble tradition to emulate, to continue, and to surpass." He encouraged members of the new generation to "show their devotion to their Mother Church and Community," by attending these special services. The parish had clearly turned its attention to the young adults as shown by the announcements and numerous events advertised in weekly church bulletins of that era.

The focus on youth continued. The Baltimore Museum of Art hosted a highly-praised concert on June 18, 1947, featuring a shining example of the younger generation—the Hellenic Byzantine Choir. Later, on December 28, 1947, the combined choirs of the Annunciation Church of Baltimore and the St. George Greek Orthodox Cathedral of

Hellenic Byzantine Choir of the "Evangelismos" Church, 1946. Father Joakim Papachristou (third row center); Musical Director Athanasios Theodorides (third row far left); Cantor James Venetos (second row far right); Choir President Joanne Souris (second row third from right); and Choir Vice President Alexander W. Vlangas (top row far right).

Philadelphia hosted a concert of Classic, Byzantine, and Modern music. It was held at the Polytechnic Auditorium at North and Guilford Avenues before an overflowing audience. Baltimore's choral group, some fifty voices strong, was led by Professor Theodorides with Chrysanthy N. Pappas, organist. Choir officers that year included: Gus D. Bisbikis, President; Michael G. Athas, Vice President; Sophie J. Mentis, Secretary; and Georgia Topal, Treasurer.

In May 1948, the EONA youth club expanded its role and produced the first issue of *The Little Herald*—a publication that brought the Greek community news of events, articles on religion, interviews, and information on social gatherings. The first editor was Toni Stavracos and feature editor was Mary Bahadouris. Earlier concerns of the church's inability to satisfy the social, cultural and religious needs of its youth were slowly being erased. The regional societies also provided an excellent forum for parishioners to attend church services and splendid socials. For instance, a number of conventions were held in Baltimore in the late 1940's. The Seventh Annual Convention of the United Chios Societies of America was held July 2-6, 1947, under the auspices of the "Andreas Siggros" Chapter No. 8 with George Mesologites as general chairman. Then, in July of 1949, the 22nd Annual Convention of the Pan-Rhodian Society of America "Apollon" came to town under the direction of the Baltimore Lodge No. 4 with Michael Nicolaides as chairman.

Parish socials during the 1940's were often held at the Greek Center, Preston and Cathedral Streets. "Madame" Potula Horianopoulos (seated fourth from left) created many of the costumes of that era.

By early 1948, Father Ahladas had departed from Baltimore to assume full-time duties as the priest of the Greek community in Norfolk, Virginia. The Baltimore parish was looking toward a bright future when it decided to hire a new assistant from among the American-born clergy to further advance its youth programs. In March of 1948, Deacon Soterios Gouvellis, a 27-year-old graduate of the Holy Cross Seminary, arrived in Baltimore with his wife, Kay Gouvellis. Many parishioners were delighted with the new assistant who spoke English and who immediately developed a strong camaraderie with the youth. The new deacon, a native of Chester, Pennsylvania, was filled with much enthusiasm, anxious to contribute to the vibrant parish.

One of Deacon Gouvellis' first duties was to accompany a parish delegation, led by Parish Council President Nicholas B. Pergantis, to City Hall where Mayor Thomas D'Alesandro, Jr., issued a proclamation designating March 25, 1948, as "Greek Independence Day in Baltimore." The following month, on Sunday, April 11, 1948, Deacon Gouvellis became the very first priest to be ordained at the altar of the Annunciation Church. Bishop Athenagoras Cavadas of Boston, along with Father Joakim Papachristou, officiated at the services. It was an impressive ceremony and the church was filled to capacity. His arrival and ordination in Baltimore not only inspired the youth of the community but also marked the beginning of a difficult time of transition for the church.

Pre-Lenten Masquerade Ball (*Apokreatiko*) of the EONA at the Greek Center, March 1946.
First president of the youth group was Mark Stanley Plakotaris (seated front row far right).

Proclamation of Greek Independence Day, March 25, 1948. Left to right: Nicholas G. Pulos, Deacon Gouvellis, Father Papachristou, Basil A. Thomas, Mayor Thomas D'Alesandro, Jr. (seated), Nicholas B. Pergantis, Council President; Constantine Maistros, George Agnew.

Ecumenical Patriarch-Elect Archbishop Athenagoras (center) with clergymen and dignitaries at the St. George Greek Orthodox Cathedral of Philadelphia. Father Joakim Papachristou (fourth from right) attended this historic gathering on January 12, 1949.

As the 1948 parish council concluded its term, outgoing President Nicholas Pergantis received an eloquent letter from Bishop Athenagoras of Boston. The letter dated January 8, 1949, stated in part: "I wish to express my warmest thanksgiving to you for your close cooperation with the Holy Archdiocese. I understand that during your service you had many things to worry about and that you expended a lot of effort to meet the demands of the ministry you undertook. This service is not rewarded in this world, and therefore I wish upon all of you the blessings of God, who records such service in the golden book of eternal life." The reference to undercurrents within the parish is noteworthy and a subtle indication of upcoming events that were about to unfold.

During this same period, the Greek Orthodox Archdiocese was in transition. Archbishop Athenagoras had been selected as the next Ecumenical Patriarch and was preparing to leave New York. One farewell gathering was held at the St. George Greek Orthodox Cathedral in Philadelphia on January 12, 1949, shortly before his departure for Constantinople. Father Papachristou, a close friend of Athenagoras, was among the group of clergy and dignitaries in attendance. The selection of the next Archbishop, however, was not finalized until October of 1949 when Patriarch Athenagoras announced the election of Metropolitan Michael of Corinth as the new spiritual leader of America. The tenure of Archbishop Michael was marked by difficult

The Ordination of Rev. Soterios Gouvellis (flanked by altar servers) was conducted by Bishop Athenagoras Cavadas of Boston (center of altar) and The Very Rev. Joakim Papachristou (in foreground holding chalice), Sunday, April 11, 1948.

The Rev. Soterios Gouvellis (Father Sam) was the first American-born priest to serve at Annunciation, 1948-1949.

Presbytera Kay Gouvellis (center) posed with young women of the Greek community, Easter 1949.

changes on many levels. Transitions from the old to the new were the order of the day. For the Baltimore parish, these changes unfortunately played out in an extreme manner.

Significant differences in style were apparent between Annunciation's new assistant, Father Gouvellis, and the many priests who had served the parish before. He was young, energetic, married, and American-born. By contrast, his superior, The Very Rev. Joakim Papachristou, age 60, typified the Old School. He was part of the immigrant generation, unmarried, extremely dignified and very imposing. The younger generation identified with Father "Sam" Gouvellis who expanded athletic activities with a church league for basketball and softball. A hall in the Greek Center was even converted into a gymnasium and sports events began to flourish under his guidance.

The presence of Father Gouvellis in Baltimore coincided with another development in the Greek Orthodox church's transition from pre-war to post-war thinking. Young people had begun to participate in the governance of church affairs. For a brief period in 1945, Peter S. Sfekas, age 29, served as council president. Later in January 1949,

another first-generation Greek-American, 34-year-old George C. Mesologites, was elected president of the parish council. As Father Gouvellis expanded his activities and role within the parish, some older members, including the senior clergyman, found his liberal attitude and ways difficult to accept. In the midst of a distinguished career, Father Joakim Papachristou possibly saw his stable position as spiritual leader threatened by this newcomer. Perhaps he felt overshadowed by the growing popularity of a youthful assistant who, despite his somewhat defiant manner, received support for his new ideas.

The situation developed into a power struggle when a group of parishioners believed the senior priest had begun exercising too much control over decision-making activities. The stage had been set for the arrival of new ideas and the departure of Old World customs. Father Papachristou and Father Gouvellis became the key actors in the ensuing drama. Findings strongly suggest that this clique (a small group of instigators) used the assistant priest as a means of antagonizing the older priest. Their objective—to dismiss Father Papachristou—was soon apparent, resulting in protests from those who remained loyal to the senior clergyman.

Directors of the Greek Ladies' Philoptochos Society, 1946-1948. Seated left to right: Virginia M. Polites, Secretary; Georgia W. Vlangas, President; Father Papachristou; Panayiotitsa N. Karangelen, Vice President; Vasiliki N. Papadopoulos, Treasurer. Standing left to right: Mary Poletis, Maria Kazaras, Despina Sophocleus, Aristea Germanakos, and Katherine Tsimas.

Mayor Thomas D'Alesandro, Jr. (seated) with the Annunciation Parish Council, 1949. Left to right: Basil A. Thomas, George Sideropoulos, Father Gouvellis, Nicholas Manos, Michael Nicolaides, George Mesologites, President; Father Papachristou, Steve Avgerinos, William Eliades.

A group of Baltimore schoolteachers hears the Rev. Joakim Papachristou discuss Greek culture and religion. From talks like this the teachers learn their pupils' heritages.

Photo from The Baltimore Sun Magazine, February 1947. The three large stained glass windows
were donated by members of the parish. Left to right: The Birth of Christ (Constantine and Theodora Pecunes);
The Annunciation of the Virgin Mary (Constantine and Potula Horianopoulos); and Christ in the Temple (Anthippi Liodis).

Father Joakim Papachristou (right) and his assistant
Father Soterios Gouvellis (left) officiated at the wedding of
Hercules Spanos to Theodora N. Pappas on September 11, 1949.

By the fall of 1949, the Greek community was polarized over the issue, and the atmosphere was filled with antagonism. For reasons not entirely clear, Father Papachristou gave his opposition added strength when he had a disagreement with Father Gouvellis and according to later court records, "ejected him from the Church in the presence of parishioners during the course of a liturgy." Their differences were now irreconcilable and by December 1949, upon the senior clergy's insistence, the young priest's employment was abruptly ended. The altar incident and termination of the assistant aroused much displeasure and discussion.

A special meeting was held on December 18, 1949, at the Highlandtown Greek School, to rally a formal protest to the Archdiocese and parish council regarding the "unfair termination" of Father Gouvellis. The meeting invitation, clearly intended for the Greeks of Highlandtown, stated that Father Gouvellis had "managed in a short period of time to bring the Hellenic Orthodox youth close to the Church…something that other priests did not accomplish over a number of years."

Father Soterios "Sam" Gouvellis conducted the marriage ceremony for
Constantine G. Konstant and Evangelia (Evelyn) Mezardash on October 16, 1949.

The demand that Father Gouvellis be reinstated was a hopeless cause as news spread quickly of his hasty reassignment to Watertown, New York. Any hopes that normalcy would return to Annunciation vanished. In fact, the departure of the assistant started a chain of events that ultimately led to the removal of the senior priest.

It is interesting that the first attempt to dismiss Father Papachristou actually failed. A general assembly was called on January 22, 1950, expressly for this purpose, but the required quorum was not present—despite the claim that a majority of parishioners were dissatisfied and refused to attend religious services performed by the senior priest. One week later, the anti-Papachristou group achieved its goal. On January 29, 1950, a special general assembly was convened at the Greek Center with Savas Kambouris presiding. This time the decision was nearly unanimous: 153 members voted to "relieve, dismiss, and transfer" Father Papachristou while only seven members voted to retain him. A highly volatile newsletter, distributed

earlier that same week, no doubt influenced the high turnout of people.

The decision to fire the priest of nearly fifteen years left many parishioners stunned, confused, and outraged. It was an assault on their faith. In New York, Archbishop Michael, who had just assumed his duties in December of 1949, began receiving telegrams and letters from key participants in the dramatic events unfolding at Annunciation. Parish Council President Michael Nicolaides, Vice President Dionysios Karavedas, General Assembly President Savas Kambouris and others informed the Archdiocese of the general assembly's decision to have their priest transferred and waited for an official reply. Even with emotions running high, the parish council's letter to Father Joakim Papachristou regarding the termination of his employment politely stated that "any further services you might render to this community will necessarily be gratuitous." Some members of the parish on both sides of the issue even visited New York to plead their case to the Archdiocese.

"KYTHERIAN DAY"-BALTIMORE, MD.-
9-19-48

The Kytherian Brotherhood posed after special church services dedicated to their patron saint, *Panayia Myrtithiotissa*, September 19, 1948.

Archbishop Michael of North and South America
served as spiritual leader from 1949 until his death in 1958.

The Very Rev. Chrysostomos Bogdis served as an
interim priest during the pastoral controversy in 1950.

Hoping the matter would subside and the situation would return to normal in Baltimore, the Archbishop did not immediately respond. Throughout February 1950, the tension only worsened as Father Papachristou, without word from his superior, believed he was still the official priest. The showdown escalated on March 1, 1950, when the parish council, without Archdiocesan approval, hired The Very Rev. Chrysostomos Bogdis as its new priest. Ignoring the council's letter of termination, Father Papachristou responded by leaving for a vacation in Florida and vowed to return by the end of March to resume his rightful duties. With no definitive response from New York as to his transfer, a crisis was at hand.

The anti-Papachristou group, determined to uphold the mandate of the general assembly, turned to the parish council that was "legally responsible to enforce the property rights of the Church." The parish council, however, refused to file suit and remained "hopelessly divided" over the matter until their individual resignations in May 1950. Parish council minutes, which could provide insight into these events, are missing during this critical period.

However, documentation surrounding this matter has been preserved in the archival records of the Baltimore City Circuit Court.

On March 23, 1950, The Greek Orthodox Community of Baltimore "Evangelismos," by Savas Kambouris, President of the General Assembly, filed a Bill of Complaint against the senior clergyman. They were successful in securing a court injunction against Father Papachristou, whose new residence since the spring of 1947 was at 1719 Lakeside Avenue. The injunction was issued on March 24, 1950—the eve of the *Feast Day of the Annunciation*. The next day, *The Baltimore Sun* covered the controversial event in an article entitled "Suit Seeks Ouster of Greek Pastor." Archbishop Michael was also kept informed through telegrams. "Local conditions have become dangerously acute from the standpoint of public safety...Father Joakim must not be permitted to serve...Reply at once so that the emotions subside." Within a week, another message was sent. "Father Papachristou anxious to resume duties. Please inform him by Western Union if he is free to serve mass tonight."

Ladies' Auxiliary of the Pan-Rhodian Society of Baltimore, July 1949. Seated left to right: Evangelia Nicolaides, Maritsa Klimentou, Stergoula Karpathiou and Athena Markulis. Standing left to right: Irene F. Arnas, Anthi S. Kambouris, Chrysanthy Lolakis, Hariklea A. Antonakas, Hariklea A. Antonas, Georgia Papavasiliou and Sophia J. Diakoulas.

"All Nations Day Festival," circa 1951. Standing left to right: Philip Lucara, Katie Paxenos, Irene Kalandros, Michael Prevas, Ruth Kampos, Basil Kotsatos, Esther Katsaros, Nicholas Petite. Seated left to right: Helen Christie, Jordan Kampos, Christine Gereny.

It is also known that at some point following the court-issued order, opponents of Father Papachristou prevented him from entering the church building. As the drama unfolded, even the local police were summoned to Preston Street to maintain order—one of the darkest moments in parish history. Brokenhearted and taken aback by these events, Father Papachristou filed his response to the Bill of Complaint on April 18, 1950, and denied the charges of being "spiritually and temperamentally incompatible" with the laymen. His concise answers provided through his attorney, James Sfekas, did not indicate a broken spirit. In fact, his determination to maintain his senior ranking at Annunciation was steadfast.

Court documents and parish records indicate that even with his successor, Father Chrysostomos Bogdis, already established at Annunciation, Father Joakim Papachristou persisted in performing sacraments and participating in religious services. The exact date of his departure is not clear, but could not have occurred before May 14, 1950, when the church registry reveals he performed his final sacrament, a baptism. After nearly fifteen years of service, the longest term of any priest during those years, he left a turbulent Greek community still torn by discord over the entire matter.

The remainder of that year saw more problems surface. The new parish council, elected in May 1950 with John Lambros as president, sought to

One of the final sacraments performed by The Very Rev. Joakim Papachristou in Baltimore was the wedding of George Tsouvalos (Tsottles) and Ermione (Erma) Karitis on April 16, 1950.

Father Chrysostomos Bogdis united Louis N. Dezes and
Mary Karayinopulos in Holy Matrimony on September 10, 1950.

The Very Rev. Philotheos B. Ahladas was the
next clergyman assigned to the parish in October 1950.

distance itself from the controversial general assembly action. As a result, when attorneys in the civil suit requested payment for their legal services, they were flatly denied and later took the parish to court. Dissension continued throughout the summer months as Father Papachristou's supporters began accusing the new priest, Father Bogdis, with instigating the earlier court injunction.

Further controversy surrounded Father Bogdis due to his own lack of decorum, and he often skulked about the church building to avoid criticism from parishioners. Realizing his declining popularity, he soon expressed a desire to return to Greece as quickly as possible. Parish attorney Basil A. Thomas worked diplomatically to resolve the various legal issues confronting the Annunciation community during these difficult times.

Needless to say, an atmosphere of contention hovered over the 1950 general assembly meetings. Luke Carman, who presided at these acrimonious gatherings, was able to maintain a semblance of order from vocal participants. Holding steadfast, the church tried to move forward with its business agenda. In the meantime, the Archdiocese began searching for a new clergyman who could aid in

calming the turmoil that enveloped the parish. It is interesting that two of the ten priests on the roster of candidates considered that year were prior clergymen who had served the parish: The Rev. Symeon Emmanuel of Portland, Maine; and The Very Rev. Constantinos Statheros of San Jose, California. Both had served brief tenures at Annunciation nearly a quarter of a century earlier.

Ultimately, the decision was made by the Archdiocese that the Baltimore and Norfolk parishes would switch priests. In October of 1950, following the hasty departure of Father Bogdis, Annunciation welcomed back The Very Rev. Philotheos Ahladas who had made a good impression while serving as assistant priest from 1946-47. Subsequently, the Annunciation Greek Orthodox community in Norfolk, Virginia, was assigned to Father Joakim Papachristou. Though not the younger Greek-American priest desired by many parishioners, the 52-year-old Father Ahladas was cordially received and worked gently to mend and revitalize the community. The 1950's showed that an impressive rejuvenation did take place. The parish would soon set aside its internal differences and aspire to greater accomplishments.

Father Ahladas returned to Baltimore and found that a renovation project, initiated by him while he was assistant priest, was now well underway. This included an extensive remodeling of the church basement and the addition of new rooms for the administrative, educational and social functions of the community. Unfortunately, he also found the parish in a less stable financial position. Sweeping changes and events—clergy terminations, a court injunction, embarrassing publicity, and parish council resignations—led to dissatisfaction and a number of parishioners protested by withdrawing their financial support.

General economic difficulties, coupled with a new movement to incorporate all church activities under one roof, ultimately led to the sale of the Greek Center at 45 W. Preston Street at the corner of Cathedral Street. After eight years of operation, the maintenance cost of this large building was also deemed impractical. On October 18, 1950, the Greek Center was sold for $38,000, with the proceeds earmarked for future expansion projects. In hindsight, considering the parish's strong need in later decades for the purchase of additional property in that same block, the sale of the Greek Center was most unfortunate.

Another change was the resignation of choir director Professor Athanasios Theodorides in the fall of 1948. His departure for another assignment left a void in the education and music programs he had designed. Following a number of interim choir directors and assistants, including Elly Ioannides (Jones), Chrysanthy N. Pappas, and Michael N. Prevas, a new era of stability began in May 1951. Georgia Topal (Topaltzas), a parishioner and graduate of the Peabody Conservatory of Music, became the first American-born choir director formally employed by Annunciation. During this period, Efrosene Brown (Kalantzopoulos) served as the church organist. Soon, the parish music program was flourishing with active Senior and Junior Choirs.

By this time, Archbishop Michael had made his first Archpastoral visit to Annunciation. On March 18, 1951, the first Sunday of the Orthodox Lenten season, he assisted Father Ahladas with church

The Senior Choir of the Annunciation Greek Orthodox community of Baltimore under the
musical leadership of Georgia Topal (front row far left). The organist was Efrosene Brown (middle row center).
This picture appeared on the front cover of *The Community Herald* published by the Annunciation Church in May of 1952.

The Lord Baltimore Chapter No. 364 of the AHEPA (American Hellenic Educational Progressive Association) was organized on December 28, 1949. Charter members gathered for this historic photograph to mark the occasion.

services and spoke to the congregation, hoping his message would bring a fresh spirit of unity to the ever-growing number of parishioners. During this era, various Greek fraternal organizations also expanded their activities. One example was the establishment by the AHEPA of a second chapter in the city. On December 28, 1949, the Lord Baltimore Chapter No. 364 of the Order of AHEPA was organized. Its first elected officers were: John Fangikis, President; Costas Michaels, Vice President; Andrew A. Papaminas, Secretary; and James Tangires, Treasurer.

Great strides in communicating news to the growing Greek community of Baltimore was also achieved during this decade. On April 23, 1950, William Campas and Mark S. Plakotaris debuted the first successful Greek-American Hour on radio station WBMD. The "Greek Hour" included church and community news, social announcements, a full coverage of news from Greece, and popular ethnic music. By 1952, the program, written and produced by John Morekas, had become an integral part of the community. Within a few years his cousin, Nitsa Morekas, joined the venture as the co-host of the program. Printed material was another vital source of information. *The Little Herald* of the EONA was combined with

the "Evangelismos" church bulletin to establish one periodical of church news and events. By September 1951, Annunciation proudly published the first issue of *The Community Herald* with Mary Bahadouris serving as editor.

In the early 1950's, the focus was once again on the youth. The EONA was revitalized in the spring of 1952 when it voted to become a member of the newly-formed national youth organization GOYA (Greek Orthodox Youth of America). The national group, established in 1950 under Archbishop Michael, developed an American identity with English as its official language. By February 1953, a junior organization for youngsters 12-18 years of age was established called JOY (Junior Orthodox Youth); it was later renamed Junior GOYA. Plans were also initiated for a Greek-American Boy Scout Troop. Through the efforts of Richard Contos and Father Ahladas, Troop No. 629 was established with Peter Moralis and George Peters, both former scouts, serving as first leaders.

This period was truly a time of transition for the Orthodox Church. The use of the English language in religious education was recommended at the 1950 Clergy-Laity Congress. The groundwork was now laid for changes across the country.

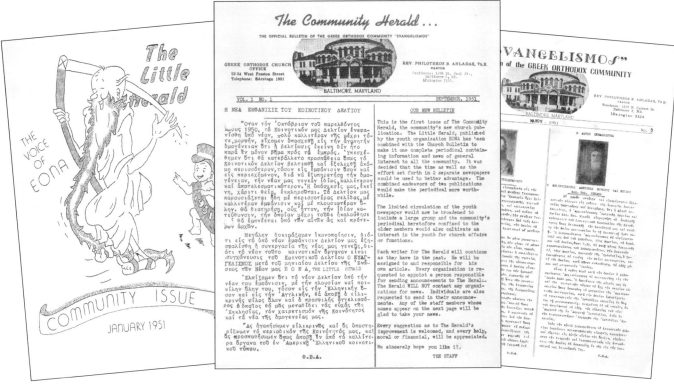

The youth newsletter (left) and church bulletin (right) were merged as *The Community Herald* in 1951.

Broadcast of the Greek-American Radio Hour with William Campas (seated) and John Morekas (standing), circa 1951. John Morekas served as host of the program for over five decades.

Demetra Moralis, Mary Bahadouris (center) and Venus Sarant pose at the entrance to the building next to the church, 1952. Mary Bahadouris would serve for three decades as editor of *The Community Herald*, later renamed *The Annunciation Herald*.

Costume Party

These girls made up a Gay Nineties group at a pre-Lenten costume party of Baltimore's Greek Orthodox community.

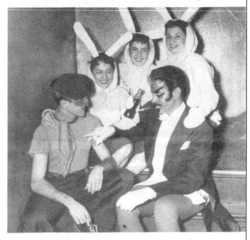

A Greek "shop dance" is a feature of the affair, held at the community's center, Preston and Cathedral streets.

An Apache and Old Nick chat with three bunnies, above, while waiting for the ballroom dance to begin, below.

No stags allowed on the dance floor, so a fisherman and a monk remove one of the younger offenders their own way.

Circus clowns have more fun than anybody, so these four ingenious girls came prepared for an enjoyable evening.

The Baltimore Sun published photographs of the Pre-Lenten Party of the EONA held at the Greek Center on March 6, 1949. Parish records show admission was $1.00 for this event.

In Baltimore, Father Ahladas was concerned for the youth to better understand Orthodox traditions. With the English language now acceptable in teaching, a strong Sunday school program was established in 1951 through a Hellenic University Club Committee under the supervision of Peter J. Prevas. Twelve qualified professionals were quickly organized into the first Sunday school staff.

The fall of 1953 saw the establishment of a PTA (Parent Teacher Association), organized with Mary H. Tsakiris as its first president, to provide financial assistance to the growing needs of the afternoon Greek school. As programs flourished, the need for an assistant priest again surfaced. From 1951-1954, the Rev. Demetrius Cassis, a retired priest and parishioner, was often called upon to assist Father Ahladas. Later, the Rev. Ernest Arambiges served as the interim clergyman for a one-month period following his ordination to the priesthood on July 1, 1954. The ceremony was conducted at his home parish of Annunciation in Baltimore with Bishop Dimitrios of Olympos officiating. Soon after, Father Ernest and Presbytera Maria Arambiges departed for their first parish assignment in Peoria, Illinois.

During these years, the Annunciation parish again recognized the need for expansion to serve the highly-concentrated Greek Orthodox population in the Highlandtown section of East Baltimore. Many additional immigrants from the Greek islands had settled there, especially since the late 1940's, due to the abundance of work provided by the various industries near the community. A Greek language school, sponsored by Annunciation, had been offered since 1926 to the families residing in Highlandtown. Now there was a definite need for a local house of worship.

After much heated debate on the issue of forming a second church, parishioners who opposed the concept slowly began to accept the validity and need for a separate parish in Highlandtown. On September 14, 1952, a special meeting was held in the Highlandtown Greek School building to initiate action. Two days later, Articles of Incorporation were filed for the newly-established "Greek Orthodox Church of St. Nicholas." Signers of the

Father Philotheos Ahladas performed the wedding ceremony of Nicholas G. Klicos to Hrysoula Cranes on October 20, 1951.

Deacon Ernest Arambiges greeted Philoptochos President Angela Hamilos following his ordination on June 24, 1954. Within a week, he was ordained as a priest at Annunciation.

The St. Nicholas Church at 520 South Ponca Street was designed by Architect Demetrius (James) Mandris, 1955.

Sakellarides was assigned as the first full-time priest. The first parish council consisted of William Eliades, President; Anthony Padussis, Vice President; Constantine Lambros, Secretary; Michael Karas, Corresponding Secretary; and Steve Nicholson, Treasurer, along with ten directors.

Continuing its support of the sister parish, Annunciation voted at a meeting in January 1956 to donate $5,000 to assist the construction project. The new St. Nicholas Church, designed by architect James Mandris, was built on the corner of Ponca and Fleet Streets replacing the Greek school building at that location. The official ceremony opening the new church for regular worship services was held on April 22, 1956. The following year, on November 3, 1957, Archbishop Michael consecrated the church in the Orthodox tradition before an overflowing congregation. The dream of establishing a second parish had become a reality.

charter were: William Apostolou, Athanasios Demetriades, Stamatios Diakidis, William Eliades, Kostas Lambros, James Latgis, Kostas Loukas, Euripides Papachristou, Soterios Plakitsis, George Sideropoulos, Vasilios Venos, and Stelianos Xintas.

Annunciation, as a gesture of support, transferred title of the Greek Community School of Highlandtown to the St. Nicholas parish which used the building initially as its church and school. The Archdiocesan charter was soon granted and in October 1953, the Rev. Demetrios N.

Even after the transfer of a number of parishioners to the new church in Highlandtown, the mother church of the Annunciation continued to grow. In fact, the years 1954 to 1956 were extremely prosperous. Through the incorporation of new ideas and programs, the church was able to solve the financial problems experienced earlier in the decade and achieve stability. New programs required the energetic spiritual leadership of the

A farewell photograph of Father Philotheos Ahladas (front row center) was taken with members of the Laconian Association, 1954.

The first wedding performed by Father George Gallos in Baltimore was for William Tangires and Choir Director Georgia Topal on August 15, 1954.

The Rev. George P. Gallos

younger generation. Dynamic changes in parish life were on the horizon by the summer of 1954. Considering these factors, Father Ahladas, a dedicated and untiring worker, realized his tenure would soon come to a close.

As he prepared to depart for reassignment in Massachusetts, the parish council began searching for a younger pastor who could effectively administer to the entire congregation, especially the youth. During these interviews, however, Annunciation was faced with a challenge—finding the right priest who would agree to serve a Greek community that had gained notoriety from its recent pastoral controversies. Accepting the challenge was the 39-year-old Rev. George P. Gallos, who had extensive training and experience with a strong focus on spirituality, culture, and music.

Father Gallos was ordained to the priesthood on October 18, 1942, in the Church of the Transfiguration in Lowell, Massachusetts, by Bishop Athenagoras Cavadas. He was a graduate of the second class at the Holy Cross Theological Seminary in Pomfret, Connecticut, in May of 1943. Among his other achievements were degrees from Macalester College in St. Paul, Minnesota, and the Hartford Seminary, a non-denominational school of theology in Connecticut. Prior to his ordination, he married Anna Gerotheou in August of 1942. He first served as the priest of the St. George Greek Orthodox Church in New Britain, Connecticut,

and by 1947 was assigned to the Annunciation Greek Orthodox Church in Rochester, New York.

Father George and Presbytera Anna Gallos and their two sons, Stephen and John, established themselves in Baltimore in August of 1954. The new Presbytera was the daughter of a clergyman who would also be employed by the parish within a few years. Father Gallos took his place as Annunciation's first full-time American-born priest of Greek descent. The importance of his arrival cannot be underestimated. Later, Louis G. Panos wrote in the parish's *50th Anniversary Souvenir Book* that Father Gallos represented the "realization of the dream held by the founding fathers that the guardianship of their religion might some day be entrusted to the hands of their children born in their newly-adopted land." A new phase of church history was about to commence.

Under the spiritual guidance of Father Gallos, many positive reforms were also begun with the help of progressive-thinking parish councils. The 1954 council under the leadership of C. G. Paris initiated the "envelope system" for the collection of Sunday offerings. In later decades, this concept evolved into the *Pledge* and later the *Stewardship* program, assuring funds for operating expenses and parish projects. Also during this period, the Mr. and Mrs. Club was established to acquaint young married couples with the teaching and traditions of the church and assist them through the problems of

The *proskinitarion* (holy icon shrine) was donated by the remaining members of the Enosis Ladies' Society in 1954.

The Very Rev. Joakim Papachristou, age 66, was laid to rest in the Greek Orthodox Cemetery on February 17, 1955.

early married life. During its tenure, the club sponsored many activities to raise funds for the renovation of the church.

While much of the church's emphasis was on its youth, the immigrant generation continued to make significant contributions to parish life. For instance, in October of 1954, the Annunciation Church received a new *proskinitarion* (holy icon shrine) from the remaining members of *Enosis*, the first ladies' society formed in the 1920's. Coordinated by Catherine P. Capsanes, President, Fevronia Petite, Secretary, and Chrissie C. Alevizatos, Treasurer, this project was completed with the remaining balance of funds in their treasury just before the group dissolved. The beautiful shrine, carved from solid oak, features the double-headed eagle—the symbol of the Byzantine Empire. Their lasting gift has been revered by thousands of worshippers entering the sanctuary for over fifty years. Tributes to the early immigrants continued as Father Gallos bestowed the title of honorary parish councilman to John Kousouris who had served on the board of directors in numerous capacities for over three decades.

Another group that began sponsoring events to benefit the parish was the Ladies' Tea Guild that took form in January of 1955. Founding members included Voula P. Rois, Amalia Paris, Chrysanthe A. Pappas, and Dorothy Mesologites. Their energies were directed toward the beautification of the church. Fundraising projects have included benefit teas, annual fashion shows, luncheons, and other events. One of the earliest sponsored teas held in February 1955 was to honor their new pastor, Father Gallos, on the occasion of his 40th birthday. The group's first fashion show was held at the Greenspring Inn on November 6, 1958, under the chairmanship of Mrs. Paul G. Stamas. Two decades later, the organization would be renamed as the Women's Guild, continuing its noteworthy efforts toward the beautification and preservation of the church.

Working in harmony with various parish councils throughout the next decade, Father Gallos would also make great strides in reaching out to young parishioners. For the first time in parish history, sermons were delivered in English on a regular basis, in addition to those spoken in Greek.

Similarly, more English was extended to the church bulletin and other communications. In 1956, journalist Louis G. Panos commented how this change assured "a wider range of reception for the message of the Church without sacrificing the beautiful traditions of past centuries." The use of English in the Divine Liturgy, however, would not occur for another decade.

The year 1955 began with a period of mourning. News of Father Joakim Papachristou's death in Virginia on Saturday, February 12, 1955, spread throughout the Greek Orthodox Archdiocese. While conducting services aboard the *S.S. Markos*, a Greek vessel docked in the port of Norfolk, he died suddenly from a heart attack. With family members still in Baltimore, his remains were brought to Annunciation and *The Community Herald* noted that "a bereaved community paid its final respects to its former pastor." On February 16, 1955, hundreds of parishioners, friends, and leading local figures gathered to pray as his body lay in state in the same church that had ended its relationship with him in 1950. Now, five years later, the community prepared a grand funeral for this remarkable and learned clergyman who greatly influenced fifteen years of parish history.

The Reverend George Gallos, assisted by three Orthodox priests from the Baltimore-Washington region, conducted the funeral service. On behalf of the past presidents, George Mesologites delivered the heartfelt eulogy. President C. G. Paris then read a resolution from the Board of Trustees expressing condolences to the surviving family members. This death marked the end of a unique era, allowing many parishioners to reflect on their former priest—a distinguished figure who had led the procession from the old to the new church in 1937. Now, on February 17, 1955, a solemn procession was led by pallbearers who carried The Very Rev. Joakim Papachristou to his final place of rest in the Greek Orthodox Cemetery on Windsor Mill Road. Soon after, his parish in Norfolk was assigned to the Rev. Anthony N. Pappas, who was ordained on March 25, 1951, at his home parish of the Annunciation in Baltimore.

Other noteworthy activities occurred in 1955—a threshold year for the first half-century of parish life. Though the congregation was more Americanized, philanthropic assistance to the homeland was not forgotten. On June 12, 1955, a special campaign to raise funds for earthquake victims in Volos, Greece, was launched with George Mesologites and Anthony Padussis as chairmen. Two years earlier, in 1953, the Ionian Relief Committee headed by Parish Council President Sam Malas, raised funds to assist victims of the earthquakes that hit the Ionian Islands that summer. Another interesting concept was also tested. A system of two Divine Liturgies was launched in October 1955 with the first sermon in English, the second sermon in Greek. After a difficult three-month trial, Father George Gallos reverted to conducting one liturgy on Sunday.

Annunciation Parish Council, 1954. Seated left to right: Anthony Trintis, Treasurer; John Mitsos, Vice President; Sam Malas, Past President; The Rev. George Gallos, C. G. Paris, President; Andrew Lygoumenos, Secretary; John Kousouris. Standing left to right: Eugenios Vagenos, Sexton; Theodore Diacumakos, Constantine Karavedas, John Sarantos, James Karukas, Athanasios Panayiotopoulos.

The general assembly agenda in the fall of 1955 covered a number of noteworthy topics. A proposal for the purchase of a 16-acre tract of land at 5704 Roland Avenue was reviewed at great length but unfortunately did not materialize. Future expansion was a crucial issue that would be addressed in the coming years. Amending the bylaws to begin officially calling the church "Annunciation," the English language version of "Evangelismos," also missed approval by a small margin. A decade would pass before this change would occur. An even more significant issue, however, was resolved on November 6, 1955. The parish assembly voted that a person must be of the "Eastern Orthodox faith" rather than of "Greek descent" in order to qualify for church membership. This change would open the congregation to a wider base of Orthodox Christians from various ethnic backgrounds.

As the parish approached 1956 and fifty years as an organized religion in Baltimore, it had allowed for more diversity. The Annunciation community was evolving again. Greek ethnicity was important, but no longer took precedence over Orthodox Christianity. It was an indication of exciting times ahead. More changes would be brought forth in a positive manner during the upcoming decade of development.

Rev. George Gallos holding *stephana* (wedding crowns) was assisted by Rev. Demetrios Sakellarides of the St. Nicholas Church at the marriage ceremony of Carolyn Marmaras to Charles Tsakalas on January 2, 1955.

Opposite Page: 50th Anniversary Dance at the American Legion Armory in Towson, October 28, 1956.

1956-1965

The Annunciation Greek Orthodox Community reached its Golden Anniversary in the spring of 1956. In his anniversary message, Father George Gallos reflected that over the course of fifty years, thousands of Orthodox Christians had entered the sanctuary to worship, to receive Holy Communion, to witness the joyous sacraments of Baptism and Holy Matrimony, and to mourn the passing of loved ones. They experienced the beauty of the Greek Orthodox faith, learned their ancestral language, and praised the glory of God. They had established organizations with philanthropic, social, and ethnic goals. It was truly a time to pay tribute to all those, living and deceased, who founded the church, supported parish activities over the years, and provided direction for growth and expansion.

The actual observance of the 50th Anniversary was celebrated in the fall of 1956. General chairman for this impressive commemoration was Peter N. Karangelen, and co-chairmen were George Mesologites and William Gereny. Mr. Karangelen hoped these special events would signal the "vigorous beginning of another half-century of progress." The celebration began on Sunday, October 21, 1956, with a special Hierarchical Divine Liturgy led by The Rt. Rev. Ezekiel, Bishop of Nazianzos. Following church services, a very successful 50th Anniversary Bazaar was held under the direction of Alexander Pappas. Featuring a variety of food and entertainment booths, the festival offered box lunches to hundreds of attendees prepared by the ladies of the Philoptochos Society. Other activities that week included a profitable automobile raffle chaired by Anestes Kampos and a tea social arranged by Mrs. C. G. Paris and Mrs. Robert Contos of the Ladies' Tea Guild.

50th Anniversary Bazaar and Commemorative Pin, 1956

Then, on Sunday, October 28, 1956, a Golden Anniversary Dance organized by Jack Pillas was held at the American Legion Armory in Towson, Maryland. Two months later, on December 16, 1956, the Lord Baltimore Hotel was the scene of the grand finale to the celebration. Under the chairmanship of William C. Gereny, parishioners attended the 50th Anniversary Banquet honoring all past presidents of the parish council. The oldest living honoree was Constantine Diamantopoulos (Diamond) who had served as president in 1908. Other guests of honor included Baltimore's Mayor Thomas D'Alesandro, Jr., and Annunciation's former pastor, Father Philotheos Ahladas. As a remembrance of the 1956 celebration, a special *Fiftieth Anniversary Souvenir Book* was later published under the direction of George Mesologites and Paul Stamas. In looking to the future of the parish, Father Gallos inspired parishioners to "meet new challenges, solve growing complex problems, and show the way to greater progress and to a higher expression of Orthodox Christianity."

During the course of the year, there were also additions and changes to the church staff. Due to the growing size of the parish, the necessity of a full-time assistant priest again became apparent. In July of 1956, the parish council acquired the services of The Reverend John N. Gerotheou who was the father-in-law of Reverend Gallos. Father Gerotheou also served as principal of the Greek school and assisted in conducting liturgical services at Annunciation for a period of five years. Two months after arriving, his daughter, Presbytera Anna G. Gallos, became the new musical director of the parish. This occurred after Georgia Tangires resigned as choir director due to family commitments as she awaited the birth of her second child. As a result, by the fall of 1956, three members of the Gallos family were shaping the parish's spiritual and musical programs. Their cooperative efforts would soon result in further advancement.

Bishop Ezekiel conducted the 50th Anniversary
Hierarchical Divine Liturgy on Sunday, October 21, 1956.

Presbytera Anna Gallos and Rev. George Gallos
at the wedding reception for John Padousis
and Katherine Poletis, February 14, 1960.

As a graduate of the Eastman School of Music
at the University of Rochester, Anna Gallos was
an exceptional church musician. She had
accomplished extensive work as a composer and
arranger of liturgical music. The choir continued to
excel and many new liturgical works written by her
were incorporated into the worship services. Two of
her many outstanding arrangements were *Kassiani's
Troparion* and the Lamentations sung on Good
Friday. It was also during this decade that music
education was incorporated into the Sunday school
curriculum. Organists during Anna Gallos' tenure
included the talented Philip N. Brous, Helen
Vounas, Lambryn Mavrikos and George Anest.

The mid-1950's witnessed significant changes
in the running of parish affairs. The church office
was reorganized with the hiring of Michael
Coulianos who was employed as Executive Secretary
for over twenty years. Administrative efficiency was
accomplished through stability in leadership. For
instance, the well-respected C. G. Paris was elected
for three consecutive terms as president from 1954-
1956. Parish council members viewed the clergy
as an integral part of the church's administration
and the first generation of Greek-American youth
increased its level of participation, assuming new
roles and responsibilities. In addition, the Orthodox

Rev. John and Presbytera Evangeline Gerotheou
were the parents of Choir Director Anna G. Gallos.
Father Gerotheou was Assistant Priest from 1956-1961.

Annunciation's Sunday School Teachers, 1956. Front *l to r* : Peter Panopoulos, Mrs. Nicholas Petrou, Anna Margaritis, Sebbie Lykos, Mrs. James Cargas. Middle *l to r* : Mrs. Peter J. Prevas, Mrs. Peter Panopoulos, Mrs. George Hayes, Mrs. Peter Coutros, Andrew Kotsatos. Back *l to r* : Nicholas Petrou, William Gereny, Nicholas Lykos, Matina Psoras, Angela Diakoulas, Mrs. James Panopoulos, Alex Zades.

faith was gaining greater respect throughout the entire nation. As an example, on March 26, 1956, following the request of Archbishop Michael, Father Gallos became the second clergyman of the Eastern Orthodox faith to ever give the prayer before the opening session of the United States Congress.

This atmosphere of mutual respect continued for the remainder of the 1950's under the presidencies of Evan Alevizatos Chriss in 1957, Paul G. Stamas in 1958, and Jack P. Pillas in 1959. During these years, more changes were implemented without much opposition. Parish general assembly records reflect the first usage of the English language as early as February of 1955. Minutes of regular parish council meetings followed a similar transition from Greek to English in the late 1950's. By January of 1959, the minutes of council meetings were consistently being recorded in the English language. Change, growth, and further expansion became topics of discussion. In

one issue of *The Community Herald*, dated July 1957, Parish Council President Evan A. Chriss urged parishioners to keep up the momentum: "This is *your* parish…this is *your* church…they can be of service and help to you only to the extent that you seek to be served."

The Annunciation congregation, moving forward into its second half-century, met the ever-changing needs of the parish with definitive action and programs. Parishioners were polled to gauge their interest on a number of topics during the late 1950's. One topic was the Greek language program. In recognition of the growing need for a Greek school to serve the families now residing in the northeastern part of the city, a branch Greek school was established at Leith Walk Public School. In 1958, a second annex school opened in the Catonsville area with relative success. Other suburban schools soon followed. The establishment of these schools was an indication that the future expansion of church facilities was on the horizon.

Great strides were made during these years to strengthen the church's relationship with the surrounding non-Greek community. This was part of a nationwide effort during the 1950's, initiated by Archbishop Michael, to have Eastern Orthodoxy recognized as a major faith following the Catholic, Protestant, and Jewish religions. On March 11, 1957, Governor Theodore McKeldin of Maryland signed a resolution passed by the Maryland General Assembly giving official recognition to the Eastern Orthodox Church as the fourth major faith within the State of Maryland. Through press releases, the March 25th celebration of Greek Independence Day was also given extensive coverage. Eastern Orthodox listings were established in various directories and Father Gallos furthered public relations by lecturing at colleges, clubs, and various civic organizations.

That spring saw the establishment of the first scholarship fund following the death of active community leader and dental surgeon, Dr. Michael S. Varipatis, on April 17, 1957. Soon after, the idea for a memorial scholarship was initiated through the efforts of the Hellenic University Club and coordinated by Nicholas Petrou and James M. Panopoulos. This first scholarship program, encouraging young students to further their studies, would lead to numerous memorial and honorary scholarships offered by other individuals and church-affiliated organizations in later years.

Two months later, His Eminence Archbishop Michael visited Baltimore the weekend of June 15-16, 1957. Great Vesper services were conducted on Saturday in which clergy and members of the Greek, Russian, and Ukrainian Orthodox churches of Baltimore participated. Following the

Acolytes posed for the 50th Anniversary Celebration, 1956. Left to right: Stephen P. Gallos, Manuel Psaris, Andrew Vendelis, James Karantzalis, James C. Pecunes, P. Paul Cocoros, Theodore A. Cavacos. Back row left to right: Eugenios Vagenos, Church Sexton; Father John Gerotheou, Assistant Priest; and Father George Gallos, Pastor.

Greek Independence Day Proclamation with Mayor Thomas D'Alesandro, Jr. (seated). Left to right: Father George Gallos, Evan Alevizatos Chriss, Paul Stamas, James Apostolides, William Gereny, C. G. Paris, President; George Mesologites, March 25, 1956.

Hierarchical Divine Liturgy on Sunday, the Archbishop bestowed the priestly rank of *Economos* upon Father George Gallos in recognition of his exemplary service to the Orthodox Church. A few years later, Father Gallos was elevated in status to a *Protopresbyter*—the highest rank a married priest can achieve in the Greek Orthodox Church.

Though the church was prospering, the one major problem still unsolved was that of expansion. With the sale of the Greek Center at the corner of Cathedral and Preston Streets in 1950, it was difficult to adequately host the social, cultural, and athletic activities of all church-related organizations. Growing enrollments of both Sunday school and Greek school compounded the problem and led to serious discussion for a modern, attractive, well-planned school and community center. Another topic that caused heated debate was the idea that perhaps it was time for the Annunciation parish to relocate to the suburbs. Throughout meetings marked by opposing views, there was clear agreement on one point—some type of decision, one way or the other, was needed quickly to guarantee the future stability of the Greek Orthodox community.

Ladies' Philoptochos Society President Ruth Kampos and her husband, Anestes Kampos, presented a donation from the parish to Archbishop Michael in New York, 1957.

MRS. PAUL G. STAMAS
Chairman

MRS. EVAN A. CHRISS, *Co-Chairman*

MRS. ROBERT G. CONTOS, *Co-Chairman*

COMMITTEES

Fashion Show Arrangements:

Mrs. Basil A. Thomas   Mrs. James Krometis
Mrs. John A. Somers   Mrs. Harry J. Anderson

Models:

Babe Constantine   Tess Malamatis
Beulah Georges   Minnie Magiros
Christine Gereny   Dotty Pavlos
Ernie Karukas   Fofy Plakotoris
Mrs. George Kent   Sylvia Sherwood
Julia Krometis   Ann Zambounis

Music:

Mrs. G. Tangiris   Mrs. George Gallos

Narrator: MRS. J. MELLUS

Fashion Show Sponsored by
THE HECHT CO. OF BALTIMORE

Fashion Show

presented by

LADIES TEA GUILD

of

ANNUNCIATION

NOVEMBER 6, 1958
GREENSPRING INN

Program booklet for the first "Fashion Show" of the Ladies' Tea Guild, November 6, 1958.

Music Director Anna Gallos conducting the Annunciation Church Choir, 1958. Before the expansion of the choir loft, musical groups often sang from the balcony as shown in this rare photograph. The balcony had the original wooden theatre-style seating which was inherited from the Associate Congregational Church.

Enrollment in Annunciation's Sunday School program was quite impressive throughout the 1950's.

Students and Teachers from various grades were photographed during the 50th Anniversary Year, 1956.

Alex Zades with Sunday school students, 1958. This image was used to illustrate the crowded conditions in the manse and the need to renovate church facilities.

Through the efforts of James Markakis and Architect James Mandris, two alternate sketches providing expansion plans for the parish were drawn up during 1957. The initial architectural renderings provided for an expansive new building with classrooms, meeting rooms, a large kitchen, a social hall-auditorium-gymnasium with stage, dressing rooms, a lodge room with an adjacent kitchen, new restrooms, a spacious boardroom, and administrative offices. In addition, the altar would be extended for a new *iconostasion* (altar screen), a new choir loft would be built, and the Maryland

Avenue entrance would be enlarged. The close of the 1950's saw the Annunciation community focus on developing these facilities for its present and future needs.

The main decisions regarding the project were reached in 1958 at three important general assembly meetings. At the special assembly held on March 30, 1958, it was resolved that the parish would remain in the city for the following reasons: the present central location most conveniently served the greatest majority; replacing the facilities elsewhere would be too costly; and urban renewal plans brought hope for improvement of the declining neighborhood around Preston Street. The second meeting for the project took place on June 8, 1958. That day, the parish assembly approved the demolition of the manse (original building adjoining the church) and voted to erect a new three-level Education and Social Building. The ambitious project was a sign of the times.

Throughout the City of Baltimore during these years, it was not uncommon to see many of the old architecturally-detailed buildings razed to make way for new office space, parking garages, high-rise apartments, and other structures. The Annunciation parish's acute need for expansion resulted in the demise of a uniquely beautiful building constructed in the late 19th century. This original manse, designed by famed architect Charles E. Cassell, and the front lawn area and landscaping that added charm to the Preston Street property would soon be gone in the name of progress.

Members of the Parish Councils of 1958 and 1959. Seated left to right: Louis Kousouris, George Rangos, Paul Stamas, Rev. George Gallos, Jack Pillas, Peter Panopoulos. Standing left to right: Spiro Leanos, Gus Klosterides, William Gereny, Nicholas S. Morekas, Evan Alevizatos Chriss, Gregory Perentesis, Michael Coulianos, Executive Secretary; George Menas.

This is our answer. This is where it is going to be.

OUR OBJECTIVES

1. To raze the Wing adjoining the Church and construct in its place an entirely new three-story building that will give us adequate recreational social facilities, including a complete and modern kitchen, and much needed Sunday School and Greek School class rooms. The school spaces have been so designed that they can be utilized for a parochial school, if demanded by future programs of the Church.

2. Modernize the space under the Church to provide, among other things, a lounge and an adequate lodge hall, with refreshment room.

3. Enlarge the Altar, so that the new Iconostasion can be properly placed to enhance the interior beauty of the Church.

We can make the foregoing become realities by achieving the following:

$235,000
Victory Goal

$300,000
Challenge Goal

The Greek Orthodox Church "Evangelismos" (Annunciation) published a special promotional booklet to educate parishioners on the expansion project approved by the general assembly in 1958. The "Objectives" page (above) shows James and Mary Markakis and their family standing at the future site of the Education Building in 1959.

Groundbreaking ceremonies for the Education Building were officially conducted on Sunday, May 24, 1959. Standing left to right: Paul Stamas, Nicholas Morekas, Spiro Leanos and Emmanuel Hondroulis (partially hidden) look on as Parish Council President Jack Pillas and Father George Gallos conduct the ceremonial groundbreaking.

In addition to the construction of the new wing, remodeling was planned in the area beneath the church, including the enlargement of the altar, for a total cost of nearly $400,000. At the general assembly meeting of October 13, 1958, it was decided to hire a consulting firm for the fundraising drive. The Building Fund campaign, using a new concept called "Fair Share Pledge," raised over $250,000 in pledges and a finance committee led by Evan A. Chriss administered the payment program. Construction of the building began with a groundbreaking ceremony on Sunday, May 24, 1959. *The Community Herald* later noted that "demolition men appeared on the site and began methodically tearing down the building adjoining the Church." The ground floor of the Church was then prepared for the improvements to be made which included breaking open the wall behind the Altar to make way for the extension.

The Education Building project progressed under the leadership of Paul G. Stamas, General Chairman, and Evan A. Chriss, Co-Chairman. A number of subcommittees carried out various phases of the work. For instance, the Expansion and Improvement Committee led by James N. Markakis oversaw the construction. The Finance Committee, chaired by Harry J. Anderson, secured the necessary mortgage on the church property so the new addition could proceed on schedule. The cornerstone for the new Education Building was laid on February 7, 1960. Officiating at the ceremony was The Rt. Rev. Athenagoras Kokkinakis, Titular Bishop of Elaia.

Highlighting Annunciation's focus on education, the newspaper account of that day's event cited that the new building would include eleven classrooms for Sunday school and parochial studies. Four months later, the construction was completed and the building opened on June 1, 1960.

Nicholas J. Anderson, President of the Worthington Chapter of AHEPA (left), presented a $5,000 check for the building fund to Father Gallos, President Jack Pillas and Evan A. Chriss, Co-Chairman of the project, 1959.

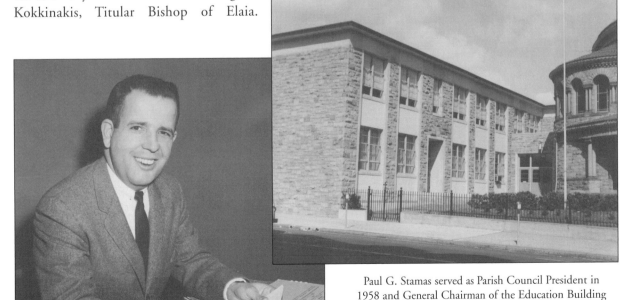

Paul G. Stamas served as Parish Council President in 1958 and General Chairman of the Education Building project. The structure was completed by June of 1960.

Archbishop Iakovos served as the spiritual leader of the Greek Orthodox Archdiocese from 1959 through 1996.

By this time, the Archdiocese had experienced a change in leadership. Following the death of Archbishop Michael in July of 1958, Bishop Iakovos of Melita was enthroned on April 1, 1959, as the new spiritual leader of the Greek Orthodox Archdiocese. Baptized as Demetrios Coucouzis in 1911 on the Island of Imvros, Turkey, he enrolled at the Theological School in Halki by the age of 15. Upon his ordination as a deacon in 1934, he assumed the ecclesiastical name of Iakovos. Deacon Iakovos Coucouzis came to America and was ordained to the priesthood in 1940. Within a few years, he became Dean of the Annunciation Greek Orthodox Cathedral of Boston where he served from 1942 through 1954. His spiritual mentor, Patriarch Athenagoras, ordained him as Bishop of Melita in December of 1954, and within five years the Holy Synod in Constantinople elected him as Archbishop Iakovos. His impressive tenure of furthering religious unity and revitalizing Christian worship in America would span over three and a half decades.

The Rt. Rev. Athenagoras Kokkinakis, Bishop of Elaia (center), was invited to conduct the laying of the cornerstone for the new Education Building. The event took place on February 7, 1960, with Father John Gerotheou (left) and Father George Gallos (right) assisting in the ceremony.

ICON—On view in the church will be this icon purported to have wept on several occasions.

THE OLD AND THE NEW—The new $400,000 social and educational center of the Greek Orthodox Church of the Annunciation will be dedicated at 1 P.M. on May 14 by Archbishop Iakovos.

PRIMATE—Archbishop Iakovos, Greek prelate, will speak at the center dedication.

Greek Primate To Dedicate Church Center

N.Y.'s 'Crying Madonna' Icon To Be Placed On Display

By JOHN D. HACKETT

More than 1,000 Marylanders of the Greek Orthodox faith are expected to visit the old Church of the Annuniciation and its new $400,000 social and educational center here for a fourfold purpose Saturday and Sunday.

They will attend special religious ceremonies; meet Archbishop Iakovos, Primate of North and South America, on his first visit to Baltimore; see the "Crying Madonna" icon which will be brought by the archbishop from New York, and attend the formal dedication ceremonies of the new center.

The weekend festivities at this largest Greek Orthodox church in Maryland, located at Maryland avenue and Preston street, will begin with a vespers service at 7.30 P.M. in the church, followed by a reception for the archbishop in the center's auditorium.

Ancient Ceremonies

The traditional and colorful pontifical liturgy of the Greek Orthodox Church will begin at approximately 9 A.M. Sunday in the church and will continue for some three hours.

Archbishop Iakovos will be celebrant, assisted by the Rev. George Gallos and the Rev. John Gerotheou of the Church of the Annunciation, and by priests from other churches in Maryland, Delaware, Pennsylvania and the District of Columbia.

Archbishop Iakovos, after com-pleting the Sunday morning liturgy, will then dedicate the social and educational center in another ancient ceremony reserved for the blessing of church property.

The chief prelate of the Western Hemisphere is expected to leave Baltimore on Sunday at approximately 4 P.M.

Dance To Follow

Parishioners and visitors will continue the celebration with a dance, starting at 9 P.M., in the Emerson Hotel sponsored by the church's board of trustees and the Philoptochos Society.

The festivities herald the volunteer work and many donations which made the new $400,000 center possible. The dance will climax some three years of fund raising activities.

Leaders in the fund campaign will be honored. They include Paul Stamas, the general chairman; Evan Chriss, associate chairman; James Markakis, building committee chairman; Emmanuel Hondrulis, special gifts chairman, and Nicholas Morekas, dedication day chairman.

Icon Display

Perhaps the greatest spectator interest will be in the "Weeping Icon." It will be on display atop a special table inside the church altar rail in front of the "iconostasis," the traditional wall of the three doors which separates the altar from the congregation in Eastern Rite churches.

This small print of the Madonna was reported to cry, the tears coming from the left eye of the Virgin while Mrs. Panagiotis Catsounis stood at prayer in her home at 41 Norfolk road in Island Park, L.I., on March 16, 1960.

The frightened woman immediately called her priest, who, seeing the print, called in his superiors, who in turn called in others.

The icon was reported to have wept again on Saturday, March 18, when some 70 persons attested to having seen tears coming from the left eye of the Madonna representation.

Archbishop Iakovos and other clergymen hesitated to give official indorsement to the manifestation.

They questioned all witnesses and finally, the archbishop confirmed that a "sign" had been manifested in the Catsounis home.

The Greek archdiocese later issued special instructions to churches in the United States and Canada that the "Akathist Hymn," the praises to the Blessed Virgin, be chanted on the evening of April 1 to mark this "sign."

Still later, after more investigation, the Holy Synod of the Ecumenical Patriarchate of Constantinople, headed by the spiritual leader of the Greek Orthodox Church, Athenagoras I, designated the reported tears as a "sign of Divine Providence."

Time For Exhibit

The icon, Father Gallos said, will be on exhibit Saturday from 9 P.M. until 11 P.M. and on Sunday from 1 P.M. until 3 P.M.

Archbishop Iakovos was born Demetrios A. Coucouzis on the Turkish island of Imbros on July 29, 1911. He was an honor graduate of the Theological School of Halki in Istanbul in 1934 and served as deacon in Derkon, Turkey, until 1939.

He came to the United States in 1939 as archdeacon and professor at the Archdiocese Theological School in Pomfret, Conn., and was ordained a priest in Bos-ton in June, 1940. He served as dean of the Cathedral of the Annunciation in Boston until 1954.

Elevated In 1956

On December 17, 1954, then director of the Holy Cross Orthodox Theological School in Brookline, Mass., he was elected Bishop of Malta and assigned to the archdiocese of Central and Western Europe.

In March, 1955, he was appointed representative to the Ecumenical Patriarchate at the World Council of Churches in Geneva.

In April, 1956, he was elevated to Metropolitan and succeeded Archbishop Michael in the Americas in February, 1959.

New Center

Archbishop Iakovos, who is an American citizen, holds a master's degree in sacred theology from the Harvard School of Di-vinity and is author of several books and pamphlets.

He is spiritual leader of some 1,150,000 Orthodox communicants and supervises some 375 churches in the United States.

The new social and educational center was started in April, 1959, completed in March, 1960, and saw a cornerstone ceremony in February, 1960.

Father Gallos said the center now serves for a Sunday school, an afternoon Greek language school, for parish meetings, luncheons and social gatherings.

Father Gallos said the church board of trustees decided to build in the downtown area because of the redevelopment plans and because the central location better serves parishioners who live in surrounding counties as well as in the city.

CHURCH WORKERS—Parishioners cooperated in helping raise funds for the center. Among the benefit luncheon planners who posed at the site with the Rev. George Gallos were, left to right, Mrs. Stephen Padussio, chairman; Mrs. George Deyes, Mrs. George Demotatis, Mrs. Nick Fochios, Father Gallos, Mrs. Louis Panos and Mrs. Gus Contantine. The center cost $400,000.

"Dedication Day" ceremonies for the new Education Building received much publicity as parishioners anticipated the first visit of Archbishop Iakovos to Baltimore for this historic occasion, May 13-14, 1961.

In the spring of 1961, the Annunciation community cordially welcomed Archbishop Iakovos to Baltimore. It was his first official visit and he was asked to officiate at the dedication ceremonies for the new Education and Social Building. On May 11, 1961, Baltimore's *Evening Sun* covered the story: "More than 1,000 Marylanders of the Greek Orthodox faith are expected to visit the old Church of the Annunciation and its new $400,000 social and educational center." Father Gallos, reflecting on the project, reiterated that his parish chose to build in the downtown area due to redevelopment plans and because the "central location better serves parishioners who live in surrounding counties as well as the city."

The Archbishop arrived in Baltimore on Saturday, May 13, 1961, and conducted special Vesper services that evening. He also brought the famous "Crying Madonna" icon from Long Island, New York. The icon was placed on display within the sanctuary for visitors to venerate. According to journalistic accounts, Orthodox Church leaders had designated the reports of tears coming from the icon as a "sign of Divine Providence." The following day, May 14, 1961, Archbishop Iakovos officiated at the Hierarchical Divine Liturgy and the dedication ceremony for the Education Building. He was assisted by Fathers Gallos and Gerotheou of Annunciation along with numerous priests from parishes throughout the region.

Later that day, the Annunciation community sponsored a luncheon honoring their new Archbishop at the Belvedere Hotel followed by a gala dance at the Emerson Hotel. During the celebration, church leaders instrumental in the building fund campaign were honored. Among them were: Paul G. Stamas, Evan A. Chriss, James N. Markakis, Emmanuel D. Hondroulis, and Nicholas S. Morekas, who served as chairman of the Dedication Day celebration. The expansion of parish facilities, another symbol of progress, had become a reality.

With the arrival of the 1960's, the completion of the new building provided for the spiritual, educational, and social needs of an ever-growing

Members of the GOYA (Greek Orthodox Youth of America) posed with Father George Gallos in 1956.
Peter Karukas, President (seated second from left); James Canelos, Vice President (seated third from right).

Annunciation's Senior Choir participated in the WBAL-TV presentation, "The Voices of Christmas," which aired on December 24-25, 1959. This photograph from the recording session appeared in *The Community Herald* in 1960.

active Greek Orthodox community. During the first half of the new decade, Peter M. Panopoulos from 1960-61, Nicholas S. Morekas from 1961-62, James N. Markakis from 1963-64, and Harry J. Anderson in 1965 served as parish council presidents. Their energies were focused on overseeing the many new aspects of church administration that resulted from the programs of the Education Building. During this decade, the Annunciation Church also expanded its horizons by developing outside contacts. Unlike the self-contained organization of the 1920's, the Greek Orthodox community's sphere of influence now included other religious denominations.

In May of 1959, Father George Gallos attended the prestigious Religious Leaders Conference in Washington, D.C. In a follow-up letter, Vice President Richard Nixon expressed his personal appreciation to Father Gallos for his attendance and involvement with the Presidential Committee. Later that year, the Annunciation Greek Orthodox Church was welcomed as a new member of The Council of Churches and Christian Education of Maryland-Delaware, Inc.

Interfaith dialogues were also initiated with leaders of other denominations through the Maryland Region of the National Conference of Christians and Jews. The Maryland Council of Churches amended its new constitution and added to its identifying provision the term "Eastern Orthodox Churches." The impact of these events was significant and provided the outside

community with a better understanding of the Greek Orthodox religion and the many customs and traditions associated with its culture.

This era was also marked by a continuous growth of internal projects. The Education Committee, under the chairmanship of Theodore J. George, was formed to help supervise activities. Parish council minutes reflect a number of committee chairpersons working to establish a formal, organized program for the new Education Building. Among the numerous sub-committees were: Library, Matina Psoras; Sunday School, Kathy Petrou; Kindergarten, Angela Diakoulas; Adult Education and Athletics, Alex Pulianas; Adult Religious Education, Peter J. Prevas; and

Baltimore Orioles All-Star Catcher Gus Triandos and his wife were the guests of honor at a banquet sponsored by the Annunciation parish at the Emerson Hotel on June 14, 1959.

Rev. George Gallos (center of altar) and Rev. Nicholas Stavrakis (foreground) conducted the wedding
of Anna Zambounis to Harry P. Pappas on December 30, 1961. Choir Director Anna Gallos (top left)
provided musical accompaniment on the refurbished pipe organ located in the renovated choir loft.

Greek Language School, Theodore J. George. By the spring of 1964, the church newsletter, *The Community Herald*, was expanded and the name was changed to *Annunciation Herald*. Having served as editor for thirteen years, Mary Bahadouris Kiladis would continue for sixteen more years writing and producing this informative church publication—a documented chronicle of parish life on Preston Street.

The early 1960's also saw the beauty of the music program enhanced. The extensive effort to rebuild the church's historic pipe organ was spearheaded by Philip N. Brous. Following general assembly approval of the project in March of 1959, members of the Adult Choir personally pledged half the $13,500-cost. Following completion of the work, a special ceremony took place on Sunday, February 18, 1962. Choir Director Anna

Gallos proudly noted that "this is the first organ dedication of its kind in any Orthodox Church anywhere…at least to our knowledge." The recent addition of the Education Building had also led to renovations resulting in a larger choir loft. This provided more space for the growing junior and senior high school choir as well as the Adult Choir.

The church music program took the spotlight again in 1964 with the recording of "The Divine Liturgy of St. John Chrysostom." Presbytera Anna Gallos composed the music as part of a regional choir convention in 1960. Later, the decision was made to record her original liturgical work using voices from the Annunciation Choirs of Baltimore. A brief explanation of the music was included on the back cover of the record album. "Based primarily on traditional Byzantine melodies, this Liturgy employs chant, some modal harmonization, and occasionally, simple counterpoint in the two-voice style." The highly-acclaimed production featured Father George Gallos, Celebrant; Presbytera Anna Gallos, Choir Master; and Lambryn Mavrikos as the parish organist.

The midnight services on Holy Saturday begin with a single candle symbolizing the Resurrection of Christ. This image of Father Gallos appeared in *The Baltimore Sun* in 1964.

The Junior Choir of the Annunciation Church singing the hymns and responses during liturgical services from the new choir loft. Presbytera Anna Gallos (seated) is shown conducting the group, circa 1962.

After two years of planning, a parish library was blessed and officially opened within the Education Building on November 25, 1962. The Library Committee, including Theodore George, Beulah Georges, Electra Pistolas, Matina Psoras, and Evelyn Venetos, worked to organize and categorize over 500 volumes in both Greek and English. Theodore J. George, an educator by profession, assumed the leadership role as director of this new venture. The parish would name the library after him in the following decade. During the early 1960's, the idea was promoted to compile Greek recipes into a book with proceeds to benefit the parish. Through the efforts and recipe contributions of parish women, the Annunciation Church published its first cookbook, *Ambrosia and Nectar*, in November 1962 under the chairmanship of Carol L. Prevas. Ten years later, a second volume of new and revised recipes was published by the parish and renamed *The Best of Greek Cookery* with Eurydice M. Canelos, Editor; and Carol L. Prevas, Associate Editor.

Though the church was committed to many tasks, not all projects proved successful at first. In the late 1950's, for example, plans were drawn up for a chapel to be built in the Greek Orthodox Cemetery. A special groundbreaking ceremony was even held in May of 1959 with The Rev. George Gallos of Annunciation officiating along with The Rev. Nicholas Stavrakis who became the next priest at the St. Nicholas Church of Highlandtown in 1957. The chapel project was estimated to cost approximately $40,000.

By January 1960, however, the Annunciation parish's financial commitment to the Education Building put this project on hold. Due to mortgage obligations at the time, it was decided that Annunciation "should not proceed for several years" with constructing a chapel. By 1961, the Cemetery Committee was placed under the jurisdiction of the parish council and two decades would pass before the goal of establishing a chapel at the Greek Orthodox Cemetery was reached.

Parishioners often gathered to prepare meals for social events using the new kitchen in the Education Building.
Left to right: Phyllis Kavros, Litsa Sfekas, Helen Stamas, Anna Kassolis, Angela Chirgott, Nora Chirgott,
Sophie Chirgott, Georgia Spanos, Sevasti Ricas, and Effie Stamas, circa 1963.

Exterior renovations included the replacement of the roof. Although the original red Spanish tiles were in satisfactory condition, the sheathing material under the tiles had deteriorated over 75 years causing water damage to the ceiling from the rain. All roofing material was replaced and a new slate roof that blended with the exterior colors was installed by the fall of 1964.

By early 1963, more innovative projects had taken form. As an alternative to yearly dues, parishioners now had the option to "pledge" their financial support either weekly, monthly, or annually. Church leaders saw this as an opportunity to be relieved of the continuous task of selling tickets and raffle books in order to apply themselves to more important parish policies and programs. With the help of outside consultants, a "pledge system" was instituted but met with limited success at that time. Fortunately, the preferred "dues" system was still generating strong revenues and by 1964 the parish was able to move forward with some much-needed repairs. For instance, Nicholas Morekas and Harry J. Anderson of the Cemetery Committee reported in November 1964 that the entrance to the cemetery had been widened and resurfaced. In addition, the front gates were repainted and soon new landscaping with low-level shrubbery replaced the outer front bushes, allowing the stone wall to show in a prominent manner.

The Social Hall was designed to quickly convert into a gymnasium. Youth groups throughout the region have played in countless basketball tournaments here since the early 1960's.

The Rev. George Gallos proudly posed in front of the doorway of the new *iconostasion* (altar screen) during his final year as priest of the Annunciation Church, 1965.

The main focus, however, soon turned to the church edifice itself. Now over seventy years old, the sanctuary was showing signs of wear and deterioration. The Building Committee, guided by leaders such as Nicholas Petrou and Nicholas Malamatis, coordinated the various phases of the work throughout 1964 and 1965. Work included a new slate roof, a new electrical system, and a general refurbishing of the interior—woodwork staining, carpeting, painting and the preparation for a new *iconostasion* (altar screen) that was installed by the summer of 1965.

Peter G. Angelos donated the cost of the ornately carved *iconostasion* as his gift to the parish. Soon after, a brass plaque below the Icon of the Annunciation on the altar screen doorway was inscribed, "In memory of Frances Melissanos Angelos." In later years, Mr. Angelos would again provide financial assistance as a great benefactor for a number of capital improvement projects. The dedication and vision of church leaders, benefactors, and volunteers to restore and preserve the building was now an established trend and would be a recurrent theme in future decades.

Fundraising for church projects also took on style and innovation. For example, in 1965 the Annunciation community was in the city spotlight as the Ladies' Tea Guild presented its 7th Annual Fashion Show and Luncheon at the Emerson Hotel. The event was held on October 12, 1965, with fashions provided by Hochschild Kohn. Chairperson Hrysoula (Judy) Klicos, along with Co-Chairpersons Georgia Anderson and Esther Kokinos, worked with six sub-committees to ensure the success of the event. In keeping with its mission, the Ladies' Tea Guild earmarked the proceeds from the affair to pay for various furnishings needed in the Education Building.

By this time, Father John Gerotheou, the assistant priest, had retired to Somerville, Massachusetts. Two years after his departure, in September of 1963, the Annunciation parish welcomed Steven Vlahos, a graduate of the Holy Cross Theological Seminary. He provided spiritual guidance for the youth groups, helped with Sunday school supervision, instructed the Greek language classes, and assisted in preparing sermons and church publications. He remained for one year at which time the Archdiocese appointed The Rev. Anastasios Voultsos as the new assistant pastor in

Guild To Sponsor Luncheon, Fashion Show

The annual fashion show and luncheon sponsored by the Ladies Tea Guild of the Greek Orthodox Church of the Annunciation will be held at noon tomorrow at the Emerson Hotel. Proceeds will be used for the new educational-recreational wing of the church. Helping to plan the program are, from left, Mrs. Harry J. Anderson, Mrs. Chris Kokinos, Mrs. Louis Elias and Mrs. Nicholas Klicos.

THE LADIES
TEA GUILD
OF THE
ANNUNCIATION
GREEK ORTHODOX
CHURCH

Presents Their

7th ANNUAL
FASHION SHOW
AND
LUNCHEON

EMERSON HOTEL
Baltimore, Maryland

Tuesday,
October 12, 1965

GALA DRESS—1835/GREECE

Newspaper clipping and program booklet
for the Ladies' Tea Guild Fashion Show, 1965.

September of 1964. Father Voultsos had come to America in 1954 and served in Norwalk, Connecticut, for ten years before coming to Baltimore. With a quiet and unassuming manner, he devoted himself to many responsibilities ranging from hospital visitations to performing liturgies and sacraments. With growing demands placed on the clergy and the passage of three years since the departure of Father Gerotheou, Father Gallos was undoubtedly relieved to have Father Voultsos as a full-time assistant priest.

Following the arrival of Father Voultsos, it is interesting to note that Father Gallos again proposed a two-liturgy system that required two choirs and two choir directors. The council approved a proposal to hire Georgia Tangires as the second musical director and the ambitious Sunday morning change was implemented. The experiment once again received unsatisfactory reviews and in some instances proved too confusing. By early 1965, Annunciation resumed its practice of celebrating one Divine Liturgy on Sunday. It was during this time period that the sister parish of

The Rev. Anastasios Voultsos was originally from Kastoria in Western Macedonia. He served as the Assistant Priest at Annunciation from 1964-1970.

A major contributor to the interior renovations of 1964-1965 was Peter G. Angelos (inset) who donated the cost of the new ornately carved *iconostasion* (altar screen). *See page 173.*

St. Nicholas also underwent a change in clergy. Following the departure of Father Nicholas Stavrakis in 1963, The Rev. Peter C. Chrisafidis assumed the spiritual leadership of the Greek community of Highlandtown where he would serve for the next seven years.

With more parishioners now speaking only English, the language issue surfaced again in the 1960's at Annunciation as well as other parishes. The matter was taken up at the Clergy-Laity Congress during the summer of 1964 and minor modifications to church services were approved by the Archdiocese. English would be allowed "in conjunction with Greek for the Epistle and Gospel readings, the Creed, and the Lord's Prayer." In addition to these changes, Father Gallos also expanded the use of English at special services and sacraments depending on the composition of the congregation in attendance. Conservative Greek-speaking parishioners were disappointed to say the least. The thorny issue of language usage would surface again for the future clergymen who would serve at Annunciation.

The varied activities of the parish youth organizations such as the GOYA and Sunday school continued to flourish during this decade. One vital area, however, the Greek school program, was in decline. The decreasing interest of students in the study of their ancestral language and the drop in enrollment was ultimately recorded in the minutes of general assemblies. By the 1960's, there were Greek schools operating from five different locations in Baltimore. In March of 1965, Paul Stamas provided an extensive report on behalf of a committee appointed to investigate the status of the Greek language schools. The parish decided to discontinue the suburban schools due to lack of sufficient registration and operational expenses. By the fall of 1966, one main school, located at the church, was serving the parish needs. This problem was not unique to Annunciation. In many Greek communities across America, concern over the success of Greek language schools was and still is a recurring topic, perhaps reflecting the changing attitudes and values of second- and third-generation Greek-Americans.

The next significant event to occur was a transition of clergy. At a parish council meeting on June 14, 1965, Father George Gallos submitted his letter of resignation to Parish Council President Harry J. Anderson. He had been offered the

Father Gallos Builds Up Parish, Now Leaving For New Challenge

By Robin Frames

The Rev. George P. Gallos, for more than a decade the pastor of Maryland's first and largest Greek Orthodox parish, soon will be moving to Massachusetts to undertake an entirely different kind of challenge.

He will leave the Greek Orthodox Church of the Annunciation in Baltimore late this summer or early in the fall to lead the St. Demetrios Community of Newton-Wellesley, a small group of Greek Orthodox Christians one fourth the size of the Maryland parish.

Father Gallos plans to remain until his successor is selected and firmly established here.

Since he came to Baltimore in 1954, his congregation has become a member of the Maryland Council of Churches, and the Greek Orthodox Church has been officially recognized in the State as the fourth major faith.

800 Families In Parish

As one admirer phrased it, "Father Gallos brought us into the big leagues."

Today the parish includes more than 800 families, some from as far away as Hagerstown, Aberdeen and Glen Burnie.

A comprehensive educational program comprises twelve grades plus kindergarten, nursery school, an adult class for those of all faiths and five afternoon Greek schools.

To meet the needs of its extensive programs and growing parish families, the Church of the Annunciation completed a $400,000 social and educational building in 1961. It is currently putting the finishing touches on a remodeling and repair project to preserve and further the beauty and safety of the original church structure at Maryland avenue and Preston street.

Needs Of The People

But Father Gallos, whose genial smile and gentle manner contrast pleasantly with his swarthy physique, places the greatest value of his Baltimore ministry in "meeting the needs of the people of the parish, as they come to me each day."

And come they do. They know that almost without exception, he can be found in his study during the midafternoon and may be reached at any time in the event of an emergency.

But pastoral counseling also presents problems in a parish as large as Annunciation.

Because of his enormous work

ORTHODOX LEADER—The Rev. George P. Gallos, pastor of the Greek Orthodox Church of the Annunciation, stands in the sanctuary in front of the newly-installed ikonostasion, a wooden altar screen carved especially for the congregation.

load, which grows each day, Father Gallos feels that he is unable "to get to know each family as well as I would like to. Yet each family is very much worth knowing, and interesting in its own special way."

Younger Man Needed

Although at 50 he is far from ready to retire, the pastor nevertheless suggests that a younger clergyman "with an abundance of energy" would be better able to cope with the work load in the giant Baltimore parish.

As a general rule, he also would like to see more sabbaticals made available to parish priests.

"A year or more to devote to rest, change, travel, study and meditation would enable many pastors to return to their parishes renewed," he said.

But he also points out the difficulty of such a plan, due to the acute shortage of ordained clergymen.

The Greek Orthodox pastor emphasizes that he would have remained at the Annunciation parish had he not received the call

to Massachusetts to help organize a strong church community.

In Borrowed Building

St. Demetrios has been in existence five years, but throughout its short history has been led by part-time priests in a borrowed church building.

In a letter to his parishioners, Father Gallos explained that his move "will give me the opportunity to do a much more thorough job than I was able to do in Baltimore—to know my parishioners better and to be a more accomplished preacher and pastor.

"It will give me more time to read and pursue advanced studies, allow more time for my family, and provide the challenge to build a new church. . . ."

In the sanctuary, Father Gallos immerses himself just as completely in the liturgy as he does in the lives of his parishioners when engaged in counseling.

A Unique Blend

He feels the Greek Orthodox Church has a unique blend of

mysticism, music and art in its worship that makes Christianity especially real.

Three years ago, when the congregation dedicated a new pipe organ, members of all faiths were invited to attend a demonstration service of the liturgy. "The church was filled," Father Gallos recalls.

Particular emphasis is placed on art. "Art enhances our worship by reminding parishioners of the events of the life of Christ and the saints. And the higher the quality of art, the more inspiring it should be to the worshiper."

During his eleven-year stay in Baltimore, Father Gallos has not only opened his church doors to others, but has participated in many discussions and joint programs with Roman Catholics, Protestants and Jews.

On National Groups

He is a member of the National Conference of Christians and Jews, and three years ago represented the National Council of Churches as well as his own church as a summer exchange preacher in Great Britain.

A native of Minneapolis, Father Gallos was educated at Macalester College, Holy Cross Greek Orthodox Seminary and the Hartford (Conn.) Theological Seminary.

He served parishes in New Britain, Conn., and Rochester, N.Y., before coming to the Church of the Annunciation here.

Father Gallos says that while the increased use of English and other liberalizations of the Orthodox rite have been well received by his parishioners, most of them speak Greek and do not want to relinquish their unique religious and cultural heritage.

"Better Americans"

"Keeping our Greek culture alive makes us better Americans," the priest observes. "It enables us to add to America's culture — which is a rich mixture of the contributions of all the immigrants who have come here."

He says that during his stay in Baltimore "the Greek community has been anything but static. As some individuals leave, more come from Greece and other parts of this country."

One of the most significant developments at Annunciation during the last decade, according to Father Gallos, is the evolvement of a "peaceful, united and growing parish."

The Baltimore Sun published this farewell tribute to Father George Gallos on Saturday, July 17, 1965. Two months later, the Gallos family departed from Baltimore for a new parish assignment in Massachusetts.

position as pastor of the St. Demetrios Greek Orthodox community in Newton-Wellesley, Massachusetts. The offer afforded him the exciting opportunity to help build a new church while allowing him the chance to pursue higher education and teach at the Holy Cross Theological Seminary. During that summer, *The Baltimore Sun* ran an extensive article entitled, "Father Gallos Builds Up Parish, Now Leaving for New Challenge." The Annunciation parish with over 800 families was about to undergo another change.

The transfer was confirmed by the Archdiocese in August of 1965, and Annunciation prepared to say goodbye to its pastor and his wife. Father George and Presbytera Anna Gallos were honored at a testimonial dinner held at the Emerson Hotel on September 15, 1965, attended by hundreds of faithful parishioners, friends, and local dignitaries. *The Baltimore Sun* article written at the time of his departure stated: "Father Gallos has not only opened his church doors to others, but has participated in many discussions and joint programs with Roman Catholics, Protestants, and Jews." One of the most significant developments was the evolvement of a united and growing community. His eleven-year pastorate in Baltimore laid the foundation on which greater achievement and progress could be built.

Consequently, the arrival of The Reverend Emmanuel E. Bouyoucas in September of 1965 as the next spiritual leader of Annunciation was a peaceful and smooth transition, unlike the turbulent departures and arrivals of earlier priests. The church had reached a new level of maturity and understanding which was accomplished, in part, through the strengthening of its relationship with the Greek Orthodox Archdiocese. Diplomacy in parish administration was helping Annunciation reach higher standards. The first stage of major development ended in 1965 with this change in clergy. Further enhancements in parish life would soon be evident as the Annunciation community of Baltimore was about to begin its next decade as a viable religious organization within the city.

The Rev. Emmanuel E. Bouyoucas

Opposite Page: During its sixth decade, the Annunciation parish sponsored a testimonial dinner honoring Lawrence Cardinal Shehan (left) and Archbishop Iakovos (right). The new pastor, Father Emmanuel Bouyoucas, was a key organizer of this historic ecumenical gathering of Catholic and Orthodox Christians on September 9, 1967.

1966–1975

Upon his arrival, the 47-year-old Father Bouyoucas became the second full-time American-born pastor of Greek descent to serve at Annunciation. As a member of the distinctive first graduating class of the Holy Cross Theological Seminary in Pomfret, Connecticut, in May of 1942, he had been named class valedictorian. In December of that year, he married Helen Smyrniotou and was later ordained to the priesthood by Bishop Athenagoras Cavadas in January of 1943. During the first two decades of his pastoral career he had served Greek communities in Portland, Maine; Kansas City, Kansas; Birmingham, Alabama; Chicago, Illinois; and Charlotte, North Carolina. Father Emmanuel and Presbytera Helen Bouyoucas, with their sons Ernest and Chris, quickly adapted to parish life in Baltimore. The groundwork of the former pastor, Father Gallos, along with the new order of progressive thinking had nurtured the transition.

More positive changes would take place in 1966. The Annunciation Church, with the parish council under the leadership of George H. Pappas, began the second stage of major development and outreach to the larger community. By the spring of 1966—the Sixtieth Anniversary of Annunciation—a very significant decision took place symbolizing a greater assimilation into the mainstream society. On April 12, 1966, two days after the celebration of *Pascha* (Easter), a special meeting was called. Through an amendment to the bylaws and charter, the parish assembly voted favorably for the long-anticipated name change. After six decades as the Greek Orthodox Church "Evangelismos," the parish would now be known as "The Greek Orthodox Church of the Annunciation." Records show that on April 25, 1966, Parish Council President George H. Pappas and Secretary Charles Pavlos filed the formal amendment to the charter with the City of Baltimore.

Other landmark changes were implemented later that year. In October of 1966, women were welcomed as voting members at general assembly meetings. The Annunciation community was truly evolving. The church initiated by the early immigrants had come of age. Soon, a number of activities were undertaken showing the parish's spirit and energy as well as the range of its programs. For instance, the interior sanctuary took on an inspiringly different look with the addition of Byzantine icons, painted by Iconographer Constantine Youssis, for the new *iconostasion* (altar screen) that was gifted to the parish in 1965. The donors of the various icons proudly participated in a special dedication ceremony following church services on Sunday, February 27, 1966.

The music program also underwent change upon Father Bouyoucas' arrival. In the fall of 1965, after the departure of Anna Gallos, Georgia Tangires returned as the next director of the church choir. She quickly reacquainted herself with the entire music program, having served as director from 1951-1956. Soon, there were four choirs from various age groups under the direction of Mrs. Tangires and her dedicated associates. Among those

Icon of the Annunciation with brass plaque dedicating the new altar screen to the memory of Frances M. Angelos.

The Rev. Emmanuel Bouyoucas (left) and his assistant, The Rev. Anastasios Voultsos, circa 1970.

One of the first sacraments following the parish's official name change from "Evangelismos" to "Annunciation" was the wedding of Basil G. Markulis to Dorothea Rosemary on Sunday, April 17, 1966. The large icon of the Virgin Mary on the rear wall of the altar was donated by the Maistros Family in 1944. The *iconostasion* was gifted by Peter G. Angelos in 1965.

directing youth choirs during the late 1960's were William Sharkey, Stacie N. Petrou, Chrysanthy P. Stevens, and Ann Sophocleus. By December 1967, the choir presented the first Candlelight Christmas Concert. Complementing the choir voices was the arrival of Fotini Arnas Nichols as new church organist in 1968. The teamwork of Georgia Tangires and Fotini Nichols would remain steadfast over the next forty years.

The year 1967 also marked the arrival of additional staff to meet the growing demands of the business office at the Annunciation Church. On June 5, 1967, Lucy Hagopian joined the Executive Secretary, Michael Coulianos, to carry out the many organizational duties required to run church operations. Parish officials immediately noted her efficiency and dedication. Though some parishioners initially were hesitant of a "non-Greek" working in the office, she was successful in reaching

out to the diverse congregation. The professional manner and strong business acumen of Lucy Hagopian would enhance parish administration for over four decades. During this time, Father Bouyoucas received noteworthy recognition. On June 4, 1967, at the 25th Anniversary gathering of the first Holy Cross Graduating Class of 1942, he was named *Protopresbyter* of the Ecumencial Patriarchal Throne—the highest rank a married priest can achieve in the Greek Orthodox Church. Accolades continued six months later when he was named as the Archdiocesan Vicar for the State of Maryland.

Earlier that year, as the congregation prepared for Holy Week, the Annunciation Church was featured in the Religion section of *The Evening Sun* on April 22, 1967. The article served to educate its readers about the Orthodox faith, religious customs, and traditions surrounding the

SERVICE—The Rev. Emmanuel E. Bouyoucas, the pastor of the Greek Orthodox Church of the Annunciation, will conduct daily services starting tomorrow in observance of the Orthodox Easter week, which ends April 30.

Palm Sunday Services Will Open Orthodox Christians' Holy Week

Left: Stained glass window depicting the "Crucifixion of Christ," donated by Constantine Lazaris in 1942.

coloring signifies the blood of Christ redeeming the world." The article also noted that Baltimore had five Eastern Orthodox congregations at that time: St. Andrew Russian Orthodox Church; Holy Trinity Russian Orthodox Church; St. Michael Ukrainian Orthodox Church; St. Nicholas Greek Orthodox Church; and the Greek Orthodox Church of the Annunciation.

Later that year, in a continued effort to foster better interfaith relationships, a testimonial dinner was held on September 9, 1967, honoring Archbishop Iakovos of the Greek Orthodox Archdiocese and Lawrence Cardinal Shehan, spiritual leader of the Roman Catholic Archdiocese of Baltimore. The event commemorated the lifting of the "anathema" which had been declared by the

celebration of Easter. Father Bouyoucas reflected that "the midnight service is literally a movement from darkness into light and, for the Orthodox Christian, a reminder that death has been conquered through the resurrection of Christ." The traditional Easter egg "symbolizes the grave and breaking it indicates a life renewed, while the red

Western and Eastern Churches upon each other in 1054—the final act that caused the Great Schism. In an atmosphere of mutual respect and understanding, Orthodox and Catholic Church leaders and laity joined in fellowship at that historic 1967 gathering. The event was held at the Blue Crest North with proceeds earmarked for the new UGOC (United Greek Orthodox Charities).

The United Greek Orthodox Charities was established at the Clergy-Laity Congress in 1966 to raise funds for education, disaster relief, care of the aged and orphans, and other philanthropic causes. Founding fathers of the Baltimore chapter were Emmanuel Hondroulis, John D. Copanos, Steve Karas, Dr. Dennis Agallianos and Capt. John P. G. Livanos with Peter J. Prevas serving as chairman of the Executive Committee. One of its first and most successful events was the Maryland premier on March 26, 1969, of the acclaimed film, "The Lion in Winter." Over 1,000 tickets were sold and $6,000 was raised for the benefit of the Hellenic College in Brookline, Massachusetts. The Rev. Dr. Leonidas Contos, President of the Hellenic College/Holy Cross Greek Orthodox School of Theology, and Spyros Skouras, National Chairman of the charities group, were among the honored guests in attendance.

Throughout this period, the Annunciation Church continued to play a prominent role in activities with other denominations. Minutes of the general assembly meeting in March 1967 related that Father Bouyoucas was very involved in interchurch activities and had lectured on Orthodoxy at several schools. During these years, the choir groups participated in the annual Holly Tour sponsored by the Central Churches of Baltimore. By the fall of 1967, the Annunciation library was in its fifth year of operation and was gaining recognition from many visitors due to its growing collection of books and material in both Greek and English. Four years later, on January 31, 1971, the library name was officially changed to the "Theodore J. George Library" in honor of its dedicated founder and organizer.

Soon, the use of English in the church liturgy was again sparking debates. Upon arriving in Baltimore, the more conservative Father Bouyoucas was abiding strictly with the decision of the 1964

Baltimore Chapter of the United Greek Orthodox Charities. Left to right: Theodore J. George, Evan A. Chriss, Emmanuel Hondroulis, Peter J. Prevas, Charles Constantine, Dr. Paul Koukoulas, and Dr. Anthony Bravos, March 1969.

Bishop Silas of Amphipolis
Metropolitan of the New Jersey Diocese

Clergy-Laity Congress. His limited usage of English became a subject of much concern for some parishioners. At the special assembly held in February 1968, a resolution was passed requesting the Archdiocese to allow English in "a substantial portion of church worship." Subsequent meetings were held to which Bishop Silas of Amphipolis, the Hierarch of New Jersey, was invited to attend and hear both sides of the controversial issue. Having been appointed by Archbishop Iakovos in November of 1965 as Bishop of the First Archdiocesan District, Bishop Silas would soon become a regular visitor to the Annunciation Church. At the parish assembly meeting on March 31, 1968, it was reported that the 1964 ruling would remain in force on a nationwide basis. For the time being, this was as far as the changes in language would go.

By the late 1960's, Annunciation, like other parishes in major cities, began experiencing problems as urban decay and racial tensions started to escalate. The assassination of civil rights leader Dr. Martin Luther King, Jr. in April 1968 led to uncertainty, fears, and riots in cities across America. The Annunciation Church soon found itself

The Islanders dance troupe entertained at the GOYA (Greek Orthodox Youth of America) Convention, May 27, 1966.
Left to right: Aristides Cederakis, Michael Fochios, Nicki Maistros, Dorothea Karageorge, Irene Daskalakis, Georgia Maistros.

Ladies' Tea Guild Fashion Show and Luncheon organizers, November 5, 1969. Clockwise from top: Sandra Pefinis, wife of Parish Council President Charles Pefinis (not in photograph); Anna Z. Pappas, Harry P. Pappas, Sylvia Lambros, Michael Lambros, Helen K. Xenakis, George Xenakis, Presbytera Helen Bouyoucas and Rev. Emmanuel Bouyoucas.

surrounded by dismal-looking buildings and city blocks long overdue for revitalization. The need for a future planning strategy that required the parish to work directly with neighborhood redevelopment led to the formation of a special church committee. This group initially organized in July of 1968 with Father Bouyoucas, Chairman; Charles Pavlos, Parish Council President; and board members Nicholas Petrou, Evan A. Chriss, James Markakis, Constantine Courpas, and Paul Sarbanes. The work would be tedious, but the ultimate long-term rewards would be greatly beneficial to the parish.

In the interim, some type of action was needed to appease parishioners' fears as attendance at evening events and services was on the decline. The parish council of 1969, under the leadership of Charles G. Pefinis, employed armed guards to stand vigil on church property during Greek school, youth group events, or other evening activities. Though the use of guards for several years received mixed reviews, it was an immediate and proactive response to a situation that eased some apprehension and allowed church activities to stay on course until larger-scale solutions emerged.

The close of the 1960's saw other decisions and activities unfold. The fall assembly of 1968 approved the increase in yearly church dues from $30 to $52. On February 9, 1969, the first church dance held in years, under the chairmanship of Alex Zades, drew a crowd of 900 to the Howard Room of the Civic Center. A few months later, on June 22, 1969, an "Appreciation Day" program was held to recognize the many volunteers who had given of their time and talents to church activities. The idea was initiated by President Charles Pefinis and sponsored by the parish council and their wives. During this period, the first Greek dance school was initiated through the efforts of Alex Zades who also served as one of eight instructors. Soon, over 100 parishioners were signed up to learn the folk dances of their heritage. In August of 1969, the first Youth Camp was held in Rocks, Maryland, under the direction of Frank G. Pappas who later reported the success of the parish outing to the general assembly.

The fall of 1969 evoked fond memories of prior decades as Annunciation warmly welcomed back Professor Athanasios P. Theodorides as a *psalti* (cantor). He had devoted his services from

1937-1948 to the Baltimore Greek community. Nationally recognized as the first to introduce four-part singing to Orthodox churches, he was the composer of inspiring liturgical hymns. Upon his retirement three years later, the Annunciation community designated Sunday, June 4, 1972, to honor this great layman. The choir, including many former members, sang original church music composed by Professor Theodorides and presented a program of his secular songs. Proceeds from the testimonial dinner were forwarded to the Holy Cross Greek Orthodox School of Theology.

A most prestigious event marked the end of the year 1969 and the close of the decade—the Theodore S. Agnew Scholarship Fund Dinner. This gala was held on December 10, 1969, under the chairmanship of Harry P. Pappas and Evan A. Chriss. The late Theodore S. Agnew was the father of United States Vice President Spiro T. Agnew who addressed the group attending this function. The senior Agnew was a charter member and past president of the Worthington Chapter No. 30 of the Order of AHEPA (American Hellenic Educational Progressive Association). That night,

the scholarship fund to benefit young adults of Greek descent received over $25,000.

Annunciation underwent a variety of changes as the 1970's began. After six years as assistant priest, Father Anastasios Voultsos retired in the summer of 1970. As a replacement, the Rev. Alexander Nathan was appointed on July 1, 1970, to serve for two years. Shortly after his arrival, Father Nathan changed his surname to Anastasiou. He worked with the Youth Committee and a new program was formulated for the Junior GOYA to renew participation in all aspects of spiritual, social, educational, and athletic life. Within the year, a completely refurbished room was designated as the Youth Office, funded primarily by the efforts of the Ladies' Tea Guild.

During the initial months following Father Anastasiou's arrival, the question of the use of English in the Divine Liturgy resurfaced again. The 20th Clergy-Laity Congress held in New York in July 1970 was the forum for a debate that became a major issue in Greek Orthodox communities everywhere. The Archdiocese realized that linguistic reforms were needed for the Orthodox Church to

THE EVENING SUN

Rev. Alexander Anastasiou (left) served from 1970-1972 as the assistant to Rev. Emmanuel Bouyoucas (right). Both were featured in a newspaper story discussing language changes in the Greek Orthodox Church, July 18, 1970.

Left to right: Rev. Emmanuel Bouyoucas of the Annunciation Church, United States Vice President Spiro T. Agnew, Bishop Silas of the New Jersey Diocese and Rev. Peter Chrisafidis of the St. Nicholas Church in Highlandtown, 1969.

maintain its viability as a major religion in America. Changes were adopted by the majority of delegates at the convention permitting the use of English "as needed in church services in accordance with the judgement of the parish in consultation with the bishop." Staunch supporters of the Greek language sounded the alarm that the Archdiocesan decree would lead to the "abolition of Greek" from the Divine Liturgy.

As the controversy made headlines in Greek-American publications throughout the United States, the Annunciation parish council and clergymen handled matters carefully and attempted to educate parishioners—dispelling the rumors of the demise of Greek in the liturgical services. Father Bouyoucas, who took part in the national debate, attempted to preserve harmony on the local level.

In a strong message to his parishioners, published in August 1970, he related: "Nowhere and at no time was the abolishment of the Greek language considered…. Language is the vessel used to transmit ideas and knowledge. The language of the country and the people must be used…. We shall use a combination of Greek and English." Annunciation succeeded by introducing a bilingual system that used either Greek or English, depending on the service and the predominant language used by those in attendance. *The Evening Sun* even featured a story on July 18, 1970, with the theme that the Greek Orthodox Church in America was now "changing with the times."

Of all the events that occurred with the arrival of the new decade, perhaps the most significant was the establishment of a third Greek Orthodox Church in Baltimore. Parishioners from both Annunciation and St. Nicholas had been moving in increasing numbers to the suburbs north of the city. A preliminary meeting was held at the home of Gabriel and Elaine Pantelides on November 29, 1969, where members interested in establishing a new church adopted guidelines and set their plan into motion. A steering committee, under the chairmanship of Constantine Alexion, communicated its intent to Annunciation and St. Nicholas church leaders, asking for their support in this new venture.

Charter records show that on June 8, 1970, Articles of Incorporation were filed for the new "Suburban Greek Orthodox Community of Baltimore, Inc." Signers of this historic document included Constantine Alexion, John L. Sitaras, Alex Pulianas, and Dr. Andrew Vendelis. The Archdiocese assigned the first full-time priest, The Rev. Sam J. Kalamaras, to the new suburban parish on November 29, 1970. Following the first Divine Liturgy held at the Cromwell Valley Elementary School, church services would be held at the Parkville Senior High School auditorium for the next five years. In the interim, leaders of the new community began plans for the ultimate construction of a formal church building.

The first parish council of the Suburban Greek Orthodox Community of Baltimore included

Constantine Alexion, President; John L. Sitaras, Vice President; Alex Pulianas, Secretary; Joanne Sitaras, Recording Secretary; Dr. Andrew Vendelis, Treasurer; and eleven directors assigned to various aspects of church administration. By December of 1971, a thirty-acre tract of land was purchased at 2504 Cub Hill Road in Baltimore County for the future church site. Three years later, at a special banquet on May 11, 1974, the name "St. Demetrios Greek Orthodox Church" was chosen. Groundbreaking ceremonies were conducted on May 12, 1974, and construction of the chapel and education center progressed rapidly throughout 1975. The first church services in the new building were held on Sunday, January 4, 1976. Officiating at this historic liturgy was The Rev. Ernest Arambiges, who had assumed full-time duties in September of 1972 as the next clergyman of Baltimore's suburban congregation.

During the initial years following the establishment of the third parish, an organization was formed to bring together and coordinate the numerous religious and lay programs of the Annunciation, St. Nicholas, and St. Demetrios Churches. Established in 1972, the Coordinating Council of Orthodox Churches (CCOC) sought to oversee the scheduling of events to assure larger participation by all parishioners. During this

The Education Center of the St. Demetrios Greek Orthodox Church on Cub Hill Road opened for use in 1976.

period, John L. Sitaras was named the council's executive secretary. The recent changes in clergy at St. Demetrios and St. Nicholas also ushered in a new era of leadership and stability. The Rev. Ernest Arambiges would serve the St. Demetrios Church for nearly a quarter of a century. Similarly, the assignment of The Rev. George E. Kalpaxis to the St. Nicholas parish in 1971 would span two decades. As a result, there were great strides in all aspects of liturgical, educational, and philanthropic work occurring at all three Greek Orthodox parishes in Baltimore during these years.

Proclamation of Greek Independence Day at Baltimore City Hall, March 25, 1970. Left to right: John Morekas, John Paterakis, Jimmie Chambers, Rev. Emmanuel Bouyoucas, John J. Karukas, Mayor Thomas D'Alesandro III, Gabriel Pantelides, Konstantine J. Prevas, Peter N. Marudas, Andrew Papaminas, and Nicholas S. Morekas.

Athenian Agora Offers Flavor of Old Greece

Ribbon-cutting ceremony for the first "Athenian Agora." Left to right: William Koutrelakos, Chairman; Father Emmanuel Bouyoucas, and Mayor William Donald Schaefer, November 20, 1971.

At Annunciation, events of the early 1970's were especially rewarding as the urban parish continued expanding its presence within the City of Baltimore. In the fall of 1971, the Sunday school sponsored a bazaar for the benefit of the church. After much planning and preparation by countless volunteers, the first "Athenian Agora" was presented on November 20 and 21, 1971. The ribbon-cutting ceremony to start the festivities was conducted by Baltimore's Mayor William Donald Schaefer, assisted by Father Bouyoucas and William Koutrelakos, general chairman of this historic first "Agora." The festival name, which translates as marketplace, was the inspiration of parishioner Nicholas Ioannou. Even the local newspapers noted the marketplace atmosphere: "Food will not be the only attraction of the agora. Featured also will be an import boutique offering jewels and accessories, art objects and wall plaques.... Byzantine icons will be on sale as well as Greek Christmas cards."

For thirty-five years, Annunciation has continued to shine in the city's spotlight with its annual festival providing people throughout the Baltimore region a unique opportunity to sample the flavor, culture, history, and religious experience of the Greek people and their Orthodox faith. The event has now expanded to include street vendors, dance troupe performances, historical and cultural displays, church tours, choir performances, a silent auction, and much more. Similarly, in a coordinated effort a few years later, the Annunciation, St. Nicholas, and St. Demetrios parishes participated in the Ethnic Weekend at Baltimore's Constellation Pier from July 7-8, 1973. Drawing large crowds to witness a proud display of ethnic culture, all three churches shared equally in

The Rev. Dean C. Martin served
as the Assistant Priest from 1972-1975.

success, fellowship, and profits. This was the forerunner of the enlarged "Greek Festival" which was part of the international festival series held annually at Baltimore's revitalized Inner Harbor through the early 1980's.

By this time, Annunciation had moved ahead on a number of administrative matters. A "Foundation Fund" was established to encourage gifts and bequests so that the parish could carry forward effectively its Christian Orthodox Mission. Literature explaining the fund stated how Annunciation would be able to "accumulate assets to generate income," in order to support future parish projects in the areas of education, culture, and religion. Records show that cash bequests, property donations, stock shares, and other legacies were being earmarked for the fund by 1972. One of the first events sponsored by Annunciation to benefit the new church endowment fund was a musical concert honoring a past parish council president, the late Sam Malas. The concert was performed on May 8, 1971, featuring his vocally talented children—Spiro Malas, a basso, and Mary Malas Aiello, a soprano.

The proud record of achievement continued at Annunciation. In August 1972, under the leadership of Parish Council President Nicholas J. Kiladis, mortgages for the Education Building as well as the interior renovations of the mid-1960's were paid in

full. Then, at the general assembly meeting in November of 1972, members authorized another long-awaited project, the air-conditioning of the church complex at a cost of over $70,000. Through the financial support of the congregation and various church organizations, funds were raised and the installation was completed by the summer of 1973. Other projects during this time included the relandscaping of the church courtyard under the chairmanship of Anthony J. Cavas and the correction of the drainage problems at the Greek Orthodox Cemetery under the supervision of George T. George.

The early 1970's also saw more changes in church personnel. Following the transfer of Father Alexander Anastasiou, the parish welcomed The Reverend Dean C. Martin as its new assistant in November of 1972. It was his first pastoral assignment and Father Martin soon proved to be a great asset to the parish, particularly with the Junior GOYA. Father Dean and Presbytera Lillian Martin were embraced by the youth. He carried out his ministry with the assistance of dedicated Junior GOYA advisors who planned bus trips, social outings, and coordinated basketball tournaments. Among them were: Eurydice and Aristides Canelos, Matina and Nicholas Mentis, and George and Helen Xenakis who were fondly nicknamed "Mr. and Mrs. X." Following the untimely death of Aristides "Otts" Canelos in February of 1973, a scoreboard in the parish gymnasium was dedicated to his beloved memory during the Junior GOYA basketball tournament later that year.

Through the efforts of the clergy, parish council, and committees, a comprehensive program of fellowship was perpetuated. Activities from 1972 through 1975 illustrate this achievement. Father Martin also began a lecture series and religious retreats with youngsters from other parishes in the region, attempting to expand activities beyond the usual social events. Continuing the trend of showing appreciation for exemplary parish members, a testimonial dinner was held on June 9, 1972, to honor Evan Alevizatos Chriss, the church's legal counsel since 1969. The following week on June 17, 1972, parishioner Lambryn Mavrikos Stergiou, a coloratura, took the spotlight as she accompanied the Metropolitan Greek Choir of New York in a stirring concert of liturgical, classical, and modern music.

Later that year, "National Youth Sunday" was designated for October 8, 1972. Michael Fochios from the Senior GOYA read the Epistle in English. The Sons of Pericles and Maids of Athena passed the collection tray and took charge of the candles. The oath of office was also administered to youth group leaders. Gay Lynn Krometis was elected president of Senior GOYA; Angie Drosinos became president of Junior GOYA. Also, Paula Canelos was voted the recipient of the first "Youth of the Year" award with a special plaque presented by Father Bouyoucas. After church services, the Junior GOYA hosted the congregation at a coffee hour and the Senior GOYA sponsored a bake sale. It was inspiring to see such enthusiasm among the future generation of church leaders.

Christmas of 1972 saw the mailing of the very first community greeting card based upon the idea proposed by Angela Koutsoutis, one of the first women to serve on the Annunciation parish council. Each holiday season for over three decades, season's greetings have been sent to homes from participating parishioners. Another musical milestone was reached in early March 1973 when the parish honored former choir director Presbytera Anna Gallos. Choirs from various cities gathered in Baltimore for a weekend of music workshops and performances of her liturgical works. Three months later, the parish council under the leadership of Nicholas J. Kiladis, designated Sunday, June 17, 1973, as Founding Fathers Day. Nearly 150 men,

age sixty-five and older, were recognized and many who were parish founders or sustaining members were presented with Memorial Medallions from the Greek Orthodox Archdiocese.

Keeping with this theme, Annunciation honored its past presidents with a special recognition dinner at the Maryland Jockey Club on March 9, 1974. The event was under the chairmanship of Mr. and Mrs. William Tangires. Other members of the organizing committee included Mr. and Mrs. Nicholas Kiladis, Mr. and Mrs. Nicholas Lykos, Mr. and Mrs. George Mesologites, and Mr. and Mrs. Dennis J. Psoras. President Nicholas C. Lykos explained the importance of the parish council leadership role in resolving issues, moving the community forward, and setting guidelines.

The congregation realized its strong position within the Archdiocese was directly attributed to the tireless, dedicated work of its leadership over seven decades. Nearly two dozen living past presidents, along with representatives of deceased church leaders, received awards. Vasiliki Sempeles, the widow of Annunciation's first parish council president, George Sempeles, was also in attendance and given special recognition that evening.

As a result of the continued growth of the Annunciation parish, a recurring issue during the early 1970's was whether or not a new community center should be acquired. The decline of the neighborhood surrounding the parish helped

Presbytera Lillian Martin, Agora 1972.

Left to right: Eurydice M., Paula, and Aristides "Otts" Canelos, October 8, 1972.

Past Presidents Dinner, March 9, 1974. Award presentations left to right: Nicholas J. Anderson accepting on behalf of his deceased father, John G. Anderson (1928); Niketas A. Konstant (1934-1936); and George C. Mesologites (1949).

advance the idea for a center in the suburbs. The Site Committee, under the chairmanship of Charles Pefinis, was directed to find a suitable location and soon made numerous proposals. One suggestion, the spacious Emerson Farm site north of the city, proved to be controversial when first proposed to the general assembly on April 15, 1973, and again on March 14, 1976.

There were mixed feelings on the subject. Some believed a suburban center would result in the "deterioration of the present facility and its ultimate closing." Others felt the need for some type of expansion was obvious, especially with the obstacles of trying to get people downtown for meetings, searching for youth campsites each year, and other problems in coordinating events.

The time had arrived for some type of change, but the Annunciation parish was not sure where to focus its energy. Throughout 1973, lengthy negotiations and debates conducted at the general assemblies resulted in frustration and produced no final decision. By the fall of 1973, a survey to determine the parish needs was circulated to church members. The results of the questionnaire prioritized the issues and concerns of the day in the following order of importance: parking, home for the elderly, purchase of property around the church, cemetery chapel, community center, and a campsite. The closeness of response percentages on a number of these items, however, added further uncertainty and confusion to the entire matter.

As the parish grappled with these issues, most available sites close to the church were eventually sold to other parties. In the course of discussion, it was proposed that Annunciation begin focusing on the acquisition of residential properties around the existing building for future expansion. The idea took root as the Ladies' Philoptochos Society had recently purchased 33 W. Preston Street, one of the row houses directly across from the church, hoping to renovate it for elderly housing. It was not until the close of the decade that Annunciation would establish a definitive course of action for major facilities expansion.

Although this issue was left temporarily unresolved, progress was achieved in another significant area—church financial policy. At the general assembly meeting in March of 1974, the Pledge Drive Committee under the chairmanship of Nicholas J. Kiladis proposed that a Membership Obligation Program be instituted in 1975. Under this system, a parishioner would be considered a member in good standing by making a "pledge" each calendar year. Payments could be made weekly, monthly, quarterly, or annually. The program was approved and overall response was extremely favorable. Father Bouyoucas commented that Annunciation became "one of the first Greek Orthodox parishes in the United States to abolish formal dues and adopt a system of 'fair share pledges' which leaves the size of contributions at the discretion of parishioners." This concept became known as the "Stewardship Program."

In the spring of 1974, as the community prepared to celebrate *Pascha* (Easter), tragedy befell Annunciation during Holy Week. Matina Varipatis Mentis and her three daughters, Maria, Jo Anne, and Georgeen, died suddenly on Holy Tuesday, April 9, 1974, in an explosion that burned and sank the Greek oil tanker *Elias* in the Delaware Bay. They were visiting relatives aboard the ship that fateful day. The Annunciation congregation was overcome with grief upon learning the tragic news. Later, on April 24, 1974, four caskets were placed on the *solea* as Father Bouyoucas conducted funeral services for these well-loved parishioners. Hundreds filled the sanctuary to pray and offer their final respects. Three months later, the July 1974 issue of the *Annunciation Herald* was dedicated to widower Nicholas G. Mentis, "a man of abiding faith and courage," as a memorial tribute to his wife and daughters who perished. "May their love of our Church and of our parish be a beacon by which all of us will be guided."

When it was announced that a Mentis Memorial Scholarship Fund had been established, substantial contributions were sent to the church office. Considering that all three girls were active participants in the youth groups, the Junior GOYA also paid its tribute to them in a most touching manner. As a labor of love, the youngsters cleaned, painted, and prepared a special room on the lower level of the Education Building to honor their memory. The dedication of the "Mentis Room" took place on Sunday, April 6, 1975, to coincide with their one-year memorial service. A few years later, with additional fundraising assistance from church leaders, the space was further remodeled. The unveiling ceremony was held following their five-year memorial service on April 1, 1979. An elegant bronze plaque marks the entrance to the room, and the memory of these "four beautiful people" has a special place in parish history. Over the years, the "Mentis Room" has served church groups for meetings, luncheons, lectures, and other events.

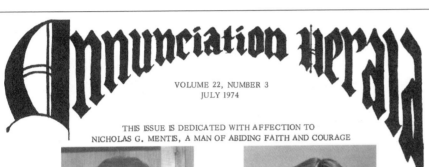

VOLUME 22, NUMBER 3
JULY 1974

THIS ISSUE IS DEDICATED WITH AFFECTION TO
NICHOLAS G. MENTIS, A MAN OF ABIDING FAITH AND COURAGE

We dedicate this issue, much of which concerns our youth groups, to these dear people, Matina Varipatis Mentis and her three daughters, Maria, JoAnne and Georgeen. May their love of our Church and of our parish be a beacon by which all of us will be guided in attaining the blessed virtues of belief in, service to, and devotion for the principles and tenets of our Faith. We pray God "to rest their souls".

A special issue of the *Annunciation Herald* was dedicated to the memory of Matina Mentis and her three daughters (clockwise from top): Maria, Georgeen, and Jo Anne. The memorial plaque at the entrance to the "Mentis Room" was unveiled at their one-year memorial service, April 6, 1975.

By the mid-1970's, the order of the day was not so much the establishment of organizations, but that of sustaining and strengthening the existing ones such as the Sunday school and Greek school programs. For instance, discussion groups had emerged for high school students as an extension of the traditional curriculum. Religious educational classes for adults were also earmarked as necessary to provide a comprehensive program for the entire community. The 1975 parish council, under the leadership of Anthony J. Cavas, continued to explore ways to improve the overall religious, educational, and social experience of the congregation. Strengthening the community for nearly seven decades was the cooperative spirit of those who revered the Orthodox faith and maintained the ministries of their parish as a foremost priority. Recognition of Annunciation's steadfastness and stability was soon to come.

The year 1975 marked the beginning of a new and exciting era in parish history. Within a matter of months, not only would Annunciation experience a complete change in spiritual leadership, but its position within the Archdiocese would undergo a major upgrade as well. In the spring of that year, it was announced that the Annunciation Church would be elevated to the status of a Cathedral. On Sunday, March 23, 1975, before an overflowing congregation, His Grace Bishop Silas of the First Archdiocesan District celebrated the Hierarchical Divine Liturgy and read the official proclamation from Archbishop Iakovos. All the Greek Orthodox parishes of Maryland were represented by delegations and participated in the services and festivities of that historic day.

In its new role, Annunciation Cathedral became the primary spiritual center of Greek Orthodoxy in the region. As the largest and oldest

1975 Parish Council with Father Bouyoucas (left) and Father Martin (right). Second row left to right: James Markakis, Angela Koutsoutis, Secretary; Constantine Courpas, Vice President; Anthony J. Cavas, President; Nicholas Lykos, Charles Constantine. Back row left to right: Nicholas Kiladis, George Coutros, Charles Pefinis, Edward Jackovitz, Treasurer; and Xenophon Maglaras.

parish in Maryland, its many significant contributions to the religious and cultural aspects of the community were noteworthy not only to the Archdiocese, but even to the Baltimore City Council that passed a resolution congratulating the parish on this auspicious occasion. Parish Council President Anthony J. Cavas proudly stated that the Cathedral designation was "a tribute to all the members of the church who had worked diligently and unselfishly for many years." Though not immediately visible, the impact of this event would prove to be considerable in the years ahead.

In the months immediately following the Cathedral designation, other notable events occurred. On May 8, 1975, a fundraising banquet was sponsored to aid the inhabitants of the Island of Cyprus which had been invaded by Turkey in July of 1974. The amount of $35,000 was raised, and hundreds of boxes of clothing and other relief items were sent to help the Greeks living on that island. Evan A. Chriss served as chairman for the State of Maryland Cyprus Relief Committee, and Dr. Constant J. Georges was chairman of the local relief committee. Later that year, on September 27, 1975, a reunion celebration of the parish's first youth group, EONA, was held. Over 150 members from the 1946-1956 era shared a nostalgic evening. Continuing the presentation of

The Rev. Emmanuel Bouyoucas with altar server Constandinos Pavlakos in background, March 23, 1975.

Bishop Silas read the proclamation designating Annunciation as a Cathedral on the Sunday of Orthodoxy, March 23, 1975.

Metropolitan Silas of the First Archdiocesan District officiated at the special services elevating
the Annunciation Greek Orthodox Church to the status of a Cathedral on Sunday, March 23, 1975.

progressive programs, Mary Bahadouris Kiladis was honored as "Church Woman of the Year" on October 3, 1975, for twenty-five years of dedicated service. It was the first time a woman of the parish had been honored with a testimonial.

During 1975, however, the parish's primary concern was focused on its clergy. Father Martin, the assistant priest of three years, was assigned a full-time position with the Holy Trinity parish in Sioux City, Iowa. On February 27, 1975, Father Dean and Presbytera Lillian Martin were given a fond farewell—a prelude to a larger goodbye later that same year. By the summer of 1975, Father Bouyoucas requested a transfer due to ill health and was soon assigned to the St. Katherine's parish in West Palm Beach, Florida. He requested that his service at Annunciation be concluded officially on September 15, 1975—exactly ten years from the date he started. His tenure was filled with great strides in development culminating with the parish's designation as a Cathedral.

An emotional farewell dinner honoring Father Emmanuel and Presbytera Helen Bouyoucas was held on Monday, September 8, 1975, at Martin's West with over 800 people in attendance. Charles Pefinis served as toastmaster and among the roster of those presenting gifts that evening were: Rodopi Smyrnioudis of the Philoptochos Society; William Koutrelakos of the Sunday School; Julia Krometis of the Ladies' Tea Guild; and Vernon Rey of the Choir. On behalf of the parish council, President Anthony J. Cavas presented a beautiful color portrait of Father Bouyoucas. Keynote speakers included: The Honorable Paul S. Sarbanes of the United States House of Representatives; Past Parish Council President Harry J. Anderson; and Parish Librarian Theodore J. George. This memorable event, under the chairmanship of John Fangikis, was a fitting tribute to Father Bouyoucas' decade of service to the Annunciation community.

The departures of both clergymen within a few months left many feeling uneasy and uncertain about the future. The immediate agenda was clear as the parish council moved quickly in search of replacements. Through careful planning with the Archdiocese, the transition began smoothly. On September 15, 1975, The Rev. Elias C. Velonis was welcomed as the new assistant priest just as Father Bouyoucas departed. The week before, on September 7, 1975, Elias Velonis had been ordained

The Rev. Elias C. Velonis served as the Assistant Priest from 1975-1979.

The first concert to benefit the newly-designated Cathedral featured the talented Johanne Markakis who gave a memorable performance of modern Greek songs, Towson State College, May 16, 1975.

to the Holy Diaconate at the Cathedral of St. George in Philadelphia. Then, on September 13, 1975, he was ordained to the priesthood in the Holy Cross Chapel in Brookline, Massachusetts. Father Elias and Presbytera Mary Velonis quickly established themselves in Baltimore. Their first child, Margo, was born in October 1975. Three years later, a son, Thomas, was also born during Father Velonis' pastorate at Annunciation.

The search for a Cathedral Dean, however, was more involved. The Baltimore parish needed an energetic and progressive-thinking clergyman to lead Annunciation as it moved toward higher accomplishments as a Cathedral. On September 11, 1975, a special parish council meeting was held to interview a prospective candidate. The interview was with a 42-year-old priest—The Reverend Constantine M. Monios of the Holy Cross Greek Orthodox Church in Mt. Lebanon, Pennsylvania. He was highly respected for his theological knowledge, organizational expertise, and inspiring communication skills. Father Monios felt it was time to move on with his pastoral career and viewed a larger parish like Baltimore as a challenge. Following a successful interview, the decision came quickly. The Annunciation community had found its new spiritual leader.

Father Constantine Monios became the new Dean of the Annunciation Cathedral in November of that historic year. He celebrated his first Divine Liturgy in Baltimore on Sunday, November 2, 1975. Father Constantine and Presbytera Mary Monios and their five children—Amalia, Harry, Athena, Michael, and Nikki—were cordially received as new members of the Cathedral family. Immediately upon arrival, Father Monios understood and appreciated the rich and poignant sense of history within the parish. In four short months, Annunciation would reach seventy years as a religious community. No one could have imagined the lasting legacy this new clergyman would create in the years ahead. Father Monios was about to begin the most impressive chapter of his pastoral career that would chart the course of Annunciation's progress for over a quarter of a century.

The Rev. Constantine M. Monios became the new
Dean of the Annunciation Cathedral in November of 1975.

Opposite Page: The need for expansion of parish facilities led to the acquisition of century-old town houses across the street from the Cathedral. Under the guidance of Father Monios, these buildings would be transformed into the Annunciation Orthodox Center within the next decade.

1976-1985

Within the first few months, Father Constantine Monios expressed overwhelming satisfaction with his new assignment and urged the congregation to "become even more aware of its great faith and heritage as Orthodox Christians." To better understand his impact on the Annunciation community, a brief overview of his background is needed. His personal history was steeped in religion dating back to 1938 when he was only five years of age. At that time, he first became an acolyte at the St. Spyridon Greek Orthodox Church in his hometown of Monessen, Pennsylvania. Deeply impressed by a moving encounter in later years with Archbishop Athenagoras, Constantine Monios entered the Holy Cross Theological Seminary in 1951, just three years after its relocation to Brookline, Massachusetts.

Later, as his theological studies neared completion, he married Mary Christodoulou of Weirton, West Virginia, in July of 1956. She was a graduate of the St. Basil Academy. Apart from its renowned home for orphans, St. Basil Academy offered a junior college to train young women for positions as Greek school teachers and secretaries on the local parish level. With this extensive schooling, Mary Monios would soon complement the pastoral work of her husband. Constantine Monios was ordained a deacon in the Church of St. Demetrios in Warren, Ohio, on October 28, 1956. Three months later, on January 30, 1957, at the Holy Cross Chapel in Brookline, Massachusetts, Deacon Constantine Monios was ordained to the Holy Priesthood by Bishop Athenagoras Kokkinakis, Dean of the Holy Cross Theological School.

Shortly after, Father Constantine Monios was assigned to the Assumption Greek Orthodox Church in Manchester, New Hampshire, and remained there until September 1960. During this period, he continued his graduate studies and received his Master's Degree in Sacred Theology from Boston University. In the fall of 1960, he was transferred to the Holy Cross Greek Orthodox Church in Mt. Lebanon, Pennsylvania, near Pittsburgh, where he would serve for the next fifteen years. During his tenure, the church building was completed and consecrated in the fall of 1971. At that time, Father Monios received the noted ecclesiastical rank of *Economos* from Archbishop Iakovos in recognition of his service to the Archdiocese. Soon, his other philanthropic works were being recognized on the national level as he was listed in the 1975-76 edition of the prestigious *Who's Who in Religion.*

With this impressive resume of accomplishments, Father Monios began his pastorate in Baltimore during the fall of 1975. The recent designation of the parish as the Greek Orthodox Cathedral for the State of Maryland mandated that expanded responsibilities were forthcoming. Under his guidance, the Annunciation community was on the path to becoming a true center of spiritual, cultural and social growth for the Orthodox faithful throughout the region. Activities during the first two years of Father Monios' pastorate illustrate this greater sense of awareness and commitment to God and Church. The pace of events was about to accelerate.

In the early months of 1976, one goal of the parish council, to make the senior citizens a more active part of the community, was realized. On February 22, 1976, nearly 200 people were welcomed to the first meeting and social function of the new Golden Age Club coordinated through Father Monios and Alex Zades, parish council liaison. The first officers were Theodore Canaras, President; Mary Canelos, Vice President; Fevronia Petite, Secretary; and Cleo BeLer, Treasurer. This club was the first of many new groups and programs the Cathedral would soon be promoting.

The Seventieth Anniversary of Annunciation was observed in the spring of 1976. On March 27, 1976, Archbishop Iakovos came to Baltimore to celebrate Great Vespers at the Cathedral with all area Orthodox clergymen participating. The following day, Sunday of the Veneration of the Cross, he officiated at the Hierarchical Divine Liturgy followed by a banquet at the Lord Baltimore Hotel under the chairmanship of Nicholas C. Lykos. Over 400 people attended to reminisce and celebrate the progress made by their parish. The keynote speaker was Konstantine J. Prevas who presented an overview of parish history. His powerful closing remarks, adapted from a poem by T. S. Elliot, inspired listeners to imagine how future generations would reflect on the parish of

Choir members posed with Father Elias Velonis (left) and Father Constantine Monios (right), circa 1976.
Organist Fifi Nichols (first row, sixth from left); Choir Director Georgia Tangires (first row, fifth from right).

1976. "Here were a decent, God-loving, God-fearing people, whose only monument was the Byzantine cross and its symbolism from generation to generation to be protected and carried on as a tradition until the very end."

During the spring of that anniversary year, other events of historic interest took place. At the Holy Friday Services on April 23, 1976, the solemn procession of the *Epitaphios* (Tomb of Christ) was held outdoors for the first time in many years and rekindled a tradition from years past that has now continued for the last three decades. The Ladies' Philoptochos Society, providing philanthropic assistance on the local and national levels, observed its own fortieth anniversary year. Under the presidency of Rodopi Smyrnioudis, the ladies' society hosted a dinner dance at the Blue Crest North in Pikesville, Maryland, on May 16, 1976, followed by a luncheon in the Cathedral social hall in October of that year.

Seventy years of community life had produced many organizations and activities. The parish council, under the leadership of Edward Jackovitz,

Feast Day of the Annunciation Vespers, March 24, 1976. Left to right: Rev. Elias C. Velonis, Rev. Michael Sekela, Rev. Ernest Arambiges and Rev. George Kalpaxis.

Left: Archbishop Iakovos at Great Vespers for the 70th Anniversary of the parish, March 27, 1976. Above: Archbishop Iakovos appeared on the cover of the April-May 1976 issue of the *Annunciation Herald*.

continued the progress of previous administrations. Records show that by 1976, over twenty committees were carrying out their respective duties at Annunciation. Among them were: Athenian Agora Steering; Stewardship Program; Special Property Acquisition; Community Site; Special Projects; Cemetery and Chapel; Foundation Fund; Building; Social Events; Youth Advisory; Young Adult; Golden Age; Sunday School; Greek School; Spiritual Renewal; Church Services (Ushers, Choir, Altar Boys); Beautification; Inter-Orthodox and Inter-Faith Committees, and others.

The diversity of interests and activities was reflected in the final events of the Seventieth Anniversary year. On September 11, 1976, all three of Baltimore's Greek Orthodox communities gathered for an evening of fellowship and ethnic dancing at the Eastwind Ballroom. Annunciation and St. Nicholas sponsored this event to benefit the newly established parish of St. Demetrios. The following month, on October 8, 1976, a testimonial dinner honoring Dr. Stephen K. Padussis was held with proceeds donated to the cemetery chapel fund project. The success of the event led to future testimonial fundraisers. Two days

later, on October 10, 1976, in a highly moving ceremony, Mr. John Green, the Cathedral sexton of African-American descent, was confirmed into the Orthodox faith during the Divine Liturgy with Mary B. Kiladis and Peter J. Prevas as his sponsors.

By this time, the music department had reestablished its programs featuring four choirs under the direction of Georgia Tangires. The Greek school also underwent restructuring. The class concept was replaced with levels of instruction which included a new adult conversational Greek course. The following month on November 21, 1976, the spotlight focused on two more dedicated volunteers. During an Archpastoral visit, Bishop Silas presented Sam Morekas with the Archdiocesan Layman's Award for nearly three decades of service to the choir. In addition, William Koutrelakos, who served as Sunday school director from 1965-1975, was awarded for twenty years of service to the Sunday school program at Annunciation.

After seventy years, Annunciation no longer stood apart from the greater community. It had evolved into a moving force in all aspects of religious and civic activities in the Baltimore region. One of Father Monios' first accomplishments upon his arrival had been the reopening of strong communications with the Russian Orthodox priests in the city. A result of this effort was the institution of the Annual Sunday of Orthodoxy Vesper Services, first held on February 27, 1977, at the St. Demetrios Greek Orthodox Church. The clergy participants included Fathers Monios and Velonis of Annunciation; Father George Kalpaxis of St. Nicholas; Father Ernest Arambiges of the host parish; Father Mark Odell of Holy Trinity Russian Orthodox Church; and Father Michael Sekela of St. Andrew Russian Orthodox Church.

Another example of this expanded role was the establishment of the Cooley's Anemia Foundation of Maryland. A cooperative spirit of harmony between leaders of the Greek and Italian communities led to the realization of this goal. By the summer of 1977, Father Monios was elected first president of this board, and a public screening program for thalassemia—a blood disorder that affects people of Mediterranean descent—was in operation by the fall season. Father Monios had also reached a personal milestone that same year. The parish recognized the twentieth anniversary of his ordination to the priesthood on Sunday,

John S. Green, the Cathedral Sexton, was confirmed into the Eastern Orthodox faith on October 10, 1976.

Cathedral Ushers and Clergy, 1977. Standing *l to r*: Stelios Hadjis, Xenophon Maglaras, William G. Coutros, George Spanos, Louis Sabracos, George Christopoulos, James Chilaris, Basil Markulis, George Panagakos, James Christopoulos, Edward Jackovitz, John Christopoulos. Seated *l to r*: Richard Kassolis, Michael DePetrillo, Arthur Thomas, Father Monios and Father Velonis.

January 30, 1977, with special presentations from various Cathedral organizations.

The social and cultural life of the Cathedral continued to flourish throughout 1977. For instance, the Ladies' Tea Guild sponsored a three-day art exhibit and sale. Nicholas Petrou was given a testimonial honoring over two decades of service to the parish. The Hellenic University Club hosted Harry Mark Petrakis, a distinguished Greek-American novelist, and Annunciation Cathedral welcomed Mama Stavritsa Zachariou, a noted Orthodox Missionary from Africa, to speak to the congregation on her fascinating experiences. The parish responded with over $1,000 in donations to her cause. Another notable event was the first Conference of the Federation of Greek Orthodox Choirs held November 12-13, 1977. Hosted by the Annunciation Cathedral and its two sister churches, twenty parishes from the diocese were represented with nearly 200 people participating in choral and organ workshops.

Organizations and personnel underwent further change that year. The Sunday school, with Father Velonis as spiritual advisor and Michael Fochios as director, was reorganized into several departments, allowing for a more progressive series of lessons at each grade level. Records show a staff of 35 people dedicating their time and energy toward the success of the program. During the summer months, Michael DePetrillo was employed on a temporary basis to assist with church-related duties. On July 3, 1977, he was received into the Orthodox faith through the sacrament of Holy Chrismation with Father Elias and Presbytera Mary Velonis as his sponsors. Mr. DePetrillo, a former Roman Catholic deacon, soon departed for his studies at the Holy Cross Seminary.

By the close of the 1970's, building priorities were set to meet the growing needs of the Cathedral. At the general assembly in November 1977, plans for the long-awaited cemetery chapel took form and were presented by George T. George and James Karayinopulos of the Cemetery Committee. This idea, first proposed in the 1950's, had now expanded to include a mausoleum. By the spring of 1978, final plans were approved and the project

Preston Street town houses as they appeared in the 1890's. These buildings would become the Annunciation Orthodox Center.

Father Monios (left) and Father Velonis (right) with Cleo BeLer who gifted 31 West Preston Street to the parish.

would be named the "Chapel of the Holy Resurrection." Vigorous fundraising drives were initiated and the Ad Hoc Committee sponsored its second testimonial to raise monies. On June 9, 1978, 1,200 people gathered at Martin's West to honor John Paterakis, President of the H & S Bakery, Inc. This event, under the chairmanship of Dr. Stephen K. Padussis, was attended by national, state, and local dignitaries and raised over $60,000 for the cemetery chapel project.

At the same time, property acquisition was on the parish agenda as many envisioned the future expansion of the Cathedral center. At a special general assembly meeting held on February 5, 1978, members voted to purchase three town houses across the street from the Cathedral—25, 27 and 29 West Preston Street. Previous dialogue between parishioner Tom Rafailides, a real estate agent, and Sidney Kaplan, owner of the properties, had set the plan into motion. Building fund monies were used as down payments and the parish assumed a mortgage for the balance. These purchases symbolized the beginning of a new era of growth for Annunciation.

Continuing the momentum, the parish was most fortunate to acquire two additional houses during these years. Through the generosity of Cleo BeLer, 31 West Preston Street was donated in memory of her husband, Peter. By March of 1979, the Ladies' Philoptochos Society, with Elizabeth Fiackos, President, donated its earlier acquisition, 33 West Preston Street, to the parish. The Annunciation Cathedral now owned five historic town houses designed by renowned Baltimore architect, John Appleton Wilson. Built in the early 1890's, these homes were owned by prominent city residents during an era when the Associate Reformed Church, a Protestant parish, occupied the Cathedral edifice.

The Property Development Committee, led by James N. Markakis, was charged with defining uses for these houses. Among the original ideas proposed were: the expansion of the parish library, the establishment of an archives to preserve the rich history of the community; a permanent social services office; a social hall for meetings and receptions; and a senior citizens center. From the start it was realized that much research, planning, and funding would be needed to allow for the best utilization of these deteriorated homes. A great help to the parish was its increased involvement in the Mid-Town Belvedere Redevelopment Association. Annunciation and other area institutions now joined together to enhance the surrounding neighborhood. It would not be until the early 1980's that this particular project would start to take form as the Annunciation Orthodox Center.

The Cathedral's expansion of events, activities and services was reflected by the pioneering projects that marked the period between 1978 and 1980. In March 1978, the Ladies' Tea Guild sponsored a colorful Ball de Masque with Eleni Venetoulis serving as Honorary Chairperson. The following month, on Sunday, April 9, 1978, the parish welcomed back Father Soterios Gouvellis to observe the thirtieth anniversary of his ordination that took place at Annunciation. That summer, the Annunciation and St. Nicholas parishes sponsored the first Inner Harbor Greek Festival at Rash Field

Parishioners enjoying the preparation of loukoumades at the Inner Harbor Greek Festival, 1978.
Left to right: Voula Sarantos, Loula Fantopoulos, Helen Sabracos and Antigone Hadjis.

from July 14-16, 1978. The parishes donated $5,000 from the proceeds to the City of Baltimore for the construction of the "Grecian Spirit," a longboat for the city's touring and promotions vessel named the *Pride of Baltimore*.

During these years, new committees were instituted at Annunciation. The Greek School Parent Teachers Organization was revitalized in September 1977 with Georgia Lambrinos as president. In 1978, the Religious Life Committee was established with Basil G. Markulis as first chairman. Its purpose was to define and meet the spiritual needs of the parish and to explore various aspects of church life. One of its earliest events was a lecture given in the spring of 1979 by The Very Rev. Kallistos Samaras who spoke on "Orthodox Spirituality in Everyday Life." By the summer of 1980, the first adult religious retreat was held in Sparks, Maryland. Soon after, the committee's survey of parishioners led to the establishment of adult religious education classes.

Another progressive concept became reality in June 1978. The new Social Services Committee, with Vasso Rider as first chairperson, worked with the clergy in providing transportation for the elderly, translating for the non-English speaking parishioners, visiting those who could not travel, bringing them to church and hosting luncheons. The committee also established contacts with local police and fire officials in the event the services of a translator were needed to assist non-English speaking Greeks involved in emergencies. Under the spiritual guidance of Father Monios and Father Velonis, these groups set lofty goals showing their commitment to enhancing the needs of a diverse congregation.

With the town house restoration and cemetery chapel projects underway, a third priority was added to the Cathedral building program. In December 1978, a gift of $20,000 was received from Kalliope H. Pappas for the construction of a chapel in the Education Building. Mrs. Pappas, the first president of the Ladies' Philoptochos Society, donated the funding in memory of her husband, Harry G. Pappas, who was among the early founders of the parish. With the library ultimately moving into an expanded facility across the street, the space would be redesigned as a chapel allowing for weekday liturgical services, sacraments, and a quiet area within the Education Building for prayer and meditation. The Chapel Committee led by James Krometis was soon formulating plans for this noteworthy endeavor.

The many building projects, together with a number of other new projects, moved forward very rapidly in 1979. The Iconography Committee, along with the design firm of Rita St. Clair Associates, was busy planning the interior redecoration of the sanctuary to conform to a more Byzantine appearance. The Property Acquisition Committee was negotiating with city authorities for the acquisition of a nearby parking garage in the next block south on Maryland Avenue. The need for additional parking was even more imperative with the opening of the Meyerhoff Symphony Hall one block southwest of the Cathedral property.

Housing for the elderly also took the spotlight. January 1979 saw the establishment of Trinity Plaza, a non-profit corporation sponsored by the three Greek Orthodox parishes in order to provide affordable senior housing. First officers included Andrew Kalathas, President; Michael Karas, Vice President; Helen Johns, Secretary; and George Spanos, Treasurer. Though a site in the 900 block of Cathedral Street was found for a building, the technical and legal aspects of securing funding proved to be quite overwhelming. Considering these issues and the diminished support from parishioners, the senior housing project was abandoned. Two decades later, the project would become a reality as an AHEPA-sponsored initiative.

Father Constantine Monios (left) and Harry P. Pappas (right) with Kalliope H. Pappas, Chapel of Holy Wisdom donor.

Holy Friday procession of the *Epitaphios* (Tomb of Christ) led by Father Monios and Father Velonis, April 20, 1979.

Nicholas Ioannou (left) and Dennis Psoras (right) were among the parish councilmen who carried the Tomb of Christ, 1979.

There were other firsts for the Cathedral in 1979. A Pan-Orthodox Blood Assurance Program was established through Social Services. The first blood drive was held in April 1979 with over 100 people participating. Under this program, any member of the Greek Orthodox community of Baltimore could receive blood, provided at least 100 pints were donated annually by parishioners. The following month, the Cathedral took part in a citywide effort coordinated by the Baltimore Rotary Club. All major faiths collected food for distribution to the needy. Within a few years, the parish would establish its own similar philanthropic outreach programs.

Also during 1979, the Ladies' Tea Guild officially changed its name to the Women's Guild of Annunciation. Under the presidency of Carolyn M. Tsakalas, group members led by Beulah Georges made a formal proposal to the parish council for the opening of a second-hand shop. In August 1979, following approval, the Second Chance Thrift Shop opened on the lower level of the Education Building near the Maryland Avenue entrance. Staffed by guild members, this successful venture continues to sell items of clothing, jewelry, and other merchandise donated by parishioners with monies going toward the Guild's beautification projects to enhance the Cathedral.

The summer of 1979 also saw the formation of a parish youth group, initially called GALA (Greek Adult League of Annunciation), comprising young adults age eighteen and older who desired to create a common bond of fellowship based on their Orthodox traditions. First officers included: James Argyropoulos, President; Ted Stavrakis, Vice President; Amalia Monios, Secretary; and Ted Stathis, Treasurer. By the summer of 1983, through the support of the Archdiocesan Office of Youth Ministry, a national youth conference was held in Dallas, Texas. Annunciation sent a contingency to the event. At this conference, the Greek Orthodox Young Adult League (YAL) took form with chapters across the nation and continues to excel in offering contemporary religious and social activities for young adults.

Another new concept was the establishment of the Cathedral Archives. Angeline Polites, a professional historian and archivist, outlined her vision for Annunciation to organize a program for historical reference and the preservation of its ethnic heritage. Under her initial guidance, an Archives Committee, led by Chrysoula Ponticas, began the task of gathering, sorting, and preserving the records of Annunciation's rich history. With the 75th Anniversary of the parish only two years away, the project was timely. By 1985, Betty Jean Alevizatos was named the Cathedral Archivist and took on the responsibility of organizing, indexing, and preserving the parish's vast collection of documents and photographs.

At the end of the decade, the parish underwent a change in clergy. After four dedicated and productive years, Father Elias Velonis, the assistant priest, accepted a full-time position at the St. Luke's parish in East Longmeadow, Massachusetts. On Sunday, October 14, 1979, over 500 people gathered at the Lord Baltimore Hotel for a farewell reception to honor Father Velonis, Presbytera Mary Velonis and their two children. Following his departure, Mark B. Arey was appointed as the new assistant. Raised in the Episcopal tradition, he converted to Orthodoxy in 1977 and later received his Master of Divinity degree from the Holy Cross School of Theology. His fluency in the Greek language and knowledge of Orthodox traditions was most impressive.

Father Elias and Presbytera Mary Velonis and their two children born in Baltimore, Margo and Thomas, October 1979.

During the last weekend in October of 1979, the Annunciation congregation witnessed two special ceremonies in the Cathedral sanctuary. On Saturday, October 27, 1979, Mark B. Arey was ordained as a deacon. The next day, Sunday, October 28, 1979, he was ordained to the Holy Priesthood. His Grace, Bishop Gerasimos of Abydos, officiated at these ceremonies. Draped in priestly vestments, Father Arey heard the officiating hierarchy and the congregation proclaim him as *Axios!* (he is worthy). Father Mark and Presbytera Katherine Arey, and their infant daughter, Zoe, were welcomed at receptions held in their honor that weekend. The arrival of Father Arey at the close of the 1970's was also symbolic of the changing composition of the congregation.

There were many in the Annunciation community who had converted from other religious backgrounds and embraced the Orthodox faith. As a result, there was a very positive response to Father Arey's assignment to the Cathedral. Many parishioners, however, still found it difficult to worship in a language they did not fully understand. Though the parish still valued its Greek heritage, more members were American-born who preferred the use of English than Greek. Another changing trend was that inter-faith marriage had been on the rise throughout the 1960's and 1970's. In fact, by the time Father Monios arrived in 1975, the number of marriages between two people of the Orthodox faith had declined greatly according to statistics taken from parish registries.

With concern to fulfill the spiritual needs of the American-born Orthodox and the converts at Annunciation, Father Monios introduced linguistic reforms in 1979. During the Divine Liturgy, the choir began to increasingly sing hymns and responses to the priest's petitions in the English language. Through an established cooperative spirit between clergy and laity, the congregation accepted the reform without much opposition. Citing the book entitled *American Congregations*, Annunciation Cathedral "successfully avoided the bitter controversies" over language that dominated many Orthodox parishes during those years.

Reflecting on four years of service at the Cathedral, Father Monios shared his thoughts with parishioners at the close of 1979. "Orthodoxy is no longer a church of foreigners. It is no longer

Bishop Gerasimos of Abydos (right photo) officiated at the Ordination of Deacon Mark Arey to the Holy Priesthood and later tonsured altar servers (above), October 28, 1979.

a church with temporary roots. It is a living, thriving, growing, and vital church. The church of immigrants has grown and matured. It is time we take our true place in American life....In the absence of a Bishop of Maryland and a Diocesan center, we become the center of Orthodoxy in this city and state....Our Liturgical cycle must be rich and spiritually uplifting. Our Cathedral activities must be responsible and complete. Programs must be generated to make the Cathedral the center of life for people of all ages." His inspiring message was an indication of the quick pace ahead.

With the arrival of the 1980's, systematic and progressive actions were taken to complete four major building projects now on the parish agenda, namely: the Orthodox center, Cathedral chapel, parking facility, and cemetery chapel-mausoleum. An architectural study of the proposed Preston Street town house renovation was submitted, layouts prepared, and initial construction bids were solicited. Final plans for the Cathedral chapel project received council approval and the work began to convert the space using the plans formulated by Rita St. Clair and Ted L. Pearson, designers. Regarding the parking facility, the property at 1205-1223 Maryland Avenue was purchased from the city for $75,000 and a

The Rev. Mark B. Arey converted from the Episcopal tradition and served as the Assistant Priest from 1979-1982.

Father Mark Arey and Father Constantine Monios
at the Resurrection Services on the main portico, 1980.

contract for nearly $200,000 was drawn up for its conversion into 120 parking spaces for the Cathedral and surrounding neighborhood. Financed through an industrial bond from the City of Baltimore, work was soon in progress.

The cemetery chapel project also moved ahead with a groundbreaking service at the Greek Orthodox Cemetery on April 26, 1980, with Metropolitan Silas of the New Jersey Diocese officiating. Later that day, a testimonial dinner to benefit the Chapel building fund was given in honor of United States Senator Paul S. Sarbanes, a member of the congregation. President August A. Krometis praised the Ad Hoc Committee that raised over $82,000 for the chapel project. The committee consisted of John Paterakis, Dr. Stephen K. Padussis, Nicholas D. Karavedas, Peter Marudas, Tom Marudas, and Konstantine J. Prevas. Later that year, the parish general assembly approved the construction phase. The project, costing in excess of $350,000, was awarded to the Mark Engineering Company in March 1981. Soon, the work was underway and scheduled for completion the following year.

Paschal egg distribution. Front *l to r* : Father Constantine Monios, Louis Sabracos, Peter G. Coutros, George P. Panagakos, Evan A. Chriss. Back *l to r* : Dean Moralis, Anthony Bruno, James Christopoulos, Basil G. Markulis (partially hidden), 1979.

The new decade, though dominated by expansion, also saw attention placed on beautifying the sanctuary. The Iconography and Beautification Committee had focused its research on ways to enhance the spiritual aspects of worship. Earlier icons and fixtures of the church were in a Westernized style—often preferred by the immigrant parishes. At the general assembly meeting on November 23, 1980, Harry C. Maistros, committee chairman, outlined a comprehensive proposal for change. Adhering to strict Orthodox tradition complemented by an atmosphere of mystique, a thorough and all-inclusive master plan for the beautification of the Cathedral was presented. To minimize disruption to weekly services, the ambitious project would be conducted in phases over the next few years. The approval of the plans ultimately resulted in a complete renovation of the interior sanctuary and reflected the parish's greater appreciation of its Byzantine heritage.

In the early part of 1981, the Cathedral chapel project was completed. On Saturday, February 7, 1981, in a special dedication ceremony conducted by Fathers Monios and Arey, Kalliope H. Pappas witnessed her dream turn into reality. The new beautifully-furnished Chapel of the Holy Wisdom, located within the Education Building, was blessed and opened for the first time. A commemorative bronze plaque was installed at the entrance dedicating the chapel to the memory of her husband, Harry G. Pappas, who served as parish council president in 1924. Kalliope Pappas, age 86, a prominent woman from the early decades, left her legacy to the parish and passed away four months later during that historic year...1981 marked the 75th Anniversary of the Annunciation community.

Realizing the importance of such a celebration, a special 75th Anniversary Committee had been established to prepare the commemorative program. A series of religious services, banquets, concerts, films, lectures, and other cultural and social events were held throughout 1981. For many, it was a time to remember. For some, a time to learn. For all, a time to pay tribute to those founders and sustainers of the parish. The 75th Anniversary Committee consisted of Evan Alevizatos Chriss and Nicholas C. Lykos, General Co-Chairmen, with the following

Iconography and Beautification Committee, 1981. Front row left to right: Georgia Economou, Carolyn Tsakalas, Efrosene Maglaras, Alice Ioannou, Sebbie Svolos, Esther Samios, Nancy Karas, Anna Z. Pappas. Back row left to right: Andrew Lygoumenos, Father Constantine Monios, Father Mark Arey, Harry C. Maistros, Chairman; and George C. Maistros.

Chapel of Holy Wisdom Committee, 1980. Seated left to right: Loretta S. Prevas, Audrey Thomas, Kalliope H. Pappas, Anna Z. Pappas, Angela N. Krometis. Standing left to right: George H. Pappas, Steven Thomas, Father Mark Arey, Father Constantine Monios, James Krometis, Chairman; and Harry P. Pappas.

The Chapel of Holy Wisdom was dedicated by Kalliope H. Pappas in memory of her husband, Harry G. Pappas, in February 1981.

associate chairmen: James N. Markakis, Capital Fund Drive; Theodore J. George, Cultural Events; Charles G. Pefinis, Social Events; Anthony J. Cavas, 75th Anniversary Album; Father Constantine Monios, Religious Events; and Peter N. Marudas, Publicity.

The eight months of celebration began and concluded with special religious ceremonies. On Sunday, March 29, 1981, Metropolitan Silas officiated at the Hierarchical Divine Liturgy followed by a 75th Anniversary Inaugural Luncheon at the Hunt Valley Inn attended by 800 parishioners and guests. This event, under the chairmanship of Edward F. Jackovitz, featured wonderful highlights of parish history, organized by the Archives Committee, which traced the community's progress from its founding in 1906. Other commemorative events that year included: GOYA's Tribute to the Philoptochos Society on Mother's Day; GALA's Tribute to the Parish Council Presidents on Father's Day; special events for Fathers Gallos and Bouyoucas; the Diamond Jubilee Ball presented by the Women's Guild; and the Greek festival under the general chairmanship of Louis Sabracos.

To celebrate the conclusion of the anniversary year, Archbishop Iakovos came to Baltimore and officiated at an Ecumenical Doxology on Saturday, November 21st, and a Hierarchical Divine Liturgy on Sunday, November 22, 1981. Following church services, Archbishop Iakovos announced the Archons of the Ecumenical Throne—the highest honor bestowed upon laymen for outstanding service to the Church. Evan A. Chriss, Theodore J. George, and James N. Markakis already held this distinguished title. That day, Nicholas Lykos, John Paterakis, Peter J. Prevas, and Harry Tsakalos joined them and the entire congregation responded with enthusiasm. A lavish banquet at Martin's West that afternoon marked the conclusion of the celebration. Later, a 75th Anniversary Album, filled with numerous parish activities and photographs surrounding this commemorative milestone, was published and distributed to the congregation.

The historic events of 1981 were also chronicled in the well-known Cathedral publication entitled *The Annunciation Herald*—reorganized in the fall of 1980 with a new group of volunteers under the guidance of Stephanie Panos, Editor.

75th Anniversary Delegation at Baltimore City Hall, March 1981. Left to right: Peter Marudas, Marinos Svolos, Michael Zotos, August Krometis, Father Mark Arey, Evan A. Chriss, 75th Anniversary Co-Chairman; Metropolitan Silas, Father Constantine Monios, Parish Council President Thomas Gleason, Tom Marudas, and George Perdikakis.

The culmination of the 75th Anniversary began with an Ecumenical Doxology at Annunciation Cathedral. The choir, acolytes, and clerygmen from various denominations participated in the evening services, Saturday, November 21, 1981.

Commemorative ice sculpture, 75th Anniversary Banquet.

Nick Kutson and his daughter, Catherine, greet the Archbishop.

Archbishop Iakovos raises the cross and blesses the congregation during the 75th Anniversary Hierarchical Divine Liturgy.
He was assisted by Archdeacon Gerasimos Michaleas (holding candles signifying the Holy Trinity), Sunday, November 22, 1981.

The excitement of the 75th Anniversary was also enhanced with the news of a sizable donation giving a tremendous boost to Annunciation's building expansion. It was the most significant and inspiring example of stewardship in the history of the parish. Mr. and Mrs. John Paterakis and Mr. and Mrs. Harry Tsakalos donated a total of $585,000 to Annunciation Cathedral for three of its projects: the Annunciation Orthodox Center - $500,000; Chapel of the Holy Resurrection at the Greek Orthodox Cemetery - $50,000; and the interior beautification of the Cathedral - $35,000.

Soon after, on Sunday, March 8, 1981, a special general assembly approved the renovation of the five Preston Street town houses, located across the street from the Cathedral, at a total cost of $1.2 million of which $500,000 had been graciously donated. During the 75th Anniversary year, the decision was reached for the establishment of the Annunciation Orthodox Center. A fundraising committee, with James Markakis as chairman, began organizing a capital fund drive within the parish in order to secure the additional $700,000 needed to complete the project. By the close of 1981, the campaign had exceeded its goal by over

$30,000 through the generosity of many supporters. Within a few years, the dream would come to fruition.

In the years leading up to the 75th Anniversary, Father Constantine Monios envisioned a magnificent tribute to the founding fathers—a well-documented, carefully researched history of the parish. At the time, a 22-year-old parishioner, Nicholas M. Prevas, was in the midst of writing his family history and was knowledgeable as to the various archival sources available to properly document immigrant history. With the guidance and support of Father Monios, Nicholas Prevas accepted the challenging task and focused his efforts on writing the 75-year history of the parish.

After two years of research and writing, *History of the Greek Orthodox Cathedral of the Annunciation* was published in the summer of 1982. Through the financial support of Peter T. Prevas, along with parishioners and family sponsors, Annunciation's history book became a reality. The 300-page volume soon received Archdiocesan recognition as one of the first complete histories of any Greek Orthodox parish in the United States. In October 1982, the parish council, under the leadership of Marinos T. Svolos, recognized this milestone achievement and officially named Nicholas M. Prevas as "Parish Historian" of the Cathedral.

The Monios Family, 1981. Front row left to right: Michael, Reverend Constantine M. Monios, Presbytera Mary Monios, and Harry. Standing left to right: Amalia, Nikki, and Athena.

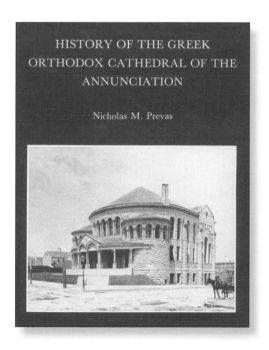

Annunciation Cathedral's 75-year history was published by Nicholas M. Prevas in August 1982.

The Cathedral Parking Garage opened on April 11, 1982. Left to right: Rev. Constantine Monios, Rev. Mark Arey, Parking Garage Chairman Harry P. Pappas, Senator Paul S. Sarbanes, and Parish Council President Marinos Svolos.

In addition to a literary work, a musical production was also receiving high praise. The Annunciation Cathedral Choir had produced a long-playing record album in May of 1981 entitled *Journey to Pascha*. Under the direction of Georgia Tangires, with Fotini Nichols as organist, nearly thirty talented parishioners took part in the recording of inspiring selections of the Easter season. Choir members were praised for their tireless effort in beautifying the liturgy and for perpetuating Byzantine music.

The accelerated pace of events was staggering, especially since Annunciation's designation as a Cathedral. Two capital improvement projects were completed in 1982. In February of that year, the parking garage facility was completed. A ribbon-cutting ceremony was held on Palm Sunday, April 11, 1982, with Senator Paul Sarbanes participating. The spring of 1982 was also a time of transition in the clergy. After a three-year tenure as assistant

pastor, Father Mark Arey bid farewell to the Annunciation community as he prepared for his first full-time parish assignment in Orange, Connecticut. On May 23, 1982, at a farewell reception honoring Father Mark, Presbytera Katherine, and Zoe Arey, various groups and committees expressed their appreciation to this outstanding and impressive clergyman with generous gifts of remembrance.

The following week, the long-awaited Chapel of the Holy Resurrection was completed to the point where a special blessing ceremony was planned. The Cemetery Committee that continued to move the project toward ultimate completion included: Constantine N. Kutson, Chairman; James Karayinopulos, George T. George, Samuel Karavedas, Joanne Deitz, and Nora Caloyianis. Officiating at the Memorial Day dedication ceremonies on Monday, May 31, 1982, were Father Ernest Arambiges of the St. Demetrios Church,

The Chapel of the Holy Resurrection at the Greek Orthodox Cemetery on Windsor Mill Road officially opened in May 1982.

The Rev. Louis J. Noplos, the longest-serving
Assistant Priest at Annunciation Cathedral, 1982-1996.

Father George Kalpaxis of the St. Nicholas Church, and Father Constantine Monios along with his new pastoral assistant, Deacon Louis Noplos, who had arrived in Baltimore earlier that week. The new deacon quickly became acquainted with the administrative functions and many diverse ministries at Annunciation. The following month in his hometown of Chicago, Illinois, Deacon Louis Noplos was ordained to the priesthood by Bishop Iakovos of Chicago at the Holy Cross Greek Orthodox Church on June 27, 1982.

By the summer of 1982, Father Louis and Presbytera Alice Noplos established themselves in Baltimore. Great learning opportunities were available to the new assistant priest under the guidance of the well-schooled senior pastor. Father Monios had recently celebrated the 25th Anniversary of his priesthood in January 1982, receiving special citations from the Governor, Mayor, and Baltimore City Council. The arrival of Father Noplos would mark the beginning of a new era of dedicated teamwork and continuity. During his tenure at Annunciation, Father and Presbytera Noplos would also celebrate the birth of their three children: Katrina in 1984; Dimitri in 1988; and Gregory in 1993. His assignment to the Annunciation Cathedral would span over fourteen years, creating an atmosphere of stability in which greater progress would be achieved.

During the early 1980's, new programs continued to be implemented. For instance, the installation of five ramps and railings to assist the handicapped entering and exiting the Cathedral was completed by August 1981. The project, costing over $5,700, was funded by The Pan-Karabournian Society. The club president, Mary L. Peters, and her dedicated members worked with Charles and Vasso Rider of the Social Services Committee to make this a reality. Later, the growing need for transportation for the elderly and handicapped parishioners led to interest in purchasing a van that could be equipped as a mini-bus. Donations from various parish organizations helped to fund the purchase. However, considering the geographic spread of parishioners throughout the region, the logistics of setting up a schedule to transport people to and from the Cathedral became impractical and the venture was abandoned.

March of 1982 saw the formal establishment of a "sister-city" relationship between Baltimore, Maryland, and Piraeus, Greece. Senator Paul S. Sarbanes, Mayor William Donald Schaefer and Thomas Marudas, Baltimore's Community Relations Director, organized a special ceremonial event held at the Walters Art Gallery emphasizing the cultural ties between Greece and the United States. As a result, "A Weekend in Piraeus" was chosen as the theme of the Greek Festival held at the Inner Harbor in July of that year with Dr. Frank Z. Thomas serving as general chairman.

Further cooperative spirit was evident as the American-Israeli Society honored Father Monios, selecting him as the goodwill ambassador to Jerusalem for 1982. During his pilgrimage to the Holy Land that spring, Patriarch Diodoros bestowed upon him the honor of Cross-bearer and Protector of the Holy Sepulchre. Following his return, Father Monios was again honored by the American-Israeli Society and Baltimore City officials at a luncheon on September 24, 1982. His enthusiasm to help improve the city and his parish neighborhood did not go unnoticed. A resolution from the Mayor and City Council proclaimed that day as "Reverend Constantine M. Monios Day" in Baltimore.

By the fall of 1982, the beautification program was producing stunning changes within the sanctuary. Various phases had been completed: installation of new icons, repainting of the walls, a

Lucy Hagopian, Cathedral Business Administrator, began her career at Annunciation in 1967.

Social Services Committee, chaired by Charles Rider (front row center), in the Cathedral courtyard, 1981.

Religious Life Committee, chaired by Basil G. Markulis (front row center), in the Cathedral courtyard, 1981.

new pulpit, a new cantor's stand, new carpeting and a new chandelier modeled after a similar fixture in the Byzantine-style Cathedral of Archangel Michael in Moscow. The Women's Guild contributed the funds for the impressive lighting fixture that featured a unique scroll concept of wrought iron and brass. Highly-respected interior designers, Rita St. Clair and Ted L. Pearson, had been hired as consultants to work with the Iconography Committee. Their research of Byzantine churches assisted in the preservation of the building's architectural beauty while remaining faithful to authentic Byzantine tradition.

During the entire process, George Maistros of the parish council, along with Anna Z. Pappas of the Iconography Committee, acted as liaisons between the designer and the contractor. Nicholas Ioannou served as the technical advisor and Father Monios provided valuable input on the religious aspects of the project. The committee oversaw the installation of seven major icons under the curved brick archways on each side of the altar. These holy images, dedicated by individuals

The impressive new chandelier installed in the sanctuary was funded by the Women's Guild of the Annunciation Cathedral.

and organizations, reinforced the new Byzantine look of the Cathedral interior. Later, new pew cushions were installed and six bronze relief medallions, crafted by Stephanie Scuris, were added to the pulpit depicting various religious symbols. More interior enhancements would be on the agenda later in the decade.

With other capital improvement projects nearing completion, the community shifted its focus to its most ambitious undertaking since the construction of the Education Building at the close of the 1950's. At the parish assembly meeting of November 14, 1982, final plans were approved for the construction of the Annunciation Orthodox Center. August A. Krometis of the Building Committee, along with President Marinos Svolos, explained the revised improvements to the design made by the architectural firm of Lapicki-Smith Associates. One notable change was the extension of the ballroom across the entire length of the center. Within a few months, the plans were turned over to the contracting firm of Peter J. Scarpulla. On Friday, March 25, 1983, the *Feast Day of the Annunciation*, a ceremonial blessing was held at the future site of the building. Construction work to transform five turn-of-the-century town houses into a multi-purpose center was about to begin and would span over the next eighteen months.

While the Greek community looked ahead, it maintained its appreciation for the past and often paid tribute to those whose services were exemplary. In keeping with this theme, a testimonial dinner to honor Constantine J. Pecunes was held on March 11, 1983. He had served as Parish Council President for a total of six terms during the years from 1941 to 1952—the longest tenure of anyone in parish history. The tribute was sponsored by the United Chios Society, an active regional society that also benefited greatly from his volunteer work.

The spring of 1983 saw great strides in the areas of outreach to the community at large. A committee headed by Loretta S. Prevas, a member of the parish council, initiated Project Philoxenia (Friends of Strangers). The Franciscan Center, located at 2212 Maryland Avenue, was chosen as the recipient of this philanthropy. The center, run by the Franciscan Sisters, provides hundreds of meals a day and offers counseling, emergency housing, a clothing bank and education programs.

Getting a backlift

These five gutted row houses on the corner of M...
Preston streets will become a church center for
Greek Orthodox Cathedral of the Annunciation.
were built in 1890, and the city required that the b...

Construction of the Annunciation Orthodox Center
(25-33 West Preston Street). The top photo shows
the preservation of the original front facades while
redesigning the interior space for a multi-purpose
parish center. The back view (inset) is taken from
Maryland Avenue and shows the Greek Orthodox
Cathedral of the Annunciation in the background.

On a quarterly basis, the Cathedral collects donations to assist the homeless serviced by the center. Similarly, parishioners embraced Project Zestasia (Warmth) when it took form in 1986, spearheaded by parishioner Melody Simmons. This project has successfully collected hundreds of boxes of clothing which are distributed to those less fortunate living within the city. These endeavors show the expansion of philanthropic work as the Cathedral strives to play a viable role within its established city neighborhood.

By the summer of 1983, the construction of the Annunciation Orthodox Center was well underway and the future looked optimistic. The events following a Friday evening youth group meeting, however, became a stark reminder of the harsh realities of modern society. On Friday, July 1, 1983,

without provocation, two young men walking on Maryland Avenue turned and shot seven bullets into a small parish group conversing outside the Cathedral. Father Louis Noplos was wounded in the leg, George Maistros was wounded in the hand and both legs, and Stelios Hadjis suffered the worst. With injuries in the arm, leg and abdominal area, his recovery period was the longest of the three victims.

Shock, disbelief, and fear overwhelmed the congregation following this near-tragic incident. Father Monios and the parish council moved quickly to disseminate accurate information to parishioners filled with great anxiety about the future. The participation of Father Louis Noplos at the liturgical service two days later sent a strong message to the parish—criminals would not frighten them from the neighborhood. Needless to say, the shooting of the assistant priest and two parishioners received local news coverage as well as a national editorial in the *Orthodox Observer.*

With the parish commitment to further build up its downtown center, it was fortunate the incident was isolated and never repeated. The parish council established a Safety and Security Committee that implemented more stringent security measures both inside and outside of the Cathedral complex. Improved lighting, mirrors in parking garages, crime prevention training sessions, and communication of evening events with police were among the new programs. Another safety measure was the installation of an intercom system later that year which was funded with a $5,000 gift from the Women's Guild.

With parishioners strongly advised to use common sense precaution when arriving and departing from the Cathedral, the events throughout the remainder of 1983 were held as scheduled. The weekend of July 8-10, 1983, resulted in another highly successful Greek Festival at the Rash Field in Baltimore's Inner Harbor. On July 17, 1983, Constandinos A. Pavlakos, a

Baltimore native, was ordained to the Holy Diaconate during the Divine Liturgy with Metropolitan Silas officiating. Deacon Pavlakos, who had married parishioner Pauline Hayes, was in his final year at the Holy Cross Seminary. The following year, on June 3, 1984, Deacon Pavlakos was ordained to the Holy Priesthood by Metropolitan Silas at the Annunciation Church in North Miami, Florida. At the Annunciation Cathedral in Baltimore, Father Monios expressed his personal pride announcing the news of the ordination. "We pray that this young man, raised in the altar of our Cathedral, will have a long and blessed ministry."

By the spring of 1984, the once-shabby block of town houses across from the Cathedral was slowly taking form into the new parish center. The Metropolitan of the Diocese had the unique opportunity to see the work in progress during this period. The Annunciation Cathedral successfully sponsored the District Clergy-Laity Congress from May 4-6, 1984, presided over by Bishop Silas and well-attended by clergy and parish leaders from throughout the region. As a result of the meeting, an extensive report, outlining numerous issues of concern dealing with the church and its role in modern society, was approved and submitted to the Archdiocese for further study.

Other events of 1984 showed the continued involvement in diverse programs. For instance, The Women's Guild sponsored a Masked Ball chaired by Litsa Weil at the Belvedere Hotel to raise funds for the restoration of the original 95-year-old Tiffany windows. The Cooley's Anemia

The Ordination of Constandinos A. Pavlakos to the Holy Diaconate took place on July 17, 1983.

The St. Demetrios Greek Orthodox Church at 2504 Cub Hill Road opened on August 26, 1984.

Scenes from the Women's Guild Masked Ball.
Above: James N. Pappas and Anastazia Karas.
Left: Litsa Weil and Mary Pillas, March 3, 1984.

Foundation sponsored its third annual dinner-dance to raise monies for screening and treating this blood disorder. On Sunday, March 11, 1984, the seventh annual Sunday of Orthodoxy services were hosted by the parish of St. Andrew Russian Orthodox Church. During this period, the St. Demetrios Greek Orthodox Church reached another milestone in its history. A sanctuary was built and formally opened for worship services on August 26, 1984. For the convenience of its growing congregation, the St. Demetrios Church also established its own cemetery on church property.

At Annunciation, church-affiliated groups continued their sponsorship of yearly traditions in 1984. For instance, keeping up its fine record of providing financial assistance, the Philoptochos Society awarded numerous scholarships to worthy students. The Golden Age Club again honored all parish fathers with special tributes to those 80 years and older. The Cathedral Greek School students

presented their annual program at the close of the school year. The members of the Junior GOYA youth group participated in a three-day outing to Ocean City, Maryland, that summer. The roster of active organizations and their diverse activities was most impressive.

Tributes to noteworthy individuals were again on the parish agenda. The Ad Hoc Committee, under the chairmanship of John Paterakis, honored Mayor William Donald Schaefer at a gathering of nearly 1,400 people at Martin's West on June 8, 1984. Recognizing the mayor's tremendous support for Annunciation's building project, the formal reception room on the first floor of the new Center would later be dedicated to him and to the memory of his parents. This event alone raised $125,000 for the Annunciation Orthodox Center and there was great anticipation as the project neared completion. The formal dedication ceremony was now less than four months away.

On Saturday, September 22, 1984, hundreds of people gathered on Preston Street to witness the dedication and blessing ceremony for the Annunciation Orthodox Center (AOC). With a backdrop of colorful flags, banners, and blue skies above, Archbishop Iakovos led the services assisted by Archdeacon Gerasimos Michaleas. Participating clergy included: Fathers Constantine Monios, Louis Noplos, George Kalpaxis, Ernest Arambiges, George Gallos, Peter Chrisafidis, Myron Manzuk, Costas Sitaras, Thomas Heath, and Stamatios Zahariou. Among the speakers who addressed the crowd were: United States Senator Paul Sarbanes; Mayor William Donald Schaefer; George Papoulias, Ambassador of Greece; George Spanos, Parish Council President; and August A. Krometis, the Annunciation Orthodox Center Building Committee Chairman. A reception and tour of the new Center was held after the special ceremony.

The following day, Archbishop Iakovos officiated at the Divine Liturgy followed by a Dedication Luncheon in the elegant ballroom of the AOC. Special acknowledgement was given to the Paterakis and Tsakalos families for their outstanding financial contribution and also to James Markakis, Building Fund Committee Chairperson; Anna Z. Pappas, Interior Design Committee Chairperson; George Perdikakis, Cathedral liaison to Scarpulla Contractors; and others for their efforts in bringing the project to completion. Father Monios reflected that the new Center would allow the parish to "expand ongoing programs, to begin new programs, and to better meet the social needs of the community."

During the establishment of the AOC facility, a number of other supporters also made substantial donations toward the construction and furnishing of the building. They included the James Hamilos and James Markakis families; Mr. and Mrs. John Copanos; Mr. Hercules Barberis; Mr. and Mrs. Terry Barberis; Mr. and Mrs. Konstantine J. Prevas; Mr. and Mrs. George Sfakianoudis; Mr. and Mrs. Evan Alevizatos Chriss; Mr. and Mrs. Harry Karvounis; Mr. Alex Kotarides; and Dr. and Mrs. Stephen K. Padussis. In addition, the Golden Age Club provided furnishings for their designated room and the Greek Ladies' Philoptochos Society provided furnishings for the Social Services office.

Dedication ceremonies for the Annunciation Orthodox Center were held on September 22, 1984. The establishment of this multi-purpose parish facility provided a significant boost to the revitalization of the Mt. Vernon Cultural District.

The Paterakis and Tsakalos families were "Founders" of the Annunciation Orthodox Center.
Antonia and John Paterakis are shown with Archbishop Iakovos on Dedication Day.

Archbishop Iakovos at the Annunciation Orthodox Center ribbon-cutting
ceremony with "Founders" Liberty and Harry Tsakalos, September 22, 1984.

A new and exciting era began with the dedication of the Annunciation Orthodox Center in the fall of 1984. The first major event to allow the general public to see the finished building was the "Athenian Agora" festival held in early October of that year. The acclaim was instant. Even the local newspapers applauded the Annunciation Cathedral for taking the bold initiative to revitalize and make good use of the buildings which greatly enhanced the appearance of the neighborhood. Within the first year of operation, the scope of activities at the AOC quickly took form.

A Cultural Events Committee was organized to promote usage of the AOC and broaden the range of cultural and educational events. Under the chairmanship of Dr. Corinna Courpas, the committee began featuring notable authors, musical performances, lectures, cultural presentations, art exhibitions, and other events to enrich parish life. Proceeds from event admissions were used to purchase furnishings throughout the Center. Many of these events have been held in the elegant second- and third-floor ballroom/banquet area. The Cathedral's new ballroom, able to accommodate social functions for nearly 300 people, was described as the "crowning jewel" of the AOC. For

over twenty years, a lease agreement with the well-known Martin's Catering firm provided the parish with a steady rental income from events held at "Martin's Preston Room" (AOC Ballroom).

As envisioned, the first floor of the AOC became the new home of the Theodore J. George Library. The multi-lingual collection of books, magazines, and other educational material resulted from three decades of acquisitions by Mr. George and other book enthusiasts. Catalogued, indexed, and presented in a professional setting, it has been acclaimed as one of the most comprehensive parish libraries in the entire Archdiocese. The Golden Age Room, a formal reception room, and office space for Social Services are also part of the first-floor area. The beautiful lobby is complemented by two large oak display cases donated in memory of Constantine J. Pecunes. Antique furnishings, donated by Mrs. Frances Haussner of Haussner's famous restaurant/museum, enhance the overall appearance of the setting. The Cathedral Archives, initially part of the first-floor library area, was later given its own expanded space on the fourth floor. Special temperature and humidity controls allow for better preservation of historical documents.

Philoptochos Society Directors, 1985. Seated *l to r* : Father Monios, Amanda Pappas, Loula Fantopoulos, President; Vasso Rider, Eli Roussos, Father Noplos. Standing *l to r* : Georgia Demos, Zena Hayes, Helen Maschas, Betty Andreadakis, Joyce Melonas, Voula Sarantos, Georgia Zissimos, Virginia Avgerinos, Estelle Tselepis, Elizabeth Fiackos, Sevasti Ricas.

The first summer camp sponsored by the Chesapeake Youth Council was held at Camp Glyndon, August 1985.

The establishment of the Annunciation Orthodox Center was not without its difficulties and challenges. In fact, the present building was the result of a redesign in architecture. After fundraising was underway during the summer of 1981, the initial architect reported that the rehabilitation "could not proceed as planned because of soil conditions under the existing buildings." The existing foundations would simply not support the new structure. This setback ultimately resulted in a redesign by a new architectural firm. With more flexibility in the layout of the interior spaces, the new parish center ultimately encompassed the use of all five buildings through interior demolition and exterior preservation of the original late 19th century facades.

The necessary changes in design ultimately increased the construction cost from the estimated $1.2 million to $1.6 million. During the fall of 1985, the first anniversary of the building's dedication, a new fundraising effort was initiated with the goal of securing an additional $500,000. The chairmen of the "Pay the Debt" Campaign were Evan Alevizatos Chriss and Marinos Svolos. With the cooperation of numerous division leaders and team captains, the solicitation of funds began

allowing parishioners to make pledge payments over a three-year period. The response to the campaign was overwhelming. Just as the generation before had focused energies on the Education Building, the community now rallied to fulfill this major challenge. The Annunciation Orthodox Center stood as a symbol of unlimited potential with ample physical space for new programs into the next century. Ultimately, the success of the AOC would depend on volunteer commitment and funding to maintain a variety of programs.

At a special reception that marked the tenth anniversary of the Cathedral's Stewardship Program, benefactors and sponsors were honored on Sunday, January 22, 1985. Annunciation was one of the first parishes in the Archdiocese to replace the dues system with a stewardship program. Larry Burgan, 1984 Stewardship Chairman, prepared a ten-year analysis of the successful program that had reached a quarter of a million dollars per year by 1984. For 1985, Committee Chairman Theodore Venetoulis announced the ambitious goal of $300,000. Meeting the yearly parish budget through stewardship reflected the greater level of parishioner satisfaction and commitment to numerous Cathedral ministries.

By early 1985, the Chesapeake Youth Council (CYC) was gaining momentum under the strong guidance of Father Louis Noplos. Volunteers worked to coordinate a cooperative program of church-related activities for the youth of the area Orthodox parishes. CYC members involved with the initial organizational efforts included: George C. Maistros, Melody Simmons, and Father Louis Noplos from Annunciation; John and Irene Voxakis from the St. Nicholas Greek Orthodox Church; and Violet Leventis and Dr. Andrew Vendelis from the St. Demetrios Greek Orthodox Church. In August of 1985, the first weeklong summer camp of the CYC was held at Camp Glyndon. Over 50 youngsters attended this first outing designed to strengthen the bond between the young people and the Church. CYC-sponsored activities, such as the very successful summer camp, have since flourished for over two decades.

Another noteworthy event occurred during the summer of 1985. Three years after his initial visit to Jerusalem, Father Constantine Monios organized the first pilgrimage for parishioners to visit the Holy Land and Constantinople. A group of eighty pilgrims departed for their journey on Saturday, June 15, 1985. During the trip, the faithful gathered in the River Jordan to be blessed by the Holy Waters, visited the Church of the Holy Sepulchre and other revered shrines, and met with Patriarch Diodoros of Jerusalem. While visiting Constantinople, the Cathedral pilgrimage was granted a private audience with Ecumenical Patriarch Dimitrios. They were the largest group to visit the Patriarchate that year. The highly-acclaimed trip would lead to future journeys as Father Monios desired to increase parishioner appreciation for their Orthodox heritage while they

Visitors to the Holy Land at the Cathedral of the Resurrection which adjoins the Holy Sepulchre in Jerusalem.

saw firsthand the places and shrines referenced in liturgical readings and services.

Later that summer, a national choir school was held at Annunciation during the week of August 10, 1985, under the direction of Father George and Presbytera Anna Gallos, and Choir Director Georgia Tangires. Musicians attended sessions on composition, vocal methods, Byzantine theory and other music-related topics. Combining its dedication to church music with outreach activities, Annunciation then hosted the first annual choral concert of the Central Maryland Ecumenical Council on November 25, 1985. The Cathedral became affiliated with this organization to continue fostering improved relations with other religious groups. Georgia Tangires later reflected that 200 singing voices filled the Cathedral during a "magnificent soul-stirring performance."

Continuing the beautification work started earlier in the decade, Mrs. Alexandria Maistros and her family took the spotlight on Sunday, August 25, 1985. That day, the new "Platytera" icon was formally dedicated. In August 1944, the Maistros family had donated the Icon of the Virgin Mary for the rear wall of the altar and now, four decades later, they gifted the Cathedral with a more fitting Byzantine-style image. Created by Iconographer George Papastamatiou, the wall-sized icon, depicting the open arms of the Theotokos and Christ Child reaching out to worshipers, rises above the *iconostasion* adding to the peaceful beauty of the sanctuary. In a special blessing ceremony, this icon was dedicated to the memory of George and Angela Maistros, Haralambos and Maria Cardiges, and Constantine G. Maistros, who had played an active role in church affairs for many years.

The Cathedral pilgrimage was also the largest single group to visit the Ecumenical Patriarch of Constantinople in 1985.

With the growing number of activities and committees, one of the least-discussed, but most important volunteer group, was the Board of Auditors. This Board is responsible to ensure that the parish's financial transactions are carried out accurately, funds are used for the purpose intended, and that all record-keeping is properly maintained. As an independent group, the auditors report directly to the parish assembly. By 1985, the Board of Auditors, under the chairmanship of C. James Condax, had recommended computerization for more efficient handling of billings, stewardship, and administrative tasks performed by the church office.

As the year 1985 came to a close, Father Monios completed ten years of service as Cathedral Dean. On Sunday, November 3, 1985, he was the guest of honor at a luncheon held in the AOC Ballroom. Father Louis Noplos organized the celebration and served as toastmaster. A portrait of Father Monios was unveiled that day and later added to the gallery of clergymen whose portraits adorned the hallway outside the Cathedral office. The portrait was a gift of love and appreciation. In just one decade, his accomplishments to enhance parish life were being praised on both the local and national level.

So much had transpired…and so much more was on the horizon as the Annunciation Cathedral approached its eightieth anniversary year. Father Monios conveyed a unique enthusiasm for spiritual and educational progress that was unprecedented. His assistant, Father Louis Noplos, was maturing in his priestly duties, managing the growing demands of youth and Sunday school programs, and proving to be a great asset in all aspects of Cathedral life. As the mother church of Orthodoxy in the region, Annunciation was playing a larger role in religious and civic affairs. It was a strong indication that greater levels of accomplishment would be evident in the upcoming decade of parish history.

In keeping with the Byzantine style of all renovations, a new "Platytera" icon was installed by the summer of 1985.

Opposite Page: The magnificent "Platytera" icon was created by Iconographer George Papastamatiou and donated by Alexandria Cardiges Maistros in memory of her husband, Constantine, and their parents.

1986-1995

In the spring of 1986, the Annunciation Cathedral had reached its eightieth year as a religious community. One changing trend among its volunteers was noteworthy. Since the mid-1970's, an increasing number of women had begun to assume greater administrative responsibilities and were serving on the parish council. The election of the first woman as parish council president occurred in 1986 when Loretta S. Prevas graciously accepted this leadership role. In an 80th Anniversary year message, she stated that the parish was serving the spiritual needs of "American-born Greek Orthodox Christians, as well as mixed married couples (Orthodox to non-Orthodox), families of diverse ethnic and religious backgrounds, and recent immigrants from Greece."

Clergy and parish leaders were aware of the challenges and growth opportunities available with such a diverse congregation. Under the guidance of Parish Council Presidents Loretta Prevas in 1986, Larry Burgan in 1987, and Charles Constantine from 1988-1989, the various religious, educational, and social committees at the Annunciation Cathedral worked to enhance existing programs while adding a number of newer projects to the growing list of ministries. Records show that volunteers and organizations were at impressively high numbers during this period.

The roster of parish ministries during 1986 included groups such as: The Greek Ladies' Philoptochos Society, Loula Fantopoulos, President; Greek Language School, Dr. Sidney Krome, Principal; Sunday School, George Rogers, Director; Music Department, Georgia Tangires, Director; Women's Guild, Alice Ioannou, President; Parent-Teacher Organization, Kerry Agathoklis, President; YAL (Young Adult League), Thomas Boardman, President; GOYA (Greek Orthodox Youth of America), Eleni Stamatakis, President; Golden Age

Holy Cross Seminary graduate Thomas Constantine, 1982.

Club, Anthea DeMedis, President; Annunciation Library, Theodore J. George, Librarian; Children's Choir, Elizabeth Rostek and Deanna Sakellaris, Directors; and the Social Services Committee, Charles Rider, Chairman.

By this time, Father Constantine Monios proudly announced that another Annunciation parishioner had joined the ranks of the priesthood. Thomas Constantine had graduated from the Holy Cross Seminary in 1982 and later married Vasiliki Vlahoyiannis on January 16, 1983. Father Monios and his assistant priests of that era—Father Elias Velonis, Father Mark Arey, and Father Louis Noplos—conducted the wedding ceremony. Then, on Saturday, November 2, 1985, Thomas Constantine was ordained to the Holy Diaconate by Metropolitan Silas at the Annunciation Cathedral. The following year, on July 6, 1986, Deacon Thomas Constantine was ordained to the Holy Priesthood at the Sts. Constantine and Helen Greek Orthodox Cathedral located in Richmond, Virginia.

Parish Council, 1986. Seated left to right: Larry Burgan, Rev. Constantine Monios, Loretta Prevas, President; Rev. Louis Noplos and Irene Michallas. Standing left to right: Dr. Pete N. Nickolas, Charles Constantine, Alex Zades, Cornelia Rogers, Anna Z. Pappas, Constantine Courpas and August Krometis.

The Greek Ladies' Philoptochos Society also took the spotlight in 1986 as it observed the fiftieth anniversary of its founding in Baltimore. On Saturday, November 1, 1986, the anniversary banquet and grand ball were held at the Omni Hotel. The next day, Metropolitan Silas officiated at the Divine Liturgy followed by a luncheon at the Annunciation Orthodox Center (AOC) Ballroom. Cornelia C. Rogers, General Chairperson for the Golden Jubilee events, reflected on fifty years of philanthropic service in her commemorative message. "The Philoptochos Society helped a struggling Greek population adapt to life in America while maintaining the Greek Orthodox faith and traditions. As friends of those in need, the society's benevolent contributions were always made in a manner that assured a person's dignity." A 50th Anniversary Album, under the chairmanship of Karolyn Krial, was published to mark the occasion.

Tessea Carman, Vasiliki Vlangas and Penelope Psoras
in the Golden Age Room at the AOC, circa 1986.

Over the years, as the parish took on responsibilities beyond the local level, the mission of the Philoptochos Society evolved. For instance, during World War II, the ladies worked in hospitals, rolled bandages, contributed to the Red Cross, worked tirelessly for the Greek War Relief, and supported other worthy causes. Later examples include generous financial aid to St. Basil Academy, the Holy Cross Seminary, and the Patriarchate of Constantinople, as well as missionary and disaster relief work on the national and international levels. The fifty-year celebration was a great tribute to the generosity shown by those who served the Greek Orthodox community of Baltimore under the banner of the Philoptochos Society.

Left to right: Rev. Louis Noplos, Rev. Elias Velonis, Rev. Constantine Monios and Rev. Mark Arey officiated
at the wedding of Holy Cross Seminarian Thomas Constantine to Vasiliki Vlahoyiannis on January 16, 1983.

The year 1986 also marked the tenth anniversary of the Golden Age Club. Parishioners who served as club presidents during its first decade included Theodore Canaras, Steve Kaludis, Dr. Andrew T. Cavacos, James Chilaris, and Anthea DeMedis. In addition to sponsoring trips and other events, Golden Age Club projects have included donations to the Cathedral choir, assisting the Cathedral library, an annual St. Photios Shrine benefit, and fundraising drives for various national Orthodox organizations.

Another group that continued to develop was the Social Services Committee. It was soon apparent that referrals from hospitals, nursing homes, and other city agencies required a full-time social worker. Through the determined support of Father Monios, the Greek Orthodox Counseling and Social Services (GOCSS) soon evolved to meet the challenge of serving the needs of Greek-Americans who were often reluctant to seek assistance due to their independent nature. Initially, an office was set up in the AOC and soon after, Stelios Spiliadis was the first professional employed by the group to

focus on care for the elderly and recent immigrants attempting to adjust to American society.

The GOCSS Board of Directors, under the leadership of Stephen J. Sfekas in 1986, outlined three levels of service: individual therapy; family therapy; and case management (health services and economic assistance). The goal was to link Greek-Americans with appropriate agencies that could effectively deal with the problems they faced. By the spring of 1988, GOCSS sponsored a conference offering human services professionals a chance to learn about the social and cultural aspects of Greek-American families. Father Monios explained his vision for the project: "What I attempted to create within the Cathedral parish…is a true reflection of the scope of the Church as it flourished during the long and productive period of its life in Byzantium. The Church was the spiritual center but it was also the center of education, philanthropy, and healing."

Cultural and religious activities were also on the agenda. From June through August 1986, the prestigious Walters Art Gallery, through the efforts of Assistant Director Dr. Gary Vikan, featured an

GOCSS Conference, 1988. Seated left to right: George Spanos, GOCSS President; Father Louis Noplos, Katerina Polichroniadis, Case Manager; Dr. John T. Chirban, Father Constantine Monios, Stelios Spiliadis, Social Worker; Dr. Stamatios Sinis. Standing left to right: William Koutrelakos, The Honorable John N. Prevas, Michael Zotos, Mary Ann Constantinides, and Stephen Sfekas.

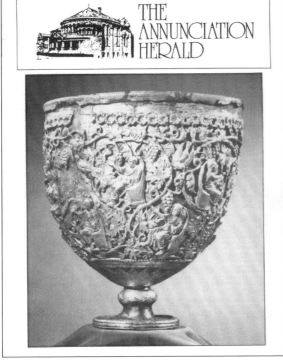

The *Annunciation Herald* of June 1986 featured
Byzantine artifacts displayed at the Walters Art Gallery.

Father Louis Noplos conducting worship services.

exhibition entitled "Silver Treasure from Early Byzantium." Father Monios, a great admirer of Byzantine art, served as an advisor to the art gallery. The Walters event was highly successful and would lead to future cooperative efforts with the Greek community. Two months later, on October 17, 1986, the Cultural Events Committee hosted the Baltimore Mandolin Orchestra in a benefit concert at the AOC. Parishioner Mary Hamilos Markakis, a member of the famed musical ensemble, served as assistant conductor.

Monthly communications show that the Annunciation Cathedral hosted a number of special activities and visitors that year. During the summer, parishioners were given the opportunity to view an extraordinary film documenting life at the Monastery of St. Catherine on Mt. Sinai. On September 21, 1986, famous Orthodox Missionary Mama Stavritsa Zachariou made a return visit to the Cathedral and received donations toward her church building project in Zaire, Africa. Two months later, the Cathedral was visited by the Foreign Minister of Greece, Karolos Papoulias, and a reception was given in his honor at the AOC on November 21, 1986. The 80th Anniversary year

also saw parishioners join together in fellowship at lectures, picnic outings, concerts, and other church-sponsored socials.

The youth programs had strong support and continued their activities throughout this period under the spiritual guidance of Father Louis Noplos who reported that the Chesapeake Youth Council had "implemented programs to perpetuate the parent/child relationship to its fullest." The 1986 summer camp numbered over 100 children participating in a well-organized schedule of events. With a focus on family, the GOYA also planned events for both parents and children. The following year saw the annual basketball tournament along with the St. John Chrysostom Oratorical Festival. Coordinated by Father Noplos, this diocese-level competition encouraged young adults to express themselves by delivering speeches about their faith, their Church, and their heritage. Metropolitan Silas of New Jersey, who was in attendance, praised this scholarly youth program.

The highlight event of 1986 was the 15th Annual Athenian Agora held in October. A team of dedicated volunteers, under the chairmanship of Irene Michallas, planned and presented a memorable festival for hundreds of visitors throughout the region; the event raised thousands of dollars to fund the Cathedral's varied projects. Soon after, the Annunciation community was also in the citywide spotlight at the Chesapeake Region Red Cross Blood Services Recognition Dinner. The Social Services Committee had sponsored blood drives for parishioners since 1979, assisting the Red Cross to fulfill its mission in the community. On December 2, 1986, Charles and Vasso Rider accepted the "Outstanding Donor Group Chairmen" award from the Red Cross on behalf of the parish. Cathedral programs were truly flourishing as Annunciation reflected on eighty years of Orthodoxy in Maryland.

The spring of 1987 marked another milestone in parish history—the 50th anniversary of the move from the old church on Homewood Avenue to the Preston Street church. The historic move had taken place on Friday, April 23, 1937. In 1987, the *Annunciation Herald* featured an article by Angeline Polites entitled "Moving—and Moving On." It provided an interesting perspective on the occasion marking a half-century of parish life on Preston Street. As part of this milestone observance, His Excellency Metropolitan Silas and The Very Rev.

Germanos Stavropoulos, Chancellor of the Diocese, visited the Cathedral on Sunday, April 5, 1987, to bestow recognition on the individuals who served as parish council presidents during this fifty-year period. A commemorative luncheon concluded the celebration.

That same week marked the Clergy-Laity Congress of the Diocese of New Jersey under the chairmanship of Evan A. Chriss. Clergy and lay delegates from thirty-five parishes met at the Annunciation Orthodox Center from April 5-7, 1987. Led by Metropolitan Silas, the weekend program was coordinated by Fathers Monios and Noplos. Those in attendance marveled at the completion of the parish's Orthodox Center and its capacity to host diocese-level events.

A few months later, the Annunciation Orthodox Center was again in the spotlight with the blessing and dedication of the Cathedral Library and Archives on Sunday, August 30, 1987. Furnishings for the Theodore J. George Library were funded by a gift from John Copanos in memory of his parents. Furnishings for the Cathedral Archives were funded by a bequest of $37,000 from the estate of Louis A. Doukas in memory of his parents, Theodore J. and Pota Doukas. In 1911, Theodore J. Doukas had served as the fifth council president of the Annunciation community. Two commemorative plaques were dedicated on

Left to right: Doreen Pecunes, Demetra Georgitsos, Nicolette Chios, Maria Georgitsos, Pauline Houliaras and Stacie Morekas entertained visitors in the Cathedral courtyard, Annual Greek Festival, 1985.

Library and Archives Staff, 1987. Seated left to right: Elizabeth Monocrusos, Gigi Conomos, Chrysoula Ponticas, Crossie George, Betty Jean Alevizatos, Cathedral Archivist. Standing left to right: Lenna Macintire, Alexandria Maistros, George Mesologites, George T. George, Father Constantine Monios, August Conomos, Theodore J. George, Parish Librarian; and Anna Z. Pappas.

August 30, 1987, and Parish Council President Larry Burgan thanked the families for their generous support. During this time period, the new icon of the Ascension, showing the resurrected Christ in wondrous glory, was added to the ceiling above the Holy Altar. This masterful creation of Iconographer George Papastamatiou was gifted to the parish by Dimitrios Coventaros.

Other innovative events were held during 1987. At Annunciation Cathedral, the spring and fall seasons that year included "Gyromania," the name for fun-filled evenings of dining on the popular "gyro" sandwiches while enjoying Greek musical entertainment. These events were organized through the assistance of the parish's Young Adult League under the direction of Geli Ioannou. Then, on Sunday, November 1, 1987, the AOC Cultural Events Committee presented a musical evening at Goucher College featuring Spiro Malas and Mary Malas Aiello. The following week on November 7, 1987, the Golden Harvest Auction Gala was held in the AOC Ballroom chaired by Tula Stamas.

Proceeds of $18,000 from the evening were contributed to the Cathedral general fund.

The late 1980's were filled with other special anniversaries. The year 1988 marked the 50th Anniversary of the Cathedral's consecration. Archbishop Athenagoras had officiated at the dedicatory service in the spring of 1938. Reflecting on that historic event, Father Monios noted that the Archbishop's diplomacy, patience, and complete self-denial were traits that impressed all who knew him. During his tenure as spiritual leader of the Archdiocese (1931-1948), Archbishop Athenagoras elevated the status and prestige of Eastern Orthodoxy as an integral religion in America. Elected as Ecumenical Patriarch in 1948, he served as the world leader of Orthodox Christians until his death on July 7, 1972. To commemorate the 50th Anniversary of the church's historic consecration, Father Constantine Monios offered special memorial prayers for the late Ecumenical Patriarch Athenagoras of Constantinople.

During 1988, members of the community made a pilgrimage to the St. Basil Academy in New York, personally delivering gifts to the needy children. On January 15, 1988, the Philoptochos Society, the Daughters of Penelope, and the Sunday school sent representatives on this goodwill mission. Fifteen parishioners, led by Dean Moralis, visited youngsters who cherished these small gifts of affection. The Archdiocese related its pride with Annunciation's commitment to its ministries. Later that year, with growing concern over the shortage of Orthodox clergymen in America, the Archdiocese proudly looked again to Annunciation. Bishop Silas was invited to the Cathedral to officiate at the ordination of parishioner Angelo C. Pappas to the Holy Diaconate on July 10, 1988.

The spring of 1988 saw many of the traditional events unfold. As *Pascha* (Easter) approached, the Social Services Committee hosted its yearly luncheon for "shut-in" members and friends. Volunteers gathered in fellowship to prepare palm crosses for distribution to the faithful on Palm Sunday. The following month, GOYA hosted its annual Mother's Day Luncheon. Within weeks, high school graduates received awards and token gifts of encouragement for their future. The annual Greek school closing exercises brought special recognition to Presbytera Mary Monios for over a decade of teaching students in the Cathedral

Greek school program. Koula Savvakis, PTO President, and Nicholas Kutson, Greek School Principal, made the presentations to the graduating class of 1988.

The parish also continued its outreach activities during the eighth decade. On April 30, 1988, the Cooley's Anemia Foundation sponsored its tenth annual dinner dance to benefit medical research, screening, and education regarding this genetic blood disorder affecting people of Mediterranean heritage. Father Constantine Monios served as Master of Ceremonies and Socrates Koutsoutis was named the Foundation's new president. Annunciation Cathedral also maintained its prominent role in the Central Maryland Ecumenical Council. The council, which began as the Baltimore Federation of Churches in 1919, was supported by contributions from local churches and governed by a Board of Directors comprising lay people and clergy from Orthodox, Roman Catholic, and Protestant traditions. In 1988, Rev. Louis Noplos and Loretta S. Prevas represented the Greek Orthodox Church.

That summer, the Greek community was in the city spotlight when the exhibition entitled *Holy Image, Holy Space: Icons and Frescoes from Greece* began its American tour in Baltimore at the Walters Art Gallery in August 1988. An Icon Exhibition Committee, representing members of all the Orthodox churches of Baltimore, raised over $40,000 to cover costs of the event. Greek diplomats, state and local officials, Orthodox

Nicholas Kutson, Principal, and Anastasia Primikirios, Teacher, with students of the Greek school program, 1988.

Cooley's Anemia Foundation Board of Directors, 1986-1988. Left to right: Evan A. Chriss, George P. Smith, Soula Lambropoulos, Philip A. Doccolo, Barbara Tucci, Norma Averza, Anita Lombardi-Reiley, Father Constantine Monios, Jackie Leone, H. Berton McCauley, Samuel Karavedas, Socrates Koutsoutis, Mary Torrieri, Joseph Giordano, Pat Panaggio.

Parish Council, 1988. Seated left to right: Rev. Constantine Monios, August Krometis, Charles Constantine, President; Dr. Pete N. Nickolas, Thomas Boardman, Rev. Louis Noplos. Standing left to right: Spyros Stavrakas, Irene Michallas, Anna Z. Pappas, Andrew J. A. Chriss, Cornelia Rogers, Larry Burgan, Dr. Constantine Chilimindris, Melody Simmons, Larry Vakoutis, Loretta S. Prevas and Andreas Savvakis.

This 1910 postcard of the Cathedral building was featured in *The Annunciation Herald*, October 1989.

clergymen throughout the region, and hundreds of visitors gathered to view what was described in *The Annunciation Herald* publication as "the most important collection of Byzantine icons ever to cross the Atlantic."

In the week prior to the Walters exhibition, Annunciation Cathedral paused to honor the millennium celebration of Russian Orthodoxy (988-1988). To mark this historic occasion, the parish hosted Russian Orthodox Vespers on August 16, 1988. Metropolitan Methody of the Moscow Patriarchate officiated at the service assisted by Bishop Clement, Patriarchal Vicar of the Russian Orthodox Church in the United States. Local Orthodox clergymen also participated in the service and the Annunciation Cathedral was filled with worshippers from their respective parishes.

Continuing the Russian Orthodox millennium theme, the Cultural Events Committee coordinated an exhibit in the AOC during the fall of 1988 featuring Russian icons. The display was a cooperative effort between the six Baltimore Orthodox communities—Annunciation, Saint Andrew, Saint Demetrios, Holy Trinity, Nativity of the Theotokos, and Saint Nicholas. Members of

these parishes graciously provided exquisite icons. Several parishioners even took part in a pilgrimage to the Soviet Union, coordinated by St. Vladimir's Academy in New York, which focused on visiting Orthodox churches and historic monasteries of that country.

As the 1980's drew to a close, another historic milestone was reached in 1989—the centenary of the Cathedral building itself. Constructed in 1889, the historic edifice had reached 100 years of existence. Informative articles on the building's architect, Charles E. Cassell, as well as a detailed analysis of architectural features with illustrations were published in *The Annunciation Herald* by Editor Stephanie Panos Link and her husband, Lawrence J. Link, Jr., an architect by profession. Their well-researched work to preserve the history of the building would be a lasting tribute to Mr. Cassell who was commissioned in the late 19th century to design the sanctuary for the original parish of the Associate Reformed Church.

To further commemorate the building's centenary, another phase of restoration and beautification took place during the spring of 1989. The work included roofing, guttering, and the

The original 1889 Tiffany stained glass window depicting the "Sermon on the Mount."

plastering and repainting of the sanctuary walls and ceiling. In addition, the crown moulding was repaired and gilded with soft and malleable 22-karat gold. A colorfully painted ceiling medallion bordered with gold leaf scrolling was added above the chandelier. Similar ornate scrollwork was installed around the perimeter of the ceiling. Improvement to the lighting in key areas of the sanctuary, such as the altar, solea, and choir loft, enhanced the recent addition of rich, authentic Byzantine-period color schemes.

In general, the beautification work complemented the original massive triple arches in front of the sanctuary, the carved oak woodwork, and the brilliant stained-glass windows—four of which are original textured glass from 1889 created by the Louis Comfort Tiffany Glass and Decorating Company of New York. The most impressive of the four original Tiffany windows is the circular stained glass depiction of the "Sermon on the Mount." The other three Tiffany windows grace the west wall of the sanctuary. The entire renovation project, spanning the decade of the 1980's, provided a dramatic and inspiring effect. After visiting the Cathedral, The Reverend George Papaioannou, a noted author and Orthodox scholar, later praised the restoration work in the publication entitled *American Congregations.* He stated in part, "The ethereal setting lends much to the worship experience" for parishioners at Annunciation.

The circular sanctuary with its curved arches and theatre-style seating originally featured a vaulted ceiling.

This view from the balcony shows the many Byzantine renovations of the Annunciation Cathedral.

By 1989, the Second Chance Shop was in its tenth year of operation. A report showed that about $10,000 from customer sales each year was being donated to the general operating fund of the parish. The chairperson for 1989, Esther Kokinos, commented on the shop's high level of success thanks to the diligent work of countless volunteers. A recent refurbishing of the shop, allowing for better display of items, also enhanced the operation. In the spirit of Christian love, the Second Chance Shop fulfills its role to the larger community through generous contributions of merchandise from parishioners.

As the summer approached, parishioners were saddened by the death of a 20-year employee. John Stanley Green, age 79, the faithful caretaker for the parish, passed away on June 18, 1989. He was well-known and loved for his kind mannerism. Mr. Green, who resided in a town house across from the Cathedral, was affectionately known as the "Mayor of Preston Street." On June 21, 1989, John Green was laid to rest in the Greek Orthodox Cemetery. Other changes occurred in personnel during those years. Manuel J. Burdusi was employed as the Office Assistant for a nine-month period between 1987-1988 following his graduation from the Holy Cross School of Theology. On March 12, 1989, he was ordained a Deacon at his home parish of St. Nicholas in East Baltimore. The following month on April 16, 1989, he was ordained to the Holy Priesthood by Metropolitan Silas at the St. Thomas Greek Orthodox Church in Cherry Hill, New Jersey. The Rev. Manuel J. Burdusi was then assigned to the St. Nicholas parish to assist Father George Kalpaxis who was nearing retirement.

Interior view of the Chapel of the Holy Resurrection at the Greek Orthodox Cemetery.
The chapel dome (inset) features the powerful image of Christ as the Pantocrator, the Ruler of all.

Cathedral *Psaltes* (Cantors) left to right: Emmanuel Smyrnioudis, Sotirios Mangos and John Avramidis, circa 1991.

At the Greek Orthodox Cemetery, the Chapel of the Holy Resurrection underwent its first phase of iconography during the summer of 1989. A notable icon of Christ Pantocrator surrounded by angels soon filled the upper dome area. The twelve Apostles and four Evangelists were added in the lower area of the dome, donated in memory or in honor of parishioners. To further beautify the space, the *iconostasion* (altar screen) and holy furnishings were soon added to the chapel. Over the decades, Annunciation Cathedral was fortunate to have numerous volunteers working on the Cemetery Committee. Some of the parishioners involved with cemetery-related projects and issues throughout the 1970's and 1980's included: George T. George, Nicholas D. Karavedas, Samuel H. Karavedas, James Karayinopulos, Constantine Kutson, and Andrew Lygoumenos, and others.

Unique events were also on the agenda at the close of the 1980's. The Hellenic Golf Invitational was initiated in 1988 through the efforts of Andy Georgelakos, Paul Cocoros, Gus Diakoulas, and others, and continues to the present. The idea originated from golf enthusiasts representing the three Greek Orthodox parishes of Baltimore. Their annual Invitational Tournament brings golfers together in fellowship and good sportsmanship to raise money for specific church-related projects. For nearly two decades, their results have been consistently impressive.

In the summer of 1989, the Cathedral hosted the National Forum of Greek Orthodox Church Musicians for a series of workshops exclusively for organists. Topics included technical instruction involving pipe and electronic organs, the piano, and various lectures on Byzantine music. The success of the workshop would lead to similar future events. During that period, another achievement took place at the sister parish of St. Demetrios as it approached the twentieth anniversary of its founding. On Sunday, July 9, 1989, Metropolitan Silas officiated at the formal blessing and dedication ceremonies for the Chapel of St. Kyriaki located on the St. Demetrios Church grounds.

Having flourished and expanded in the 1980's, the Annunciation Cathedral accelerated its pace in the 1990's. The new decade began with the annual observance of the Feast Day of St. Basil the Great on January 1, 1990. The yearly *Vasilopita* Luncheon was sponsored two weeks later by the Philoptochos Society and organized by long-time members Angela Zades, Dorothy Demetrakis, and Cornelia Rogers. Father Monios and Father Noplos led the traditional singing of the Greek New Year's carol entitled *Ayios Vasilis Erhete* (St. Basil is coming). The parish priests were accompanied by their dedicated *psaltes* (cantors)—John Avramidis, Sotirios Mangos, and Emmanuel Smyrnioudis.

The summer of 1990 marked a most historic occasion for the Archdiocese, namely, the first-time visit to America of an Ecumenical Patriarch from Constantinople. The visit of Patriarch Dimitrios I coincided with the 30th Clergy-Laity Congress held in Washington, D.C., from July 8-12, 1990.

Ecumenical Patriarch Dimitrios I of Constantinople

Annunciation parishioners were among the 4,000 Orthodox faithful who attended the Patriarchal Divine Liturgy on Sunday, July 8, 1990. Cathedral delegates to the congress included Parish Council President August A. Krometis, Anna Z. Pappas, and Peter Marudas. Members of the Young Adult League and their spiritual advisor, Father Noplos, also took part in the Archdiocesan YAL conference that immediately preceded the Clergy-Laity Congress.

During that week in the nation's capital, Father Constantine Monios, one of eighteen priests on the Archdiocesan Presbyters' Council, received a private audience with Patriarch Dimitrios. Father Monios later reflected upon his notable visit. "The throne of Constantinople is, for all Orthodox Christians, a direct link from Apostolic times to the present. My own life and ministry have been refreshed and strengthened as I lived these moments in history." Later that year, Father Monios would make his own career history. On November 1, 1990, as the parish busily prepared for its annual

Women's Guild 35th Anniversary, June 1990. Seated *l to r* : Dr. Corinna Z. Courpas, President; Aphrodite S. Panos, Chrysanthe A. Pappas, Eleanor Grivakis, Litsa Weil. Standing *l to r* : Ceres Chriss, Esther Kokinos, Hrysoula Klicos, Helen Xintas, Cornelia Rogers, Julia Krometis, Mary Pillas, Bess Stamas, Carolyn Tsakalas, Helen Padussis and Anna Z. Pappas.

festival, Father Constantine Monios quietly observed his fifteenth year at Annunciation. With this achievement, he surpassed the record held by The Very Rev. Joakim Papachristou (1935-1950) as the priest with the longest tenure. Soon, Father Monios would receive numerous accolades for his key role in developing many progressive programs.

One of the strongest Cathedral ministries also marked a milestone that same year. The Women's Guild proudly celebrated its 35th Anniversary with a special reception and general meeting on June 14, 1990, at the home of Vice President Nancy Chilimindris. Then, on September 15, 1990, the Women's Guild held a gala costume ball, entitled "Return to Tara," inspired by the movie *Gone with the Wind*. This event, under the direction of Litsa Weil, raised $18,000 for the repair of the Cathedral courtyard. Under the presidency of Dr. Corinna Z. Courpas in 1990, the Guild proudly reflected on 35 years of devotion to its mission of raising funds to refurbish, renovate, and maintain the beauty of the Cathedral furnishings.

During the fall of 1990, attention was placed on the much-needed repairs to the Cathedral's parking garage now in its eighth year of operation.

Structural problems were brought to light at the parish assembly held in September of 1990. Yorgos Spiliotis assumed chairmanship of the garage repairs while the Finance Committee made arrangements to secure the payments for the $70,000-project. The work was soon accomplished and rental income from the garage tenant, the University of Baltimore, helped defray the costs. The repair and upkeep of facilities, especially when dealing with older building structures, would be a recurrent issue faced by Annunciation. Planning, funding, and carrying out these repairs in a timely manner, with minimal disruption to parish activities, would be challenging, to say the least.

Cultural and religious events were also met with enthusiasm and well-supported. For instance, in October 1990, a Byzantine Studies Conference was held at the Walters Art Gallery. The forum allowed anyone interested in Byzantine history to gather and share information. The AOC Cultural Events Committee presented the Greek *Karaghiozis* (puppetry) with the assistance of the Maryland State Arts Council and the Mayor's Advisory Committee on Art and Culture. Parishioners such as Corinna Courpas, Kerry Agathoklis, and Litsa Weil actively promoted the project. The Cathedral also extended

"Return to Tara," September 1990. Theodoros and Nora C. Vlahoyiannis, Drs. Anthony and Corinna Courpas, and Stamos Courpas.

its congratulations to the St. Andrew Orthodox Church celebrating the 50th Anniversary of its founding. On Saturday, November 10, 1990, Father Monios joined Father Myron Manzuk of the St. Andrew parish and other clergymen at special Vesper services to mark their golden anniversary.

The following year began with a visit from Philoptochos National President Dina Skouras Oldknow who was the honored guest at the Annual Vasilopita Luncheon on January 13, 1991. The national president, overseeing 450 chapters, encouraged more Orthodox women to take part in the exemplary work carried out by the Baltimore group. During this period, a new program was instituted throughout the Archdiocese. Each year during the month of February, one Sunday would be henceforth dedicated to renewing the spiritual relationship and baptismal vows between Godparents and their Godchildren. At Annunciation Cathedral, the event includes a special ceremony often followed by a parish luncheon sponsored by the Sunday school.

Throughout 1991, the Annunciation Cathedral was in the spotlight among prominent city parishes. In his report, Parish Council President Thomas Marudas outlined the spring agenda. For example, Father Monios was invited to preach a Lenten sermon at the Old St. Paul's Episcopal Church on March 20, 1991. The following month, on April 15, 1991, the Advertising and Professional Club of Baltimore honored Father Constantine Monios with a distinguished civic award for his ecumenical work in Baltimore City. Continuing its outreach program, a "Multi-Ethnic City" forum was held at the Annunciation Orthodox Center on May 1, 1991, in cooperation with the Citizens and Housing Association. The former Mayor of Baltimore, Thomas J. D'Alesandro III, served as moderator to explore how ethnic differences and similarities shape the educational, cultural, and political institutions within the city.

A few weeks later, the Central Maryland Ecumenical Council bestowed more recognition upon Annunciation's senior clergyman. The

Philoptochos Directors, 1990. Front left to right: Father Constantine Monios, Litsa Pakas, Angela Koutsoutis, Joyce Melonas, Freda Metaxas, Cornelia Rogers, President; Julia Krometis, Helen Maschas, Georgia Zissimos. Back left to right: Virginia Avgerinos, Loula Fantopoulos, Dorothy Demetrakis, Estelle Constantine, Stacey Mesologites, Gloria George, Angela Zades, Father Louis Noplos.

Portrait of The Rev. Constantine M. Monios, 1985.

The Rev. George Kalpaxis at the Cemetery Chapel.

Reverend Constantine Monios was selected as the 1991 recipient of their Ecumenical Leadership Award for outstanding work promoting interfaith understanding and cooperation. The award was presented at a special dinner on May 20, 1991.

During this time, the Philoptochos Society, as an expression of its admiration, established the annual Father Constantine Monios Scholarship to the Hellenic College/Holy Cross School of Theology in Brookline, Massachusetts. This noteworthy scholarship has helped various young men of the community pursue their educational journey and religious studies toward the goal of becoming a priest of the Greek Orthodox Church.

The year 1991 also marked the retirement of Rev. George Kalpaxis from the St. Nicholas Greek Orthodox Church after twenty years of excellent service to his parish and nearly fifty years as a Greek Orthodox clergyman. He was honored at a testimonial dinner on May 9, 1991, at Martin's Eastwind with hundreds of Orthodox faithful in attendance. Father Kalpaxis spoke with gratitude and pledged to continue serving the Church by remaining in Baltimore and assisting his brother priests. As his successor, The Reverend Manuel J. Burdusi

assumed the full-time position as spiritual leader of the St. Nicholas Church on Ponca Street in February of 1991. Through successful fundraising efforts, along with generous contributions and pledges from its growing congregation, the parish was able to acquire additional properties in the Highlandtown neighborhood for its expansion. Today, the thriving St. Nicholas Greek Orthodox Church boasts a membership of 850 families.

Rev. Louis Noplos with Deacon Angelo Pappas (left) who served Annunciation from 1988-1992. Seminarian Constantine "Dean" Moralis (right) began his theological studies in 1988 and by 1994 would become the Cathedral Lay Assistant. Photograph taken Easter season of 1991.

During the summer of 1991, the work at the Chapel of the Holy Resurrection within the cemetery was progressing. A listing of icons and furnishings for the chapel, including items still available to be pledged, was distributed to the faithful. The response was positive and soon the cemetery chapel was transformed with beautiful iconography and ecclesiastical furnishings to enhance the worship experience. During that summer, a Bible Study program was sponsored for parishioners and coordinated through the efforts of Deacon Angelo Pappas. The following year, he would be ordained to the priesthood at the Holy Cross Greek Orthodox School of Theology on March 25, 1992, by Bishop Methodios of Boston. Soon after, the Cathedral family bid farewell to Father Angelo and Presbytera Mary Pappas as they departed for their first parish assignment in Portsmouth, New Hampshire.

The fall of 1991 marked the 20th Anniversary of the Athenian Agora festival. John Gavrilis, Samuel Karavedas, and Theodore Stavrakis served as co-chairmen of the event held November 1-3, 1991. One of the festival highlights was the new *Evangelakia* Dance Troupe, spearheaded under the guidance of Nicki Sharkey. This group of enthusiastic teenage parishioners in vivid costumes entertained and pleased the crowds in attendance. Their success led to the formation of another dance troupe called the *Filakia*, directed by Dr. Savas Tsakiris, exclusively for parish children ages 9 to 12.

Evangelakia Dance Troupe, under the guidance of Nicki Sharkey, entertained audiences with their intricate routines, 1992.

More culture was spotlighted when the "Gold of Greece" exhibit opened at the Walters Art Gallery in late November 1991. The traveling exhibit featured over 200 examples of jewelry and ornamental objects spanning centuries of Hellenistic culture. For the Baltimore exhibit, Georgia and George P. Stamas coordinated a memorable gala that raised over $90,000. The following summer, *Gates of Mystery: The Art of Holy Russia* was the next exhibit at the Walters Art Gallery that received outstanding reviews by parishioners and the community-at-large.

The news of the death of Patriarch Dimitrios of Constantinople on October 2, 1991, quickly spread throughout the Orthodox Christian world. He had served as Ecumenical Patriarch for nearly three decades, having been elected to the Patriarchal Throne in 1972. The Annunciation Cathedral reverently paused to memorialize the spiritual leader who had visited America during the summer of 1990. As his successor, Bartholomaios I (Bartholomew I) was enthroned as the new Ecumenical Patriarch on November 2, 1991. He was a 1961 graduate of the Theological Academy in Halki, Turkey. By 1973, he was elevated in status to a Bishop and held the highest position in the Holy Synod. Before the close of the 1990's, Patriarch Bartholomew, the spiritual father of Orthodox Christians worldwide, would visit the Annunciation Cathedral on Preston Street in Baltimore—a religious event of great historic significance to the entire region.

The year 1992 began with a first-time social function that received immediate acclaim. On January 18, 1992, the Women's Guild presented "Taverna Night." This family-oriented event featuring Greek musical entertainment, delicious platters of Greek appetizers, and plenty of fellowship was a tremendous success and continues on a yearly basis in the elegant ballroom of the Annunciation Orthodox Center. In the prior month, the Adult Bible Study sponsored a New Year's Eve family gathering in the Cathedral Social Hall. Events such as these helped to perpetuate the strong sense of community offered to parishioners through church-affiliated organizations.

The months ahead were once again filled with memorable tributes. On February 16, 1992, Alex Zades was the guest of honor at the Stavrakas Scholarship Dinner sponsored by the Worthington

Ecumenical Patriarch Bartholomew I of Constantinople

Chapter of AHEPA. His services included two terms as parish council president with over twenty years on the board of directors; president of AHEPA; president of the Golden Age Club; Sunday school advisor; youth group advisor; and chairman of the Agora. Mr. Zades received awards for over four decades of volunteer service to the Greek community. A few months later, on June 24, 1992, the AHEPA sponsored a Testimonial and Awards Banquet featuring keynote speaker Spiro T. Agnew, former Vice President of the United States. Among the eleven scholarship recipients that evening was 25-year-old Constantine Moralis—the future Dean of the Annunciation Cathedral.

The spring and fall of 1992 marked a number of noteworthy anniversaries. Father Louis Noplos was honored at a luncheon reception on May 31, 1992, for reaching his 10th Anniversary as assistant priest. On behalf of the Cathedral family, Parish Council President Basil M. Pappas presented a portrait of Reverend Louis Noplos that was soon placed among the photograph gallery of clergymen. That fall, Lucy Hagopian, Cathedral Business Administrator, was formally recognized for 25 years of employment at the Cathedral office. At the

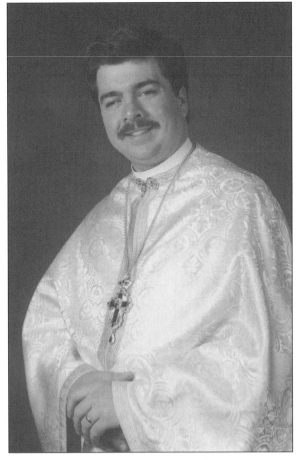

Portrait of The Rev. Louis J. Noplos, 1992.

Left to right: Rev. Constantine Monios, Nicholas J. Anderson, Argyroula Anderson, Presbytera Mary Monios, March 1988.

coffee hour held in her honor on September 13, 1992, parish organizations presented her with appreciation gifts and Father Monios spoke glowingly of her "cheerful, efficient, and dedicated service" to the Cathedral family.

Momentum continued when Annunciation honored its past priest, Father George Gallos, on the fiftieth anniversary of his ordination to the priesthood. The event was held on Church Music Sunday, October 11, 1992, during the annual conference of the Eastern Federation of Greek Orthodox Choirs. Over 100 voices sang at the Divine Liturgy and paid tribute to Father Gallos who served as the Federation's spiritual advisor for many years. Six years earlier, his support of liturgical music was also recognized when he received the distinguished St. Romanos Medallion from the National Forum of Greek Orthodox Church Musicians. Father George and Presbytera Anna Gallos, the parish's former choir director, were both honored at a reception planned by Theodore Dourakos and his wife, Constance, an active member of the Annunciation Choir.

That same month also saw Father Monios bestow special accolades upon retiring Greek school instructor Argyroula Anderson. Father Monios stated, "Please accept the greatest measure of our sincere gratitude for thirty years (1962-1992) of outstanding service to our Cathedral and our children as a dedicated teacher in our Greek Language Program." Continuing this trend, Head Usher Basil G. Markulis and the entire group of parish ushers were honored at a special appreciation coffee hour held on November 15, 1992. The ushers provide a valuable service by maintaining order and handling the quiet movement of parishioners in and out of the sanctuary during church services, particularly the overflowing crowds of worshippers who attend during Holy Week.

The year 1992 included a number of noteworthy youth accomplishments. The Parent Teacher Organization of the Greek School published a "Youth Yearbook" under the supervision of Vasi Lea Karas. The Chesapeake Youth Council sponsored a Tri-Parish GOYA Retreat from April 10-12, 1992, in Ocean City, Maryland. Eighty young adults, between 13 to 18 years of age, attended from the three Baltimore churches with Rev. Angelo Artemas, Archdiocesan Youth Director, leading the retreat. In July, members of GOYA and their advisors visited the famous Walt Disney World in Orlando, Florida. During the fall, the Young Adult Leagues of Annunciation, St. Nicholas, St. Demetrios, along with the Saints Constantine and Helen Church of Annapolis, sponsored the Diocese YAL Conference at the Hunt Valley Inn from October 16-18, 1992. Eleven clergymen and eleven seminarians, joined by Metropolitan Silas, welcomed participants from four area Orthodox parishes to this event.

In the midst of much activity, parishioners were given the opportunity to participate in another pilgrimage to the Holy Land. The 1992 pilgrimage was held the first two weeks in June and included visits to Cairo, Sinai, and Jerusalem. Over twenty-two faithful traveled as a group under the guidance of Father Monios. Among the trip highlights were visits to the pyramids, the Great Sphinx at Giza, the St. Catherine's Monastery at Mt. Sinai, and the Holy Sepulchre in Jerusalem. The Cathedral pilgrims each received their symbolic baptism in the River Jordan performed by Father Monios. Another religious excursion would be held the following year with a different itinerary.

By the fall of 1992, the parish council reported that further beautification work had been accomplished. The four sets of exterior doors, now over 100 years old, had undergone major refinishing and restoration thanks to a generous donation from the Women's Guild. Soon after, the two sets of interior doors underwent similar preservation work. Within six months, the Women's Guild focused its energies to repair, refinish, restore and re-cushion the three sections of pews in the sanctuary. During this period, the parish council also signed a contract to proceed with the creation of a major icon of the Resurrection of Christ for the west wall of the sanctuary, including six Great Hierarchs for the lower portion of the wall. Nikolaos Brisnovalis, a noted iconographer from Astoria, New York, was chosen for the task and preparations for this magnificent undertaking were soon underway.

It should be noted that in the spring of 1992, the Annunciation Cathedral formally received designation as a National Historic Landmark. The special plaque from Baltimore City's Commission on Historic and Architectural Preservation was installed on the building exterior near the far right set of entrance doors. By the fall season, the Cathedral was again in the national spotlight. The *Orthodox Observer* published a glowing article in November 1992 stating that Annunciation "provides its parishioners and the community-at-large with an array of programs, services, and activities." Even the renowned Handel Choir of Baltimore was invited that year for a presentation of "The Messiah." On December 19, 1992, the sanctuary was filled to capacity for this holiday tribute. Considering the varied events of 1992, the title of the article in the *Orthodox Observer*, "A Parish with Something for Everyone," was most appropriate.

Members of the Cathedral pilgrimage received their symbolic baptism in the River Jordan, June 1992. Left to right: Father Constantine Monios, Lenna Macintire, Anastasia August, Betty Jean Alevizatos, Soula Lambropoulos, James Krometis.

The Cathedral was designated a National Historic Landmark in 1992. Commemorative plaque enlarged on page 390.

By this time, the IOCC (International Orthodox Christian Charities) was established by the Standing Conference of Canonical Orthodox Bishops in the Americas (SCOBA) as the official humanitarian aid organization of Orthodox Christians. The mission of the IOCC is to assist the world's most vulnerable people: orphans, refugees and displaced persons, elderly, children, individuals with disabilities, hospitals and schools. A Baltimore chapter was initially established in December 1992 at 711 West 40th Street in the Rotunda. One of its first endeavors was to collect funds for the 1993 Lenten Appeal. Records show that the projects of the IOCC quickly received notable support from the Annunciation congregation.

The year 1993 began with a unique religious gathering in Baltimore. On January 10, 1993, local newspapers reported that "two thousand years of religious differences—but shared beliefs in justice and peace" came together yesterday as "Christian, Jewish, and Muslim clergy prayed for an end to the ethnic hostilities in the Balkans." *The Baltimore Sun* elaborated how prayer services began at Annunciation Cathedral with Metropolitan Silas and The Very Rev. Maximos Moses, Chancellor of the Greek Orthodox Diocese of New Jersey, participating. Afterwards, services were also held at a mosque, then at a synagogue, and ultimately concluded at the historic Basilica of the Assumption on Cathedral Street in Baltimore. Archbishop William H. Keeler, spiritual leader of the Roman Catholic Archdiocese of Baltimore, organized this notable event.

Later that month, the Cathedral hosted Bishop Kallistos Ware on the weekend of January 30-31, 1993. Bishop Kallistos is a well-known theologian, writer, and teacher. English-born into the Anglican faith as Timothy Ware, he converted to Orthodoxy

Bishop Kallistos Ware performed church services and conducted a lecture series for parishioners, January 1993.

in 1958 and was later ordained as a priest taking solemn monastic vows. Two of his books, *The Orthodox Way* and *The Orthodox Church*, have been acclaimed as definitive sources on Eastern Orthodox history and theology. He spoke at various events that weekend in which a number of seminarians from the Hellenic College participated. Among them was Baltimorean Constantine (Dean) Moralis who assisted with preparations for the Vesper services. Later that year, Dean Moralis conducted a series of seminars at the Cathedral to better acquaint parishioners with the meaning of Holy Week. The following year, he would be assigned as the Lay Assistant at his home parish of the Annunciation.

A full range of emotions marked the fall of 1993. The sanctuary was filled with joy during the annual observance of Church Music Sunday on October 3, 1993. That day, Fotini Nichols was honored for completing 25 years as choir organist. Later that month, the parish mourned the death of Emmanuel Smyrnioudis, age 78, who passed away

on October 14, 1993. He had served as *psalti* (cantor) for over twenty-five years. In 1985, he was elevated to the rank of *Protopsaltis* (First Cantor). As an expression of love to this dedicated man who faithfully served the parish, the Ladies' Philoptochos Society hosted the *makaria* (traditional Orthodox funeral luncheon) in his memory. Within a few years, Peter Constantinou and Stefanos G. Niktas would be added to the roster of talented cantors serving at the Annunciation Cathedral.

A special parish assembly in October 1993 authorized the start of construction to update and refurbish the kitchen facilities and the "Mentis Room" on the lower level of the Education Building. A Capital Fund Drive was then initiated to secure $250,000 in pledges in order to retire the debt incurred for these reconstruction projects. Harris J. George, Chairman of the Kitchen Committee, and Gary T. Padussis, Chairman of the Fundraising Committee, along with Basil M. Pappas, Parish Council President, would make numerous appeals to parishioners throughout the course of 1994 and 1995.

"Hotel Preston" at 35 West Preston Street was the first in a series of new property acquisitions for the parish, 1993.

The Philoptochos Society, the Women's Guild, and other organizations soon contributed generously toward the cause. Parish council minutes, however, show that support from parishioners through financial pledges toward the projects took much longer to receive than anticipated. By March of 1995, the parish council commenced with the kitchen project despite being $30,000 short of the pledge goal. The project was considered long overdue, especially with the acute need to improve the food service operation at the yearly parish festival. Funding for the project was eventually reached, but the lack of large-scale support was an indication of the financial challenges the parish would need to address.

A series of property acquisitions would also begin in the early 1990's to allow for the future expansion of physical facilities. A special parish assembly on August 3, 1992, authorized the parish council, under the leadership of Basil M. Pappas, to negotiate the purchase of 35 West Preston Street (known as Hotel Preston). Records show that by May 3, 1993, the parish had officially purchased this property adjacent to the Annunciation Orthodox Center. Soon, energy was focused on the next two town houses farther up the block owned by the Theatre Project. By the summer of 1994, parish leaders were involved in detailed negotiations with the property owners.

Needless to say, when the general assembly convened on November 14, 1994, there was much concern over the affordability of these crucial properties. That day, the congregation in attendance was most grateful when Father Monios reported the news that a generous donation of $40,000 was made by Peter and Georgia Angelos to acquire these historic buildings. As a result, the parish assembly was able to approve the purchase of 37 and 39 West Preston Street without incurring additional debt. The donation was made in loving memory of Georgia Angelos' grandfather, John Kousouris, who was one of the early stewards of the church. Future expansion now seemed within reach. Only two more townhouses, 41 and 43 West Preston Street, remained in that block and would be acquired by the parish later in the decade.

The completion of the Icon of the Resurrection, along with six icons depicting the Hierarchs of the Orthodox Church, was announced in January of 1994. The project, coordinated by the

The Icon of the Resurrection, along with Six Hierarchs of the Church and Archangel Michael (above the doorway), was created for the west wall of the sanctuary by Iconographer Nikolaos Brisnovalis. Dedication ceremonies were held on April 17, 1994.

Iconography and Beautification Committee under the chairmanship of Harry Maistros, resulted in an inspiring enhancement to the west wall. The Resurrection Icon, donated by the Laconian Association, shows Christ in his glorious Resurrection lifting Adam and Eve from the tomb. Other donations included the following: St. John Chrysostom (Marmaras and Kousouris families); St. Basil the Great (Drs. William and Susan Prevas and family); St. Gregory the Theologian (Nicholas and Argyroula Anderson); St. Nectarios (Peter T. Prevas); St. Nicholas (Tsakalas family); and St. Spyridon (Morekas family). The formal dedication ceremony was held on April 17, 1994. Soon after, the addition of recessed lighting would greatly enhance these breathtaking holy images.

The spring of 1994 was also a time to reflect and pay tribute to noteworthy ministries and volunteers. On April 10, 1994, the Preston Room

Father George Gallos was invited to Annunciation for the observance of his 50th anniversary as a priest, October 1992.

of the AOC was the site of a luncheon to recognize Theodore J. George and the parish library that began as an inspiration upon the discovery of books being discarded during the construction of the Education Building in the late 1950's. Coordinators for the 1994 event were Betty Jean Alevizatos and Elizabeth Monocrusos. Two noted authors, The Rev. Anthony Coniaris and Marilyn Rouvelas, were also invited as guest speakers. Theodore J. George proudly reflected on the growth of the library collection and acknowledged the many volunteers who assisted in keeping his dream alive. Within a few years, Mr. George would retire from his volunteer position, thus concluding his outstanding record of over four decades of service to the Cathedral community.

The following month, on May 21, 1994, Baltimore seminarian Constantine (Dean) Moralis, the son of Peter Moralis and Sarah Vrachalus Moralis, graduated from the Hellenic College/ Holy Cross School of Theology with a Master of Divinity Degree. Soon after, the Annunciation Cathedral employed Dean Moralis as its new Lay Assistant. Among his duties was the administering and enhancing of the parish youth programs and establishing campus ministries. Supervised by Fathers Monios and Noplos, Dean Moralis would gain valuable experience in parish administration to prepare for his future pastoral career. The results of his efforts were soon apparent.

By the summer of 1994, Cathedral children under seven years of age were invited to the first meeting of HOPE (Hellenic Orthodox Primary Enrichment). Youngsters between seven and twelve years of age were organized as the JOY (Junior Orthodox Youth). In addition, Dean Moralis would oversee the GOYA (Greek Orthodox Youth of America) for ages 13-17 and the YAL (Young Adult League) for those 18-35. The latter groups were successful in revitalizing their activities. Then, by September of 1994, the campus ministry program became operational. A number of educational institutions took part in the newly-formed OCF (Orthodox Christian Fellowship). Among them were Towson University, University of Maryland, and The Johns Hopkins University. In the spring of 1995, Loyola College was included in the new OCF ministry.

By this time, Father Monios announced with great pride that the Annunciation Cathedral had

Filakia Dance Troupe under the guidance of Dr. Savas Tsakiris. Left to right: Effie Panselinos, Jennifer Zizos, Eleni Makris, Nina Diemer, Angela Moniodis (background), Despina Moniodis, Dorothea Tsakiris, Elizabeth Arkuszeski, 1995.

been chosen as one of twelve parishes from various denominations to be recognized for its progressive programs. A chapter was devoted to the development of the Annunciation parish in a new book entitled *American Congregations*, published in 1994 by the University of Chicago Press. The Cultural Events Committee later announced that The Rev. George Papaioannou, who wrote the chapter, would speak at a lecture in the AOC on March 30, 1995. As the noted author of *The Odyssey of Hellenism in America* (1985) and other historical publications, Father Papaioannou served as priest at the St. George Greek Orthodox Church in Bethesda, Maryland, and was well-received by the audience in attendance that evening.

The year 1995 was also marked by a number of notable events. The *Evangelakia* and *Filakia*, popular dance troupes of the Annunciation Cathedral, took first place honors in the 5th Annual Greek Folk Dance Festival of the New Jersey Diocese held on January 21-22, 1995. The following month, hundreds of parishioners attended the Annual Cathedral Ball at Martin's Eastwind on February 25, 1995, and enjoyed a wonderful evening of fellowship with Greek and American dance music. The parish council expressed its sincere thanks to Mr. and Mrs. Louis Sabracos and their children, Demitra and Jeff Eagan, who were the chairpersons of the Cathedral Ball for over a decade with highly successful results.

Later, Charles "Skip" Stover would assume chairmanship of the parish's annual dance, carefully planning and promoting this social event.

At the general assembly held on March 20, 1995, Harry P. Pappas, chairman of the Parking Garage Committee, reported that lease agreements were in place to generate additional revenues for the Cathedral. One example was the $30,000-annual lease with MedChi (Medical Chirurgical Society) for use of the parking garage. The parking sticker program was then initiated to maintain a record of vehicles parked on Cathedral property. The parish assembly commended the Parking Garage Committee which also included August Krometis, Timothy Chriss and Theodore Vlahoyiannis.

Regarding the Annunciation Orthodox Center, Chairman Michael Mallis reported that new wall covering, carpeting, painting, and the repair and refinishing of the dance floor in the Preston Room had been completed. Renovations were paid from invested rental money received from Martin's Caterers for their use of the Preston Room. The Building Committee also reported on the feasibility of installing an elevator to access all three levels of the Cathedral and Education Building complex. With the cost projected in excess of $250,000, a motion was passed to form a committee to survey the parishioners to determine if an elevator was needed. Within five years, the project would become a reality.

Outdoor Midnight Resurrection Service on Holy Saturday, 1993.
Soula Lambropoulos (left) worshipping at the Easter Divine Liturgy.

Father Constantine Monios at the burial site of Patriarch
Athenagoras I at the Patriarchate in Constantinople, 1994.

Spiritual renewal was also afforded to parishioners in a variety of venues throughout the mid-1990's. Annunciation Cathedral welcomed Metropolitan Demetrios of Vresthena for his first visit to Baltimore the weekend of March 31, 1995. He was the keynote speaker at the first annual Lenten retreat sponsored by the Adult Bible Study Group on April 1, 1995. Well-known as a prolific author, the Metropolitan had served as a professor of Biblical Studies and Christian Origins at the Holy Cross Seminary. The following day, he conducted a Hierarchical Divine Liturgy and spoke at the luncheon given in his honor. The retreat program, coordinated through the efforts of Jeanne Tsakalos, would lead to similar well-attended and highly acclaimed retreats in future years.

With the success of the August 1994 pilgrimage to the Holy Land, which included an excursion to the Theological Seminary in Halki, plans were initiated for another trip. During the period from June 26 to July 10, 1995, visits were made to the historic cities of Rome and Constantinople—the two great centers of Christianity. In Rome, at a combined prayer service on June 29, 1995, parishioners had the inspiring opportunity to worship at St. Peter's Basilica in the presence of Pope John Paul II and Ecumenical Patriarch Bartholomew. Afterwards, the two great Churchmen blessed the multitudes in

Father Constantine Monios (left) and *Proskinitria* (Pilgrim) Rose A. Sitaras (right) received a private audience with Patriarch Diodoros I of Jerusalem during the Cathedral's pilgrimage to the Holy Land, August 1994.

Members of the Cathedral pilgrimage at the Church of "Hagia Sophia," July 1995. This magnificent edifice in Constantinople stands as the supreme architectural expression of Eastern Orthodox Christianity.

Cathedral Lay Assistant Dean Moralis (far right) with members of the Annunciation Cathedral
GOYA (Greek Orthodox Youth of America) and their advisors, Boston, Massachusetts, March 1995.

St. Peter's Square. Later, in Constantinople, the pilgrims visited the Patriarchal Center and the magnificent Cathedral of St. George. A highlight of the journey occurred when they received an inspiring hour-long audience with His All Holiness, Patriarch Bartholomew.

In the meantime, the parish's lay assistant, Dean Moralis, coordinated a group of enthusiastic young adults for the "Summer Byzantine Venture" sponsored by the Ionian Village. After nearly twenty years of operation, this Archdiocesan initiative has remained committed to serving the Orthodox youth and teaching them the religious and ethnic ideals of their rich Greek Orthodox heritage. On July 2, 1995, an energetic group of 14- to 16-year-olds, led by Dean Moralis, departed for a two-week trip to the Ionian Village Camp near Patras, Greece.

In the midst of these activities, the parish council, under the leadership of Paul Agathoklis, made a request for an unprecedented meeting. On May 8, 1995, a gathering of twenty past parish council presidents was asked to critique the activities of the Annunciation community, identifying strengths and weaknesses, and to make

recommendations to the parish council. The committee was under the chairmanship of Marinos Svolos. As the parish approached its ninetieth year as a religious community, the areas of concern were identified as follows: stewardship and finances; inter-faith marriages; increased usage of the English language; the need for a welcoming committee; and promoting the benefits of volunteerism. Their insightful report issued in October 1995 laid the groundwork for future enhancements and changes in parish operations.

The fall of 1995 was filled with a variety of unique activities. Through the efforts of the Catholic Archdiocese, Pope John Paul II visited Baltimore on October 8, 1995. *The Baltimore Sun* reported that the "most traveled Pope in history came to Baltimore, the birthplace of American Catholicism, and presided over a day of celebration, pageantry and prayer." The Pontiff received a jubilant welcome from thousands of people representing many faiths at the historic mass held at Oriole Park at Camden Yards. Entertainment was also provided by various ethnic dance troupes. The *Evangelakia* dancers led by Nicki Sharkey and Gus Letras represented the Annunciation Cathedral.

The following week, on October 15, 1995, the International Orthodox Christian Charities (IOCC) and all Orthodox churches in the Maryland and Washington, D.C., region sponsored a walk-a-thon. Nearly $6,000 was raised for the worldwide philanthropic work of the IOCC. Later that month, the consecration of the sister parish of St. Demetrios on Cub Hill Road was held during the weekend of October 28-29, 1995. Metropolitan Silas presided at the dedication services assisted by Rev. Ernest Arambiges of the St. Demetrios Church and numerous Orthodox clergymen. The solemn consecration ceremonies were followed by a dinner-dance celebration at the Sheraton Baltimore North in Towson, Maryland.

Toward the end of 1995, the Annunciation community mourned the death of its former pastor, The Rev. George P. Gallos, who had served in Baltimore from 1954-1965. At 80 years of age, he fell asleep in the Lord while serving the Holy Trinity Greek Orthodox community of St. Augustine, Florida. Throughout Annunciation's history, certain spiritual leaders have stood out for their progressive programs to enhance the religious and cultural aspects of church life. Father Gallos was among that distinctive group of clergymen. He had designated Baltimore as his final resting place and on

November 21, 1995, the Annunciation Cathedral was filled with respectful mourners as Metropolitan Silas of the Diocese of New Jersey officiated at his funeral service. The Reverend George P. Gallos was laid to rest in the Greek Orthodox Cemetery on Windsor Mill Road.

A few weeks later at the parish assembly held on December 4, 1995, a number of noteworthy items were discussed. Lay Assistant Dean Moralis outlined his various youth-related initiatives throughout 1995. This report was followed by Father Monios' announcement that the ordination of Dean Moralis to the Holy Diaconate would take place at Annunciation in the coming months. Parish Council President Paul Agathoklis commended numerous committees and noted that Dr. Stephen Padussis and Kathryn Belitsos had agreed to serve as co-chairpersons of the newly-formed Elevator Committee. In addition, Parish Council Secretary Annabelle Setren was praised for the detailed reports she provided the Cathedral office for publication in the monthly newsletters.

A more somber tone of the assembly, however, dealt with the financial position of the parish. Concern was voiced by some in attendance that the proposed budget for 1996 contained an

Greek School, 1993-1994. Faculty/Advisors included: Father Monios, Stephanie Vakoutis, Christos Motsiopoulos, Kaliopi Grund, Dr. Yula Ponticas, Michael Adam, Lena Efthimiou, Dimitra K. Poulos, Anastasia Primikirios, Nicholas Kutson and Father Noplos.

overly optimistic projection of stewardship funding. The assembly also reviewed a detailed inventory of Cathedral debts, including items such as roof repairs, garage repairs, property mortgages, and kitchen remodeling. Following review and revisions, the budget then reflected a deficit of $180,000. It was decided that special communications would be sent to parishioners in early 1996 explaining the budget deficit and asking the community to respond accordingly. Through determination and hard work, the financial situation confronting the parish would be effectively handled within a few years.

The activities of 1995 culminated with a grand event on Sunday, December 10, 1995—a testimonial banquet honoring The Reverend Constantine Monios and the celebration of his 20th anniversary as Dean of the Annunciation Cathedral. The Rev. Louis Noplos, Assistant Priest, and Dean Moralis, Lay Assistant, served as co-chairmen of the Planning Committee. Over a dozen parishioners served on the committee to ensure the success of the event. Months of planning and preparation resulted in a memorable tribute. Past Parish Council President Basil M. Pappas

served as toastmaster and Martin's West was filled to capacity with local dignitaries, family, friends, and parishioners from all area Orthodox churches.

That evening, well-deserved accolades were given to Father Constantine Monios to mark his 20-year pastorate at Annunciation. Among them were special citations presented on behalf of Patriarch Bartholomew, Archbishop Iakovos, Metropolitan Silas of New Jersey and William Cardinal Keeler of the Catholic Archdiocese. The outpouring of love was evident by the applause that filled the room as the senior-ranking Orthodox clergyman in Maryland proceeded to the podium. In his customary eloquent manner, Father Monios delivered his remarks and inspired listeners with his vision for the continued growth of Orthodoxy in the State of Maryland. It was apparent that the Annunciation Cathedral was striving for higher levels of religious, cultural, and philanthropic achievement. In three short months, the parish would reach another historic milestone…the 90th anniversary of its founding in Baltimore. The next decade, which would culminate with the celebration of the parish's centennial in 2006, was about to begin.

Father Constantine Monios enjoying a relaxing moment, 1996.

Opposite Page: A momentous event in parish history was the visit of Ecumenical Patriarch Bartholomew, the spiritual leader of Orthodox Christians worldwide. Over 1,000 people attended the Patriarchal Doxology held at the Annunciation Cathedral on October 23, 1997.

1996-2006

As the new parish council took its affirmation of office during the Ninetieth Anniversary year, the main topic of concern dealt with the financial status of the Cathedral. Over the next few years, council members, under the leadership of Gary T. Padussis, worked diligently with clergy, laity, and Cathedral organizations to improve the financial stability of the parish. Soon, the stewardship program was the focus of attention and parishioners responded through increased pledges and substantial donations. The administrative staff, led by Lucy Hagopian along with committee chairpersons, worked to devise cost-cutting initiatives. It was truly a concerted effort to reverse the budget deficit. In monthly newsletters, parish council updates also proved to be effective. Topics addressed by Father Monios, Parish Council President Gary T. Padussis, and Vice President Annabelle Setren increased awareness and the importance of Cathedral ministries.

During this period, building repairs requiring immediate attention also compounded the parish's financial concerns. Heavy snow from the blizzard in January of 1996 caused the decorative roof pediment to break off, fall into the courtyard, and damage the area beneath the main portico. Later, at the parish assembly of April 17, 1996, Harris J. George of the Insurance Committee was commended for working diligently to see that the insurance carrier reimbursed the Cathedral for the damages sustained during the winter snowstorm. In addition, the dome of the cemetery chapel had begun to leak causing damage to the iconography within the structure. The Building Committee, under the chairmanship of Lawrence J. Link, Jr., reported on these items in detail as well as other restoration work needed for the Cathedral exterior. As a result, the parish council wisely sought the advice of a structural engineer who provided an in-depth report identifying key areas

The Ordination of Constantine (Dean) Moralis to the Holy Diaconate took place on February 11, 1996.
Left to right: Metropolitan Silas of New Jersey (seated), Rev. Louis Noplos, Deacon Constantine Moralis, and
Rev. Constantine Monios. Four months later, Deacon Moralis was ordained to the Holy Priesthood at Annunciation.

Parish Council, 1996. Front row *l to r*: Father Monios, Father Noplos, Annabelle Setren, Vice President; Irene Michallas,
Betty Jean Alevizatos, Secretary; Esther Samios, Soula Lambropoulos, Gary T. Padussis, President. Back row *l to r*: Father Moralis,
Michael Bouloubassis, August A. Krometis, Treasurer; Theodore Stavrakis, John Gavrilis, Anna Z. Pappas and Paul Agathoklis.

of concern including the issue of moisture within the Cathedral building itself.

The extensive report provided an outline on ways to address problems, seek estimates on repairs, communicate project costs, and raise the necessary funds to take corrective measures. Repairs were needed for roofing, guttering, flashing and masonry work to prevent further damage. Considering the growing number of items on the maintenance list, an "Emergency Replacement and Repair Fund Drive" was initiated and ultimately proved successful in raising monies to complete the repair work. Even the air conditioning system was upgraded with the installation of two new units and repairs were made to the remaining two units.

As the 90th Anniversary year began, Father Monios announced with great pride that Constantine "Dean" Moralis, the Cathedral's Lay Assistant, would soon be ordained as a Deacon. After serious contemplation and prayer, Dean Moralis stated he would focus his entire life to the Church and would soon take his place among a distinctive group of unmarried Orthodox clergymen in America. On Sunday, February 11, 1996, Dean Moralis was ordained to the Holy Diaconate in a moving ceremony celebrated by Metropolitan Silas. Dedicated to his future pastoral mission, plans were quickly set for his ordination to the priesthood four months later.

On Sunday, June 9, 1996, before an overflowing congregation, Deacon Constantine Moralis, age 29, was ordained to the Holy Priesthood with Metropolitan Silas of New Jersey officiating. Those present at the ordination ceremony responded with the traditional *Axios!* (he is worthy). Best wishes were bestowed upon Father Moralis in the summer 1996 edition of the parish newsletter. "Now an ordained priest, he has made this community very proud of his many accomplishments in so short a time—and he was born, baptized, and grew up in this parish. We wish him a wonderful future…and know he will always serve his Church and Christ with much love." From June through September of that historic year, Annunciation had three priests—Fathers Monios, Noplos, and Moralis—to serve the growing roster of nearly 1,200 families.

The 90th Anniversary of the Annunciation Cathedral was formally observed on Sunday, March 17, 1996, with a special Doxology service.

George and Stacey Mesologites (left) with Theodore and Gloria George (right) at the Cathedral Ball, 1996.

Greek School PTO Officers, 1996-1997. Front *l to r* : Evie Williams, Christine Grimes. Back *l to r* : Soula Makris, Vasi Lea Karas, Mary Valmas, President; Denise Damalas.

The names of all *proistamenoi* (senior clergymen), as well as parish council presidents during the 90-year period, were commemorated in prayers. The events of that day were a clear indication of the varied ministries in place after nine decades as a religious community. For example, the Women's Guild sponsored the *Artoclasia* followed by a well-attended general membership meeting. The flourishing Golden Age Club met in its designated room at the

Annunciation Orthodox Center (AOC). Later, a Young People's Concert was held as well as a meeting to discuss the upcoming Ionian Village excursion planned for that summer. The diversity of parish activities was outstanding.

During that same month, on March 11, 1996, the Clergy-Laity Conference of the New Jersey Diocese was held at the AOC. Evan A. Chriss, Cathedral Legal Counsel, who was elected to serve on the Archdiocesan Council, chaired the event. Two weeks later, on March 23, 1996, the Growing in Faith Bible Study sponsored its second retreat with Father Anthony Coniaris as guest speaker. The March 1996 newsletter included a four-page insert, entitled "Tracing 90 Years of Progress," written by Parish Historian Nicholas M. Prevas. This article, which later appeared in the national *Hellenic Chronicle* newspaper, offered readers an insightful overview of parish history. This decade, filled with challenges and significant changes, would soon prove to be one of the most exciting and productive periods in the life of the Annunciation Cathedral.

The 90th Anniversary year also coincided with the establishment of a Greek Independence Day parade in Baltimore. On Sunday, March 24, 1996, the first parade was formally held in Highlandtown near the St. Nicholas Greek Orthodox Church. George Demetrides initiated the concept sponsored by the Lord Baltimore Chapter #364 of the Order of AHEPA. Participants from all three Greek Orthodox Churches and various affiliated organizations marched

through Baltimore's "Greektown" in a proud display of their ethnic heritage celebrating Greece's 1821 battle cry for independence from 400 years of Ottoman rule. By 1999, under the direction of Steve G. Mavronis and George J. Stakias, the popularity of Baltimore's parade reached new heights. Renamed the Mid-Atlantic Greek Independence Day Parade in 2000, the event continues to attract thousands of spectators and over one hundred participating groups from throughout the region. In recent years, Emmanuel B. Matsos, representing Annunciation Cathedral, has also played a key role in organizing the event.

The summer of 1996 saw the retirement of 85-year-old Archbishop Iakovos after 37 years as spiritual leader of the Greek Orthodox Archdiocese. According to the Archdiocesan web site, www.goarch.org, his dynamic tenure was "distinguished by his leadership in furthering religious unity, revitalizing Christian worship, and championing human and civil rights." As his successor, Metropolitan Spyridon of Italy was

Cathedral Acolytes were led by
Gregory Valsamakis (Valmas) on
Holy Friday, April 12, 1996.

It is a yearly tradition for the decorated
Tomb of Christ to be processed around
the block with solemnity on Holy Friday.

enthroned as the next Archbishop of America on September 21, 1996. He was born in 1944 in Warren, Ohio, and later graduated from the famed Halki Seminary in 1966. By 1985, he was elected titular Bishop of Apamea and served as auxiliary bishop to the Archdiocese of Australia and subsequently as Exarchate of Italy.

The assignment of the new American-born spiritual leader to the Greek Orthodox Archdiocese was noted in the September 1996 issue of Annunciation's newsletter. "Archbishop Spyridon is known for his dedication to the Ecumenical Patriarchate and for his energetic career and creativity. He is very much involved with the Ecumenical movement. We pray that God will bless his new ministry as our Archbishop." During this period, the Ecumenical Patriarchate formally divided the American Archdiocese into four jurisdictions: Canada, centered in Toronto; Central America, centered in Mexico City; South America, centered in Buenos Aires; and the United States, headquartered in New York under the jurisdiction of Archbishop Spyridon. The Greek Orthodox Church in America was beginning a new era of its own history.

Archbishop Spyridon served as the spiritual leader of the Greek Orthodox Archdiocese from 1996-1999.

Philoptochos Society Directors, 1996. Seated left to right: Joyce Melonas, Patty Arkuszeski, Secretary; Vasi Lea Karas, Vice President; Kyriake Agathoklis, President; Rena Marmaras, Treasurer. Standing left to right: Elizabeth Monocrusos, Constance Rogers, Zena Hayes, Kay Maistros, Helen Maschas, Angela Zades, Bess Stamas.

Junior Choir, 1996. Front row *l to r* : Effie Syntax, Argie Hajiantoni, Christina Panageotou, Shane Cole, Michael Chrysovergis, Maria Makris. Second row *l to r* : Katie Prevas, Vasilios Matsos, Steven Agathoklis, Zoe Lintzeris, Gia Vakoutis, Alexander Creticos. Third row *l to r* : James Prevas, Anastasia Georgandis, Christina Moniodis, Stephanie Diemer, Dimitri Valmas. Back row *l to r* : Ian Cole, Katrina Noplos, Eleni Rizakos, Despina Hyde, Alex Marcuri, Constantine Lignos, Director Stephanie S. Vakoutis.

Parish Acolytes and Clergy, 1997. Front row *l to r* : Vasilios Matsos, Nicholas Klicos, Chris Morris, Thomas Popomaronis, Steven Agathoklis, Nicholas Karas. Second row *l to r* : Father Dean Moralis, Thomas Prevas, Athanasios Spanos, Christopher McPherson, Dimitri Valmas, Chris Grimes, Demetri Karas, Father Constantine Monios. Back row *l to r* : Costa Karas, Gregory Valmas, Benjamin Prevas, James Prevas, Robert Morris, Alex Constantinides, Andrew Frankos-Rey, Alex Haziminas.

Archbishop Spyridon quickly became familiar with the Cathedral of the Annunciation and its programs through regular communication with Father Monios. During this period, numerous Cathedral volunteers were recognized. The Archdiocesan Department of Religious Education posthumously awarded the late Peter J. Prevas, an educator by profession, with a Certificate of Recognition for 50 years of service. In the fall of 1996, Theodore J. George, now 80 years of age, retired after 42 years as librarian. Also, Constantine Kutson was commended for devoting fifteen years as the chairman of the Cemetery Committee. Then, on Church Music Sunday, October 6, 1996, Georgia Tangires was honored for fifty years of service to the Cathedral music program with a testimonial luncheon in the Preston Room of the AOC. Among those presenting gifts to Mrs. Tangires was Stephanie Stamas Vakoutis who was applauded for her own dedicated service as director of the Junior Choir for over a decade.

During this period, there was a growing need for uniformed off-duty police officers to patrol the Mt. Vernon district around the Cathedral on Sunday mornings. To help defray the cost of such an initiative, the parish council hosted a number of fundraising events including several well-attended community brunches first sponsored in August of 1996. Among the policemen patrolling the area was Officer Nicholas Louloudis, an active member of the Greek community.

As the 90th Anniversary year concluded, the Annunciation parish also celebrated the 25th Anniversary of the Athenian Agora. Theodore Stavrakis served as chairman and Rena Marmaras served as co-chairperson. The three-day extravaganza was held September 20-22, 1996. To mark the occasion, a Silver Anniversary album entitled "Athenian Agora XXV" was published and contained numerous images from parish festivals held since the "Agora" was initiated in 1971. The commemorative album was dedicated to all

Festival participants, 1995, left to right: Stephanie Diemer, Christina Moniodis, Katrina Noplos, Angela Moniodis.

Festival booth, 1996, left to right: Nicholas Gialamas, Stasa Gialamas, Koula Savvakis, Anastasia August.

"Evangelos and Evangelia" (far right), created by Harry C. Maistros and named by Dimitra Skleres and Alex Zades, were used in festival advertisements for many years.

past chairpersons and countless volunteers who had "unselfishly donated their time and efforts over the years." Chairperson Theodore Stavrakis noted that the festival remained an opportunity for parishioners to "come together in fellowship and to offer hospitality to our neighbors in the community in which we live."

By this time, changes in personnel at the sister parish of St. Demetrios had a direct impact on Annunciation. After nearly a quarter of a century serving the suburban parish, The Rev. Ernest Arambiges announced his retirement. He conducted his final Divine Liturgy as *proistamenos* of St. Demetrios on Sunday, June 9, 1996. Members of his church led by Dr. Peter L. Sitaras, Helen Makres, Michael Athas and Master of Ceremonies Basilios Trintis gave a banquet in his honor. Subsequently, Metropolitan Silas assigned Annunciation's assistant priest, Father Louis Noplos, to serve as the new spiritual leader of the St. Demetrios Greek Orthodox Church effective September 15, 1996.

Two months later on Sunday, November 17, 1996, Father Louis, Presbytera Alice, Katrina, Dimitri, and Gregory Noplos returned to Annunciation Cathedral for a lavish farewell banquet in the AOC Ballroom under the chairmanship of Fathers Monios and Moralis. Anna Z. Pappas served as the event coordinator, assisted by committee members Lucy Hagopian, Soula Lambropoulos, and Parish Council President Gary T. Padussis. Nearly a dozen Cathedral organizations made formal presentations to their beloved assistant priest at the emotional farewell tribute. His exemplary service to the Cathedral had spanned over fourteen years and remains the longest of any assistant priest in parish history.

During the late 1990's, major projects like the installation of an elevator were faced with challenges. An elevator was deemed important to assist elderly and handicapped parishioners in accessing the three levels of the Cathedral complex. A feasibility study and a survey of parishioners had taken place since the inception of the idea in 1993. The project, however, was placed on hold at the

A Retirement Banquet for Rev. Ernest Arambiges was sponsored by the St. Demetrios Church in June 1996.
Left to right: Dr. Peter L. Sitaras, Helen Makres, Metropolitan Silas, Presbytera Maria and Father Ernest Arambiges.

Evangelakia Dance Troupe, 1997. Front left to right: Marianna Agathoklis, Stamatia Letras, Tina Koundouriotis, Alexis Vakoutis, Anastasia Kutson. Back left to right: Gus Prevas, Steve Stamas, Gregory Valmas, Costa Karas, Marc Tsakiris, Alex Constantinides.

Filakia Dance Troupe at the Greek Independence Day Parade, Highlandtown. Left to right: Demetra Kosmakos, Maria Makris, Instructor Dr. Savas Tsakiris, Maria Marmaras, Christina Moniodis, Martha Panselinos, Eleni Rizakos, Gia Vakoutis, March 29, 1998.

Rev. Louis and Presbytera Alice Noplos with their children,
Katrina, Dimitri and Gregory (left to right). Their farewell
banquet was held in the AOC Ballroom, November 17, 1996.

Following the departure of Father Louis Noplos in 1996,
Father Moralis (right), a native Baltimorean, became
the primary assistant priest to Father Monios (left).

spring 1996 assembly meeting due to financial concerns. Then, in early 1997, a special parish assembly again dealt with the topic of the proposed elevator. This time, however, there was the added support of an Ad Hoc Committee formed in November 1996 under the chairmanship of Kathryn Belitsos. The committee's presentation to the assembly on February 2, 1997, addressed the issue of the elevator location, outlined the estimated costs, and proposed a strategy for fundraising. Soon after, the committee was successful in finding a space large enough to connect all three floors by an elevator without compromising other areas of the building.

Continuing forward, upcoming goals were outlined and communicated in the January 1997 newsletter: stewardship computer software, pay-off of the debt, additional exterior lighting for the Cathedral, the promotion of trusts and charitable contributions, and continued cost-cutting on budget items. The parish council also gave its approval to correct the problem of water leakage to the downstairs portion of the parking garage from the upper deck. Michael Constantine, chairman of the Garage Committee, explained that the project would cost about $14,000 and span over four months with no interruption to parking.

The spring of 1997 was marked by a superb tribute entitled "An Evening with Jeanne and Nicholas Tsakalos." The banquet, underwritten by John Paterakis and Peter Angelos, was held on May 30, 1997, and raised $275,000 for the Capital Projects Fund of the parish. This gave a tremendous boost to major interior renovations that were being planned for 1998. The following week, the Baltimore-Piraeus Sister City Committee celebrated its 15th anniversary with an art exhibition at Baltimore City Hall. The opening reception was held on June 6, 1997, showcasing the art books and rare prints from the collection of parishioner George Lintzeris. In keeping with the cultural theme, the Maryland Historical Society opened an exhibition in August of 1997 entitled "An Immigrant Odyssey: The Maryland Greek-American Experience." The special exhibit included images from the collection of the Cathedral Archives and other private sources.

That same month, on August 12, 1997, Archbishop Spyridon made his first pastoral visit to the Annunciation Cathedral to discuss a most

The arrival of Ecumenical Patriarch Bartholomew (left) was anticipated with much excitement by Father Constantine Monios (right) and the congregation. This historic visit of October 23, 1997, was denoted with a bronze plaque (shown right) in the left entrance foyer of the Cathedral sanctuary.

HIS ALL HOLINESS
ECUMENICAL PATRIARCH BARTHOLOMEW
ON THE OCCASION OF
THE 75TH ANNIVERSARY
OF THE
GREEK ORTHODOX ARCHDIOCESE OF AMERICA
VISITED
THE CATHEDRAL OF THE ANNUNCIATION
ON
OCTOBER 23, 1997

historic event—one that mandated overwhelming coordination between the Greek Orthodox community, the Catholic Archdiocese of Baltimore, Baltimore City officials, and other government agencies. The Archbishop announced that during a monthlong tour of the United States, His All Holiness Ecumenical Patriarch Bartholomew of Constantinople would visit the Greek Orthodox Cathedral of the Annunciation on Preston Street. The clergy, office staff, and dozens of volunteers at Annunciation Cathedral pooled their talents and focused all energies in anticipation of that historic day…Thursday, October 23, 1997.

That morning, the glorious autumn weather was an early indication of the outstanding success of the Patriarch's visit. His arrival at the Cathedral was a poignant moment. Parish youngsters, dressed in colorful Grecian costumes, lined the red-carpeted entrance and showered him with rose petals. In a gesture of humility and love, the Patriarch then reached into the flower baskets and sprinkled rose petals upon the children. Months of planning culminated the moment Patriarch

Bartholomew entered the Annunciation Cathedral and officially began the Patriarchal Doxology. The sanctuary was completely filled by 1,000 people representing a number of parishes in the region, city and state officials, clerics from various denominations, and other notable dignitaries.

The remainder of that day's agenda included a visit to Baltimore City Hall to meet Mayor Kurt Schmoke and representatives of the major Christian charities based in Baltimore. This was followed by a luncheon at the Baltimore Convention Center attended by nearly 2,000 people; special Ecumenical Services at the Roman Catholic Basilica of the Assumption on Cathedral Street; a reception at the Walters Art Gallery; and a dinner at the residence of William Cardinal Keeler. In reflecting upon the event, Father Monios recalled October 23, 1997, as the most significant day in the history of the Cathedral, second only to its consecration. He expressed his overwhelming gratitude to all those who assisted in the many aspects of hosting the world leader of Orthodox Christianity.

Ecumenical Patriarch Bartholomew I at the Roman Catholic
Basilica of the Assumption in Baltimore, October 23, 1997.

Official Patriarchal Seal

Patriarchal Doxology conducted by Ecumenical Patriarch Bartholomew at the Annunciation Cathedral, October 23, 1997.

Parish children in costumes were showered with flower petals
by Patriarch Bartholomew in the Cathedral courtyard.

William Cardinal Keeler (left) and
Ecumenical Patriarch Batholomew
at the Basilica of the Assumption.

Patriarch Bartholomew (center) and Mayor Kurt Schmoke (standing left) posed with dozens
of Orthodox faithful from area parishes at Baltimore City Hall during the historic visit in 1997.

Orthodox clerygmen throughout the region and representatives from various religious denominations
were among the 1,000 people who attended the Patriarchal Doxology at the Annunciation Cathedral in 1997.

Ecumenical Patriarch Bartholomew presided from the Bishop's Throne—a place of honor reserved
for Hierarchs. The double-headed eagle on the side of the throne is symbolic of the Byzantine Empire.

Choir Director Georgia Tangires (seated right) and Organist Fotini Nichols (seated left)
and members of the special choir group that participated during the Patriarchal Visit of 1997.

The following year, a 95-page commemorative issue of *The Annunciation Herald*, dedicated to the Patriarchal visit, was published with Stephanie Panos Link as editor. The impressive chronicle gave a behind-the-scenes look at the event and the enormous amount of preparation that went into each phase of that historic day. In a moving editorial she wrote, "From the moment the Patriarchal motorcade entered Baltimore, His All Holiness was received with red carpet treatment by the entire community. Mayor Schmoke, Governor Glendening, Senators Sarbanes and Mikulski, and our Roman Catholic brethren, represented by William Cardinal Keeler, opened their arms for this charismatic leader of 300 million Orthodox Christians worldwide."

Almost two months later, the news of the death of The Reverend Emmanuel E. Bouyoucas in West Palm Beach, Florida, on December 18, 1997, was a time of reflection for many parishioners. Father

Bouyoucas had served the Annunciation parish from 1965-1975. His tenure as *proistamenos* (senior clergyman) was marked by a number of improvement projects, philanthropic events, increased spiritual education for parishioners, cooperative efforts among all three Greek Orthodox churches, and the elevation of the parish to Cathedral status. His funeral was held at the St. Catherine Greek Orthodox Church in West Palm Beach, Florida, where he had last served. At Annunciation Cathedral in Baltimore, the name of "Emmanuel the Protopresbyter" was added to the memorial prayers chanted by Fathers Monios and Moralis during that month.

The year 1998 began with a notable event. On January 11, 1998, His Eminence Archbishop Spyridon again visited the Annunciation Cathedral and celebrated the Hierarchical Divine Liturgy. Other participating clergy included: Fathers Monios and Moralis of Annunciation, Father

Orthodox Clergymen at the St. Nicholas Church. Front *l to r* : Rev. Costas Kostaris, Rev. Ray Velencia, Rev. Constantine Monios, Rev. George Kalpaxis, Rev. Petros Kakaris, Rev. Dean Moralis. Back *l to r* : Rev. Anastasios Kousoulas, Rev. Louis Noplos, Rev. Manuel Burdusi of the host parish; Rev. Duane Johnson and Rev. Michael Roshak, December 5, 1997.

Manuel Burdusi of St. Nicholas, Archimandrite John Heropoulos, Deacon Elias Villas, and retired clergymen Father Ernest Arambiges and Father George Kalpaxis. In his message to parishioners, Archbishop Spyridon eloquently stated that "conveying the Orthodox faith to our children is our greatest challenge – as parents, as members of the Church family, and as practicing Orthodox Christians. The only reality that saves us is the Church, a community gathered in the name of God, a community which is the body of Jesus Christ."

A few months later, Annunciation Cathedral was once again blessed by the generosity of parishioners Peter and Georgia Angelos. With the expansion of numerous area institutions, parking became a key concern. It was announced that the Angelos family had purchased the Crestar (Loyola Bank) property in the 1300 block of North Charles Street and donated the adjacent parking lot portion of the property to the Cathedral in loving memory of Mrs. Angelos' grandfather, John Kousouris. Now,

the parish would develop this into a much-needed flat parking lot. Also during that spring, on May 3, 1998, the Central Maryland Ecumenical Council hosted is annual Awards Banquet at the AOC. The "Christian Life Award," honoring a life of works and deeds exemplifying a steadfast commitment to Christian faith, was bestowed upon parishioners Nicholas and Jeanne Tsakalos.

Two weeks later, on May 18, 1998, Patriarch Ilia II, spiritual leader of the Orthodox Church in the Republic of Georgia, visited Baltimore. He met with officials at the offices of the IOCC (International Orthodox Christian Charities) in the Rotunda Building to express his appreciation for the assistance given to the people of the Republic of Georgia by the IOCC. He then proceeded to the Annunciation Cathedral where he officiated at special prayer services. His ascent to the Bishop's Throne within the sanctuary that day marked the second time in seven months that a Patriarch had visited the Annunciation Cathedral.

The visit of Patriarch Ilia was the last major event prior to the start of extensive interior refurbishing of the sanctuary. In fact, to expedite the various work phases, the sanctuary was closed during the summer months of 1998, and church services were held in the Social Hall of the Education Building. Project Manager Anna Z. Pappas, who also served as co-chairman of the Iconography Committee during these years, coordinated the renovations of 1998. The renovations would complement the work done in the summer of 1996 when the *iconostasion* (altar screen) received a unique *faux* glaze application, transforming its color from a medium oak to a rich mahogany in order to blend with the wall colors added in the prior decade.

The first project was the removal of all church pews for restoration and repair. Other phases of work included the restoration of wooden furnishings, floor sanding and refinishing, new carpeting and pew cushions, refurbishing of the balcony chairs, and interior painting. Nearly twenty contractors were involved in various tasks. Police Department Col. John Gavrilis was responsible for additional security and a fire prevention system; George C. Maistros coordinated the lighting, sound, and improved intercom system; and William Paterakis supervised the mechanical portion of the project. The Ad Hoc Committee and the Women's Guild were among the main benefactors of the renovations. The results were most impressive and parishioners commented favorably when church services resumed in the main sanctuary on Sunday, September 20, 1998.

During this period, the parish council received news of a sizable donation toward another capital improvement project—the installation of an elevator within the Cathedral. At that time, it was determined that $350,000 would be needed to see this project through to completion—$300,000 for

The Ionian Village Summer Camp, located near Patras, Greece, with Father Dean Moralis (first row, eighth from left), 1998. Ministered by the Greek Orthodox Archdiocese of America, the facility offers spiritual, historical and social venues for young adults.

The *iconostasion* (altar screen) of the Annunciation Cathedral underwent a renovation in 1996 with a *faux* glaze application that transformed its appearance to a rich mahogany color.

construction and $50,000 placed in an escrow account for maintenance. By the summer of 1998, the Peter G. Angelos family had donated half the cost of the elevator which accelerated the timetable for completion. By May of 1999, the parish council reported that the Whiting-Turner Contracting Company, under the supervision of the Elevator Committee led by Kathryn Janos Belitsos, had begun the project. Her dream for easier access to all three levels of the Cathedral complex would soon come to fruition.

Another noteworthy endeavor in the late 1990's was the establishment of the Cathedral's web site, www.goannun.org, which was officially launched in October of 1998. The web site provided computer-savvy parishioners with a variety of news, educational information, religious articles, and links to various Archdiocesan sites. It was truly a sign of the changing times as more parishes across the United States began to establish communication and educational sessions with Orthodox Christians through the use of the Internet.

Balcony view of interior shows scaffolding during the extensive renovations in the summer of 1998.

The Cathedral Pilgrimage to the Holy Land was led by Father Constantine Monios (front row sixth from left).

View from "Mount of Olives" in Jerusalem shows the "Dome of the Rock" in the background, June 22, 1998.

WAITING FOR A BLESSING

ALGERINA PERNA : SUN STAFF

Little angels: *At Baltimore's Greek Orthodox Cathedral of the Annunciation, twins (from left) Steven and Alexander Pappas, 3, and George Roros, 3, hold one of 100 quilts parishioners made for children with AIDS and other illnesses. The boys are waiting to take the quilt to the altar for a blessing from the Rev. Constantine Monios, dean of the cathedral.*

The Quilt Project of the Philoptochos Society was publicized in *The Baltimore Sun* on December 7, 1998.

In the fall of 1998, the Philoptochos Society took the spotlight with the establishment of its "ABC Quilts Project." The concept was modeled after a project in New Hampshire that brought comfort and assistance to children afflicted with AIDS and other serious illnesses. Parish records show that on November 21, 1998, "one hundred eleven volunteers gathered in the social hall to sew, to pin, to cut and to iron." The organizing committee members included: Kerry Agathoklis, Penny Frankos, Koula Savvakis, Bess Stamas, and Diane Tseckares.

The following month on December 6, 1998, the Feast Day of St. Nicholas, one hundred quilts were presented for blessing on the Holy Altar prior to being delivered to at-risk infants in area hospitals. The overwhelming success of this philanthropic endeavor caught the attention of the media with a *Baltimore Sun* article on November 23, 1998, followed by a front-page feature story on December 7, 1998. The Philoptochos Quilt Project, with over 1,600 quilts made by Cathedral volunteers since its inception, has gained enormous popularity among parishioners and continues on a yearly basis.

During 1998, a most historic event had taken place for the Greek Orthodox Archdiocese—the selection of the first bishop of the Greek Orthodox Church in America to come from the ranks of married priests. On June 13, 1998, The Rev. George Papaioannou, a widower, was ordained to the episcopacy by Archbishop Spyridon and was bestowed with the official title of Bishop George of Komanon. Bishop George had served as the priest of the St. George Greek Orthodox Church in Bethesda, Maryland, for over twenty-five years. His enthronement as Bishop of New Jersey took place on March 13, 1999, filling the void caused by the retirement of Metropolitan Silas in 1996. That same month, Bishop George visited the Cathedral for the *Feast of the Annunciation* and presided over Great Vespers and the Divine Liturgy.

Later that year, on October 22, 1999, at the Diocesan Clergy-Laity Assembly, Bishop George presented his vision, ideas, and programs for the

Father Constantine Monios welcomed Bishop George of New Jersey (right) to Annunciation Cathedral, March 24, 1999.

Archbishop Spyridon (seated) with priests and cantors. Front *l to r* : Rev. Costas Kostaris, Rev. Constantine Monios, Rev. George Papaioannou, Rev. Louis Noplos, Cantor Sotirios Mangos. Back *l to r* : Cantor Stefanos Niktas, Rev. Manuel Burdusi, Rev. George Kalpaxis, Rev. Anastasios Kousoulas, Rev. Kosmas Karavellas, Cantor Peter Constantinou, 1997.

future of the Diocese. Foremost on the agenda were plans to establish a Diocesan Center. Bishop George made a return visit to Annunciation Cathedral on Sunday, October 31, 1999, to celebrate a Hierarchical Divine Liturgy. Sadly, his tenure as Bishop of the New Jersey Diocese would be short-lived. On Sunday, November 21, 1999, while speaking at the stewardship dinner of his former parish of St. George in Bethesda, Maryland, Bishop George became ill, collapsed, and fell asleep in the Lord the following morning. On Saturday, November 27, 1999, Bishop George, age 66, was laid to rest in the Gate of Heaven Cemetery in Aspen Hill, Maryland. It would be a few years before a new spiritual leader would be chosen to succeed him.

Archbishop Demetrios became the new spiritual leader of the Greek Orthodox Archdiocese of America in the fall of 1999.

During this period the Greek Orthodox Archdiocese also underwent change. After a three-year tenure overshadowed by criticism and dissatisfaction from both clergy and laity, Archbishop Spyridon was reassigned as the Metropolitan of Chaldea in Turkey. As his replacement, the twelve-member Synod of the Ecumenical Patriarchate elected Metropolitan Demetrios of Vresthena as the new Archbishop for America on August 19, 1999. Archbishop Demetrios, age 71, was born in Thessaloniki, Greece, in 1928. The son of Christos and Georgia Trakatellis, he graduated from the University of Athens School of Theology with honors in 1950. He was ordained a deacon in 1960 and a priest in 1964.

Later, on September 17, 1967, he was consecrated as titular Bishop of Vresthena (Greece). He came to the United States in 1965, enrolled at Harvard University, and received a Ph.D. in 1972. Five years later, he was awarded his Doctorate in Theology from the University of Athens. Upon his enthronement on September 18, 1999, he became the sixth Archbishop to serve the Greek Orthodox Archdiocese since 1922. Archbishop Demetrios soon traveled throughout the United States working with clergy and laity to strengthen and advance the work of the Orthodox Church. Well-versed in Orthodox traditions and the author of numerous books, he often lectured in academic and ecclesiastical venues. In 1995, as the Metropolitan of Vresthena, he was the keynote speaker at Annunciation's first lenten retreat. His first official visit to Annunciation Cathedral as the new Archbishop would take place in the spring of 2000.

The momentum at Annunciation continued throughout the year 1999. With the vast renovation project of 1998 completed, plans were formulated to address issues concerning the rehabilitation of the Education Building. Volunteer enthusiasm for the future was evident in the March 1999 newsletter. "Along with President Gary T. Padussis and other veteran members, all with a track record of success, the council will continue its emphasis on the youth, the cohesiveness of the three parishes, the cemetery, and anything the community brings to its attention." It was also noted with pride that new parish council members of the next generation— Zaharoula Kokinos, Christos Panagiotopoulos, Ernest Rafailides and Evangelos D. Sidou among

Father Dean Moralis symbolized the growing number of second-generation Greek-Americans assuming spiritual and administrative roles within the Orthodox Church.

others—were contributing fresh, innovative ideas. The atmosphere was upbeat as Annunciation stood poised to meet the challenges of the new millennium.

In the spring of 1999, after four decades of dedicated volunteer work as Legal Counsel of the parish, Evan Alevizatos Chriss stepped down from this important role. He was given tremendous thanks and praise for handling many of the delicate matters concerning the business administration of the parish. Following his departure, a Legal Committee comprising attorneys from the community, under the chairmanship of Evangelos D. Sidou, would now be called upon to render legal opinions and advice on business matters.

During this decade, Larry Burgan, a past parish council president and convert to the Orthodox faith, served as the Cathedral Sexton. He served in this capacity from 1995 until his death in the summer of 1999. Soon after, George Kariotis, the uncle of The Rev. Dean Moralis, assumed duties as the new Cathedral Sexton. Mr. Kariotis continues to faithfully carry out the countless behind-the-scenes responsibilities of this important role in the parish.

More honors were on the agenda as John Morekas, well-known radio host of the Greek-American Radio Hour in Baltimore, observed the anniversary of his broadcasting career that now spanned over five decades. Following church services on April 25, 1999, Father Monios spoke glowingly of John Morekas' role with the Greek Hour—a varied radio program that served to unite Baltimore's Greek population. The Laconian Association hosted the coffee hour in honor of Mr. Morekas, an active member of the regional group. Both John Morekas, along with his co-host and cousin, Nitsa Morekas, would continue as radio announcers for nearly seven more years before bidding farewell to the airwaves in the spring of 2006.

By the summer of 1999, the installation of a new copper dome on the cemetery chapel finally corrected the moisture and condensation problem that had damaged some of the inside iconography. The iconography repair work was well underway and would be completed by the fall. Great financial assistance was also provided to the cemetery projects that year in the form of a $100,000-donation from the estate of Peter T. Prevas. At the Cathedral complex, the Building Committee recommended that Morris Associates, Architects & Planners, spearhead the corrective measures needed for the Education Building. The removal of asbestos and the replacement of the roof, along with repainting and general repairs, were the main agenda items to be addressed. In looking ahead, the planning of "Glendi 2000," a tri-parish gala to mark the start of the new millennium, was underway with Sandra Hondroulis of the parish council representing the Annunciation Cathedral.

Fellowship and charitable work between the parishes were also evident. One example was the yearly success of the Hellenic Golf Invitational. By 1999, August A. Krometis reported that proceeds from the first ten annual tournaments had enabled the golfing venture to donate over $125,000 toward the work of the Chesapeake Youth Council. To prepare for the youth activities of 1999-2000, GOYA elected new officers: Jennifer Zizos, President; George Makris, Vice President; Elizabeth Stamas and Nina Diemer, Secretaries; Angela Moniodis, Treasurer; and Eleni Makris, Historian. On October 30, 1999, the Eastern Federation of Greek Orthodox Choirs held a conference at Oriole Park at Camden Yards with Joanne Souris Deitz as chairperson. Greek-American comedian, Basile Katsikis, was the featured entertainer for Greek Orthodox musicians from throughout the region.

28TH ANNUAL
ATHENIAN AGORA
THE 1999
GREEK FESTIVAL

"A Weekend
in Greece!"

November 5, 6, 7

The Greek Orthodox Cathedral of the Annunciation
24 West Preston Street
Baltimore, Maryland 21201

"Athenian Agora" opening ceremony with Mayor Kurt Schmoke (right of Father Monios) and Police Commissioner Thomas Frazier (back row far right), November 6, 1998. Each year, a program booklet is published (shown left) as a guide for festival patrons.

As Parish Council President Gary T. Padussis neared the conclusion of his fourth consecutive term of office, he received praise for his volunteer service. In the November 1999 newsletter, it was noted that "his contributions were many during his nine years on the Council. He was instrumental in re-establishing the Ad Hoc Committee…which spearheaded many of the capital improvements… He played a major role in helping to procure the Crestar parking lot on Maryland Avenue for Cathedral use. He was in tune to the need for an elevator and acted on that need…He was a major

participant in supporting the Patriarchal visit." Foremost, Mr. Padussis was commended for putting his financial talents to use during his presidency. Father Monios noted that the Cathedral "has no long-term debt and operates on a balanced budget."

The new millennium began with a grand celebration on January 1, 2000. Over 1,200 people from all three Greek Orthodox parishes in Baltimore gathered at Martin's West for "Glendi 2000." The popular Greek-American orchestra, Zephyros, provided the musical entertainment. In observing the Feast of St. Basil the Great, the evening's agenda included "The Celebration of the Vasilopita" (*vasilopita* meaning the bread of Saint Basil). Sweet spices added to the bread represent the joy of everlasting life. In addressing the large gathering, Father Constantine Monios commented, "The observance of the Vasilopita tradition is a wonderful way to begin each New Year, both at home and with our Church community. It allows us time to reflect on all of God's gifts and share them, in the spirit of St. Basil the Great...."

Within a week, a new fifteen-member parish council was installed at the yearly affirmation ceremony. The oath was administered on Sunday, January 9, 2000, with the following elected as officers: Michael Bouloubassis, President; Larry Vakoutis, Vice President; Evangelos D. Sidou, Treasurer; and Thomas Boardman, Secretary. The important role played by the parish council to properly administer the business affairs of the Cathedral cannot be underestimated. A pamphlet of parish ministries, published by the Stewardship Committee, listed nearly 50 separate programs on Annunciation's agenda by the year 2000. The impressive roster was an indication that more expansion was on the horizon.

That same month, the clergy congratulated leaders of the Golden Age Club for providing senior parishioners with such a diverse agenda. Fathers Monios and Moralis administered the affirmation of office on January 16, 2000, to the following: Nicholas Pavlos, President; Nicholas J. Kiladis, Vice

President; Christopher Apesos, Treasurer; Marlene Apesos, Corresponding Secretary; and Angela Koutsoutis, Recording Secretary. Three months later, on April 2, 2000, under the presidency of Maria Donnelly, the Women's Guild was in the spotlight with an *Artoclasia* and coffee hour held in celebration of the 45th Anniversary of its group that year. All past presidents were presented with a corsage and recognized for their devoted service.

One of the most significant events that year was the long-awaited dedication of the new elevator that took place on Sunday, January 16, 2000. Ceremonial ribbon-cuttings were conducted with the following participants: Kathryn J. Belitsos, Elevator Committee Chairperson, and her husband, Dr. Nicholas Belitsos; and John and Louis Angelos, the sons of Peter and Georgia Angelos, Elevator Great Benefactors. Other members of the Elevator Committee recognized that day for their dedicated focus included Soula Lambropoulos, Gary T. Padussis, Carolyn Tsakalas, Dr. Constantine Chilimindris, Anna Z. Pappas, Lawrence J. Link, Jr., and the late Dr. Stephen K. Padussis who was involved in the planning stages of the project.

Annunciation Parish Council, 2000. Seated left to right: Evangelos Sidou, Treasurer; Larry Vakoutis, Vice President; Rev. Dean Moralis, Rev. Constantine Monios, Michael Bouloubassis, President; Thomas Boardman, Secretary. Second row left to right: Zaharoula Kokinos, Sandra Hondroulis, Ernest Rafailides, Nicholas Pavlos, Charles Stover, Chrysoula Ponticas. Back row left to right: Dr. Savas Tsakiris, Christos Panagiotopoulos, Chris Cotsonis, Perry Galanakis, Dimitri Cavathas.

Elevator Dedication left to right: John and Louis Angelos representing their parents, Peter and Georgia Angelos; Father Moralis, Father Monios, Kathryn Janos Belitsos and Dr. Nicholas J. Belitsos, Sunday, January 16, 2000.

Chairperson Kathryn Janos Belitsos reflected that the elevator would "facilitate the flow of spiritual life for years to come."

A number of other noteworthy activities also took place in 2000. The Annunciation Cathedral hosted the Ionian Village Reunion the weekend of March 10-12, 2000. Over 100 young people from throughout the United States gathered in Baltimore. Father Moralis commented that the Ionian Village experience remained "an incredible way to learn about the Orthodox faith and Greek culture." On March 26, 2000, The Greek Independence Day "Millennium Parade 2000" was held in Greektown with thousands of spectators in attendance. Among the noted dignitaries on the reviewing stand at the St. Nicholas Greek Orthodox Church was Bishop Dimitrios of Xanthos, Auxiliary Bishop to Archbishop Demetrios. Other clergymen in attendance included Father Manuel Burdusi, Father Louis Noplos, Father Constantine Monios,

Special plaques honoring members of the Angelos and Belitsos families for their generosity toward the Cathedral Elevator Project, January 2000.

Annunciation Girls' Basketball Team, 2000. Left to right: Christina Moniodis, Maria Makris, Aritee Poletis Bond, Coach; Elizabeth Stamas, Dorothea Tsakiris, Natalie Constantinides, Eleni Makris, Angela Moniodis, Gia Vakoutis, Martha Panselinos, and Jennifer Zizos.

Annunciation Boys' Basketball Team, 1999. Front row left to right: Nicholas Kourtsounis, Dimitri Valmas, Tim Chryssikos, Alex Haziminas, Leslie John Constantinides. Standing left to right: Costa Karas, Nick Panteleakis, Alex Prevas, Jonathan Marmaras, George Makris, and Demetri Karas.

Archbishop Demetrios (right) venerating the
Holy Gospel during Orthros, Sunday, April 16, 2000.

During his visit, Archbishop Demetrios elevated
Rev. Dean Moralis to the status of Father Confessor.

Father Dean Moralis, Father Michael Roshak and
Father James Kyriakakis.

The following month, on April 15, 2000,
Archbishop Demetrios made his first official visit to
Baltimore. He conducted the Hierarchical Divine
Liturgy on Sunday, April 16, 2000, followed by a
luncheon held in the AOC Ballroom. That evening
and on Monday, he presided at the Diocese of New

Jersey Clergy-Laity Congress. During his visit, the
Archbishop elevated Father Dean Moralis to the
dignity of Father Confessor, blessed the new
Cathedral Sextons, George Kariotis and Sohrab
Madani, and invoked the grace of the Holy Spirit
upon three cantors—Peter Constantinou, Peter
Manousos, and Michael Tsakalos. In addition, six of
the altar servers were tonsured as readers, namely,
Alexander Creticos, Constantine Lignos, George
Makris, Vasilios Matsos, Athanasios Spanos, and
Dimitri Valmas.

Two more Hierarchs graced Annunciation
Cathedral with visits during the spring and summer
months. Metropolitan Savva of Warsaw and All
Poland visited on May 22, 2000, and presided over
a Doxology service. Then, Archbishop Stylianos of
Australia officiated at a special service on July 15,
2000, in commemoration of the International
Dialogue between Orthodox and Roman Catholic
Church leaders. This historic event was part of the
Orthodox-Catholic Dialogue Commission held
from July 9-19, 2000, at Mount St. Mary's College
and Seminary in Emmittsburg, Maryland.

Six altar servers were tonsured by the Archbishop at the conclusion of the Hierarchical Divine Liturgy, April 16, 2000.

At the spring 2000 parish assembly, Parish Council President Michael Bouloubassis outlined a number of projects centered on the improvement of the Education Building. The Building and Maintenance Committee, led by Thomas P. Zizos, organized a group of volunteers for the impressive cleanup of the catacombs, lower level storage area, and the kitchen. The asbestos removal from the Mentis Room was completed and plans were underway for further renovations to enhance the space for general use. It was also reported that the parish now had complete control of the parking lot at Maryland Avenue and Preston Street—already a contributing factor to an increase in church attendance. The following month, on Sunday, June 11, 2000, a special coffee hour was planned for Theodore J. George, the retired parish librarian, in recogniton of his devoted service to the parish.

Another topic discussed by the assembly on May 7, 2000, was a parish survey. At the fall 1999 assembly gathering, an overwhelming majority of parishioners voted that a survey should be conducted to determine preferences and opinions concerning a number of areas of parish life. It was then unanimously approved by the spring 2000 assembly to increase the budget by $5,000 to cover the cost of implementing the survey before the end of the year. The following parishioners pledged donations to cover the cost: Betty Jean Alevizatos, Evan A. and Ceres Chriss, Arthur and Tina Constantinides, Mark and Maria Jensen, Charles and Sandra Pefinis, and Mary and Steve Karas, Jr.

By September of 2000, the survey was mailed through the assistance of RESI, a research institute of Towson University that was hired to tabulate the results. The survey questions were divided into categories including church services, Cathedral programs, Sunday school, Greek language instruction, parish communications and demographics.

The varied activities of the year 2000 culminated with the 25th Anniversary of Father Constantine Monios as Cathedral Dean. The observance took place in the sanctuary on November 5, 2000. Parish Historian Nicholas M. Prevas gave an overview of Father Monios' tenure along with highlights of Cathedral life from 1975-2000. Parish Council President Michael Bouloubassis addressed the congregation and announced that the Social Hall of the Education Building would be lovingly dedicated and renamed "The Father Constantine M. Monios Hall." A commemorative plaque was unveiled and later installed near the hall entrance. To conclude the tribute, Father Dean Moralis outlined Father Monios' service to the Parish, Diocese, Archdiocese, and Patriarchate. Then, in a highly moving moment, Father Moralis raised the hand of his mentor and spiritual father and proclaimed *Axios!* (he is worthy). The congregation enthusiastically responded. Later, a reception honoring the senior clergyman was held at the Preston Room of the Annunciation Orthodox Center.

As the year 2001 began, the IOCC (International Orthodox Christian Charities) relocated to an expanded office at 110 West Road in Towson, Maryland. A formal dedication ceremony was held on January 12, 2001, led by Bishop Dimitrios of Xanthos. Among the participating clergy at the ceremony was The Rev. James Kyriakakis who came to Baltimore in 1998 to assume duties as the Director of Development for

Front *l to r* : Archbishop Demetrios, William Cardinal Keeler.
Back *l to r* : Gary T. Padussis, Father Constantine Monios,
Parish Council President Michael A. Bouloubassis, April 2000.

Archbishop Stylianos of Australia and Senator Paul S. Sarbanes
following the Doxology Service for the International Dialogue
between Orthodox and Catholic Church Leaders, July 15, 2000.

the IOCC. Father Monios, who was acquainted with Father Kyriakakis from their school years at the Holy Cross Theological Seminary, warmly welcomed Father James and Presbytera Sophia into Cathedral life. In fact, Father Kyriakakis was often invited to participate in liturgical services. By June of 2001, as Father Monios' declining health began to limit his capabilities, Father Kyriakakis officially assumed duties as the Liturgical Priest at Annunciation on a regular basis.

At the parish assembly held on April 29, 2001, a number of noteworthy items were reported. The Golden Age Club, which observed the 25th Anniversary of its founding that year, continued to be active. The club's yearly Easter egg-dyeing project received publicity in *The Baltimore Sun*. The Loaves and Fishes group once again provided food casseroles for the Franciscan Center and "Our Daily Bread." The winter 2001 initiatives for Projects Philoxenia and Zestasia were successful. The second annual Orthodox Youth Day encompassed parishes from the tri-state area and was being planned for June at King's Dominion in Virginia. Also, the Baltimore-Piraeus Sister Cities group would visit the Archdiocese and the Metropolitan Museum of Art in New York in early May of 2001.

A main topic at the spring 2001 assembly concerned the recent parish survey. Out of 2,300 surveys mailed, 950 completed surveys were returned—an impressive response rate of over 40 percent. During Holy Week of 2001, RESI had mailed the "Final Report," dated February 2001, to parishioners. According to the report, "an emphasis on engaging the youth of the parish was viewed as a major step toward moving the Cathedral forward." Creating a more "welcoming environment for those that were not of the Orthodox faith" was also suggested. There was also concern expressed for the "safety of the surrounding area." Two words that emerged frequently in the survey were "communication" and "outreach." RESI officials observed, "This is accomplished by communicating the needs of the church and its parishioners to its members and reaching out to members of all ages. Such actions will create the links that will help the Cathedral community remain strong and grow."

A topic of debate soon centered around the final survey question: "Please address any concerns or issues that we have not addressed, or any other comments you would like to add." Records show that 22 percent, or 210, out of the 950 survey respondents submitted various replies ranging from single sentences to complete pages expounding their personal suggestions for improvement. Considering the size and composition of the congregation, it was not surprising to see such great diversity in responses—from glowing accolades about clergymen and parish ministries to the outright demands for an overhaul of programs including a few suggestions to remove or reassign the priests. Even though the RESI report noted that subjective comments "do not necessarily represent the views of all parishioners," some felt it was unsettling and detrimental to see such negativity printed and distributed to the congregation.

Realizing the need to address all survey issues in a constructive manner, the spring 2001 parish assembly voted to have the parish council appoint an eleven-member committee to evaluate the results. Nearly thirty people responded to the call for volunteers. By August of 2001, Parish Council President Michael Bouloubassis convened the first meeting allowing all interested volunteers to participate. The new Survey Analysis Committee

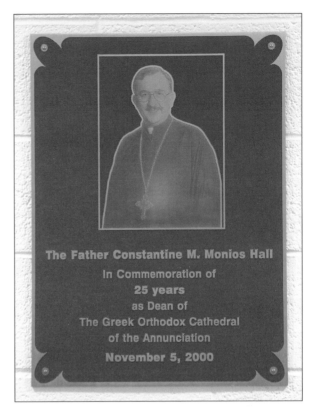

The Social Hall was renamed in honor of Father Monios for his 25th Anniversary as Cathedral Dean in November 2000.

A group of parishioners representing the Baltimore-Piraeus Sister Cities initiative visited the Archdiocesan Chapel during a special trip to New York City on May 8, 2001.

Ribbon-cutting ceremony rededicating the Mentis Room with Father Moralis (left) and Father Monios (right), July 15, 2001.

more ceiling height, was accomplished at a cost of $55,000. Some of the other new features were ceramic floor tile, brighter lighting with dimming capabilities, storage spaces, an entertainment center, and a small hospitality area.

The rededication ceremonies took place on July 15, 2001, with four special ribbon-cuttings. Participants included Irene Mentis Moshos, Michael Bouloubassis, Parish Council President; Diana Pillas, Women's Guild President; and Fathers Monios and Moralis. Major donors to the project included the Cathedral Women's Guild, Lt. Col. and Mrs. August A. Krometis, Mr. and Mrs. James Krometis, Mr. and Mrs. Nicholas Mentis, Mr. and Mrs. Gary T. Padussis, Mr. and Mrs. Basil M. Pappas, Mr. and Mrs. James N. Pappas, and Mr. John Paterakis. In reflecting on the project, Architect Paula Morris commented, "This project had special meaning for me because I recall with such fondness the many hours spent with the Mentis family in that very room. Whether it was for Junior GOYA activities, dances, or festival preparations, the room still echoes with their laughter, their compassion, and their faith."

To mark the beginning of the Orthodox Ecclesiastical Year on September 1, 2001, the Feast of Indiction was observed with a Divine Liturgy followed by an Orthodox Prayer-Fellowship Breakfast. Father Moralis read an Archpastoral proclamation from Archbishop Demetrios followed by welcome remarks and an opening discussion by Father Monios. Two keynote speakers included Reverend Gregory Mathewes-Green of the Holy Cross Antiochian Orthodox Church and Reverend James Kyriakakis representing the International Orthodox Christian Charities. The success of this event lead to a special yearly observance attended by Orthodox Christians from area churches.

Ten days later, the tragedies of the terrorist attacks in New York, Washington, D.C., and Pennsylvania on September 11, 2001, brought the world to a halt. Churches throughout the City of Baltimore, including Annunciation Cathedral, opened their doors to people seeking solace. The following day, prayer services were held to remember the victims and the families who lost loved ones in those senseless brutal attacks on humanity. At the time, final preparations were already in place for the annual parish festival on September 14-16, 2001. There were mixed

was led by: Basil M. Pappas, Chairman; Dimitri Cavathas, Co-Chairman; Despina Horst, Secretary; and Eleni Roros, Assistant Secretary. For over eight months, five work groups analyzed the data, considered the additional comments, and established guidelines for recommendations. By the following summer, parishioners would learn the outcome of their work.

In the meantime, other noteworthy projects were brought to completion. The summer of 2001 saw the rededication of the Mentis Room. This multi-purpose room had been dedicated in 1975 as a memorial tribute to the mother and her three young daughters who tragically lost their lives. Now, a quarter of a century later, it was evident that the room deserved a revitalization effort. Sandra Hondroulis served as the project liaison for the parish council. Paula Canelos Morris and her husband, William F. Morris, were the architectural consultants. Fundraising was initiated and a complete overhaul of the room, which included emotions as to whether or not to proceed with the event. Baltimore City officials encouraged church leaders not to cancel, feeling the festival would give people a place to gather in fellowship during a time of uncertainty.

Moving forward, the Annunciation Cathedral made the bold decision to host the festival. However, out of respect for the victims of 9/11, music and dancing was limited to a small number of youth group performances that weekend. The IOCC and Red Cross were the recipients of a portion of the festival proceeds. The following month, on October 21, 2001, a 40-day Memorial Service was held for the victims of 9/11. Over $2,000 was raised that day for relief efforts. By this time, the Greek Orthodox Archdiocese had established the "September 11th Relief Fund" and Orthodox faithful throughout America responded generously. Fundraising was also initiated to assist the St. Nicholas Greek Orthodox Church, located in the heart of New York's financial district, which was demolished during the collapse of the nearby World Trade Center Towers.

Throughout these difficult times, people turned to their clergy for spiritual guidance and comfort. Fathers Monios and Moralis met with parishioners, especially the youth, to help ease their worries. Father Monios' moving sermon, delivered on Sunday, September 16, 2001, had such a profound impact on the congregation that the entire text was reprinted in the November 2001 parish newsletter. In his concluding remarks he stated, "This Church would not be here if our ancestors yielded to enemy forces. They were willing to fight, even at the cost of their lives, in order to maintain the dignity of life and to instruct their children in all good things. I think many of us had our eyes opened this week because we had become complacent about our safety and security. Do not be complacent about anything, especially about your life…. I know your hearts are heavy, so is mine. I know there are images in your mind that you will never forget . . . . I also know that if we really wish to give tribute to those who have fallen asleep in the Lord…you must go on with your life…." Those who heard the passionate sermon continued to talk about it for weeks to come.

Nearly forty children from area Orthodox churches, along with clergy and volunteer counselors, participated in the first Winter Bible Camp program held at Annunciation Cathedral, December 27-28, 2001.

Parish Council, 2002. Front row left to right: Zaharoula Kokinos, Secretary; Larry Vakoutis, Rev. Dean Moralis, Rev. Constantine Monios, Rev. James Kyriakakis, Thomas Boardman, Vice President; Despina Horst, James Pappas, Ernest Rafailides, Treasurer. Back row left to right: Georgeann Morekas, Christos Panagiotopoulos, Dr. Savas Tsakiris, Paul Agathoklis, Thomas Zizos, Perry Galanakis, Constantine Letras, Evangelos Sidou, President; and Chrysoula Ponticas.

Parish Council President Evangelos D. Sidou (left) and Father Constantine Monios, Vasilopita Sunday, Jan. 20, 2002.

The fall of 2001 was also a time to reflect upon volunteer service. On National Church Music Sunday, October 7, 2001, choir officers were formally recognized: Vernon Rey, President; James Georges, Vice President; Cynthia Stathopoulos, Secretary; and Esther Samios, Treasurer. In addition, those with over thirty years of choir service were noted: Tasia Cavas, Mary Constantine, Stella Hansard, Fotini Nichols, Gus Letras, and Vernon Rey. Special awards were also bestowed upon Anita Tsakalas for 38 years and Cantor Sotirios Mangos for 45 years of service. In the Education Department, the Greek language school underwent a change in leadership. Christos Motsiopoulos stepped down after serving for five years as the principal in order to resume teaching the Greek language. By the fall of 2001, Dina-Athena Vakiaros became the new principal, followed by Calliopi Topaltzas who assumed the leadership of the Greek language program in 2006.

At the fall general assembly held on Sunday, October 28, 2001, various initiatives were discussed at length. Over the summer months, repairs were made to the Cathedral's windows including the replacement of rotting wood and painting; similar work ensued on the windows of the AOC building. The roofs of the Cathedral and Education Building were scheduled for repairs in 2002. With all work estimated at $90,000, it was decided that the Cathedral Major Repairs and Replacement Fund would pay for these projects. Property acquisition was also on the agenda. Parish Council President Michael Bouloubassis gave an overview of prior attempts to acquire the final two Preston Street town houses across from the Cathedral. It was reported that Nos. 41 and 43 West Preston Street were again for sale. Ownership of these buildings was deemed critical for the future development of the other three buildings (Nos. 35, 37, and 39 West Preston Street) acquired by the parish in the 1990's.

A motion was made by James Galanakis for the Annunciation Cathedral to acquire 41-43 West Preston Street for the sum of $147,000. It was also announced that a donor had come forward with a pledge of $47,000 toward this goal. The parish would then assume a $100,000 mortgage. The motion passed with the stipulation that a Capital Fund Drive Committee would raise the monies needed. Soon after, a purchase agreement was signed for the acquisition of the buildings. After years of anticipation, the Annunciation Cathedral finally became the owner of the entire block of town houses up to, but not including, the southwest corner property, No. 45 West Preston Street.

Another interesting topic of the fall 2001 assembly soon developed into debate on the national level. The issue concerned the Archdiocesan Charter and the procedures for implementing changes to that document. Peter Marudas introduced a resolution to request the Archdiocese to "publish the text of any proposed revised Charter and to distribute copies with a study guide" by mid-December 2001. This would give the parishes an opportunity to prepare their delegates for the upcoming 2002 Archdiocesan Clergy-Laity Conference. In addition, parish representatives to the conference were instructed by the assembly gathering to support adoption of the following, "No revised charter shall be approved or adopted by the Archdiocese unless it has been approved by the Clergy-Laity Congress pursuant to the 1977 Charter which was still in effect."

The December 2001 issue of *Baltimore Magazine* ran a special story entitled "Clergy with Clout." Father Constantine Monios, spiritual leader of one of the ten largest Orthodox parishes in the nation, was among the featured clergymen. That year, the Annunciation community quietly marked 95 years of existence as a religious organization in Baltimore. The article described the diversity of the congregation with a membership of 1,400 families and an operating budget of $670,000. Outreach programs to the lesser fortunate within the city, including Project Philoxenia, Loaves and Fishes, and Project Zestasia, received praise. In reflecting on his parish, Father Monios boasted, "We have great participation from our people—the whole congregation is very hands-on…Part of the beauty of the ministry of this cathedral is that everybody feels it's their church."

The start of 2002 was a time to commemorate the early immigrants. On Sunday, January 20, 2002, the parish observed the 90th Anniversary of the Greek Section at Woodlawn Cemetery—the first Orthodox burial grounds founded in 1912. That day, special memorial services were held for those who were buried in the historic "Greek Circle." The anniversary tribute coincided with the publication of *Gone But Not Forgotten*, a 200-page history of this first parish cemetery written by Nicholas M. Prevas. The book was dedicated to the memory of his father, Michael N. Prevas, who had assisted him over the years with his research.

The history of Annunciation's first cemetery was written by Parish Historian Nicholas M. Prevas.

The Greek Section at Woodlawn, with over 600 burials, contained only 230 tombstones. Nicholas M. Prevas used tombstones as reference points, along with cemetery office records, to find the location of unmarked graves.

The monument above for Giordanis Papadopoulos, who died in 1922, was one of many restored tombstones (see right).

In the book's foreword, Father Constantine Monios stated, "I am confident many of our faithful will find their way to the Greek Section...to witness firsthand this historic cemetery that countless Orthodox Christians have visited for nine decades."

Favorable reviews of the cemetery book were printed in the *National Herald*, a weekly Greek-American newspaper from New York, triggering renewed interest in the preservation of the historic burial grounds. In fact, all proceeds from the sales of the publication were set aside for the upkeep of the "Greek Section" at Woodlawn. The project was truly a Prevas family endeavor. In the summer of 2001, the initial restoration work began through a generous donation from the author's mother,

Zinovia Markulis Prevas, in memory of her husband, Michael. The W. S. Tegeler Monument Company, under the supervision of Walter S. Tegeler III, carried out the tedious and detailed work. The parish council of the Annunciation Cathedral designated Nicholas M. Prevas to coordinate various aspects of the restoration with officials at the Woodlawn Cemetery.

The Greek Section — North Avon
Greek Orthodox Cathedral of the Annunciation

This historic first cemetery of Baltimore's Greek Community
consists of four burial grounds

Greek Circle — est. 1912
Greek Plot — est. 1916
Holy Trinity — est. 1924
New Greek Plot — est. 1936

On May 29, 1932, Archbishop Athenagoras consecrated this
sacred burial ground. Since January of 1912, over 600
Orthodox Christians have been laid to rest here.

May their memory be eternal.

Gift of Zinovia M. Prevas, in loving memory of her husband Michael.
January 2002 — 90th Anniversary of the Greek Circle.

Zinovia M. Prevas and her son, Nicholas, at the tribute for
the 90th Anniversary of the parish cemetery, January 20, 2002.
That day, the historical marker for the Greek Section at Woodlawn
Cemetery was dedicated to the memory of Michael N. Prevas.

By the 90th Anniversary tribute, the cleaning, straightening, and repairing of broken monuments were well underway with impressive results. One unique aspect of the restoration was the installation of eighty bricks placed in the form of a circle to mark the original boundary of the "Greek Circle." A special bronze plaque was blessed at the tribute in January of 2002 and later installed at the cemetery. As a result of this project, parishioners with relatives interred in unmarked graves were able to locate exact burial sites using the diagram found in the book. Some were even inspired to place markers denoting the final place of rest for their ancestors who helped to shape the early history of the Greek Orthodox community.

As Father Constantine Monios described the importance of the memorial tribute offered through the publication of *Gone But Not Forgotten*, no one could have imagined that within six months his own name would be added to the memorial hymns of the parish. The Woodlawn Cemetery project, a topic that fascinated the senior clergyman, was in fact one of the final church-sponsored events he attended. With his health declining steadily throughout 2001, he suffered a broken ankle in February of 2002 and was confined to his home for a gradual recuperation. Parish council minutes during this period even noted his hopeful resumption of duties by the summer of 2002.

Soon, however, it was learned that Father Constantine Monios was also undergoing chemotherapy treatments for cancer. As parishioners became aware of the severity of his condition, he received hundreds of get-well wishes and prayers for a speedy recovery. As this scenario unfolded, Father Dean Moralis, the assistant priest mentored by Father Monios, found himself assuming the role as spiritual leader for the entire congregation. Father Moralis, along with Father James Kyriakakis, the Liturgical Priest, worked closely with the 2002 parish council led by President Evangelos D. Sidou. To the credit of clergy and parish leaders, the running of church affairs remained on course throughout the uncertainty of Father Monios' health in the early months of 2002.

Moving forward, the Annunciation Cathedral sponsored a luncheon program on Sunday, February 24, 2002, to benefit the newly established Ethiopian Orthodox Church of Baltimore. Ethiopian music, songs and dances were presented to the congregation. Event proceeds were earmarked for the Ethiopian Church building fund. One week earlier, the Golden Age Club, under the leadership of Nicholas J. Kiladis, sponsored its annual coffee hour for the benefit of the St. Photios Shrine. Various other Golden Age events for 2002 included a trip to Florida, a potluck dinner, and a memorial service. During Great Lent, the congregation

Over 50 parishioners joined in the "Walk for Kenya" on April 14, 2002, to raise funds for the parish team that traveled to Chavogere, Kenya, to help construct a school for the Orthodox Christian Mission Center.

welcomed His Grace, Bishop Dimitrios of Xanthos. He officiated at Great Vespers commemorating the Sunday of Orthodoxy and the Feast Day of the Annunciation on March 24-25, 2002.

By this time, an exciting new initiative had taken form. The first Missions Committee meeting was held under the direction of Father Dean Moralis. Soon, a mission trip to Chavogere, Kenya, was planned from May 24-June 8, 2002, through the Orthodox Christian Mission Center (OCMC). The objective was to help construct an eight-room secondary school adjacent to the St. Mark Orthodox Church and the Chavogere Orthodox Medical Clinic. To help defray travel expenses for the fifteen-member parish team, a "Walk for Kenya" fundraiser was held on April 14, 2002, with Jo Marie Gafos as chairperson. Over fifty parishioners participated and nearly $12,000 was raised. Continuing the parish's focus on missionary work, Seminarian Alexander Maistros traveled to the Hogar Rafael Ayau Orthodox Orphanage in Guatemala the next year and was joined by parishioner Evangelos Ioannou.

The following week, discussion about the Archdiocesan Charter was the main focus at the spring parish assembly held on April 21, 2002. Evan A. Chriss expressed his concern over the lack of clergy and laity involved in the drafting of the new proposed charter. The timing of its distribution was also noted as being too late for most Greek Orthodox parishes to act upon it and respond appropriately. As a result, the Annunciation parish assembly voted to support the continued use of the 1977 charter. Furthermore, no revisions to the charter would be acceptable unless those proposed changes and amendments were initiated and approved by the Clergy-Laity Congress. That day, Thomas Boardman, Despina Horst, and Ernest Rafailides were selected as the parish representatives to the summer session in Los Angeles, California.

That same month, the Annunciation Cathedral hosted a prestigious program in commemoration of the Tenth Anniversary of the International Orthodox Christian Charities. IOCC is the official humanitarian aid agency of SCOBA (Standing Conference of Canonical Orthodox Bishops in

Archbishop Demetrios and Chairpersons Jeanne and Nicholas Tsakalos, IOCC 10th Anniversary Banquet, April 18, 2002.

the Americas). Archbishop Demetrios, IOCC Chairman, noted that during its first ten years of operation, the IOCC had contributed more than $140 million in programs throughout 21 countries. At this event held on Thursday, April 18, 2002, Chairpersons Jeanne and Nicholas Tsakalos presented Archbishop Demetrios with a special icon of St. Sava, the 13th-century founder of the Serbian Orthodox Church. The icon had been hand-painted in a Serbian workshop supported by an IOCC program.

The IOCC dinner program held in the AOC Ballroom was preceded by Lenten Vespers in the Annunciation Cathedral presided over by Archbishop Demetrios, along with Bishop Dimitrios of Xanthos and nineteen area Orthodox clergymen. It was a highly emotional moment when Father Constantine Monios, a longtime supporter of the IOCC and Dean of the Annunciation Cathedral, entered the sanctuary for the first time in months. Though extremely weakened by his illness, he spoke briefly to the Orthodox faithful in attendance offering words of encouragement for the future of the IOCC and his beloved parish. Many in the congregation were moved to tears. . . it would be his final public appearance.

Some of the guests in attendance at the IOCC Banquet held in the ballroom of the Annunciation Orthodox Center.

The Very Rev. Constantine M. Monios, 68, led Cathedral of the Annunciation

By MICHAEL STROH
AND JOHN RIVERA
SUN STAFF

The Very Rev. Constantine M. Monios, dean of the Cathedral of the Annunciation and the senior-ranking Greek Orthodox clergyman in Maryland, died yesterday afternoon of prostate cancer. He was 68 and lived in Cockeysville.

A man who first dreamed of becoming a priest at the age of five, Father Monios served as the head of the cathedral on Maryland Avenue and Preston Street for almost 27 years and was widely admired by parishioners and priests alike.

"He was enormously respected and loved by his congregation," said Sen. Paul S. Sarbanes, a longtime parishioner who has known Father Monios since the priest arrived in Baltimore in 1975. "He was also regarded as one of the leading Orthodox priests in the country."

One of just two priests serving the more than 1,200 families who attend the cathedral, Father Monios frequently worked 12-hour days ministering to his congregation and running the church.

Despite his hectic schedule, he always found the time to make each baptism, wedding or funeral something special.

"One liturgy wasn't like the next one to him. He tried to make each one different," said the Rev. Dean Moralis, who has worked alongside Father Monios for the past seven years.

Active in ecumenical and interfaith relations, Father Monios served as mentor to many Greek Orthodox priests in the Baltimore area.

"He showed you how to be a pastor, not just a priest," said the Rev. Louis Noplos of St. Demetrios Greek Orthodox Church in Cub Hill, who had worked with Father Monios for nearly 15 years. "A pastor is more of a shepherd. He was there to teach us to be shepherds of our flocks."

SUN FILE : 1998
Father Monios was known for his skill as an orator.

The Rev. Manuel Burdusi of St. Nicholas Greek Orthodox Church in Highlandtown said one of Father Monios' greatest gifts was his ability to intently listen to anyone who approached him for counsel.

"You felt like you mattered the most to him at that particular time," Father Burdusi said. "I know it's a hard thing for me to do in my own church, when I've got a hundred things on my mind."

Another of his gifts was as an orator, those who knew him say. His sermons — and especially eulogies — were legendary among his congregation.

"He was so great at delivering eulogies, you almost wanted to die just so someone could tape it," said Lou Panos of Timonium, a parishioner at the cathedral nearly all of his 76 years.

Panos recalled that when his cousin died, Father Monios sat him down and asked him to describe the man. "He didn't make a note," Panos said. But later Father Monios gave a stirring eulogy using practically every detail of their conversation. "He was a great source of strength for members of the congregation," Panos said.

Born in Monessen, Pa., Father Monios was the child of immigrants from the Greek island of Chois.

Growing up in the town's small, tight-knit Greek community, little "Costa," as Father Monios was known then, quickly acquired a love of his Greek tradition, especially when it came to the church.

Enchanted by its sights and sounds, he became an altar boy at 5 and entertained dreams of becoming a priest even then. Not long afterward, his destiny was sealed.

In a chance encounter he would recount the rest of his life, a 14-year-old Costa met the then-head of the Greek Orthodox church in America, the Archbishop Athenagoras, who looked into the boy's eyes and told him that one day he would be a priest. Four years later, Father Monios entered Holy Cross Greek Orthodox Seminary in Brookline, Mass., and was ordained in 1957.

Afterward he sent a picture of himself in priestly garb to the archbishop as thanks.

After serving in several parishes in the Northeast, Father Monios arrived at the Annunciation Cathedral in 1975.

Father Monios was nationally known for his work on the National Presbyters Council, one of many ecclesiastical and professional organizations he served on over the years.

"Really, all of America is mourning for our priest here in Baltimore," said Father Burdusi of St. Nicholas.

Funeral services are tentatively scheduled to be held at the Cathedral of the Annunciation on Wednesday morning.

Father Monios is survived by his wife of 46 years, the former Mary Christodoulou; three daughters Athena Stem of New Freedom, Pa; Amalia Monios and Nikki Anagnostou, both of Perry Hall; two sons, Harry Monios and Michael Monios, both of Perry Hall; and nine grandchildren.

A memorial tribute to Father Constantine Monios, the senior-ranking Orthodox clergyman in Maryland, was published in *The Baltimore Sun* on Saturday, June 22, 2002. He served the Annunciation Cathedral from 1975-2002.

As summer began on Friday, June 21, 2002, The Very Rev. Constantine M. Monios, age 68, fell asleep in the Lord. News of his death spread quickly throughout Baltimore and the Archdiocese. One of his final wishes was for all parish events to proceed as planned. The following morning, parishioners gathered at the Greek Orthodox Cemetery for the traditional Saturday of Souls. The name of "Constantine the Protopresbyter" was added to the memorial hymns chanted that day. Father Dean Moralis, along with cantors, a few seminarians, and parishioners, then proceeded to the Woodlawn Cemetery for the scheduled dedication of the new plaque commemorating the establishment of the "Greek Section" burial grounds ninety years earlier.

On Sunday, June 23, 2002, the Cathedral was filled for the Feast of Pentecost as parishioners sought to comfort each other over the death of their spiritual father. The Rev. Dean Moralis displayed exemplary strength in fulfilling his priestly duties in the difficult days and weeks ahead. In keeping with Father Monios' wishes to stay the course, Lucy Hagopian, Cathedral Business Administrator, was honored that day for reaching the 35th anniversary of her service to the community. As a tribute to her Armenian heritage, the parish forwarded donations collected during the coffee hour to an orphanage in Armenia. During the activities of that emotional weekend, the clergy and parish council worked closely with the Archdiocese to finalize arrangements for the funeral of the senior-ranking Orthodox clergyman in the State of Maryland.

The viewing for Father Constantine Monios was held at the Annunciation Cathedral from June 24-25, 2002, where hundreds of mourners gathered to pray and offer final respects to their beloved priest. On Wednesday, June 26, 2002, the funeral services were conducted with His Eminence Archbishop Demetrios of America presiding, along with Bishop Dimitrios of Xanthos and forty Orthodox priests. It was the first time in parish history that a clergyman had died during his pastorate at Annunciation. The funeral of The Very Rev. Constantine M. Monios was one of the largest in the history of Baltimore's Greek Orthodox community. Eulogies given by Father Dean Moralis, New Jersey Diocese Chancellor Rev. Alexander Leondis, and Archbishop Demetrios described him as a progressive-thinking, energetic,

Father Constantine and Presbytera Mary Monios were married for 46 years and were well known throughout the Greek Orthodox Archdiocese of America.

and vibrant pastor. His sermons were considered legendary among his congregation. He was a special clergyman who had touched the lives of thousands of people.

During the span of his career, Father Monios had received numerous accolades for his dedication to the Church, including the distinguished title of *Protopresbyter,* from both the Greek Orthodox Archdiocese as well as the Ecumenical Patriarchate of Constantinople. During his early years at Annunciation, realizing that Baltimore would be his permanent home, Father Monios had the remains of deceased family members brought from their burial sites in Pennsylvania and West Virginia to be reinterred in Baltimore's Greek Orthodox Cemetery on Windsor Mill Road. On June 26, 2002, The Very Rev. Constantine M. Monios was laid to rest near his beloved parents and brother in the same cemetery where he had conducted so many hundreds of burials and comforted countless Orthodox Christians during the course of his impressive pastorate.

Forty-Day Memorial Service for Father Constantine Monios. Left to right: Rev. Christopher Flesoras of Roseville, CA, Rev. James Kyriakakis, Rev. Alexander G. Leondis, Chancellor of the Diocese of New Jersey; His Eminence Archbishop Demetrios, Rev. George Kalpaxis, Rev. John Chakos of Pittsburgh, PA, and Rev. Dean Moralis, Sunday, August 4, 2002.

A few days after the funeral, well-known journalist Jacques Kelly published a remembrance of Father Monios in *The Baltimore Sun*. It stated in part: "I'll think of all the good he accomplished every time I pass the corner of Maryland Avenue and Preston Street. I'll think of him when I walk past the handsome gray granite building he so enriched, where he celebrated liturgies and baptized so many children....I'll think of him when I walk along a row of once shabby rooming houses he and his congregation cleaned up and made into a parish center. When I was around Father Monios, I sensed a man of deep conviction. He saw the best; he saw the possibilities. He saw the light, not the darkness." Those eloquent words were a source of comfort for a grieving parish. The dynamic legacy of The Reverend Constantine Monios, spanning a remarkable quarter of a century in Baltimore, had come to a close.

The next period of Annunciation's history began with the announcement anticipated by many parishioners. The Rev. Dean Moralis, a lifelong member of the Greek Orthodox Cathedral of the Annunciation, had been selected by Archbishop Demetrios to lead the congregation. On Monday, July 8, 2002, *The Baltimore Sun* ran the story

entitled "Church's New Leader a Familiar Face." The article described how Father Moralis, with great respect for the traditions that Father Constantine Monios had nurtured, was now following in the footsteps of his mentor and predecessor. His installation as Dean of Annunciation Cathedral was planned for August 4, 2002, immediately following the 40-day Memorial Service for Father Monios. It would prove to be a day of overwhelming emotions for all who witnessed the solemn ceremonies.

His Eminence Archbishop Demetrios of America, accompanied by Deacon Panteleimon Papadopoulos, presided over church services on August 4, 2002, and conducted the traditional 40-day Memorial Service. A special Memorial Tribute to Father Constantine Monios was published and distributed to the congregation that day. Following the memorial service, Father Dean Moralis was then elevated to the dignity and status of Archimandrite and installed as the Dean of the Annunciation Cathedral. He began a new chapter in his pastoral career as the twentieth *proistamenos* (senior clergyman) to serve the Annunciation community since its founding ninety-six years earlier. Afterwards, the Philoptochos Society hosted

The Rev. Constantine "Dean" Moralis, a lifelong member of the Greek Orthodox Cathedral of the Annunciation, was named as the new spiritual leader of the parish. On August 4, 2002, he was installed as Cathedral Dean and elevated to the dignity and status of Archimandrite. This photograph appeared in *The Baltimore Sun* on Monday, July 8, 2002.

a reception in loving memory of Father Constantine Monios and in honor of Father Dean Moralis.

A number of Orthodox clergymen participated in the events of that historic Sunday including Rev. Louis Noplos, Rev. George Kalpaxis, and Rev. James Kyriakakis from Baltimore. Also present were Rev. Alexander G. Leondis, Chancellor of the Diocese of New Jersey; Rev. John Chakos of Holy Cross in Pittsburgh, Pennsylvania, representing Father Monios' former parish; and Rev. Christopher Flesoras of Saint Anna in Roseville, California, a longtime friend of Father Dean Moralis. That day, The Very Rev. Constantine Moralis became the first Archimandrite to serve the parish in nearly five decades. In addition, Archbishop Demetrios elevated Father Louis Noplos to the rank of *Protopresbyter*, and Stefanos G. Niktas was elevated to the rank of *Protopsaltis* (First Cantor).

By this time, a number of items were on Annunciation's business agenda. A special parish assembly on Sunday, July 14, 2002, focused on two

Stefanos G. Niktas was elevated to the rank of *Protopsaltis* (First Cantor) by Archbishop Demetrios in August of 2002.

improvement projects—repairing the flat roof of the Education Building and the resurfacing of the existing second-level parking garage deck at 1205 Maryland Avenue. Both were approved, the projects commenced, and were completed by the fall of 2002. During the summer of 2002, the Survey Committee mailed its findings with over forty recommendations dealing with various areas covered in the survey such as liturgical services, church organizations and programs, education, community outreach, and communications. Recommendations were forwarded to those individuals and committees responsible for various ministries. Soon, efforts were underway to improve the noted aspects of parish life within the budgeted resources available.

Further changes in personnel were also on the agenda as the Annunciation Cathedral settled into a new era of spiritual leadership. Panagiotis (Peter) J. Thornberg, a native of Washington, D.C., was welcomed in August of 2002 as the new Pastoral Assistant. As a recent graduate of the Holy Cross Greek Orthodox School of Theology, he had earned a Master of Divinity Degree with distinction and participated in numerous retreats and youth activities at the Diocesan and Archdiocesan level.

Two months later, on October 13, 2002, Peter Thornberg married Katherine Anaipakos. The ceremony took place at her home parish of the Saint George Antiochian Orthodox Church in El Paso, Texas. The Annunciation congregation cordially welcomed the new Pastoral Assistant and his wife as they established themselves in Baltimore during the fall of 2002.

The Philoptochos Society was in the spotlight a few weeks later. In addressing the congregation on November 3, 2002, Philoptochos President Koula Savvakis discussed the need for additional funding to support their work efforts. Some of the recipients of monies from the ladies' group included the Hellenic College/Holy Cross, St. Basil Academy, the IOCC, the Children's Medical Fund, and UNICEF. Locally, the group provides food to the less fortunate, distributes quilts to area hospitals through the ABC Quilts program, and supplies meals to area Orthodox college students through a Campus Ministries program. In addition, they send a monthly stipend to support Baltimore seminarians, offer scholarships, and provide emotional and financial support to families in need. The Philoptochos Society continues to flourish as parishioners respond to these worthy causes.

Pastoral Assistant Peter Thornberg and Katherine Anaipakos were united in Holy Matrimony at the St. George Antiochian Orthodox Church in El Paso, Texas, on October 13, 2002.

Philoptochos Society Meeting and Luncheon with
President Koula Savvakis (seated third from right)
and Father Dean Moralis (center), January 14, 2003.

By this time, the Religious Education Program of the Annunciation Cathedral had begun its 2002-2003 season. Perry Galanakis, Director of the Sunday school, along with Co-Directors Despina Matsos, Eleni Roros, and Abigail Tsamoutalis, coordinated the educational agenda for parish students of all ages. The teaching levels included pre-nursery, nursery, kindergarten, first through seventh grades and one class for eighth through twelfth grades. Teaching themes ranged from "God Loves Us" at the nursery level to "Contemporary Issues Facing Orthodox Christians" for teenaged students. In addition, the parish boasted a program for Adult Religious Education.

Further achievements were clearly evident by the reports given at the fall parish assembly held on November 17, 2002. Parish Council President Evangelos Sidou reported the Cathedral was maintaining its sound financial status. Treasurer Ernest Rafailides added that the proposed 2003 budget was approaching an impressive $700,000. During 2002, the parish had acquired 41 and 43 West Preston Street, and a special thanks was given to John Diakoulas of the Acropolis Construction Company for ensuring that the vacant properties were secured from potential vandalism. It was hoped that the parish would soon formulate

Preparation of Easter boxes by the Philoptochos Society
for parish college students and military personnel away
from home, *l to r* : Tasia Cavas, Stacey Mesologites,
Dottie Panos, Bess Stamas, Maria Anagnostou,
Jean Frank and Jeanette Drosinos, 2003.

Choir Sopranos Ann Sophocleus (left) and
Diane Tseckares (right) were the featured performers
at a concert in the AOC Ballroom, April 12, 2003.

Nos. 35, 37, 39, 41 and 43 West Preston Street were acquired between 1993-2002 for the future expansion of Cathedral programs.

definitive plans for the use of Nos. 35, 37, 39, 41, and 43 West Preston Street...the five town houses adjacent to the magnificent Annunciation Orthodox Center.

The physical repairs made to the Cathedral complex during 2002 were also on the business agenda, and the Building Committee was thanked for overseeing the maintenance of all Cathedral facilities. It was noted that the organized work of the Survey Committee had resulted in a plan of action. One new concept, the Welcoming Committee, was already in progress as a result of the survey. The Cemetery Committee, commended by the assembly for maintaining the burial grounds, soon found itself focused on handling the visible deterioration of the front entrance to the Chapel of the Holy Resurrection. Ultimately, the matter would be handled within a few years with an impressive face-lift to the chapel entrance.

With the arrival of 2003, the Centennial Committee, under the general chairmanship of Gary T. Padussis, had begun planning the celebration for the parish's 100th Anniversary in 2006. The observance of this historic milestone would span the course of twelve months beginning with the 99th year in March of 2005 and culminate

with the actual 100th Anniversary in March of 2006. It would be an opportunity for the community to join in fellowship at religious services, lectures, musical galas, historical tributes, museum visits, and family-oriented events. A special website, www.goannun100.org, was launched to provide more details on centennial events as they were finalized.

The spring of 2003 proved to be memorable with the return visit of a former assistant pastor, Rev. Mark Arey. He was invited to be the keynote speaker at the 9th Annual Lenten Retreat sponsored by the "Growing in Faith" Bible study group on April 5, 2003. Father Arey, the pastor of the St. George Tropeoforos Greek Orthodox Church in Manhattan, New York, shared his insights on St. John's apocalyptic writings in the Book of Revelation. The following week, the spotlight was on talented sopranos from the Cathedral's choir. On April 12, 2003, a concert featuring Ann Sophocleus and Diane Tseckares was held. The event was coordinated by Koula Savvakis and Anastasia August and included a cabaret-style fare in the AOC Ballroom.

The completion of a number of projects was noted at the spring parish assembly held on June 2,

2003. Parish Council President Evangelos Sidou commended the Building and Maintenance Committee, under the leadership of Thomas P. Zizos, for its diligent work. All roofing was completed and the ceiling near the Cathedral office was repaired. The Klicos Painting Company, under the supervision of Andreas Savvakis, repainted the classrooms, hallways, offices, and boardroom. It was noted that a structural engineer was called upon to conduct a load-bearing test for the aging garage structure. In addition, flooding in the catacomb area of the basement was slated for corrective measures. Soon after, John Diakoulas of the Acropolis Construction Company coordinated the repairs to alleviate further water damage. The summer of 2003 also saw the reconfiguration and repaving of the flat parking lot, courtesy of the Peter Angelos family.

By this time, a Five-Year Planning Committee had been established with George F. Pappas as Chairman and Thomas Boardman as Vice Chairman. Their work focused on developing a strategic plan for the expansion of Cathedral properties. In one phase of work, the progress of the Building, Garage, Annunciation Orthodox Center, and Cemetery Committees was reviewed to assess short-term as well as long-term goals and expenses associated with these programs. Throughout this period, youth ministries encompassing spiritual,

Annunciation GOYA gathering, 2002.
Front *l to r* : Christina Zizos, Gia Vakoutis, Eleni Rizakos. Middle row *l to r* : Nicholas Marsh, Shane Cole, Nicholas Klicos. Back row *l to r* : Steven Agathoklis, Alexander Creticos, Nicholas Karas.

GOYA Christmas carolers led by Pastoral Assistant Peter Thornberg (far right), December 2003.

social, and athletic programs were active under the guidance of Pastoral Assistant Peter Thornberg. Over 50 children had attended the Winter Bible Camp in December of 2002, and the JOY and HOPE groups were meeting regularly as Mr. Thornberg continued developing a good rapport with the youngest parishioners. In 2003, he also implemented the concept of "Little Angels," geared for infants and toddlers up to three years of age.

Other initiatives taken by the Annunciation Cathedral during this time included the increased use of computers. E-bulletins were sent out announcing news and events to parishioners who provided the office with their e-mail addresses. Under the direction of Father Moralis, Alex Solomotis coordinated numerous enhancements and updates to the Cathedral's web site. Computer technology was vital in allowing clergy to better communicate with parishioners in a timely manner. Keeping this goal in mind, Father Moralis sought the assistance of other knowledgeable parishioners. Savas J. Karas offered technical expertise and assistance to the clergy and office staff in dealing with computer-related issues, software upgrades and equipment maintenance.

In the spring of 2003, it was announced that Archimandrite Evangelos Kourounis would be elected as the Metropolitan of New Jersey. He was born in New York City on September 20, 1961, to John and Magdalene Kourounis who originated from the Island of Kalymnos in the Dodecanese. Graduating from Hellenic College in 1983, he continued his graduate studies at the Holy Cross School of Theology and received a Master of Divinity Degree in 1986. His ordination to the Holy Diaconate took place on February 1, 1987. Two years later, on July 30, 1989, Deacon Evangelos Kourounis was ordained to the Holy Priesthood by Bishop Philotheos of Meloa. By the spring of 1991, he was elevated to the dignity and status of Archimandrite by Archbishop Iakovos. During the two years prior to his election to the Episcopacy, Metropolitan Evangelos served as Dean of the Greek Orthodox Cathedral of St. Demetrios located in Astoria, New York.

Sunday, May 11, 2003, marked the historic enthronement of Metropolitan Evangelos as the spiritual leader of the Greek Orthodox Metropolis of New Jersey. His Eminence Archbishop Demetrios, along with several other Hierarchs,

His Eminence Metropolitan Evangelos, Spiritual Leader of the Metropolis of New Jersey, was enthroned in 2003.

conducted the ceremony at the Greek Orthodox Cathedral of St. John the Theologian in Tenafly, New Jersey. Metropolitan Evangelos succeeded Metropolitan Silas and Bishop George of New Jersey as spiritual leader of the region. Earlier that year, the Diocese of New Jersey had been elevated to a "Metropolis" under the terms of the new 2003 charter granted to the Archdiocese. The Metropolis of New Jersey comprises over 50 parishes in New Jersey, the Philadelphia region of Pennsylvania, Delaware, Maryland, and Virginia.

By the summer of 2003, Metropolitan Evangelos would make his first visit to the Annunciation Cathedral in Baltimore during the 21st National Young Adult League (YAL) Conference held from July 3-6, 2003. The Young Adult League chapters of Baltimore and Washington, D.C., hosted the conference at the Renaissance Hotel at Harborplace in Baltimore. From across America, nearly 500 young people, ages 18-35, attended numerous workshops geared to the theme "Sign of the Cross: Vision and Victory." Ernest Rafailides served as the general chairperson with Kyriakos Marudas and Andrea Liacouras as co-chairpersons. A Hierarchical Divine Liturgy at the Annunciation Cathedral on July 6, 2003, was

Hierarchical Divine Liturgy during the weekend of the National YAL (Young Adult League) Conference in Baltimore. Left to right: Rev. Christopher Flesoras, Rev. George Kalpaxis, Deacon Luke Melackrinos, Archbishop Demetrios of America, Metropolitan Evangelos of New Jersey, Deacon Evangelos Evangelidis, The Very Reverend Constantine Moralis, and Rev. Dr. Nicholas J. Verdaris, Annunciation Cathedral, Sunday, July 6, 2003.

Cardinal William H. Keeler of the Catholic Archdiocese (center) with The Very Rev. Constantine Moralis (left) and Baltimore City Police Officer Nicholas Louloudis (right) at Annunciation Cathedral, YAL Conference, July 2003.

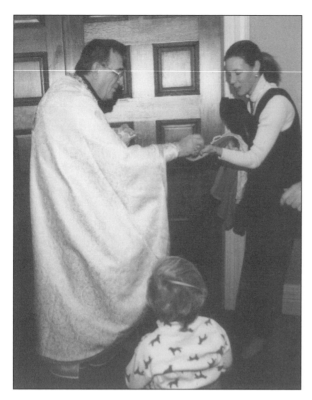

The Rev. James Kyriakakis served as Liturgical Priest at Annunciation Cathedral from 2001- 2003.

the highlight of the conference. His Eminence Archbishop Demetrios of America and His Eminence Metropolitan Evangelos of New Jersey presided over the services. The conference ended with a parish-wide Bible study held in the sanctuary that afternoon.

In the month preceding the YAL Conference, the Annunciation community bid farewell to the Rev. James Kyriakakis who had served as a Liturgical Priest for the parish since 2001. On Sunday, June 29, 2003, a special coffee hour was given in his honor to thank him for his service to the parish. He would be remembered for his informative speeches on Orthodox theology and presentations at parish Bible study gatherings. Father James and Presbytera Sophia Kyriakakis returned to Katy, Texas, to be closer to their children and grandchildren. Sadly, the following year, on May 20, 2004, Father James Kyriakakis fell asleep in the Lord and his funeral was chanted at the Annunciation Cathedral in Houston, Texas.

Throughout the summer of 2003, dozens of volunteers began preparing for the Athenian Agora festival scheduled for September 19-21. Utilizing the Cathedral, Education Building, and

Annunciation Orthodox Center, a lavish presentation of culture, ethnic heritage, Greek food, and entertainment was planned by the festival committee under the general chairmanship of Aritee Poletis Bond. The festival was to begin on Friday, September 19, 2003, with both inside and outside activities. As the day approached, however, weather forecasters grimly predicted that the fury of Hurricane Isabel would hit the Baltimore region at the same time. The brunt of the storm arrived the evening of September 18th. By the next morning, it was being reported that less than five miles away, areas of the Inner Harbor and Fells Point were under floodwaters. Fortunately, the Mt. Vernon district surrounding the Annunciation Cathedral was spared from power outages and major damage.

Parish leaders were encouraged by city officials to proceed with the festival. It would be a place for people to escape from the effects of the violent storm of the night before and enjoy the hospitality of the Greek community. Volunteers quickly assembled and the event started by midday on Friday, September 19, 2003, just as sunshine appeared in the skies above. The prayers of hard-working parishioners were answered. Soon, record crowds gathered under the tents on Preston Street, visited display booths, and enjoyed Greek cuisine and exhibits the entire weekend. At the fall general assembly on October 20, 2003, Father Dean Moralis praised the community for pulling together through difficult times to accomplish a successful three-day festival despite the advent of Hurricane Isabel. On behalf of Aritee Bond, Joanne S. Deitz presented the "Agora 2003" report projecting a net income of $36,000.

A number of other parish programs were highlighted at the fall assembly. For instance, Peter Thornberg reported that the August 2003 Chesapeake Youth Camp, under the leadership of George C. Maistros, was attended by 130 children. He also reported that a Pan-Orthodox teen retreat, hosted by the GOYA, would be held in mid-November. Father Moralis spoke on the work of the Missions Committee. On November 16, 2003, Father Alexios Inyagwa and Father Neophytos Kongai, both from Kenya, were invited as guest speakers. Father Inyagwa, the 2002 mission team's host, later participated in the celebration of Holy Week services at the Annunciation Cathedal in the spring of 2004.

Interior view of the Theodore J. George Library located on the first floor of the Annunciation Orthodox Center.

Alex Pulianas (left) and Demetrios Campanides (right) are among the volunteer assistants at the parish library.

By this time, records reflect that the new 2003 Archdiocesan Charter became a point of debate and discussion at Annunciation. At the fall 2003 general assembly, Peter Marudas, concerned over the manner in which the charter was implemented by the Archdiocese that year, proposed a resolution that the charter be "brought to the 2004 Clergy-Laity Congress for review and discussion." After debate on the validity of bringing this topic to the parish assembly, Thomas Boardman, Chairman of the Parish Assembly, ruled that a motion introducing such a resolution was out of order. This resulted in an appeal on the matter from Evan A. Chriss, the parish's former Legal Counsel. A vote was taken to see if the assembly wished to proceed with the appeal. By a narrow margin, the assembly voted to uphold the ruling of the chairman. As a result, discussion on the pros and cons of the Archdiocesan charter came to a close.

At that same gathering, parishioners were encouraged by William Koutrelakos to make greater use of the Theodore J. George Library located within the Annunciation Orthodox Center (AOC).

Demetrios Campanides, George Mesologites, Alex Pulianas, and Nicholas Ioannou of the library staff were formally acknowledged for their volunteer work. It was apparent that the programs held after church services within the Education Building, coupled with the new flat parking lot which was easily accessible from the Maryland Avenue side of the building, had led to a decrease in walking traffic over to the AOC. To enhance the parish library, plans were soon formulated to establish a book-store in the Cathedral building with the hope of generating more interest in the vast literary holdings

Georgeann N. Morekas
Parish Council President, 2004-2006.

of the parish—13,000 books, video tapes, and other educational material. As a new era was about to begin for the library, its founder Theodore J. George passed away on December 24, 2003.

Another historic first occurred for the Annunciation community in the spring of 2004. Metropolitan Evangelos of New Jersey became the first Hierarch of the Greek Orthodox Church to celebrate the "Akathyst Hymn" (Salutations to the Virgin Mary) at the Annunciation Cathedral. Prior to church services on Friday evening, March 26, 2004, members of the parish council under the leadership of Georgeann N. Morekas met with the new Metropolitan. Ms. Morekas was the second woman to serve as Parish Council President. Elected in 2004, she was following in the footsteps of her father, Nicholas S. Morekas, and grandfather, George J. Karangelen, who also had served as presidents of the Annunciation community. Other parish council officers for 2004 included Ernest Rafailides, Vice President; James N. Pappas, Treasurer; and Despina Horst, Secretary.

Following the beautiful "Akathyst Hymn," a reception was held in the Father Constantine Monios Hall in honor of Metropolitan Evangelos. The social event was coordinated by a devoted group of parishioners affectionately called the "Brooklyn Ladies" due to the section of Baltimore in which most of them resided. The volunteer group included Pat Bartsocas, Metaxia Cossis, Eleftheria Houliaras, Panagiota Spanomanolis, Eve Stamatakis, Katina Tsimopoulos and Panagiota Vavaroutsos. For over a decade, these ladies faithfully provided refreshments following the Friday evening Salutations to the Virgin Mary conducted during Great Lent. Similarly, at social gatherings after church, particularly memorial coffee hours, Maria Anagnostou has served as "parish hostess," preparing buffet tables with food and refreshments for a number of years.

In a special letter to Cathedral parishioners, dated March 24, 2004, Father Dean Moralis related that "a dream of this parish has been to institute a bookstore housed in the confines of our Cathedral building." At that time, a Bookstore Committee was formed to coordinate various aspects of the project which were estimated to cost $13,000. The major benefactor was Irene Lambros Langley, whose gracious donation was made in honor of her parents, John M. and Mary Lambros. Other parishioner donations served to move the project forward quickly. Among them was the contractor, John Diakoulas, who converted the festival storage area in the lower level hallway into a bookstore. Later that summer, on Sunday, August 8, 2004, the official opening of the bookstore took place with the unveiling of the dedication plaque naming it "The Father Dean Moralis Bookstore."

By the spring of 2004, the Archdiocesan charter was debated again…this time in the courts. Dissatisfied by the new 2003 charter approved by the Patriarchate in Constantinople, 34 individuals—members or supporters of the Orthodox Christian Laity (OCL)—independently

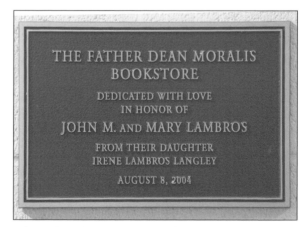

The Cathedral Bookstore, named for Father Moralis, opened on the lower level of the Education Building in August 2004.

Annunciation Cathedral GOYA (Greek Orthodox Youth of America) Officers, 2004-2005.
Front row *l to r* : Leonidia Rizakos, Recording Secretary; Angeleke Vakiaros, Historian; Demitra Sourlis, Vice President.
Back row *l to r* : Nicholas Karas, President; Alexander Motsiopoulos, Treasurer; Shane Cole, Corresponding Secretary.

filed a lawsuit against the Greek Orthodox Archdiocese. The OCL is a group of Eastern Orthodox laity and clergy that promotes autonomy and self-governance of a unified Orthodox Church in the United States. Established in 1987, the OCL was helping to fund their legal action that asked the courts to "invalidate the new charter and force the Church to operate under its old constitution from 1977." The suit brought to the surface complaints from lay activists that they had been excluded from decision-making. They asserted that the new charter resulted in more centralized power and rejected amendments proposed at the 2002 Clergy-Laity Congress that "attempted to carve out a minimal degree of influence for U.S. parishioners" in handling their own administrative matters.

News that individuals affiliated with the Orthodox Christian Laity had started a legal proceeding against the Greek Orthodox Archdiocese was met with mixed feelings in many parishes, especially those who had accepted and implemented the new charter. *The Baltimore Sun* story on February 4, 2004, undoubtedly triggered emotions at Annunciation: "In a power struggle with international implications, members of the U.S. Greek Orthodox Church filed suit against their archbishop yesterday in New York seeking greater self-governance and autonomy from the church's leadership in Istanbul." Among those at the news conference were Evan A. Chriss and Peter Marudas, long-time parishioners of Annunciation. Two months later, the *National Herald* covered the story on April 17, 2004, with an analysis written by Theodore Kalmoukos: "The plaintiffs have diminished the Church's role by associating it with a secular court.... Nobody disputes the integrity or intentions of the plaintiffs. What is inconceivable is their very act to sue their own Church."

The Annunciation Girls' Basketball Team, 2004. Seated left to right: Father Dean Moralis and Pastoral Assistant Peter Thornberg. Standing left to right: Demitra Sourlis, Alexandra Kranis, Kerrie Handakas, Christina Zizos, Demetra Kosmakos, Kalli Parrish, Maria Makris, Allie Boardman, Leonidia Rizakos, and John Nakajima, Coach.

The Annunciation Boys' Basketball Team, 2004. Kneeling left to right: Jamie Stratakis, Michael DeRito, Shane Cole, George Sourlis, Alexander Marsh, Alexander Motsiopoulos, Nicholas Marsh. Standing left to right: George Kinigopoulos, Coach; Steven Kinigopoulos, Andrew Zavage, Dionysios Kranis, Nicholas Karas, Christopher Grimes, Nicholas Klicos, Steven Agathoklis, and Gus Stratakis, Coach.

Needless to say, there was debate at the parish level over various aspects of the legal actions, the charter amendments, and the responses by church leaders to the entire situation. At Annunciation's general assembly meeting on April 26, 2004, Evan A. Chriss, a staunch supporter of the OCL movement, introduced another resolution for consideration. He proposed that the controversial Archdiocesan charter be placed as the first item of business on the agenda of the Biennial Clergy-Laity Congress in New York that summer. Any show of support to confront the Archdiocese over the 2003 charter had now waned. By a vote of 88 to 20, debate on the resolution brought before the parish assembly was stopped. Four months later, the New York State Supreme Court sided with the Greek Orthodox Archdiocese and dismissed the lawsuit, ruling that the court has no authority to interfere in an internal church dispute. Later in 2006, the Appellate Division of the New York Supreme Court affirmed the 2004 decision to dismiss the lawsuit because "it involves a question of internal governance of a hierarchical Church."

In the meantime, the 37th Biennial Clergy-Laity Congress was held in New York City from July 25-30, 2004. Representatives from the Annunciation Cathedral included Father Dean Moralis, Parish Council President Georgeann Morekas, Parish Council Secretary Despina Horst, George Maistros, Diane Tseckares, Patti Arkuszeski, and Koula Savvakis. Later, Despina Horst reported to the parish assembly on the various workshops at the conference. The educational sessions included topics such as Parish Management, Foreign Missions, Outreach, Living and Sharing our Faith in the Home, Fundraising, God in Pop Culture, and Technology in Christian Education. It was noted that educational materials were available on the Archdiocesan web site with the Cathedral web site maintaining links to many of these sources.

Another major undertaking was the updating of the Parish Directory. A comprehensive listing of current parishioners' names and addresses, telephone numbers, and e-mail addresses was published in a 106-page booklet in August of 2004. The directory also included pastoral guidelines regarding the sacramental life of the Church. Cathedral Business Administrator Lucy Hagopian, part-time assistant Alice Alefrankis Birkel, and volunteers Basil and Dorothea Markulis worked

The 2004 Parish Directory cover shows the *Epigonation,* an embroidered diamond-shaped cloth with the image of Christ, worn by higher-ranking Orthodox clergymen.

diligently to complete this project. The Markulis' had served as volunteers in the Cathedral office since 2001. Soon, their tireless work would be acknowledged in a formal manner. On May 8, 2006, at the first Greek Orthodox Metropolis of New Jersey Awards Banquet, Basil and Dorothea Markulis were each presented with a special icon/plaque which stated in part, "Your unassuming faith and devotion to your Church is indeed the *par excellence* example of Christian stewardship."

A number of noteworthy events took place in the fall of 2004. The Department of Internet Ministries of the Greek Orthodox Archdiocese established a new e-bulletin for parishes. Shortly after, in September of 2004, Annunciation launched its new web site incorporating these enhancements and other updates. The following month, the Cathedral Women's Guild, under the presidency of Frances Apostolo, officially celebrated the 50th Anniversary of its founding in 1955. On Sunday, October 24, 2004, an *Artoclasia* was held followed by a luncheon in the AOC Ballroom. As a historic tribute, Women's Guild Secretary Maryanth

The Ordination to the Holy Diaconate of Panagiotis (Peter) J. Thornberg took place at his home parish, Saints Constantine and Helen Greek Orthodox Church, Washington, D.C., November 14, 2004.

Constantine, assisted by Cathedral Archivist Betty Jean Alevizatos, prepared a nostalgic display of photographs for the lobby showcases in the Annunciation Orthodox Center.

At the fall parish assembly held on November 11, 2004, Agora Chairperson Aritee Poletis Bond reported that despite the inclement weather once again brought on by the hurricane season, the September 2004 event was considered a success. A profit of over $50,000 was realized. Considering the volatile weather patterns during September, it was decided to move the festival to its original month of November. The personal achievements of Father Dean Moralis were also noted at the parish assembly that day. He had recently been elected Vice President of the St. Basil Academy Board of Trustees, and Archbishop Demetrios had assigned him to the Board of Trustees for the Hellenic College/Holy Cross School of Theology. By 2006, Father Moralis was also elected to serve on the Archdiocesan Council for the Metropolis of New Jersey.

By this time, Parish Council President Georgeann N. Morekas reported that a Seminarian

Deacon Peter J. Thornberg and his wife, Katherine, 2004.

Assistance Fund had been established to assist seminarians from the Cathedral community with the cost of their tuition and books for theological studies. Concerning the future of the parking garage, James N. Pappas, Garage Committee Chairman, reported that options being reviewed ranged from maintenance-only repairs to razing the structure and starting over with a fresh design. More research was needed before a recommendation would be made. Also on the agenda was a new initiative modeled after similar ventures in other cities. The concept of a "Hellenic Heritage Museum" was discussed for the preservation and display of artifacts and memorabilia associated with Greek heritage. A committee, spearheaded by Harry C. Maistros, was soon formed to determine objectives and methods to categorize and store donations to the museum. Possible future space for the museum is being considered within the remaining five Preston Street town houses acquired during the last decade.

During the fall of 2004, a much-anticipated announcement was made concerning the future role of Peter J. Thornberg at the Annunciation Cathedral. On Sunday, November 14, 2004, at his home parish of Sts. Constantine and Helen Greek Orthodox Church in Washington D.C., Panagiotis (Peter) J. Thornberg was ordained to the Holy Diaconate. Officiating at the service was His Grace Bishop Savas of Troas assisted by The Rev. Nicholas Manousakis, The Very Rev. Constantine Moralis, and Deacon Michael Tervo. During this period, Deacon Peter Thornberg often traveled with Metropolitan Evangelos on Sundays performing the duties associated with his new role as a Deacon of the Orthodox Church. Officially assigned to the Annunciation Cathedral, Deacon Peter Thornberg was able to assist Father Dean Moralis with the many responsibilities of a large congregation.

With the approaching holiday season, the Cathedral's new cookbook, "Greek Home Cooking in America," became a popular gift item for many parishioners. The project, coordinated by Eurydice M. Canelos, featured over 600 recipes and was an instant success when it premiered at the parish's three-day festival in September of 2004. By this time, the Annunciation parish had begun hosting a series of Greek cooking classes entitled "Hellene Cuisine." Dr. Susan Prevas, Mary Kariotis and Anna Z. Pappas were key coordinators of this ambitious project. A variety of well-attended and informative cooking classes are now held regularly in an atmosphere of fellowship.

In late December of 2004, following the massive earthquakes and tsunami tidal waves that hit Southeast Asia, the International Orthodox

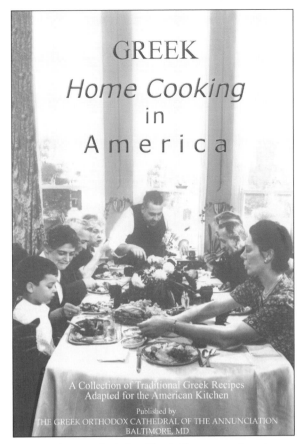

GREEK
Home Cooking
in
America

A Collection of Traditional Greek Recipes
Adapted for the American Kitchen
Published by
THE GREEK ORTHODOX CATHEDRAL OF THE ANNUNCIATION
BALTIMORE, MD

The latest Cathedral cookbook (front cover shown)
was published in 2004 under the guidance of Eurydice
Mitchell Canelos and her daughter, Paula Canelos Morris.

Christian Charities (IOCC) received an overwhelming response to its request for humanitarian aid from Orthodox faithful across America. Locally, Father Moralis appealed to parishioners for support through the preparation of "Gifts of the Heart" health kits—basic necessities such as soap, washcloths, hand towels, toothbrushes, band-aids, etc. He stated, "Our goal is to assemble 1,000 kits to be sent on behalf of you, assisting those who have been devastated by the loss of their homes and livelihoods." Parishioners rallied to the cause with impressive results.

Records show that on February 6, 2005, over 1,900 health kits were loaded onto trucks for ultimate delivery to Southeast Asia. Later that year, when Hurricane Katrina began pounding the Gulf Coast states on August 25, 2005, the parish again responded. Within a month, Father Moralis reported that parishioners had prepared over 1,000 additional health kits with essential items for survival. By October of that year, all donations, including seventy quilts made by the Philoptochos

Anastasia August (foreground) decorates the "kouvouklion," the tomb of Christ, with orchids, carnations and baby's breath at the Greek Orthodox Cathedral of the Annunciation in Baltimore.

Faithful carry on Easter traditions

Above: The ornately carved *Kouvouklion* (canopy) symbolizing the Tomb of Christ, is carried in solemn procession on Holy Friday and contains the *Epitaphios*, a large cloth icon depicting the entombed Savior.

Left: Parishioners decorating the symbolic tomb were featured in an article in *The Baltimore Sun*, April 30, 2005.

Society, were promptly delivered to Mobile, Alabama, and Biloxi, Mississippi, with a privately chartered airplane. Under the guidance of Father Moralis, parishioners George M. Anagnostou and William C. Gereny coordinated the delivery efforts of the Annunciation Cathedral.

There was a sense of excitement with the arrival of 2005. Special events to celebrate "100 Years of Orthodoxy" in the State of Maryland were about to commence. Father Moralis set the reminiscent tone in the March 2005 parish newsletter article entitled "The Foundation of Faith in Baltimore." In his remarks he stated, "Early pioneering Greeks, many

who worked as confectioners in Baltimore, knew the importance of having a place of worship…. Our community mirrors others where humble beginnings became a reality…. The immigrants dreamed, knew what would lie ahead, and set the foundation to make the "Evangelismos" (Annunciation) Church into the strong Cathedral parish it is today…. I am amazed at the accomplishments of our community. Truly there is nowhere else on earth like our church. We have a community that is a world in itself—containing the love of Christ…. It has been said that a church gains more beauty by the sacraments that are celebrated within its walls and our Church—

whether in the Union Hall, on Homewood Avenue or on Preston Street—has beautified the lives of each of us." Although it was a unique year in parish history, the events of 2005 would also play out like other years with joyful and sorrowful occasions sometimes overlapping within a matter of days or weeks. The Cathedral registries provide a few noteworthy examples.

Parishioners were saddened to learn the news of the death of longtime *psalti* (cantor) Sotirios J. Mangos on February 11, 2005. His faithful service to the Orthodox Church spanned nearly five decades. The funeral of Sotirios Mangos was held at the Cathedral of the Annunciation, and he was laid to rest in the Greek Orthodox Cemetery on February 15, 2005. Within a month, the mood of the parish turned to celebration with the news that Deacon Peter and Katherine Thornberg had welcomed the arrival of a daughter, Sophia Eleni Thornberg, on March 4, 2005. Later that year, she was baptized at the Annunciation Cathedral on Saturday, July 30, 2005, and the entire parish was invited to witness the event.

In March of 2005, Maryland's Democratic Senator Paul S. Sarbanes, a member of the Annunciation parish, announced he would retire from the United States Senate at the conclusion of his fifth term in January 2007. He had made history in November of 2000 when he won reelection to an unprecedented 5th term of office giving him the distinction of being Maryland's longest-serving United States Senator. Senator Sarbanes has also been active in numerous fund-raising initiatives at the Annunciation Cathedral and has served on long-range planning committees for the parish. His departure from the Senate marks a noteworthy transition in the story of Greek-American politics. In 2006, his son, John Sarbanes, entered the political arena and was elected to the Democratic seat in Maryland's Third Congressional District for the U.S. House of Representatives.

The spring of 2005 saw the passing of two great spiritual leaders. Upon learning of the death of Pope John Paul II, the Greek Orthodox Archdiocese issued an official statement on April 2, 2005. "We participate in the sorrow of the Roman Catholic Church during this difficult time…and join the world in offering prayers knowing that he is now in the world of eternal rest." During the Pope's tenure that began in 1978, the relationship between the

Greek School Principal Dina-Athena Vakiaros (center) with Deacon Thornberg (left) and Father Moralis (right), 2005.

Roman Catholic Church and the Eastern Orthodox Church saw significant improvement with efforts toward reconciliation. In a recent gesture, the historic relics of St. John Chrysostom and St. Gregory the Theologian became symbolic of this cooperative spirit.

Taken from the great city of Constantinople by crusaders in 1204, the relics ended up in Rome where they had been kept in St. Peter's Basilica. Following the request of Patriarch Bartholomew, Pope John Paul II agreed to return the relics to the Orthodox Church where they were enshrined at the Patriarchal Cathedral of St. George in the fall of 2004. Five months later, on April 2, 2005, the Catholic Church Leader passed away at the age of 85. Pope John Paul II would be remembered for remaining steadfast on "traditional values while offering love, compassion, and forgiveness."

Greek Orthodox Archbishop Iakovos, 93

ASSOCIATED PRESS

STAMFORD, Conn. — Archbishop Iakovos, who transformed the Greek Orthodox Church in the Americas while championing religious unity and human rights, died Sunday at Stamford Hospital of a pulmonary ailment, the Greek Orthodox Archdiocese of America announced.

Archbishop Iakovos, who was 93, headed the Greek Orthodox Archdiocese of North and South America, with an estimated 2 million followers, from 1959 until 1996. He was apparently forced into retirement over his support for the idea of uniting the Eastern Orthodox branches in a single American church.

He met with Pope John XXIII after his 1959 enthronement, becoming the first Greek Orthodox archbishop in 350 years to meet with a Roman Catholic pope, and spent nine years as a president of the World Council of Churches.

A native of the island of Imvros, Turkey, who became a U.S. citizen in 1950, Archbishop Iakovos marched with the Rev. Martin Luther King Jr. in Selma, Ala., in 1965, and received the Medal of Freedom from President Carter in 1980.

"Ecumenism," he said in 1960, "is the hope for international understanding, for humanitarian allegiance, for true peace based on justice and dignity, and for God's continued presence and involvement in modern history."

The heads of the Baltimore area's three Greek Orthodox churches were together at a spiritual retreat Sunday when they learned of the archbishop's death. They said they prayed and shared memories about him.

"All three of us were ordained under his tenure," said the Rev. Manuel Burdusi of St. Nicholas Greek Orthodox Church in Bal-

ASSOCIATED PRESS 1989
Archbishop Iakovos transformed the Greek Orthodox Church in the Americas.

timore. "In the same way that the Catholic Church is mourning the pope, we're now mourning the loss of our spiritual father."

The Rev. Louis Noplos, of St. Demetrios Greek Orthodox Church in Cub Hill, remembered from his time as a seminary student seeing the archbishop at an orphanage in New York.

"When he saw the kids playing baseball, he walked over, picked up a bat and hit one with them, still in robes and all," Father Noplos said. "That's the kind of person he was."

As an altar boy, the Rev. Constantine Moralis first met Archbishop Iakovos 25 years ago at the Baltimore church he now leads — the Greek Orthodox Cathedral of the Annunciation. "He was able to capture the hearts of young and old. ... He was very endearing," Father Moralis said.

The three priests planned to attend the archbishop's funeral Mass on Thursday at the Archdiocesan Cathedral of the Holy Trinity in New York City, and said they will have memorial

services at their churches Sunday.

During his long tenure, Archbishop Iakovos led the Greek Orthodox Church out of immigrant isolation and into the mainstream of American religious life, playing a leading role in bringing English into the liturgy.

"It's the end of the golden age of Orthodoxy in America," said the Rev. George Poulos, who leads a church in Stamford and wrote a book on Archbishop Iakovos. "There's no one on the horizon who can equal his abilities and his character and his faith."

Archbishop Iakovos started a youth movement in the United States and created the Ionian Village in Greece, a summer camp that has been visited by more than 16,000 Greek-American children.

"He was in spiritual perpetual motion," Father Poulos said.

Born Demetrios Coucouzis, he took the name Iakovos, which means James, when he was ordained a deacon in 1934. He spoke several languages and could hold children as well as adults spellbound by his sermons, Father Poulos said.

One of those children was George Stephanopoulos, an altar boy who would become an adviser to President Bill Clinton and then an ABC news commentator.

"What I remember more than anything else is the voice," Mr. Stephanopoulos said. "To a young child, he sounded like the voice of God — deep, measured, but rounded with gentle tones."

Archbishop Iakovos was instrumental in setting up dialogues among Orthodox churches and Anglicans, Lutherans, Southern Baptists and other denominations. He met every U.S. president from Dwight D. Eisenhower through Clinton, and was one of the U.S. Christian leaders who met with

Pope John Paul II in a historic gathering in South Carolina in 1987.

He sought to maintain Orthodox traditions, such as opposing the ordination of women, while at the same time championing human rights and improved race relations.

Archbishop Iakovos came into conflict with Ecumenical Patriarch Bartholomew, the titular leader of world Orthodoxy, in 1994 after he convened a meeting of 29 bishops from the 10 North American branches of Eastern Orthodoxy.

In an unprecedented move, the bishops recommended placing all of the churches under one administrative umbrella while maintaining ties to their separate "mother churches" in Greece, Russia and the other countries.

It is widely assumed that Patriarch Bartholomew forced Archbishop Iakovos to resign in 1996 because he had endorsed the idea.

Subsequently, church officials split the North and South American Greek Orthodox archdiocese into four sections, and Metropolitan Spyridon was appointed archbishop of America, serving followers only in the United States. He resigned in 1999 and was replaced by the current archbishop, Demetrios.

In a statement, Archbishop Demetrios hailed the longtime religious leader as "a superb archbishop who offered to the church an intense, continuous, multifaceted and creative pastoral activity."

Archbishop Iakovos will lie in state at the cathedral in New York today and tomorrow, and his funeral will be at 11 a.m. Thursday morning, the Archdiocese of America said. Interment will be Friday morning in Brookline, Mass.

Sun staff writer William Wan contributed to this article.

A memorial tribute to Archbishop Iakovos was published in *The Baltimore Sun* on April 14, 2005. His tenure as Spiritual Leader spanned from 1959-1996. He has the distinction of being the longest-serving Archbishop in the history of the Greek Orthodox Archdiocese of America.

The following week, on April 10, 2005, Archbishop Iakovos, former Archbishop of the Greek Orthodox Archdiocese from 1959-1996, fell asleep in the Lord. In New York, Archbishop Demetrios communicated the news to all parishes in a special encyclical that stated in part: "Archbishop Iakovos was a believer in the uniting and healing power of the love of God. Throughout his ministry, he brought together people of faith, establishing helpful dialogues with Roman Catholic, Protestant, and Jewish communities.... His commitment to human rights and religious freedom was demonstrated by his response to the needs of Greek Cypriot refugees following the invasion of Cyprus in 1974.... He was an ecumenical leader, a friend of presidents, and a tremendous contributor to the global witness of our Orthodox faith."

Annunciation Cathedral, along with hundreds of churches across America, conducted a *Trisagion* (Thrice-Holy) Memorial Service, and on April 14, 2005, the day of the Archbishop's funeral, bells were tolled in a solemn mode to mark his passing. The death of the former Archbishop in 2005 gave parishioners a chance to reflect on earlier decades in parish history. Archbishop Iakovos had participated in a number of historic milestones including the dedication of the Education Building in 1961, issuing the Cathedral status in 1975, attending the 75th Anniversary celebration in 1981, and the dedication of the Annunciation Orthodox Center in 1984. His tenure would be remembered for many years to come.

Moving forward with the parish agenda, Parish Council President Georgeann Morekas highlighted a number of projects at the spring general assembly held on June 13, 2005. For instance, the mortgage-burning ceremony for the properties at 41-43 W. Preston Street had taken place. Other completed items included the upgrading of the fire detection system, repairing of the cemetery chapel doors, and clearing away overgrown shrubs and trees along the cemetery property line adjoining the Lorraine Park Cemetery. The installation of new lighting and painting of the Father Constantine Monios Hall was also noted. Esther Samios stated that a written report enumerating the values of all aspects of real and tangible property within the Cathedral, Chapel of the Holy Wisdom, Education Building, and Chapel of the Holy Resurrection (cemetery) had been completed. Religious items, icons, and

Members of the Centennial Committee seated *l to r*: Melody Simmons, Carolyn Tsakalas, Gary T. Padussis, General Chairman; Father Dean Moralis, Georgeann Morekas, Jeanne Tsakalos, Peter Sotirakos. Standing *l to r*: Anna Z. Pappas and Gayle Economos.

Bishop Kallistos Ware was the featured speaker at the Eleventh Annual Lenten Retreat held on April 2, 2005.

stained glass windows were included in the assessment. The "replacement value" report compiled for insurance purposes would be helpful as the parish assessed its long-range needs.

Parish assembly minutes also included the report of James N. Pappas on the Clergy-Laity Meeting of the Metropolis of New Jersey held on March 27-28, 2005, in Towson, Maryland. Representatives from all three Greek Orthodox parishes in Baltimore attended, and Metropolitan Evangelos offered several ideas including a new Metropolis Camp for the youth, strengthening of liturgical traditions, stronger support for the monasteries, and exploring the feasibility of parishes to provide adult day care. The report of Father Dean Moralis also looked to the future with his vision of expanded ministries: the ability to broadcast the Liturgy on-line, increased Bible studies, adult catechism, grief counseling, and

the need for a formal strategy to organize future disaster relief efforts. He also stated that in today's modern world, "a stronger Internet presence was needed to more easily access spiritual information."

In the midst of the regular parish activities, the Centennial Celebration of the Annunciation Cathedral officially began in the spring of 2005. Three years of planning had resulted in a varied agenda of activities for parishioners of all ages. The Centennial Executive Committee led by Chairman Gary T. Padussis also included the following: Father Dean Moralis, Deacon Peter J. Thornberg, Parish Council President Georgeann N. Morekas, James E. Caminis, Dimitrios A. Cavathas, Gayle V. Economos, Mary Kariotis, Constance M. Klicos, Anna Z. Pappas, Ernest Rafailides, Evangelos Sidou, Melody Simmons, Peter Sotirakos, Carolyn Tsakalas, and Jeanne Tsakalos.

Friday, March 18, 2005, officially marked the 99th anniversary of the Annunciation Cathedral. That evening's quiet and solemn service, Salutations to the Virgin Mary, was chosen to begin the year-long calendar of special events. Following church services, a reception was held in the Father Constantine Monios Hall where Parish Historian Nicholas M. Prevas gave a presentation on his research documenting the early history of the community. This set the tone for later historical events interspersed throughout the year. Two days later marked the Sunday of Orthodoxy. At the special services held on Sunday evening, March 20, 2005, combined Orthodox choirs from the region participated followed by a reception in the ballroom of the Annunciation Orthodox Center (AOC).

In keeping with the centennial theme, two displays were premiered that weekend in the main lobby showcases of the AOC. "The Immigrant Odyssey...Steamships of our Ancestors" featured passenger lists, along with photographs of steamships and the immigrants who made these historic journeys across the Atlantic. Other steamship memorabilia were included, courtesy of the Steamship Historical Society of America located at the University of Baltimore. The second display, "A Memorial Tribute to The Very Rev. Joakim Papachristou," featured rare documentation and photographs of this notable parish priest. The year 2005 marked the 50th anniversary of his death and a special memorial service was conducted on Sunday, March 6, 2005, to mark the occasion.

A few weeks later, on April 2, 2005, the "Growing in Faith" Bible Study group sponsored its Eleventh Annual Lenten Retreat. Under the chairmanship of Jeanne Tsakalos, Bishop Kallistos Ware was invited as the keynote speaker. The "Birth and Growth of the Early Church" and the "Book of Acts" were the themes of the afternoon retreat. Bishop Kallistos, a celebrated theologian, had visited Annunciation Cathedral previously and again commanded a large audience of listeners. The next day, April 3, 2005, marked the historic 10th Anniversary of the Greek Independence Day Parade in Baltimore. *The Baltimore Sun* reported on the event. "The gray skies...were no match for the abundantly colorful Greek costumes and the frigid wind and spotty drizzle failed to dampen the enthusiasm of participants and spectators." The Annunciation Cathedral and other area Orthodox churches were well-represented by marching groups and parishioners along the parade route.

Greek Independence Day Parade, 2005. Holding banner *l to r* : Angeleke Vakiaros, Michael Matsos, Nikole Koutouvalis. Back *l to r* : Nicki Sharkey, Alexander Marsh, Leonidia Rizakos, Nicholas Karas, Alexander Motsiopoulos, Tina Koundouriotis.

Greek Independence Day Parade. Front row *l to r* : Rev. Louis Noplos, Rev. Anargyros Stavropoulos, Chancellor of the Metropolis of New Jersey; Metropolitan Evangelos of New Jersey, Very Rev. Constantine Moralis, Rev. Manuel Burdusi. Second row *l to r* : Rev. Anastasios Kousoulas, Deacon Peter Thornberg, and Michael Bishop, Sunday, April 3, 2005.

One of the highlights of the Centennial Celebration was the return visit on April 23, 2005, to the former Greek Orthodox house of worship at Homewood Avenue and Chase Street, now owned by the Highway Christian (Apostolic) Church.

Later that same month on April 23, 2005, the parish reenacted a fascinating segment of its history that had taken place sixty-eight years earlier on April 23, 1937. On that day in 1937, a farewell liturgical service was held in the old Homewood Avenue Church followed by a procession to the new Preston Street Church. Father Dean Moralis, desiring to give his congregation a chance to revisit the first Greek Orthodox house of worship, organized the details of a most memorable afternoon. The Highway Christian Church, under the spiritual leadership of Bishop Charles Brown, cordially welcomed members of the Annunciation community to their place of worship for this special occasion. Shuttle buses transported over 250 Cathedral parishioners to the corner of Homewood Avenue and Chase Street where Vesper services were held with the Highway Christian congregation. A coordinated effort with the Baltimore City Police Department allowed attendees to reenact the historic one-mile walk back to Preston Street that was led in 1937 by Father Joakim Papachristou.

Amazingly, a transom window installed by the Annunciation parish had been left in the entrance hall at 1100 Homewood Avenue after the Greek

Father Dean Moralis coordinated the nostalgic return to Homewood Avenue. That day, a Vesper service was held with members of the Greek Orthodox and Apostolic parishes. Some of the attendees are shown above.

Reenactment of the historic 1937 procession from Homewood Avenue to Preston Street. Front row left to right:
Georgeann N. Morekas, Parish Council President; George Kariotis, Charlie Flannery, Diana Motsiopoulos. Altar servers
in the background left to right: Alexander Pappas, Dimitri Sidou, Alexander Motsiopoulos, Steven Pappas, April 23, 2005.

Members of the 2005 Parish Council prepare for the reenactment ceremony with icons used in the original procession
on April 23, 1937. Left to right: Spero Demetrides, Larry Vakoutis, Thomas Zizos, and Betty Jean Alevizatos.

community sold the building in 1941. Four Greek words, *Arhi Sofias Fovos Kyriou* (The Beginning of Wisdom is the Fear of the Lord), had greeted non-Greek worshippers in that building for nearly 65 years. Nicholas M. Prevas had discovered the existence of the window while conducting research in the early 1980's. As the centennial year approached, Father Dean Moralis envisioned obtaining and preserving the historic stained glass window—a tangible link to the first church of the immigrant generation. His dream came true as the Highway Christian Church graciously agreed to allow the removal and transfer of the transom window to Preston Street. In appreciation, Father Moralis, on behalf of the Annunciation Cathedral, presented Bishop Brown with a donation to assist his parish ministries.

Marchers in the historic 2005 procession then arrived in the courtyard of the Annunciation Cathedral to find the transom window installed above the entrance to the Education Building. People were moved to tears upon seeing the profound inscription. The relocation and installation of the window was a gift from Parish Council President Georgeann Morekas and her mother, Helen Karangelen Morekas, in memory of George J. Karangelen and Nicholas S. Morekas, past Parish Council Presidents. Under the threat of

storm clouds, a special blessing ceremony was held. The congregation then entered the sanctuary for the remainder of the Vesper services within minutes of a driving rainstorm. Parish Historian Nicholas M. Prevas, who had recounted the parish's early years at Homewood Avenue that afternoon, concluded his presentation with the story of the purchase of the Preston Street Church.

That day, a special Citizen Citation from Mayor Martin O'Malley was presented to Mr. Prevas for his years of dedicated research and documentation of parish history. Senator Paul Sarbanes, one of the guests in attendance, also read a special proclamation in honor of Mr. Prevas' volunteer work. "Because of your commitment, our community is fortunate to have this most valuable resource from which generations yet to come can draw upon to better understand the religious, ethnic, and cultural foundations of the Parish." Later, in addressing the congregation, Nicholas Prevas noted that Penelope Psoras, a 105-year-old parishioner, was able to attend the special events of that day. Her vivid recollections throughout numerous interviews during the 1990's had greatly assisted him in researching various segments of the parish's early history.

The next two centennial events that were on the agenda followed the celebration of *Pascha* (Easter). The Discovery Day at the Walters Art Museum was held on May 21, 2005, under the chairmanship of Athena Sidou. With participants from all three Greek Orthodox parishes of Baltimore, nearly 200 individuals attended and enjoyed the various activities geared for youngsters of the Greek community between the ages of 5-12.

The historic stained glass transom window adorns the entrance to the Education Building on Preston Street.

Commemorative plaque for the transom window brought from the Homewood Avenue Church on April 23, 2005.

Parish youngsters enjoyed arts and crafts activities at the Discovery Day at Walters Art Museum on May 21, 2005.

World-renowned tenor Mario Frangoulis performed at the Joseph Meyerhoff Symphony Hall on May 28, 2005.

The event began with a tour of Greek and Byzantine art splendidly displayed at the museum. Children learned about Greek mythology's many gods and heroes with a performance entitled "The Golden Lyre." Arts and crafts activities were also on the agenda making it a fun-filled afternoon.

The following week, on Saturday, May 28, 2005, the Joseph Meyerhoff Symphony Hall was the scene of an evening of musical entertainment featuring the world-renowned tenor, Mario Frangoulis. Carolyn Tsakalas served as Chairperson and Constance M. Dourakos as Co-Chairperson of the centennial concert event. Mr. Frangoulis who was accompanied by the Baltimore Symphony Orchestra sang over twenty selections. His unique style connected the world of opera and Broadway; his musical renditions varied in Italian, Spanish, Greek and English. As an added attraction, soprano Nicole Cabell sang a number of duets with Mario Frangoulis. Others who helped to ensure the success of the program included: Gayle V. Economos,

Publicity; Alice Ioannou, Concert Reception; Harry C. Maistros, Decorations; Georgeann N. Morekas, Program and Sponsors; and Lucy Hagopian, Cathedral Business Administrator. Over twenty volunteers, led by Eleni Flannery, Koula Savvakis, and Diane Tseckares, handled ticket sales.

The details involved in coordinating various aspects of the concert were challenging to say the least. As in many ambitious endeavors, expenses turned out to be greater than anticipated. Fortunately, a number of individuals made generous donations to offset the cost of the concert production; Georgia and Peter Angelos and John Paterakis, Sr., were Grand Benefactors. In addition, Betsy and Tony Aikaterinidis, Martin's Caterers, Mary H. Markakis, Georgeann N. Morekas, Donna and Gary Padussis, Anna and Harry Pappas, Michael Ruck, Georgia and George Stamas, and Connie and Savas Tsakiris were acknowledged as benefactors. In a rousing finale to the show, Mario Frangoulis invited Centennial Chairman Gary T.

Padussis to the stage to join him in singing an old Greek favorite, *To Periyiali to Kryfo* (The Secret Seashore). The audience joined in and the memorable event concluded with a standing ovation.

The following month, on Sunday, June 12, 2005, the Annunciation Cathedral was the scene of another historic ordination. Before a filled sanctuary, Deacon Panagiotis (Peter) J. Thornberg was ordained to the Holy Priesthood by His Eminence Metropolitan Evangelos of New Jersey. Other visiting clergymen included: Father Anargyros Stavropoulos, Chancellor of the Metropolis of New Jersey; Father Basil Kissal, Holy Trinity Cathedral of Charlotte, North Carolina; and Father Michael Prevas, Greek Orthodox Church of the Resurrection in Castro Valley, California. At the conclusion of the ceremony, the congregation exclaimed the traditional *Axios!* (he is worthy). Parishioners then had the opportunity to congratulate their new assistant pastor at a reception. The Rev. Peter J. Thornberg became the twelfth assistant priest to serve the Annunciation community since the arrival of the first assistant, Father Philotheos Ahladas, in the 1940's.

The Ordination of Reverend Peter J. Thornberg (right) was officiated by Metropolitan Evangelos (left) on June 12, 2005.

His Eminence Metropolitan Evangelos of New Jersey (center) with clergymen left to right: Rev. Michael Prevas, Rev. Basil Kissal, Rev. Anargyros Stavropoulos, Chancellor of the Metropolis of New Jersey; Rev. Peter J. Thornberg, The Very Rev. Constantine Moralis, Rev. George Kalpaxis, and Rev. Stanley Voyiaziakis, Sunday, June 12, 2005.

"An Evening of Sacred Orthodox Music" was held on October 15, 2005. This musical tribute during the centennial celebration featured arrangements of sacred hymns by a variety of composers including Choir Director Georgia Tangires.

More centennial events took place later that year. On Saturday, October 15, 2005, the Annunciation Cathedral Choir presented "An Evening of Sacred Orthodox Music." Chairpersons for the event were Georgia Tangires and Jeanne Tsakalos. In his message to parishioners, Father Moralis wrote, "It is most fitting that a musical tribute be part of our celebration. Music has always been an important aspect of church history and plays a key role in all liturgical services." The music of various composers such as Dr. Dino Anagnost, Athanasios P. Theodorides, Anna Gallos, Steve Cardiasmenos, Frank Desby, and Georgia Tangires was presented.

One of the highlights of the evening was the performance of Quartet No. 1 for clarinet, violin, viola, and cello by Bernard Crusell. The featured clarinetist was David Drosinos of the Baltimore Symphony Orchestra, a Cathedral parishioner, who was described in the program guide as a "versatile and seasoned clarinetist who has enchanted audiences from Maryland to Moscow." The exemplary concert performance would be remembered for years to come.

A few weeks later, Dr. Gary Vikan, a preeminent Byzantine scholar and longtime friend of the Annunciation Cathedral, was invited to lecture on Sunday, October 30, 2005. Under the chairmanship of Maryanth Constantine, the event was held in the AOC Ballroom following the Divine Liturgy. Dr. Vikan presented an informative slide lecture on understanding iconography entitled "Strolling through Byzantium – Theology in Color." The following month, parishioners found themselves involved in the final preparation for the 2005 Greek Festival. The three-day event was held November 11-13, 2005, with Irene Lambros Langley serving as general chairperson. This special 100th Anniversary year festival was promoted as "Visit a Greek Village…And Never Leave Baltimore." The decision to change the festival from September to November proved favorable as record crowds were in attendance that weekend.

The momentum continued with two more centennial events in November of that year. On Friday, November 18, 2005, parish children were invited to a 100th Birthday Party in the Father Constantine Monios Hall. Refreshments, games,

Parish children were invited to attend a 100th Birthday Party for the Annunciation Cathedral on Friday, November 18, 2005.

and other fun-filled activities were geared to children ages 4-12. Nora Vlahoyiannis and her mother, Dr. Corinna Z. Courpas, served as chairpersons of this event. The following weekend, on Saturday, November 26, 2005, the Walters Art Museum was the scene of a formal evening of dinner and cultural displays. Under the chairmanship of Frances Apostolo, this event featured a special exhibition, "The Golden Age of Russian Icons – Novgorod the Great," from Russia and a special collection of Byzantine art from the Dumbarton Oaks Museum in Washington, D.C. A highlight of the evening was the slide lecture by Dr. Graham Mann, Curator of Byzantine Art for the Walters Art Museum.

By this time, the fall parish assembly had taken place. One of the main topics of business at the assembly on November 2, 2005, was the restoration of the entrance to the cemetery chapel. Repairs slated for the spring and summer of 2006 included replacing the doors, the installation of a permanent entranceway awning, exterior concrete repairs, reconstruction of the front of the building and general painting. The project was estimated at $65,000. In his report, John Diakoulas of the

Acropolis Construction Company graciously announced his donation of $12,000 toward this project. Another noteworthy item discussed was the end of the lease agreement with Martin's Caterers for their use of the AOC Ballroom. For future events, the parish would need to explore catering options and establish policies to ensure consistent, quality catering.

The following Sunday, November 6, 2005, the Annunciation Cathedral sponsored its first Veterans Day Observance to honor all those who had served in the military. Parishioners were asked to submit the names of family members to be included in a special brochure that listed both living and deceased veterans. It was also a day to pay tribute to one of Annunciation's former pastors. A ten-year memorial service was held for Father George Gallos who had passed away in 1995 in St. Augustine, Florida. Father Gallos' legacy would be honored in a lasting manner three months later. On Sunday, February 26, 2006, the Education Building was rededicated as the "Father George P. Gallos Education and Resource Center." This memorial tribute was most appropriate since the building was established in 1960 under his spiritual guidance.

Evangelakia Dancers seated *l to r* : Angeleke Vakiaros, Melanie Sheridan, Courtney Nichols, Sydney Nichols, Maria Kafarakis, Nikole Koutouvalis. Standing *l to r* : Demitra Sourlis, Leonidia Rizakos, Alexander Motsiopoulos, Nicholas Karas, Nicki Sharkey and Tina Koundouriotis, Instructors; Alexander Marsh, Emmanuel Motsiopoulos, Michael Matsos, and John Frangos, 2005.

Diamantia Dancers, 2006. Seated left to right: Eva Pitsoulakis, Anastasia Emmanuelidis, Sophia Halkias, Irene Spanos. Middle row left to right: Panteli Damalas, George Roros, Dimitri Sidou, Alexander DeRito, Yanni Panagiotopoulos. Back row left to right: Tereza Roros, Christopher Rizakos, Stavros Rizakos, and Maria Pitsoulakis.

Flags of America, Greece, Maryland, and the Patriarchate were flown at the AOC during the Centennial Celebration.

The year 2006 marked the 100th Anniversary of the Annunciation Cathedral. On the first evening of the New Year, parishioners were invited to celebrate at a dinner dance in the ballroom of Annunciation Orthodox Center. With musical entertainment by Zephyros, the event featured Greek folk dancing, the traditional *Vasilopita* (St. Basil's bread), plenty of food and refreshments, and a clown in colorful costume who entertained the children. Michael A. Bouloubassis served as the chairman of this gala attended by nearly 200 people. Alexander Karas photographed the event along with other centennial events. His photography would be used in the Centennial Commemorative Album under the chairmanship of Melody Simmons. By this time, the Album Committee had been busy soliciting advertisements from parishioners and businesses for inclusion in the publication. In addition, family photographs were planned for a special section of the album along with a detailed chronicle of the year's centennial events.

On Sunday, January 8, 2006, the affirmation of office was administered to the new parish council of the Annunciation Cathedral. The officers elected

The Centennial "Glendi" in the AOC Ballroom featured Greek dancing to the lively music of Zephyros, Sunday, January 1, 2006.

Annunciation Cathedral Parish Council, 2006. Front row *l to r* : Larry Vakoutis, Alex Levas, Thomas Zizos, Emmanuel Matsos, Dina-Athena Vakiaros, Betty Jean Alevizatos, Joanne Deitz, Alec Hajimihalis, Dimitri Topaltzas. Second row *l to r*: Dr. Christos Ballas, The Very Rev. Constantine Moralis, Despina Horst, Vice President; James Pappas, Treasurer. Top row *l to r* : Metropolitan Evangelos, Georgeann N. Morekas, President; Diana Motsiopoulos, Secretary; Constantine Letras, The Rev. Peter J. Thornberg.

during the historic centennial year were Georgeann N. Morekas, President; Despina Horst, Vice President; James N. Pappas, Treasurer; and Diana Motsiopoulos, Secretary. Other dedicated council members included Betty Jean Alevizatos, Dr. Christos Ballas, Joanne Deitz, Alec Hajimihalis, Constantine Letras, Alex Levas, Emmanuel Matsos, Dimitri Topaltzas, Dina-Athena Vakiaros, Larry Vakoutis, and Thomas Zizos. Members of the parish council set policies, discuss current issues, and plan activities to enhance the ministries of the Cathedral, all of which benefit the spiritual and educational growth of their fellow parishioners.

The culmination of the centennial celebration took place the weekend of March 18-19, 2006. Father Dean Moralis set the tone for the celebration in the March 2006 parish newsletter. His article entitled "A Crucial Challenge to You" stated in part: "We have shared stories of our past and learned more about the intriguing aspects of our history. Through the records of the Cathedral, we note the names of our faithful who have laid the cornerstone of our faith. Our forefathers came to America and were determined to preserve their Orthodox Christianity and traditions in the New World. Looking around our magnificent Cathedral...we readily see the accomplishments of their dreams.

Inspired by our predecessors, we continue to set higher goals as we move ahead…. The blessings of this church are truly infinite…."

The actual 100th Anniversary of the parish occurred on Saturday, March 18, 2006. That day, *The Baltimore Sun* ran a front-page story highlighting the occasion. "Members of Maryland's first Greek Orthodox parish are to mark its centenary with a service tomorrow." The article featured a rare image showing the ornately covered "Book of Gospels" used by the immigrant congregation—a gift dating back to 1908 from charter member Leonidas A. Dezes. Journalist Matthew Hay Brown noted that "Annunciation remains a spiritual base for the Greek community, a meeting place, and a means of maintaining a common heritage through religious services, language and religious training, festivals, and celebrations." The centennial observance began quietly on Saturday evening with Vesper services officiated by Metropolitan Evangelos of the Metropolis of New Jersey. A reception followed in the Father Constantine Monios Hall where parishioners, friends, and visiting Orthodox clergymen gathered in anticipation of the next day's grand finale.

Members of Maryland's first Greek Orthodox parish are to mark its centenary with a service tomorrow

The Very Rev. Constantine Moralis, dean of the Greek Orthodox Cathedral of the Annunciation, steps toward the altar of the church at Preston Street and Maryland Avenue. The Baltimore native, 39, grew up as a member of the congregation.
ALGERINA PERNA [SUN PHOTOGRAPHER]

Celebrating a century

BY MATTHEW HAY BROWN
[SUN REPORTER]

One hundred years ago today, a cross section of Baltimore's nascent Greek community came together at the Union Hall that stood then on East Fayette Street.

Greeks, many from the Peloponnesian prefecture of Laconia, had been coming to the city since the 1890s. Already they had attracted itinerant priests to conduct services and perform sacraments in private homes and rented halls. Now they were ready to form a church — the first in Maryland for their Eastern Orthodox Christian faith.

That initial congregation of immigrant confectioners and fruit dealers, laborers and bootblacks, heard the Divine Liturgy and raised $400. In time, their Ekklisia tou Evangelismou would grow into the Greek Orthodox Cathedral of the Annunciation. Today the church, now on Preston Street at Maryland Avenue, is one of the largest Greek Orthodox parishes in the nation, with 1,300 families participating in a full range of religious, educational and charitable programs.

"I don't think the 150 people who gathered in that Union Hall could have imagined this place today," said the Very Rev. Constantine Moralis, would dean of th pl

The church, still a focal point of the city's Greek community, will celebrate 100 years of Orthodoxy in Maryland tomorrow with a Divine Liturgy to be led by Metropolitan Evangelos Kourounis. Up to 1,000 people are expected to attend a banquet with Metropolitan Evangelos, who heads the Greek Orthodox Metropolis of New Jersey, Cardinal William H. Keeler, the Roman Catholic archbishop of Baltimore, and other

Please see GREEK, 6A]

The celebration of Annunciation Cathedral's Centennial was featured on the front page of *The Baltimore Sun* on Saturday, March 18, 2006. That weekend marked the much-anticipated grand finale to a yearlong agenda of centennial-related events sponsored by the parish.

A token remembrance of the Centennial Celebration was the special Commemorative Coin (shown front and back) distributed to all guests at the Grand Banquet on Sunday, March 19, 2006.

Centennial Hierarchical Great Vespers were celebrated at the Greek Orthodox Cathedral of the Annunciation on Saturday, March 18, 2006, with Metropolitan Evangelos of New Jersey (far right at Bishop's throne) presiding. Over a dozen clergymen participated in this historic event for the Greek Orthodox community of Baltimore.

On Sunday morning, March 19, 2006, in contrast to the humble gathering that took place 100 years earlier, the magnificent Byzantine-style Cathedral of the Annunciation was adorned with banners and floral arrangements to mark the auspicious occasion. Metropolitan Evangelos commenced the Hierarchical Divine Liturgy before an overflowing congregation. Three years of planning would culminate in the hours ahead. Following the conclusion of church services, over 850 people attended the Centennial Grand Banquet at the Marriott Waterfront Hotel at 700 Aliceanna Street in the Fells Point district of Baltimore. Under the leadership of Anna Z. Pappas, a banquet committee of over twenty volunteers ensured that all details were coordinated for a successful event.

Upon arrival at the Marriott Hotel, guests enjoyed historic displays recounting highlights of parish history and received a commemorative coin to mark their attendance that day. The embossed coin had a depiction of the "Evangelismos" (Annunciation) on one side and the Cathedral building on the other. The procession of honored

Father Elias Velonis, former Assistant Pastor at Annunciation, and Lucy Hagopian, the parish Business Administrator of four decades, at the Centennial Grand Banquet, March 19, 2006.

Dignitaries at the Centennial Grand Banquet, Marriott Waterfront Hotel, March 19, 2006. Front *l to r*: Mayor Martin O' Malley, The Very Rev. Constantine Moralis, Senator Paul S. Sarbanes, Metropolitan Evangelos of New Jersey, Cardinal William H. Keeler, John Sarbanes, Christine Sarbanes. Back *l to r*: Minister Karolos Gadis from the Embassy of Greece, Lt. Governor Michael Steele.

guests then entered the grand ballroom followed by the presentation of the flags of Greece and the United States. The Cathedral Choir sang the national anthems as well as the inspiring Hymn of the Annunciation, *Simeron tis Sotirias Imon to Kefaleon* (Today is the Beginning of our Salvation). Michael Tsakalos served as the Master of Ceremonies and introduced the honored guests seated at the dais. During the afternoon program, many were invited to the podium to share their thoughts on the centennial observance.

The roster of dignitaries included: Metropolitan Evangelos of New Jersey; William Cardinal Keeler, Archbishop of Baltimore; Archimandrite Constantine Moralis and Reverend Peter Thornberg of the Annunciation Cathedral; Martin O'Malley, Mayor of Baltimore City; Paul S. Sarbanes, United States Senator; and Michael S. Steele, Lt. Governor of Maryland. Other speakers included: Georgeann N. Morekas, Parish Council President; Gary T. Padussis, Centennial Chairman; The Rev. Elias Velonis, former Assistant Priest of the Annunciation Cathedral; Anna Z. Pappas, Centennial Grand Banquet Chairman; Minister Karolos Gadis, Deputy Chief of Missions for the Hellenic Republic, Embassy of Greece; and

Nicholas M. Prevas, Parish Historian. Also seated at the dais were Presbytera Katherine Thornberg, Diane Tseckares, Philoptochos President; Mrs. Donna Padussis; Demitra Sourlis, GOYA President; and Leonidia Rizakos, GOYA Vice President.

A highlight of the afternoon was the history program in which Nicholas M. Prevas traced Annunciation's 100 years of progress. After he spoke, the lights were dimmed, music filled the room, and the Centennial slide presentation began. Savas J. Karas, under the guidance of Father Dean Moralis and Nicholas Prevas, produced the show. For thirty minutes, the audience was spellbound as historic images, carefully sequenced into decades, were projected on two large screens in the grand ballroom. Parishioners from bygone eras were momentarily brought to life with stirring background music synchronized by Emmanuel B. Matsos. The show's dramatic ending, a breathtaking image of the original circular Tiffany window followed by a slide that proclaimed "Happy 100th Birthday to our beloved Annunciation Cathedral!" resulted in a standing ovation.

As a memento of the Centennial Grand Banquet, an elegant program booklet was produced under the direction of Maryanth Constantine and dedicated to the clergy who had served the parish and to the laity who committed themselves to establishing the Annunciation Cathedral. The booklet included a listing of centennial events with chairpersons and committee members, donors to the centennial, the names of the clergymen who had served during the first 100 years, a brief synopsis of parish history, images from select centennial-year events, and congratulatory letters from dignitaries. In his message, Metropolitan Evangelos stated in part: "You stand ready to seize the opportunity for even greater labors of love and philanthropic outreach, as well as increased growth in the faith, particularly for our precious youth. I am confident that your vibrant and significant parish will continue to be a beacon of light...." The high caliber of the grand banquet set the standard for other parishes to emulate.

The Centennial Celebration had energized the Annunciation community. Father Dean Moralis reflected upon the legacy the congregation of 2006 would leave for future generations. Continuing to excel in religious, philanthropic, and cultural ministries, the parish remains dedicated to its role as Maryland's Greek Orthodox Cathedral. Under the spiritual guidance of The Very Reverend Constantine Moralis, complemented by progressive parish councils and a myriad of volunteers, Annunciation Cathedral is one of the foremost parishes in the Greek Orthodox Archdiocese. The future of the parish is filled with great promise.

Michael Tsakalos, Master of Ceremonies of the Centennial Banquet, March 19, 2006.

Nicholas M. Prevas highlighted Annunciation Cathedral's 100-year history.

Left to right: Sophia, George, and Demitra Sourlis entertained guests during the dinner hour at the Centennial Banquet.

Ten decades ago, in the spring of 1906, the humble story of a Greek Orthodox church began in a rented hall on East Fayette Street in the City of Baltimore. At that historic gathering, a visiting priest from the nation's capital and 150 immigrants dedicated to their role as Orthodox Christians established the "Evangelismos" (Annunciation) Church. Over the course of 100 years, clergymen, parish leaders, volunteers, and organizations have all changed. One important aspect of parish life, however, has remained steadfast—the desire to preserve and perpetuate the sacred traditions of the Eastern Orthodox faith.

This chronicle of the first century clearly illustrates the focus and determination of an immigrant parish that has evolved into a vibrant religious community. The founders of the Annunciation Church could never have imagined the challenges and opportunities the congregation would face by the 50th Anniversary in 1956 or the 75th Anniversary in 1981. Nor could they have envisioned the impressive roster of Cathedral ministries in place by 2006. The next quarter-century of parish history is already unfolding. May the Greek Orthodox Cathedral of the Annunciation, the *"House of God…Gateway to Heaven,"* be blessed with continued progress as it advances toward its next milestone in 2031…the observance of its 125th year as a religious community in the State of Maryland.

The Very Reverend Archimandrite Constantine Moralis
serves as the *proistamenos* (senior cleryman) of the
Greek Orthodox Cathedral of the Annunciation.

The entrance inscription, *House of God...Gateway to Heaven*, inspires all those who enter the Cathedral sanctuary.

Special Historical Collections

Ecumenical Patriarchs of Constantinople

During the 100-year history of the Annunciation Cathedral, the following Patriarchs have served as Spiritual Leaders of Orthodox Christians worldwide.

Joakim III	1901-1912	Photios II	1929-1935
Germanos V	1913-1918	Benjamin I	1936-1946
Meletios IV	1921-1923	Maximos V	1946-1948
Gregory VII	1923-1924	Athenagoras I	1949-1972
Constantine VI	1924-1925	Dimitrios I	1972-1991
Basil III	1925-1929	Bartholomew I	1991-

His All Holiness Ecumenical Patriarch Bartholomew, Archbishop of Constantinople and New Rome, was enthroned on November 2, 1991. Six years later, he visited the Annunciation Cathedral in Baltimore. This photograph was taken during that historic visit on October 23, 1997.

Archbishops of the
Greek Orthodox Archdiocese of America

Archbishop Alexander
1922-1930

Archbishop Athenagoras
1931-1948

Archbishop Michael
1949-1958

Archbishop Iakovos
1959-1996

Archbishop Spyridon
1996-1999

Archbishop Demetrios
1999-

Metropolis of New Jersey

The Greek Orthodox Diocese of New Jersey was established in 1977 and was originally housed at the headquarters of the Greek Orthodox Archdiocese in New York City. Bishop Silas of Amphipolis was elected as the first Bishop of the Diocese of New Jersey, and in 1979 he was elevated by the Ecumenical Patriarchate of Constantinople to Titular Metropolitan of New Jersey. Metropolitan Silas served as the spiritual leader of the Diocese until his retirement in 1996. Three years later, in March of 1999, Bishop George (Papaioannou) of Komanon was enthroned as the second Bishop to serve the Diocese. He relocated the site of the Diocese from New York to the State of New Jersey.

With the death of Bishop George in November of 1999, Archbishop Demetrios temporarily administered the affairs of the Diocese for the next few years. In 2003, The Very Reverend Archimandrite Evangelos Kourounis was canonically elected by the Holy Synod of the Ecumenical Patriarchate, ordained to the Episcopacy, and enthroned as the first Metropolitan and Spiritual Leader of the new Greek Orthodox Metropolis of New Jersey. Under the terms of the charter granted to the Archdiocese of America in 2003, over fifty parishes in New Jersey, Maryland, Delaware, Virginia, and the Greater Philadelphia area comprise the Metropolis of New Jersey.

Metropolitan Silas
1977-1996

Bishop George of Komanon
1999

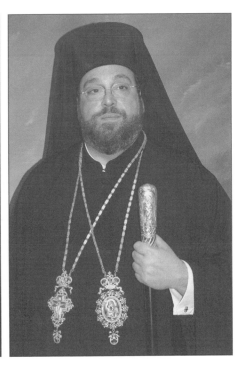

Metropolitan Evangelos
2003-

Clergy of the Annunciation Cathedral
1906–2006

Twenty priests have served as *proistamenoi* (senior clergymen) of the Annunciation Cathedral during its 100-year history. In the Orthodox Church, graduates of the theological schools are allowed to marry prior to their ordination to the Holy Diaconate and Holy Priesthood. The married priests usually bear the title of "Reverend." In this parish history, most unmarried clergymen attained higher rankings, such as the dignity and status of Archimandrite, and are titled "Very Reverend." The longest tenure of any *proistamenos* was The Rev. Constantine M. Monios who served for over twenty-six years (1975-2002). His successor, The Very Rev. Constantine Moralis, is the first Archimandrite to serve the Annunciation community in nearly five decades.

The Very Rev. Joakim Alexopoulos
March 1906 – April 1907
Visiting priest from Washington, D.C.

The Rev. Constantine Douropoulos
May 1907 – May 1911
First full-time priest

The Very Rev. Parthenios Rodopoulos
May 1911 – June 1913

The Very Rev. Chrysanthos Kaplanis
June 1913 – January 1914

The Very Rev. Iakovos Leloudas
January 1915 – August 1920

The Very Rev. Christos Angelopoulos
September 1920 – November 1920

The Very Rev. Polykarpos Marinakis
November 1920 – April 1921

The Very Rev. Iakovos Leloudas
April 1921 – April 1922

The Very Rev. Christos Angelopoulos
May 1922 – August 1923

The Rev. Athanasios Avlonitis
September 1923 – February 1924

The Rev. Symeon Emmanuel
March 1924 – September 1925

The Very Rev. Constantinos Statheros
September 1925 – September 1926

The Rev. Philimon Sevastiades
September 1926 – December 1928

The Very Rev. Nikiforos Pavlou
January 1929 – May 1932

The Very Rev. Joakim Malahias
April 1932 – December 1932

The Rev. Michael G. Andreades
January 1933 – September 1935

The Very Rev. Joakim Papachristou
October 1935 – March 1950

The Very Rev. Chrysostomos Bogdis
March 1950 – September 1950

The Very Rev. Philotheos B. Ahladas
October 1950 – July 1954

The Rev. George P. Gallos
August 1954 – September 1965

The Rev. Emmanuel E. Bouyoucas
September 1965 – September 1975

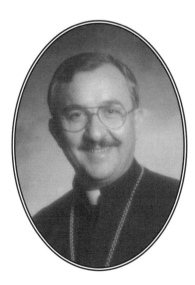

The Rev. Constantine M. Monios
November 1975 – June 2002

The Very Rev. Constantine Moralis
August 2002 –

Assistant Priests

1946-2006

By the fourth decade, the Annunciation community required the services of a full-time assistant priest. The first assistant, Father Philotheos Ahladas, later returned as the senior clergyman of the parish. The second assistant, Father Soterios Gouvellis, was the first American-born priest to serve at Annunciation. The longest tenure was Father Louis Noplos who served a fourteen-year period from 1982-1996.

**The Very Rev.
Philotheos B. Ahladas**
July 1946 – December 1947

The Rev. Soterios Gouvellis
April 1948 – December 1949

The Rev. Demetrius Cassis
1951-1954 (part-time)

The Rev. John Gerotheou
July 1956 – September 1961

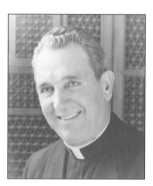

The Rev. Anastasios Voultsos
September 1964 – July 1970

**The Rev.
Alexander Anastasiou**
July 1970 – June 1972

The Rev. Dean C. Martin
November 1972 – February 1975

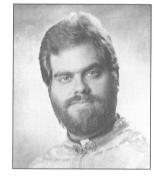

The Rev. Elias C. Velonis
September 1975 – October 1979

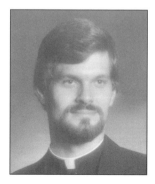

The Rev. Mark B. Arey
October 1979 – May 1982

The Rev. Louis J. Noplos
June 1982 – September 1996

The Rev. Constantine Moralis
June 1996 – July 2002

The Rev. Peter J. Thornberg
June 2005 – September 2006

A Memorial Tribute to
The Very Reverend Constantine M. Monios
1933-2002

His pastorate of twenty-six years (1975-2002) was the
longest in the history of the Annunciation Cathedral.

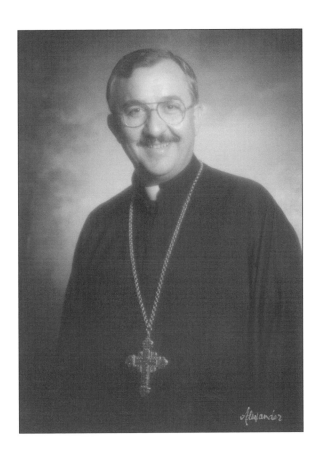

Well known throughout the Greek Orthodox Archdiocese, Father Constantine Monios was highly respected for his theological knowledge, organizational expertise, and motivational skills. During the course of his 45-year ministry as an Orthodox clergyman, he received many awards and honors for his outstanding dedication to the Church. Both the Greek Orthodox Archdiocese as well as the Ecumenical Patriarchate of Constantinople bestowed the title of *Protopresbyter* upon him. With his distinguished position as Dean of the Cathedral, he was also honored with the title "Very Reverend." Father Constantine Monios ranked highly in *Who's Who in Religion* and the International *Who's Who of Professionals*. His life was faithfully devoted to his family, his Cathedral family, the Baltimore and Maryland religious communities, the Diocese, and the Archdiocese of America.

Born in Monessen, Pennsylvania, on October 25, 1933, Father Monios was the second child of Michael Monios and Amalia Chrysopoulos Monios who had immigrated to America from the Island of Chios, Greece. Growing up in a small Greek community, where ties to family and culture were highly regarded, little "Costa"

Constantine "Costa" Monios, at four years of age,
with his older brother, Harry Monios, age seven,
Monessen, Pennyslvania, May 21, 1937.

Mary N. Christodoulou and Constantine M. Monios
were united in Holy Matrimony at the All Saints Greek
Orthodox Church in Weirton, West Virginia, July 15, 1956.

acquired a love of Greek tradition. When he was only five, Costa became an altar boy at the St. Spyridon Greek Orthodox Church in Monessen. Fascinated by the altar and the Church, he had dreams even then of becoming a priest. Through his adolescence he continued his altar duties, was active in the church choir, and worked in his father's grocery store. He was an outstanding student, graduating with honors.

In 1947, a decisive moment occurred for the 14-year-old Constantine while attending a choir conference. It was there that he met the renowned Athenagoras, then Archbishop of America, who solemnly remarked that this youth would become a priest. When the overwhelmed young boy asked His Eminence how he knew, the Archbishop responded that it was in young Costa's eyes. Four years later, in 1951, Constantine Monios entered the Holy Cross Seminary to begin pursuit of the priesthood. On July 15, 1956, he married Mary N. Christodoulou of Weirton, West Virginia, a graduate of St. Basil Academy, whom he met during their college years. During the last year of his seminary program, Constantine M. Monios was ordained to the Holy

Priesthood on January 30, 1957, at the Chapel of the Holy Cross in Brookline, Massachusetts.

Father Constantine Monios' first pastoral assignment was at the Dormition of the Virgin Mary Greek Orthodox Church in Manchester, New Hampshire. With the able assistance of Presbytera Mary Monios, he also taught the Greek school and performed the administrative duties of the parish. In June of 1957, he graduated from the Holy Cross Seminary and by that fall was enrolled in the Boston University where he obtained a Master's Degree in Sacred Theology in May of 1960. In September of 1960, he was then transferred to the Holy Cross Greek Orthodox Church in Mt. Lebanon, Pennsylvania, near Pittsburgh, and served that community for fifteen years. During his tenure, the size of the congregation doubled, the church building was completed, a half-dozen young men were inspired to study the priesthood, and he received the ecclesiastical rank of *Economos* in recognition of his service to the Archdiocese.

The year 1975 marked the beginning of a new era in the life of Father Monios as well as the Annunciation Greek Orthodox Community in

Holy Cross Graduate Constantine Monios receiving his commencement hood from Archimandrite Gerasimos Papadopoulos (later Bishop of Abydos) in Boston, June 1957.

Holy Cross Graduation Day. The Rev. Constantine Monios with his mother, Amalia (left), and Presbytera Mary (right) at their home in Manchester, New Hampshire, June 1957.

Baltimore. Six months after the Baltimore parish was elevated to the status of Cathedral, it underwent a change in clergy. As the primary spiritual center of Greek Orthodoxy in the region, the Baltimore parish needed a progressive-thinking pastor to lead the Cathedral family. At the same time, Father Monios felt it was time to move on with his pastoral career and began looking toward a larger parish like Baltimore as a challenge. Following a successful interview, the decision came quickly. His relationship with the Annunciation Cathedral began on November 1, 1975. Father and Presbytera Monios and their five children—Amalia, Harry, Athena, Michael, and Nikki—were cordially welcomed as participants in the life of the Annunciation parish.

The record of progress during Father Monios' pastorate at Annunciation remains a true example of the cooperative spirit between clergy and laity. Under his guidance, the parish undertook a variety of capital improvement projects such as the construction of the Annunciation Orthodox Center, the completion of the Chapel of the Holy Resurrection and Mausoleum at the Greek Orthodox Cemetery, and the enhancement of the

iconography in both the Cathedral and Cemetery Chapel. Other projects included the completion of the Chapel of Holy Wisdom in the Education Building, the beautification and restoration of the historic Cathedral edifice, the purchase of a parking garage, and the acquisition of a parking lot.

In an article published in the *Orthodox Observer* in 1992, Annunciation was described as "A Parish with Something for Everyone." A few examples included: Greek Language and Sunday School; Adult and Junior Choirs; Youth and Senior Programs; Orthodox Christian Fellowships; Adult Bible Studies; Ethnic Dance Troupes; Summer Camps; Ionian Village Travel Programs; International Orthodox Christian Charities, and others. The many diverse programs of the parish had one common element. All of them received guidance for their continual growth from Father Monios— a clergyman who touched the lives of so many thousands of people over the course of his ministry.

As Dean of the Annunciation Cathedral, Father Monios remained active in organizations in both his ecclesiastical and professional life. He played key leadership roles in the National Presbyters Council,

Left to right: Seminarians John Liadis and Byron Papanikolaou assisting The Rev. Constantine Monios, Dormition of the Virgin Mary Greek Orthodox Church, Manchester, New Hampshire, Holy Friday, 1957.

Clergy of the Central Churches of Baltimore, National Conference of Christians and Jews, Ecumenical Institute, Metropolitan Orthodox and Catholic Dialogue, Maryland Interfaith Project, Central Maryland Ecumenical Council, Cooley's Anemia Foundation of Maryland, and the Greek Orthodox Counseling and Social Services. He was also designated Cross-Bearer of Jerusalem and the Archdiocesan representative to the World Council of Churches in Bucharest, Rumania.

In addition to these successes, Father Monios was an ardent lover of Byzantine art. He served as an advisor to several committees at the Walters Art Museum for Byzantine exhibitions and led numerous inspirational pilgrimages to the Holy Land, Constantinople, Mt. Sinai, Russia, and elsewhere with members of the Cathedral family. Another of his gifts was his eloquent manner as a skilled orator. Those who heard his inspiring sermons will never forget the passion he projected to his listeners. His spiritual leadership and humanitarian nature enriched the entire Orthodox Community of Maryland.

On Friday, June 21, 2002, The Very Rev. Constantine M. Monios, age 68, fell asleep in the Lord. The news of his death spread quickly throughout Baltimore and the Archdiocese. It was the first time in Annunciation's history that a clergyman had died during his actual tenure as pastor. The viewing for Father Monios was held at Annunciation Cathedral on June 24th and June 25th where hundreds of mourners gathered to pray and offer final respects to their beloved priest. Funeral services were held on June 26, 2002, with Archbishop Demetrios of America officiating, along with Bishop Dimitrios of Xanthos and forty Orthodox priests. The funeral of Father Constantine Monios was one of the largest in the history of Baltimore's Greek Orthodox Community.

Several years earlier, Father Monios realized that Baltimore would be his final destination in life. His strong sense of family history compelled him to have the remains of his deceased family members brought from their burial sites in Pennsylvania and West Virginia to be reinterred in the Greek Orthodox Cemetery on Windsor Mill Road. On Wednesday, June 26, 2002, The Very Reverend

Father Constantine blessing the faithful with Holy Water at the ceremonial unveiling of the new Mentis Room, 1979.

Father Constantine bestows his blessings upon a new Orthodox Christian member of the congregation, 1994.

Constantine M. Monios was laid to rest with his beloved family members in the same cemetery where he had conducted so many hundreds of burials and comforted countless Orthodox Christians during the course of his impressive pastorate in Baltimore. Father Monios was survived by Presbytera Mary, his loving wife of 46 years, along with his devoted children: Amalia; Harry and his wife, Rhoula; Athena and her husband, Michael Stem; Michael and his wife, Sandy; and Nikki and her husband, George Anagnostou. He was also blessed with eleven grandchildren: Constantine N. Monios and Evangelia Tripolitis; Anthony, Nicholas, and Christopher Stem; Constantine J. and Zachary M. Monios; and Maria, Connie, Manuel, and John Anagnostou.

A few days following his funeral, journalist Jacques Kelly published a remembrance of Father Monios in *The Baltimore Sun*. His eloquent article summed up the feelings of so many parishioners. It stated in part: "I'll think of all the good he accomplished every time I pass the corner of Maryland Avenue and Preston Street. I'll think of him when I walk past the handsome gray granite building that he so enriched, where he celebrated liturgies and baptized so many children.... When I was around Father Monios, I sensed a man of deep conviction. He saw the best; he saw the possibilities. He saw the light, not the darkness...."

The poignant thoughts and inspirational sermons of Father Constantine Monios continue to resonate in our minds. In one message to parishioners published in *The Annunciation Herald* in May of 1983, he presented the following challenge. "Turn your life away from those acts which draw us far from Christ and His love and become Christ-centered people whose only wish and desire will be to live this life with the joy and expectation of our resurrection in Christ. Let us truly believe that one day we too will pass from death to life." When Father Constantine passed from death to eternal life in the summer of 2002, the congregation deeply mourned his passing. On the occasion of his 40-Day Memorial Service on Sunday, August 4, 2002, a memorial tribute was distributed to the congregation as a keepsake remembrance of their beloved priest.

Father Monios was known for his organizational skills
and his ability to inspire parish volunteers. Photo c. 1997.

Father Constantine Monios enjoying a private audience
with Patriarch Bartholomew I in Constantinople, 1998.

Four years later, in the summer of 2006, a 300-page commemorative issue of *The Annunciation Herald* was dedicated to the last quarter-century of parish life under Father Monios' spiritual leadership. In reflecting on his pastorate, Metropolitan Evangelos of New Jersey stated, "For over 26 years, Father Constantine played an integral role in the development of the Annunciation Cathedral community and truly nurtured the spiritual lives of his parishioners. He loved his people and knew that being a priest was one of the greatest honors in his life…. His boundless energy enabled our Diocese to continue its progress and move forward with enhanced programs to serve the faithful…. He served the Church with great enthusiasm, vision, and dedication…."

In 1975, immediately upon his arrival in Baltimore, Father Constantine Monios understood and appreciated the rich, interesting, and poignant sense of history within the parish. The longest tenure of any priest at Annunciation had been 15 years, a record held by The Very Rev. Joakim Papachristou who served from 1935 to 1950. With that impressive record, could anyone imagine surpassing it? Father Monios imagined it…and made it a reality. He fell in love with the Baltimore parish—a vibrant community that embraced him upon arrival and followed him with reverence for over a quarter of a century.

May his memory be eternal.

A Memorial Tribute to
The Very Reverend Joakim D. Papachristou
1888-1955

His pastorate of fifteen years (1935-1950) was the
second longest in the history of the Annunciation Cathedral.

Born in Proussa, Asia Minor, in 1888, he was baptized as Christos Papadopoulos, the son of Dimitrios Papadopoulos and Maria Valassis Papadopoulos. Following his graduation in 1914 from the Theological Academy of the Ecumenical Patriarchate in Halki, Turkey, he became a Deacon of the Orthodox Church and took the ecclesiastical name, Joakim. Research has shown that Deacon Joakim Papadopoulos was fluent in the Greek, French and English languages. He taught at the French Hellenic University in Constantinople during his Diaconate. In the midst of political turmoil in Asia Minor, he secured passage to America in the fall of 1922. By December of 1922, he was ordained a priest by Archbishop Alexander in New York and later changed his surname to Papachristou. He was an Archimandrite of the Greek Orthodox Church who also held distinctive scholastic honors by earning a Doctor of Divinity degree. Later, he continued his education by taking numerous post-graduate courses at American universities.

The *S.S. Madonna* of the Fabre Line (French) departed from Constantinople on October 12, 1922. Deacon Joakim Papadopoulos, listed as 32 years of age, was on the roster of passengers. Three weeks later, on November 1, 1922, the steamship arrived in New York. The following month, Deacon Joakim was ordained as a priest and later changed his surname to Papachristou.

THE ANNUNCIATION OF THE HOLY VIRGIN
(SAN JULIAN ST.) LOS ANGELES - 1912

Father Joakim Papachristou's first parish assignment was
the Greek Orthodox Community of Los Angeles, California,
organized in 1908. By 1912, the parish had established a church
at 1216 San Julian Street where he served from 1922-1929.

The Very Rev. Joakim Papachristou, 1926. After departing
from the West Coast in 1929, he served brief tenures at three
Greek Orthodox communities: New Castle, Pennyslvania
(1929-1931); Detroit, Michigan (1931-1933); and Jamaica,
New York (1933-1935). Archbishop Athenagoras then
assigned him to Baltimore in October of 1935.

Father Joakim with his brothers, Themistocles (left) and
John (right), Los Angeles, June 23, 1926. Themistocles, who
lived in Baltimore during Father Papachristou's pastorate
at Annunciation, was killed in a car accident in 1943.

The Very Rev. Joakim Papachristou, circa 1940.
His parents, Dimitrios and Maria, resided with him at
7702 Harford Road. Both of his parents passed away in the
spring of 1938 and were laid to rest in the Greek Section
at Woodlawn Cemetery. In July of 1943, his brother,
Themistocles, was also buried there.

Father Joakim and his widowed sister, Katherine Apostolides
(Apostol), with her children left to right: Olympia, George and
Mary, circa 1942. Following the death of Katherine's husband,
William Apostolides, in Los Angeles, California, in December
1931, Father Papachristou sent for his sister and her children
to join him in Detroit. By the fall of 1935, the entire
family had established themselves in Baltimore.

CHURCH PHONE: VErnon 0409   RES. HAMILTON 3434

REV. JOAKIM PAPACHRISTOU, D. D.
ARCHIMANDRITES

CHURCH ADDRESS   RESIDENCE ADDRESS
1106 HOMEWOOD AVENUE   7702 HARFORD ROAD
                                 BALTIMORE, MARYLAND

The first business card of Father Papachristou (1935-1936) in
Baltimore listed the Homewood Avenue Church. By the spring of
1937, the Annunciation community would relocate to Preston Street.

Archbishop Athenagoras (left) and The Very Reverend Joakim Papachristou (holding the 1908 Book of Gospels) led the procession to the corner of Preston and Cathedral Streets for the dedication of the Greek Center on Sunday, September 6, 1942. Standing in back: George B. Petite (left) and Aristides W. Canelos (right).

REV. JOAKIM D. PAPACHRISTOU, D. D.

Rector of The Greek Orthodox Community

45 WEST PRESTON STREET

BALTIMORE, MD. 18 Απριλ. 1945

Ἀγαπητέ μου Νῖκο
Πολὺ θερμὰ εὐχαριστῶ γιατί συχνότερα πέρνω γράμμα ἀπὸ
σένα παρα ἀπὸ τὰ ἄλλα παιδιά.
Ἰδιαιτέρως με συνεκίνησε τὸ δῶρον σου τὸ Πασχαλινόν
γιὰ τὴν Ἐκκλησίαν μας,
Η Ἐκκλησία μας στολίστικε ὠραῖα καὶ περιμένει τὰ παιδιά
Της τοὺς Στρατιῶτας Της νά τα ὑποδεχθῆ νά τα ἀγκαλιάση
καὶ νά τα πάρη στη διοικησί Της,
Οἱ Δικοί σου ὅλοι εἶναι καλὰ, Τὰ Παιδιὰ τὰ βλέπω ταντικά, Τὸν Χέρη τὸν ἔχω στὸ στρατόπεδο τοῦ CAMP RITCHIE
που πηγαίνω ταντικά καὶ δίδω προσευχὴν καὶ Λειτουργία
γιὰ τὰ Ὀρθόδοξα παιδιά μας,
Ὁ Πόλεμος τελειώνει μὲ τὴν βοήθειαν τοῦ Θεοῦ καὶ
πολὺ γρήγορα θὰ εὐτυχήσω νά σε ἰδῶ μαζὺ μὲ τὰ ἄλλα παιδιὰ στὴν Πόλιν μας καὶ τὴν Κοινότητά μας, ποῦ σας περιμένει νὰ ἑορτάσει τὴν ἐπιστροφήν σας.
Τὸ κοριτσάκι τοῦ ἀδελφοῦ Γεωργη, εἶναι μιὰ χαρὰ.
λυπήθηκα ποῦ δέν το ἐβάπτισα ἐγὼ, διότι ἤθελαν νά το
βαπτίσουν στὴν Νέαν Ὑόρκην.
Ἀπὸ τὴν Ἑλλάδα ποῦ τόσον ἀγαπᾶς πέρνουμε τώρα τα-
κτικά γράμματα καὶ μανθάνομεν καὶ εὐχάριστα καὶ λυπη-
ρά, ὅπως τὰ περιμέναμε.

με ἀγάπην & εὐχας
ὁ Ἱερεύς σου
Ἀρχ. Παπαχρίστου

Letter written by The Very Rev. Joakim Papachristou on April 18, 1945,
to Nicholas J. Anderson, a 25-year-old parishioner serving in the United States Army.

My Dear Niko:

I thank you very warmly because I receive letters from you more often than the other young men. I was especially touched by your Easter gift to our church. Our church is beautifully decorated and awaiting her children, her soldiers, to welcome them, to embrace them and to receive them in her care. Your family is well. I see the children often. Harry [Anderson] is at Camp Ritchie and I go there often and offer prayers and liturgies to our Orthodox youth. The war is ending, with the help of God, and very soon I will be glad to see you and the other young men of our city and our community which await you to celebrate your return. The little girl of your brother, George, is a joy. I was sorry that I could not baptize her since they wanted to baptize her in New York. From Greece, that you love so much, we now receive frequent letters and we learn of happiness and of sadness, as we expected.

With love and blessings

Your priest,
Archimandrite J. Papachristou

Some of the major accomplishments during Father Papachristou's pastorate in Baltimore included: organizing the Philoptochos Society (1936); purchasing the Preston Street Church (1937); initiating Greek War Relief efforts (1940); purchasing the Greek Center (1942); and establishing the Greek Orthodox Cemetery (1943). In addition, he strengthened the Greek school and the Sunday school programs. During the 1940's, the Annunciation community received recognition as a prominent congregation within the City of Baltimore. After serving a fifteen-year tenure as the spiritual leader of Baltimore's Greek Orthodox Community, division within the parish led to Father Papachristou's controversial dismissal in January of 1950. Ultimately, the Greek Orthodox Archdiocese transferred him to the Annunciation Greek Orthodox Church in Norfolk, Virginia.

Five years later, on February 12, 1955, Father Joakim Papachristou, age 66, fell asleep in the Lord. With family members residing in Baltimore, his funeral services were held at the Annunciation Church on Preston Street. Following his wishes, he was laid to rest in the Greek Orthodox Cemetery on Windsor Mill Road. It is interesting to note that arrangements for his memorial marker were made in advance. While serving in Baltimore, Father Papachristou had acquired an elegant marble tombstone for himself that was kept in storage in the catacombs of the church basement.

On Thursday, February 17, 1955, a large number of Orthodox Christians gathered at the Annunciation Church to attend the funeral services of their former pastor. In the eulogy, Father George Gallos reflected on how the church of immigrants had evolved during Father Papachristou's tenure. "There came to this community in October of 1935 a man of God named Father Joakim…. He found a community of some 300 members and a small struggling church inadequate for the needs of its parishioners. He left a community of over 1,200 members and a large, beautiful church, which he was instrumental in acquiring and beautifying….

"As a celebrant of the Liturgy, as a preacher, as one learned in the history and doctrines of our Church, he had few equals and fewer peers. His erudition was respected not only by members of our own clergy, but by clergy of all faiths. He chose to enter the ranks of the unmarried priesthood. Yet fate made him the protector of his widowed sister and her three children for whom he worked and sacrificed and gave affection…." The eulogy concluded with a poetic recitation: "The pains of death are past, Labour and sorrow cease, and Life's long warfare closed at last, Thy soul is found in peace."

The 50th Anniversary of Father Joakim Papachristou's death was formally observed at the Annunciation Cathedral with a *Trisagion* (Thrice-Holy) Memorial Service on Sunday, March 6, 2005. A "Memorial Tribute" featuring many of the images and documents contained in this book was displayed in the main lobby showcase of the Annunciation Orthodox Center during the Centennial Celebration of 2005-2006. His impressive pastorate laid the foundation for greater progress witnessed in future decades.

May his memory be eternal.

Parish Council Presidents
1906-2006

The role of the Parish Council President is a serious undertaking—resolving issues, initiating new programs, working in harmony with clergy and volunteers, and setting a strong example for others. There have been 72 individuals who have served as Parish Council Presidents of the Annunciation Cathedral during its first century of progress.

George Sempeles
1906-1907

Constantine Diamond
1908

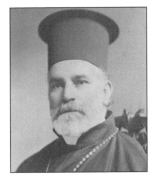

The Rev. Constantine Douropoulos
1909

Professor Aristogeiton Soho
1910

Theodore J. Doukas
1911

Antonios D. Konstant
1912

No photograph available

Aristides Goutopoulos (Houtos)
1913

No photograph available

John Coliviras
1914-1915

Leonidas A. Dezes
1915-1916

George Katsaros
1917-1918

George Poulitsas
1918

George P. Stavropoulos
1919-1921

Stylianos M. Pamfilis
1922-1923

Harry G. Pappas
1924-1925

Nicholas D. Couzantino
1925

Peter Lambropoulos
1925-1926

Andrew Alexander
1926-1927

Basil D. Constant
1927-1928

John G. Anderson
1928-1929

Constantine A. Cavacos
1929-1930

Leonidas Christakos
1930-1931; 1932-1933

George B. Petite
1931-1932

James T. George
1933

Anthony N. Raptis
1933-1934

Niketas A. Konstant
1934-1936

John G. Lambros
1936-1939; 1950

Constantine G. Mesologites
1939

George J. Karangelen
1939-1940

Constantine J. Pecunes
1941-1944; 1951-1952

Nicholas L. Karangelen
1944

Michael Nicolaides
1944; 1950

Peter S. Sfekas
1945

Nicholas Manos
1945

Dionysios Karavedas
1945-1946

James P. Karukas
1947

Nicholas B. Pergantis
1948

George C. Mesologites
1949

Anthony J. Xintas
1952

Sam Malas
1953

C. G. Paris
1954-1956

Evan Alevizatos Chriss
1957; 1967

Paul G. Stamas
1958

Jack P. Pillas
1959

Peter M. Panopoulos
1960-1961

Nicholas S. Morekas
1961-1962

James N. Markakis
1963-1964

Harry J. Anderson
1965

George H. Pappas
1966

Charles T. Pavlos
1968

Charles G. Pefinis
1969

Alex E. Zades
1970; 1978

Aristides W. Canelos
1971-1972

Nicholas J. Kiladis
1972-1973

Nicholas C. Lykos
1974

Anthony J. Cavas
1975

Edward F. Jackovitz
1976-1977

Harry P. Pappas
1979

August A. Krometis
1980; 1990

Dr. Thomas Gleason
1981

Marinos Svolos
1982-1983

George Spanos
1984

Constantine Courpas
1985

Loretta S. Prevas
1986

Larry Burgan
1987

Charles Constantine
1988-1989

Thomas Marudas
1991

Basil M. Pappas
1992-1994

Paul Agathoklis
1995

Gary T. Padussis
1996-1999

Michael A. Bouloubassis
2000-2001

Evangelos D. Sidou
2002-2003

Georgeann N. Morekas
2004-2006

Presidents of the Philoptochos Society
1936-2006

For seventy years, the Annunciation community has had a *Philoptochos* (Friends of the Poor) Society. The concept of a ladies' philanthropic organization within each Greek Orthodox parish began as a national movement in 1932 by the late Ecumenical Patriarch Athenagoras. Established in Baltimore by 1936, the initial goals of the society were to help the poor and needy families and provide comfort to the sick and elderly of the parish. Over the years, the scope of the society has expanded to serve the wider community as well as providing aid for national and international philanthropic causes.

Kalliope H. Pappas	1936-1938	Zoe Mavrides	1966-1968
Penelope Georgelakos	1939-1940	Anna Kassolis	1968-1970
Katherine J. Prevas	1940	Esther Kokinos	1970-1972
Penelope Georgelakos	1940	Hrysoula Klicos	1972-1974
Cleopatra S. Cardiges	1940-1942	Rodopi Smyrnioudis	1974-1977
Kounia Kalandros	1942-1944	Elizabeth Fiackos	1977-1981
Penelope Georgelakos	1944-1946	Vasso Rider	1981-1985
Georgia W. Vlangas	1946-1948	Loula Fantopoulos	1985-1989
Maria Nikoludis	1948-1950	Cornelia Rogers	1989-1991
Angela Hamilos	1950-1954	Julia Krometis	1991-1995
Ruth Kampos	1954-1958	Kyriake Agathoklis	1996-1999
Penelope Kent	1958-1960	Koula Savvakis	2000-2002
Fevronia Petite	1960-1962	Diane Tseckares	2003-2006
Despina Sophocleus	1962-1966		

Philoptochos Society Directors, 1936. Seated left to right: Helen G. Perentesis, Vice President; Kalliope H. Pappas, President; Panayiotitsa N. Karangelen, Secretary. Standing left to right: Helen A. Dezes, Theodora N. Konstant, Stavroula P. Spanakos, and Theodora H. Cardiges, Assistant Secretary.

Annunciation Cathedral Women's Guild
1955-2006

For over fifty years, the Annunciation community has been fortunate to have women of the parish dedicated to the purpose of raising funds for the restoration and continued improvement of the various Cathedral-owned buildings and properties. Established in January of 1955 as the Ladies' Tea Guild, the founders of the organization were Voula P. Rois, Amalia Nicholson Paris, Chrysanthe Alevizatos Pappas, and Dorothy Mesologites. The Ladies' Tea Guild, renamed the Women's Guild in 1979, has raised thousands of dollars for the beautification of the Church by hosting teas, fashion shows, luncheons, and other social events promoting Christian fellowship within the congregation.

Chairpersons and Presidents of the Women's Guild at the Diamond Jubilee Ball held
during the 75th Anniversary celebration of the Annunciation Cathedral, October 3, 1981.

Chairpersons of the Ladies' Tea Guild

Bess Stamas	1958
Helen Padussis	1959
Virginia Constantine	1960
Fi Pappas	1961
Amanda Stamas	1962
Matina Mentis	1963-1964
Hrysoula Klicos	1965
Aphrodite S. Panos	1966
Ceres R. Chriss	1967
Eva Andriotis	1968
Sylvia Lambros	1969
Jean Frank	1970
Esther Kokinos	1971
Eleanor Grivakis	1972
Fifi S. Reichhart	1973-1974
Julia Krometis	1975
Evangeline Sakles	1976-1977
Litsa Weil	1978

Presidents of the Women's Guild

Carolyn M. Tsakalas	1979
Beulah Georges	1980
Helen Xintas	1981
Cornelia Rogers	1982-1983
Mary Pillas	1984
Alice Ioannou	1985-1987
Anna Z. Pappas	1988
Corinna Courpas	1989-1990
Anastazia Pappas	1991
Annabelle Setren	1992
Eleni Flannery	1993
Constance Rogers	1994
Pamela Nopulos	1995
Susan Pappas	1996
Amalia Lucas	1997
Angelique Pefinis-Newport	1998
Maria Donnelly	1999
Christie Williams	2000
Diana Pillas	2001
Melody Simmons	2002
Tracy German	2003
Frances Apostolo	2004
Pamela Stevens	2005-2006

Women's Guild Christmas Luncheon, Towson Golf and Country Club, December 2, 1995.
Kneeling *l to r*: Anastazia Pappas, Annabelle Setren, Constance Rogers, Eleni Flannery, Pamela Nopulos.
Seated *l to r*: Ceres Chriss, Eleanor Grivakis, Cornelia Rogers, Chrysanthe Pappas, Julia Krometis, Evangeline
Sakles, Carolyn Tsakalas. Standing *l to r*: Anna Z. Pappas, Virginia Constantine, Aphrodite Panos, Eva Andriotis,
Esther Kokinos, Alice Ioannou, Fi Pappas, Hrysoula Klicos, Mary Pillas, and Dr. Corinna Z. Courpas.

Presidents of the Golden Age Club
1976-2006

For thirty years, the Golden Age Club has provided a venue for senior citizens of the Annunciation community to gather in fellowship for religious, educational, social, and philanthropic programs. Under the leadership of the following individuals, the Golden Age Club of the Annunciation Cathedral has been successful in raising funds to support the work of numerous parish ministries as well as various national organizations affiliated with the Greek Orthodox Church.

Theodore Canaras	1976	Wallace Vlassis	1992
Steve Kaludis	1977-1979	Esther Kokinos	1993-1995
Dr. Andrew T. Cavacos	1980-1981	Angela Zades	1996-1997
James Chilaris	1982-1984	Mary Lambrow	1998-1999
Anthea C. DeMedis	1985-1986	Nicholas Pavlos	2000-2001
James Chilaris	1987	Nicholas J. Kiladis	2002-2005
Alex E. Zades	1988-1989	Irene Michallas	2006
Andrew Lygoumenos	1990-1991		

Members of the Golden Age Club visited the St. Photios National Greek Orthodox Shrine in St. Augustine, Florida, in October of 1982. The St. Photios Shrine is dedicated to the memory of the first Greek colony that settled there in 1768 and honors all Greek pioneers who came to the New World to establish Greek Orthodox church communities. Each year, the Golden Age Club hosts a fundraising benefit to assist this national shrine in preserving the traditions of the Greek heritage and teachings of the Greek Orthodox Church. The 1982 Club President, James Chilaris, is seated in the front (second from right).

A Tribute to the Homewood Avenue Church
1909-1937

First Greek Orthodox House of Worship in the State of Maryland

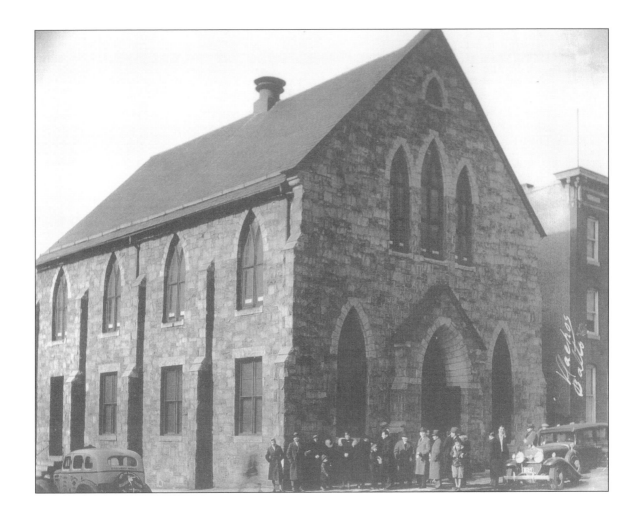

The church building at 1100-1104 Homewood Avenue, at the corner of Chase Street, was purchased from the Greenmount Avenue Methodist Episcopal Church on October 5, 1909. The first Orthodox clergyman to conduct liturgical services there was The Reverend Constantine Douropoulos. The Holy Synod of Athens, Greece, had sent him to America to serve the "Evangelismos" (Annunciation) parish in the spring of 1907. By 1909, Father Douropoulos was elected Parish Council President and signed the legal documents for the acquisition of the Homewood Avenue Church. This was most unusual during an era when laymen were typically in control of church administration.

After the departure of Father Douropoulos in 1911, thirteen clergymen would serve the parish at the corner of Homewood Avenue and Chase Street. They included: The Very Rev. Parthenios Rodopoulos, The Very Rev. Chrysanthos Kaplanis, The Very Rev. Iakovos Leloudas, The Very Rev. Polykarpos Marinakis, The Very Rev. Christos Angelopoulos, The Rev. Athanasios Avlonitis, The Rev. Symeon Emmanuel, The Very Rev. Constantinos Statheros, The Rev. Philimon Sevastiades, The Very Rev. Nikiforos Pavlou, The Very Rev. Joakim Malahias, The Rev. Michael G. Andreades, and The Very Rev. Joakim Papachristou.

The Beginning of Wisdom is the Fear of the Lord (Book of Proverbs 1:7) is the translation of the Greek phrase on the stained glass window originally installed at the Homewood Avenue Church. On April 23, 2005, as part of the reenactment of the 1937 procession from Homewood Avenue to Preston Street, this stained glass window was rededicated and installed above the entrance to the Education Building on Preston Street.

The original Icon of the Annunciation was part of the *iconostasion* (altar screen) at the
Homewood Avenue Church. This icon has now been framed and is displayed
in the Cathedral lobby for parishioners to see as they exit the sanctuary.

The ornate cover for the Book of Gospels was gifted
to the parish in 1908 by Leonidas Dezes. The book itself
is printed in Greek and contains the Gospels of St. John,
St. Luke, St. Mark, and St. Matthew, copyrighted in 1921.

Christ as the Pantocrator, the Ruler of all, surrounded by the four
Evangelists—Matthew, Mark, Luke, and John— is depicted in
the introductory pages of the historic Book of Gospels.

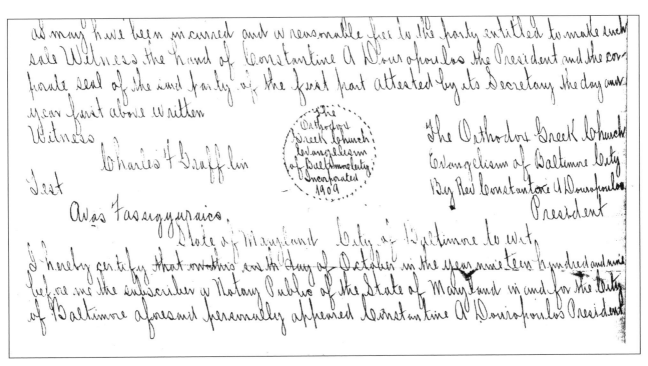

The 1909 mortgage document to the Provident Bank, securing the acquisition of the Homewood Avenue Church, was
signed "The Orthodox Greek Church Evangelism of Baltimore City by Rev. Constantine A. Douropoulos, President."
The priest's signature was witnessed by the parish secretary, Anastasios Gavaris, whose name was quite misspelled.

The only known interior view of the Homewood Avenue Church was taken on Holy Friday, April 14, 1922, showing The Very Rev. Iakovos Leloudas at the services of the *Apokathelosis* (Lowering of the Body of Christ from the Cross).

The *iconostasion* (altar screen) would later be modified and used at the Preston Street Church from 1937-1965. The identity of the altar server has remained a mystery since this photograph was first uncovered thirty years ago.

ΕΛΛΗΝΙΚΗ ΟΡΘΟΔΟΞΟΣ ΚΟΙΝΟΤΗΣ ΒΑΛΤΙΜΩΡΗΣ

"Ο ΕΥΑΓΓΕΛΙΣΜΟΣ"

HOMEWOOD AVE. AND CHASE ST.

ΠΡΟΣ ΤΑΣ ΕΛΛΗΝΙΔΑΣ ΚΑΙ ΤΟΥΣ ΕΛΛΗΝΑΣ ΤΗΣ ΠΟΛΕΩΣ ΒΑΛΤΙΜΩΡΗΣ ΚΑΙ ΤΩΝ ΠΕΡΙΧΩΡΩΝ

———————

Γεγονὸς παρήγορον! Διὰ πρώτην φορὰν ἀπὸ τῆς ἀφίξεώς του εἰς τὸν Νέον Κόσμον, ὁ Σεβασμιώτατος Ἀρχιεπίσκοπος κ. κ. Ἀθηναγόρας θὰ ἐπισκεφθῇ τὴν παροικίαν μας. Ἡ ἐπίσκεψίς του θὰ εἶναι ἐπίσημος.

Θὰ μᾶς ἐπισκεφθῇ ὡς καλὸς Ποιμενάρχης, ὡς φιλόστοργος Πατήρ, ἀλλὰ καὶ ὡς δυνατὸς Ἐκκλησιαστικὸς Ἄρχων, διὰ νὰ τακτοποιήσῃ τὰ πάντα. Θὰ ἱερουργήσῃ εἰς τὴν Ἐκκλησίαν μας, θὰ μᾶς εὐλογήσῃ, θὰ κηρύξῃ τὸν Θεῖον λόγον διὰ νὰ μᾶς ἐμπνεύσῃ, θὰ συνδιαλεχθῇ μαζύ μας, ὡς Πατὴρ πρὸς τέκνα, διὰ νὰ μᾶς δώσῃ τὰς ὡραίας του συμβουλὰς καὶ τὰς συνετὰς ὑποθήκας αὐτοῦ.

Ἡ Κυριακὴ τῆς εἰκοστῆς ἐνάτης (29) Μαΐου θὰ εἶναι ἡμέρα εὐοίωνος διὰ τὴν Κοινότητά μας καὶ ἀπαρχὴ νέας καρποφόρου σταδιοδρομίας, ἀπό τε θρησκευτικῆς καὶ ἐθνικῆς ἀπόψεως.

Ὁ Ἐξοχώτατος Πρεσβευτής μας κ. Χαράλαμπος Σιμόπουλος μὲ πολλὴν εὐγένειαν ἀπεδέχθη τὴν πρόσκλησιν ὅπως παρευρεθῇ εἰς τὴν λειτουργίαν τοῦ Ἀρχιεπισκόπου, πρὸς τιμὴν τοῦ Ἑλληνισμοῦ Βαλτιμώρης.

Αἱ δύο λοιπὸν κεφαλαί, τῆς θρησκείας μας καὶ τῆς πατρίδος μας, θὰ εἶναι παροῦσαι κατὰ τὴν 29ην Μαΐου εἰς τὴν παροικίαν μας.

Ποία Ἑλληνὶς ἢ ποῖος Ἕλλην Ὀρθόδοξος δὲν θὰ θεωρήσῃ ἠθικὴν ὑποχρέωσίν του νὰ προσέλθῃ κατὰ τὴν ὡς ἄνω ἡμέραν εἰς τὴν Ἱερὰν Ἐκκλησίαν διὰ νὰ ἀπολαύσῃ πραγματικῆς ψυχικῆς χαρᾶς; Ποῖος δὲν θὰ θελήσῃ νὰ ἴδῃ ἐκ τοῦ πλησίον τοὺς ἀντιπροσώπους τοῦ Ἔθνους καὶ τῆς Ἐκκλησίας καὶ νὰ ἀνταλλάξῃ δυὸ λόγια μαζύ των; Δὲν φανταζόμεθα ὅτι θὰ ὑπάρξῃ Ἕλλην ὁ ὁποῖος θὰ παρίδῃ τὴν ὡραίαν καὶ μοναδικὴν αὐτὴν εὐκαιρίαν. Ὅλως ἀντιθέτως, ἔχομεν τὴν πεποίθησιν, ὅτι ὁλόκληρος ὁ Ἑλληνισμὸς Βαλτιμώρης καὶ περιχώρων θὰ προσέλθῃ οἰκογενειακῶς εἰς τὴν Ἱερὰν Ἐκκλησίαν, διὰ νὰ ἀποδείξῃ εἰς ἀμφοτέρους τοὺς ἀντιπροσώπους ὅτι τὸ πῦρ τῆς πίστεως πρὸς τὴν Ὀρθοδοξίαν καὶ τῆς ἀγάπης πρὸς τὴν Πατρίδα ὄχι μόνον δὲν ἔσβυσεν, ἀλλὰ καὶ ἀναδίδει φλόγας, ἐφόσον οἱ ἁρμόδιοι ἀρχηγοί του συνδαυλίζουν αὐτό.

Κανεὶς λοιπὸν ἂς μὴ λείψῃ ἀπὸ μίαν τοιαύτην ἐθνικοθρησκευτικὴν συγκέντρωσιν. Ὅλαι καὶ ὅλοι προσέλθετε εἰς τὴν Θείαν Λειτουργίαν.

ΜΗ ΛΗΣΜΟΝΕΙΤΕ ΤΗΝ 29ΗΝ ΜΑΪΟΥ ΗΜΕΡΑΝ ΚΥΡΙΑΚΗΝ

ΤΟ ΔΙΟΙΚΗΤΙΚΟΝ ΣΥΜΒΟΥΛΙΟΝ

The first visit of Archbishop Athenagoras to Baltimore was announced with pride in this special bulletin distributed to members of the Greek community by the Parish Council of 1932. The announcement stated in part: "Solacing event! For the first time since his arrival in the New World, His Eminence Archbishop Athenagoras will visit our parish…. Sunday, the twenty-ninth of May [1932] will be a benevolent day for our Community…both religiously and ethnically. His Excellency Ambassador Mr. Charalambos Simopoulos has graciously accepted the invitation to attend the Archbishop's liturgy, in honor of the Hellenes of Baltimore…. Everyone, come to the Divine Liturgy."

Following the Hierarchical Divine Liturgy conducted at the Homewood Avenue Church,
Archbishop Athenagoras (center) posed with Charalambos Simopoulos, Greek Ambassador from
Washington, D.C., (left) and Annunciation's priest, The Very Rev. Joakim Malahias (right). Back row left to right:
Parish Council President George B. Petite and Archdiocesan Chancellor Parthenios Komninos, Sunday, May 29, 1932.

ΜΙΚΡΗ ΜΟΥ ΕΚΚΛΗΣΙΑ ΣΕ ΑΠΟΧΑΙΡΕΤΩ

Δὲν ἀπέχει πολὺ ἡ ἡμέρα ποῦ θ' ἀποχαιρετήσωμεν τὴν μικρά μας Ἐκκλησιά, τὸ χθεσινό Κοινοτικό Κέντρο τῆς πίστεως καὶ τῶν ἐθνικῶν μας παραδόσεων, ποῦ ἐξυπηρέτησε ἀρκετὰ ἱκανοποιητικὰ μ'ὅλη τὴν στενοχώρια τοῦ χώρου της, μ' ὅλας τὰς ἀτελείας της γιὰ χρόνια πολλὰ Παροικία ποῦ ἔφθασε νὰ ἔχῃ χιλιάδες Ψυχές.

Κάτω ἀπὸ τὴν ταπεινὴ της στέγη πόσες μὰ πόσες ἀπηχήσεις χαρᾶς καὶ πόνου, πόσες προσευχές, πόσες δεήσεις, πόσα ἀντίθετα συναισθήματα εὐτυχισμένων καὶ δυστυχισμένων Ἀδελφῶν μας δὲν ἀντήχησαν ... Πόσες πονεμένες ψυχές γονατισμένες μπρός στὸ Εἰκονοστάσιό Της δὲν ἀνεζήτησαν τὴν παρηγοριὰ καὶ ἀνακούφισι;

Εἶσαι μικρή καὶ πτωχή ἀλλὰ στάθηκες καὶ μεγάλη πνευματικὴ κολυμβήθρα τῆς Ὀρθοδόξου θρησκείας μας, στὰ ἱερὰ νάματα τῆς ὁποίας ἐβάπτισες τῆς ἑκατοντάδες τῶν παιδιῶν μας ποῦ φέραμε στὸ κόσμο, καὶ τοῦτο μονάχα εἶναι ἀρκετὸ γιὰ νὰ σε θυμούμεθα γιὰ πάντα, νὰ θυμούμεθα ποῦ γιὰ πρώτη φορὰ στὴ μικρή μας Ἐκκλησιά μάθαμε τὰ παιδιά μας νὰ σταυρώνουν τὰ χέρια των πρὸς προσευχὴ καὶ νὰ λατρεύουν τὸν Θεὸν τῶν Πατέρων μας, νὰ θυμούμεθα ὅτι μέσα στῆς ἀκατάλληλες αἴθουσές σου ἐδιδάσκαμε γιὰ πολλὰ χρόνια Ἑλληνικὰ γράμματα καὶ Ἑλληνικές ἱστορίες καὶ παραδόσεις τοῦ ἱστορικοῦ Ἔθνους μας.

Ἦσο γιὰ πολλὰ χρόνια ἡ κιβωτός τοῦ ἔκρυβες τὰ κειμήλια Πίστεως καὶ Πατρίδος.

Ἐσὺ βρέθηκες στὴ ξενιτειά μας ὁ μοναδικός Ναὸς σὲ μιὰ μεγάλη περιφέρεια ποῦ μᾶς συνεκράτησες γιὰ πολλὰ χρόνια ἡνωμένους καὶ ὅταν χωριστήκαμε πάλιν σὺ μᾶς ἥνωσες γιὰ νὰ μένουμε γιὰ πάντα ἡνωμένοι.

Ἡ ἀνάμνησίς σου δέθηκε σφυχτά πολὺ σφυχτά μέσα στὴ καρδιά μας καὶ ὅπου καὶ ἂν πᾶμε, ὅσο μεγάλο καὶ ὡραῖο κ' ἂν εἶναι ἐκεῖνο ποῦ θὰ Σὲ ἀντικαταστήσῃ, δὲν πρέπει νὰ Σὲ ξεχάσωμε ποτέ, πρέπει ἡ εἰκόνα σου νὰ στολίζῃ ὅλα τὰ Ὀρθόδοξα Ἑλληνικὰ σπήτια τῆς Παροικίας μας.

Πρέπει σὲ ἕνα μέρος τῆς καρδιᾶς μας τὸ ποιὸ βαθὺ νὰ κρύψωμε αἰώνια τὴν ἱερά ἀνάμνησί ΣΟΥ.

Μικρή μου Ἐκκλησία μὲ βαθειά συγκίνησι εὐλαβικὰ Σὲ ἀποχαιρετῶ .
                                        ΠΡΟΣΚΥΝΗΤΗΣ ΣΟΥ

GOODBYE MY SMALL CHURCH

*Not far is the day that we will say goodbye to our small
Church. Yesterday's community center of our faith and
our national traditions has served us very well, despite
the smallness of its space and its imperfections, for many
years—a parish that came to know thousands of souls.*

*Under its humble roof, how many sounds of joy and
pain, how many prayers, how many invocations, how many
conflicting emotions of our happy or unhappy brothers and
sisters were heard? How many pained souls knelt in front
of Her Iconostasio seeking solace and relief?*

*You are small and poor, but you also have been the great
spiritual baptismal font of our Orthodox religion, baptizing
in its Holy Communion wine the hundreds of children
we birthed, and this alone is enough for us to remember you
forever. To remember that in our small Church we taught
our children to put their hands together in prayer and to worship
the God of our Fathers. To remember that in your unsuitable
classrooms we taught for many years the Greek letters and the
Greek history and traditions of our historic Nation.*

*For many years you have been the Ark that hid the
heirlooms of faith and country. You were the only Church
in a large area within a foreign land, and you kept us united
for many years, and even when we divided it was you that
brought us together so that we are always united.*

*Your memory is kept very close to our heart, and wherever we go,
no matter how big or beautiful will be the Church that ultimately
takes your place, we should never forget you, and your picture
should adorn all the Greek Orthodox houses of our Parish.*

*In a deep place within our heart, we must cherish
your memory forever. My small Church, it is with deep
emotion that I respectfully say goodbye to you.*

Your Pilgrim

A farewell tribute to the Homewood Avenue Church (opposite page) was published in the
program booklet for the Fifteenth Annual Ball sponsored by the Greek Orthodox Community
"Evangelismos" of Baltimore, Sunday, March 7, 1937, at the Alcazar Ballroom. The eloquent
poem was simply signed "Your Pilgrim." The writer is unknown. (See translation above.)

Twenty-eight years after its acquisition in 1909, the final liturgical services were conducted at the Homewood Avenue Church on Friday, April 23, 1937—two days before the celebration of Palm Sunday. The Very Rev. Joakim Papachristou, assisted by The Rev. Thomas Daniels of the Saints Constantine and Helen Greek Orthodox Church of Washington, D.C., officiated at the historic ceremony that evening. This was followed by a parish procession to the new church building nearly one mile away at 24 West Preston Street. The only known photograph of the event appeared in *The Baltimore Sun* the following morning (see below).

The Annunciation community had acquired its new church in February of 1937 from the Mid-Atlantic Conference of Congregational Churches for $40,500. The decisive actions of the Greek community during the early months of 1937 saved the historic edifice from the wrecking ball. With these events, the Annunciation congregation bid an emotional farewell to its first house of worship and began a new era of progress in its new home at the corner of Maryland Avenue and Preston Street where it has expanded its ministries and flourished for seven decades.

Greek Congregation Moves Into New Home Of Worship

The formal procession from the Homewood Avenue Church to the Preston Street Church, April 23, 1937.
The Icon of the Annunciation was carried by Gus Karavedas (left) and Theodore Padussis (right).

A Pictorial History of the
Annunciation Cathedral Building

The Associate Reformed Church was built on Preston Street in 1889 as a Protestant house of worship.
Charles E. Cassell, a well-known architect of that period, designed this magnificent edifice in the Romanesque style
with Byzantine touches. This photograph was published in 1893 in the book *Reminiscences of Baltimore* by Jacob Frey.

Brief History of the Architect
Charles E. Cassell (1838-1916)

Charles Emmett Cassell, the son of Charles E. and Sarah W. Cassell, was born in Portsmouth, Virginia, in 1838. The family name was originally Casselli, having emigrated from Genoa, Italy, to Norfolk, Virginia, in the 1820's. Charles Emmett Cassell was trained as a naval architect and received a degree in engineering at the age of 15 from the University of Virginia.

During the Civil War, he served as a captain in the Engineering Corps under General George Pickett of the Confederate Army. Cassell designed the naval waterworks at Old Point Comfort, Virginia. Upon secession of the Southern states, he kept the plans from falling into the hands of the Union and was later branded as a traitor for this action. Following the Civil War, he fled to the South American City of Bogota, then part of Chile, to avoid execution for treason. While in South America, he served in the Chilean Navy.

After being pardoned for his wartime offense, he returned to Virginia where he married Sally Bowles, the daughter of a prominent Episcopalian clergyman. He practiced architecture in St. Louis before coming to Baltimore with his wife in 1868. The couple resided at 1407 Park Avenue in the Bolton Hill district. They had three daughters, Mary, Sally, Matty, and a son, John, who later became an architect. Charles Cassell soon found himself a widower with four children when his wife, Sally, died in a flu epidemic—quite typical throughout this era in history.

Charles Cassell was a founding member of the Baltimore Chapter of the American Institute of Architects (AIA) in 1870 and was raised to fellowship by 1905. His office was at 404 and 405 Law Building at the northeast corner of Charles and Saratoga Streets. He practiced architecture with his son, John (Charles E. Cassell & Son), from 1905 until his son's death caused by influenza around 1909. Charles E. Cassell continued to practice until his own death from pneumonia in August of 1916. Mr. Cassell, age 78, was buried in his family's lot in Cedar Grove Cemetery located in Portsmouth, Virginia.

Some of his noteworthy architectural achievements in the Baltimore area include: Friends School near the intersection of North and Park Avenues, Stafford Hotel on Mt. Vernon Place, Graham-Hughes House in the Mt. Vernon district, Brexton Apartments, Stewart's Department Store (Howard Street), All Saint's Episcopal Chapel in Reisterstown, Maryland, and the Romanesque-style Associate Reformed Church on Preston Street built in 1889. The latter was an architectural masterpiece that was left vacant in 1934 and slated to become a gasoline filling station. Fortunately, the Greek Orthodox Community of Baltimore intervened and was successful in purchasing the church building in the spring of 1937, thus preserving this fine example of Romanesque architecture.

Bibliographic sources for the brief history of Charles E. Cassell: Haynie, Neal, "Architect Charles E. Cassell was designer of All Saint's Chapel," *The Bell Tower*, July 2000, page 8, published by the All Saint's Episcopal Church of Reisterstown, Maryland; Link, Stephanie Panos, "About Our Building's Architect: A Historical Frame of Reference," *The Annunciation Herald* (Vol. 38, No. 2), October 1989; Wollon, James, Jr., A biography of Charles E. Cassell researched on-line at www.baltimorearchitecture.org, copyright 2005 by the Baltimore Architecture Foundation.

In 1900, the Associate Reformed Church and the First Congregational Church of Baltimore merged under the name of the Associate Congregational Church headquartered at 24 West Preston Street. This photograph, showing the original manse (building adjoining church), was taken in 1910.

Associate Congregational Church, 1923. During the early 1920's, the Greek Orthodox community explored the possibility of acquiring this church. At that time, the cost of $80,000 was beyond their financial means. Note the abundance of ivy growing on the left side of the building and the sign on the lawn which states to passersby: "Find your purpose and fling your life into it and you will make your life richer thereby."

This view of the church building clearly shows the streetcar lines above, automobiles of that era parked on Maryland Avenue, and the Lyric Opera House at the corner of Mt. Royal Avenue (far right), circa 1920's.

Associate Congregational Church, circa 1920's. One sign reads "Not So Long Ago" which appears to be a presentation for an upcoming Sunday. The sign on the right advertised that Raymond Griffith would be starring in "Hands Up–The Most Laughs Ever Received in One Laugh Fest – Friday 8 p.m."

Associate Congregational Church, circa 1935. The building, left vacant in 1934, was scheduled for demolition to make way for a gasoline station. The Greek community saved the church by purchasing it in February of 1937.

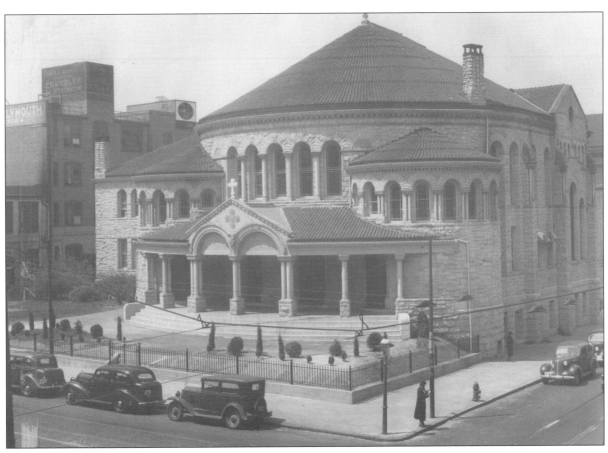

The Annunciation parish renovated the church building, both inside and out. At the corner of Maryland Avenue, the original steps were removed and the area was landscaped and fenced. This photograph was taken in May of 1937.

Famous Old Church Is Renovated By New Owners

VACANT for nearly three years and fated to give way to a filing station, the old Associate Congregational Church at Maryland avenue and Preston streets, shown above, has been renovated by the Greek Orthodox Congregation at a cost of $12,000. The stone has been cleaned, a new railing built, and new evergreens planted on the front lawn.

The purchase of the historic church edifice at the corner of Maryland Avenue and Preston Street
by the Greek Orthodox Community of Baltimore was noted in *The Baltimore Sun*, May 6, 1937.

Outdoor Resurrection Service for the celebration of *Pascha* (Easter), Annunciation Cathedral, April 18, 1993.

The Greek Orthodox Cathedral of the Annunciation marked thirty years of Cathedral status on March 23, 2005.

Greek Orthodox Cathedral

Patriarch Athenagoras

This circular stone church is one of the most unusual buildings in Baltimore. Designed by Charles E. Cassell in Romanesque style with Byzantine touches, it was built for the Associate Reformed Church in 1889. Eighteen polished granite columns support the porch roof and carved foliage ornaments the porch, windows, doors and buttresses.

Left vacant in 1934 and slated to be razed for a filling station, the church was saved through the intervention of the Greek Orthodox congregation, which purchased it in 1937. A Greek inscription, meaning "House of God, Gateway to Heaven," was carved into the stone above the entrance. The altar was transformed into an orthodox one, glowing with icons and relics from the famous Greek monasteries of Mt. Athos.

In 1938, the church was consecrated in the Orthodox tradition by Archbishop Athenagoras of the Archdiocese of North and South America. He was later named Patriarch of Constantinople, the highest honor in Eastern Orthodoxy.

The Greek Orthodox parish, oldest and largest in Maryland, was elevated to the rank of the Greek Orthodox Cathedral in 1975. It is one of the oldest Greek Orthodox parishes in the United States.

Icon of the Annunciation for which the Cathedral is named

 Greek Orthodox Cathedral of the Annunciation, Sponsor
William Donald Schaefer, Mayor

In 1992, the Commission for Historical Architectural Preservation bestowed historic designation upon the Annunciation Cathedral. The commemorative plaque (shown above) is located near the far right entrance doors.

Interior Views of the Annunciation Cathedral

The Annunciation Cathedral building, constructed in 1889, marked 100 years of existence in 1989. On the occasion of its centenary, The Reverend Constantine Monios, an ardent lover of history, wrote an insightful article entitled "One Hundred Years." The following excerpt from his article is a splendid introduction to the interior images of the sanctuary included in this section.

"This year [1989] we remember the fifty-two-year history of this Sanctuary as the house of our Orthodox faithful but also remember the one hundred years it has served as a House of God. The Christian body that contracted for the construction of this Sanctuary was the Associate Congregational Church [formerly the Associate Reformed Church]. Charles E. Cassell, noted Baltimore architect, designed the Church…. Cassell once worked under the famous American architect Stanford White. The inspiration for this design seems to come from the traditional rotunda churches that were once built in the Byzantine Empire. Whatever his inspiration, the future destiny of the Church was well served, for it did adapt beautifully to an Orthodox Church.

"The original construction cost of the Church was $137,000.00, a very respectable sum for 1889. To reproduce this Church today…would cost well into the millions of dollars. This handsome building was constructed of Maryland granite from Port Deposit, Maryland. The construction firm was that of Jefferson J. Walsh, known as J. J. Walsh and Sons, housed in Mt. Washington…. The same firm built the B&O Train Station [Mt. Royal Station] at about the same time.

"Little is known about the life of the first group of Christians who occupied the Church. Evidently they [the Protestant congregation of the Associate Reformed Church] were an affluent community to have been able to build such a magnificent complex of buildings. Beside the Church itself, there was another well-designed and handsome building [the manse] which served as office and classroom space. The large [west] wall to the left of the existing choir loft had a fine wood panel covering which opened to provide more space for choir and parishioners. In 1959, this building was demolished in order that the new office and classroom building could be erected. Granite was preserved and is now part of the façade which faces the courtyard. More of that granite was used when the altar area was expanded.

"A further indication of the wealth of that early congregation is that of the four Louis C. Tiffany windows which grace the [sanctuary]. According to Alastair Duncan in his book *Tiffany Windows*, published in 1980, the windows, by theme are: 'Sermon on the Mount,' 'Christ Knocking on the Door,' 'Christ the Counselor,' and 'Good Shepherd.'

"As one looks about the interior of the Sanctuary, one will notice the magnificent polished columns made from Tennessee granite. Similar columns grace the portico and exterior walls of the Cathedral. All the columns, both inside the building and out are graced with carved capitals, no two of which are alike. Each was individually handcrafted. We have inherited these features from the original construction. The sweeping graceful oak balcony and the century-old pews still show the great care taken in the execution of the woodwork. The vaulted brick arches lend great majesty to the interior space…. The great art of the past and the great art of the present have served to make this holy space one of the outstanding churches of Baltimore."

The Rev. Constantine M. Monios, 1989

Two of the earliest known photographs of the church interior were taken at a double wedding on November 20, 1938. This image shows The Very Rev. Joakim Papachristou preparing for the arrival of the wedding party. Beautiful palms and flowers adorn the solea.

This image shows the double wedding ceremony of Mary Constantine to Jack Pillas and Josephine Constantine to Louis Sharkey along with their bridal party on November 20, 1938. The plain glass windows on the far right would be replaced with stained glass four years later in 1942.

Interior view of the Greek Orthodox Church "Evangelismos" (Annunciation), circa 1940.
By 1944, a wall-sized icon of the Virgin Mary was added to enhance the beauty of the sanctuary.

The Very Rev. Joakim Papachristou at the lectern. The rectangular solea was later remodeled into a curved shape during the renovations of the early 1960's to complement the curved pews and balcony.

Episcopal crown of Metropolitan Silas resting on the Holy Gospel
in the altar of the Annunciation Cathedral, Sunday, May 6, 1984.

Interior view of the Greek Orthodox Cathedral of the Annunciation, 2005.

Looking into the Holy Altar of the Annunciation Cathedral, 2005.

View from the cantors' stand showing polished granite columns
and the circular stained glass window in the background, 2005.

The "Sermon on the Mount" is the most impressive of the four original
Louis C. Tiffany windows that grace the interior of the sanctuary.

The architectural detail of the original carved capitals
atop the granite columns that flank the Holy Altar.

Stained glass windows were installed on the east wall during the early 1940's
to replace the plain-colored glass windows inherited from the prior owners.
For details on the three windows shown and their donors, see page 128.

Greek Orthodox Churches of Maryland

Greek Orthodox Cathedral of the Annunciation
Baltimore, Maryland
Established March 18, 1906

Saints Constantine and Helen Greek Orthodox Church
Annapolis, Maryland
Established January 3, 1945

Saint Nicholas Greek Orthodox Church
Baltimore, Maryland
Established September 16, 1952

Saint George Greek Orthodox Church
Bethesda, Maryland
Established September 1, 1967

Saint Demetrios Greek Orthodox Church
Baltimore, Maryland
Established June 8, 1970

Saint Theodore Greek Orthodox Church
Lanham, Maryland
Established December 4, 1973

Saint George Greek Orthodox Church
Ocean City, Maryland
Established June 22, 1985

Saints Peter and Paul Greek Orthodox Church
Frederick, Maryland
Established April 7, 1991

Saints Mary Magdalene and Markella Greek Orthodox Church
Darlington, Maryland
Established April 12, 2004

Bibliography

Archdiocesan and Local Church Records

Greek Orthodox Archdiocese of America, New York, New York – www.goarch.org.

> Archives of the Archdiocese: Annunciation Cathedral File; Deceased Clergy Files; Photographic Collection of Clergy, Bishops, Archbishops and Ecumenical Patriarchs; Greek Orthodox Ladies Philoptochos Society, Annunciation Cathedral File.

Greek Orthodox Cathedral of the Annunciation, Baltimore, Maryland – www.goannun.org.

> Cathedral Archives: Organizational records, various documents, and photographs of church-affiliated societies, *topika somatia* (regional societies), Greek-American fraternal groups (AHEPA and GAPA), social events, parish leaders, and clergymen. The Archives is a repository for all historical records of the parish such as capital improvement initiatives, religious, social and philanthropic ministries, Diocesan and Archdiocesan events.

> Registries of Baptisms, Weddings, and Funerals, 1911-2005.

> Correspondence regarding the acquisition of the Associate Congregational Church by the Greek Orthodox community: Letters dated February 10-11-18-19, 1937; March 4-5, 1937.

> Event brochures, pamphlets, and assorted mementos collected by the author, 1981-2006.

> Minutes of Parish Council Meetings, 1922-1949; 1950-2006.

> Minutes of General Assembly Meetings, 1922-1949; 1950-2005.

> Parish Monthly Newsletters, 1990-2006.

> Parish Weekly Bulletins, 1946-2006.

> Publications: *The Community Herald*, 1951-1964; *Annunciation Herald*, 1964-1976; and *The Annunciation Herald*, 1976-1990, 1992, 1993, 1998.

> Official Register of the Interior Decorations, Furniture, Icons, Vestments and other Articles within the Greek Orthodox Church "Evangelismos," published in the Fortieth Anniversary Celebration Book, 1946, pages 81-89.

Greek Orthodox Metropolis of New Jersey – www. nj.goarch.org.

Orthodox Research Institute – www.orthodoxresearchinstitute.org/resources/hierarchs.

Books

Akrotirianakis, Stavros. *Byzantium Comes to Southern California*: The Los Angeles Greek Community and the Building of the Saint Sophia Cathedral. Light and Life Publishing Company, Minneapolis, Minnesota, 1994.

Anuta, Michael J. *Ships of our Ancestors*. Baltimore: Genealogical Publishing Company, 1983.

Bodnar, John. *The Transplanted : A History of Immigrants in Urban America.* Bloomington: Indiana University Press, 1985.

Burgess, Thomas. *Greeks in America*. Boston: Sherman, French & Company, 1913.

Canoutas, Seraphim G. *Greek-American Guides*. New York: 1907, 1909, and 1911 (in Greek).

Canoutas, Seraphim G. *Hellenism in America*. New York: 1918 (in Greek).

Chebithes, V. I. *The AHEPA*. Washington, D.C., May 1925.

Dracos, Helen C. *The House on Palmer Street.* Hellenic College Press: Brookline, Massachusetts, 1993.

Fairchild, Henry Pratt. *Greek Immigration to the United States.* New Haven: Yale University Press, 1911.

Handlin, Oscar. *A Pictorial History of Immigration.* New York: Crown Publishers, Inc., 1972.

Jones, Maldwyn Allen. *American Immigration.* Chicago: University of Chicago Press, 1960.

Kotakis, Spyridon A. *The Greeks in America.* Chicago, 1908 (in Greek).

Leber, George J. *The History of the Order of AHEPA.* Washington, D.C., 1972.

Leonhart, James Chancellor. *One Hundred Years of Baltimore City College*, Baltimore: H. G. Roebuck and Sons, 1939.

Mazacoufa, Demetrius. *The Story of the Greeks in America.* Atlanta: Argonne Press, 1977.

Monos, Dimitris. *The Greek Americans.* New York: Chelsea House Publishers, 1988.

Moskos, Charles C. *Greek Americans: Struggle and Success.* Englewood Cliffs, New Jersey: Prentice-Hall, Inc., 1980.

Moskos, Charles C. *Greek Americans: Struggle and Success.* Second Edition. New Brunswick, New Jersey: Transaction Publishers, 1989.

Papaioannou, George. *The Odyssey of Hellenism in America.* Thessaloniki, Greece, Patriarchal Institute for Patristic Studies, 1985.

Papaioannou, George. *From Mars Hill to Manhattan.* Light and Life Publishing Company, Minneapolis, Minnesota, 1976.

Prevas, Nicholas M. *History of the Greek Orthodox Cathedral of the Annunciation.* Baltimore, Maryland, John D. Lucas Printing Company, 1982.

Prevas, Nicholas M. *Gone But Not Forgotten* – A Definitive History of the Greek Section at Woodlawn Cemetery. Baltimore Maryland, Annunciation Cathedral, 2001.

Saloutos, Theodore. *The Greeks in the United States.* Cambridge: Harvard University Press, 1964.

Voultsos, Mary. *Greek Immigrant Passengers* 1885-1910, Volume One. Worcester, Massachusetts, 1991. Pages 57-64 of this volume reference reports on emigration to the United States from Greece and the attitude of the Greek government toward the exodus of its people.

Wind, James P. and Lewis, James W. *American Congregations* – Portraits of Twelve Religious Communities. The University of Chicago Press, 1994. Chapter Nine: History of the Greek Orthodox Cathedral of the Annunciation by The Rev. George Papaioannou.

Xenides, J. P. *The Greeks in America.* New York: George H. Doran Company, 1922.

Cemeteries

Greek Orthodox Cemetery, Windsor Mill Road, Baltimore Maryland
Purchase Agreement, Cemetery Committee Minutes, Rules and Regulations, and Records of Interments filed at the Annunciation Cathedral Office.

New Cathedral Cemetery, 4300 Old Frederick Road, Baltimore, Maryland
Book of Interments, 1899, documenting the burial of first Greek immigrant. (*See p. 9.*)

Woodlawn Cemetery Company, 2130 Woodlawn Drive, Baltimore, Maryland
Interment Card Files; Greek Church (Evangelismos) File, 1912-2002; Greek Church No. 2 (Holy Trinity) File, 1923-1929; Accounts Receivable Books, Cash Receipt Journals, and Ledger Book of Cemetery Burials, 1912-1943.

Court and Government Records

Baltimore City Archives. Market Records and Stall Receipts, 1890-1910.

Charter Records, Superior Court of Baltimore City.

> Greek Orthodox Cathedral of the Annunciation incorporated on June 4, 1909
> as the Greek Orthodox Church "Evangelism," Liber S.C.L. 50, Folios 505-507.
> Charter amendments during the first fifty years occurred on September 26, 1909,
> October 12, 1923, May 1, 1942, December 5, 1946, and November 21, 1956.

> Greek-American organizations chartered in Baltimore City, 1918-1930.
> For specific references, see Prevas, Nicholas M. *History of the Greek Orthodox*
> *Cathedral of the Annunciation*, 1982, pages 253-254.

Court Cases, Maryland State Archives, Annapolis, Maryland.

> State of Maryland v. George Saradopoulos, 1913,
> Case No. 65, Indictment filed Feb. 7, 1913, Criminal Court of Baltimore City. *(See p. 26.)*

> Basil Constant, et al. v. The Orthodox Greek Church Evangelism, 1918,
> Case No. 58 A/368/1918-A-9257, Circuit Court of Baltimore City. *(See p. 39.)*

> The Rev. Iakovos Leloudas, et al. v. The Rev. Christos Angelopoulos, 1922,
> Case No. 62 A/225/1922-A-11625, Circuit Court of Baltimore City. *(See p. 48.)*

> Greek Orthodox Community "Evangelismos" v. The Rev. Joakim Papachristou, 1950,
> Case No. 90A/142/1950-A-31159, Circuit Court of Baltimore City. *(See p. 131.)*

Court of Common Pleas of Baltimore City. Marriage License Records: Dockets 1890-1920.

Enoch Pratt Central Library, Baltimore, Maryland.

> Baltimore City Directories published by R. L. Polk & Company.

> Indexes for newspaper publications: The Baltimore Sun; Baltimore News; Baltimore News-Post;
> and News American located in the Microfilm Research Department.

Land Records, Superior Court of Baltimore City.

> Deeds, Mortgages, and Lease Agreements regarding properties owned by the
> Annunciation Cathedral. First house of worship on Homewood Avenue purchased
> October 5, 1909; Preston Street Church building acquired February 26, 1937.

Maryland Historical Society, Baltimore, Maryland.

> Baltimore Business Directories showing names, occupations, and addresses of businesses.
> Photograph Collection: For selected images see Photo Credits.

Maryland State Archives, Annapolis, Maryland.

> Administration Accounts 1914, Baltimore City Register of Wills. *(See p. 27.)*
> Baltimore City Directories, 1899-1919.
> Birth, Marriage, and Death Indexes for Baltimore City, 1900-1920.
> Naturalization Indexes for Superior Court of Baltimore City, 1890-1910.

National Archives, Washington, D.C.

> Book of Indexes to New York Passenger Lists, 1906-1942. Microfilm T612 (807 rolls).
> Alphabetical indexes to passenger manifests grouped chronologically by shipping line.

> Index to Passenger Steamship Arrivals in New York: 1897-1902; 1902-1943.

Morton Allan Directory of European Passenger Steamship Arrivals: 1890-1930 at the Port of New York; 1904-1926 at the Ports of New York, Philadelphia, Boston and Baltimore.

United States Federal Census Records: 1880, 1900, 1910, 1920, and 1930.

Passenger Records of Orthodox Clergymen researched on-line at www.ellisislandrecords.org.

Alexopoulos, Joakim, age 32, arrived on January 1, 1906, on the S.S. St. Louis.

Alexopoulos, Joakim, age 41, arrived on May 4, 1915, on the S.S. Carpathia.

Angelopoulos, Christos, age 42, arrived on November 9, 1907, on the S.S. Konigen Luise.

Avlonitis, Athanasios, age 50, arrived on December 4, 1919, on the S.S. Themistocles.

Douropoulos, Constantine, age 45, arrived on May 10, 1907, on the S.S. Sofia Hohenberg.
 Note: First full-time priest assigned to the Annunciation parish.

Emmanuel, Symeon, age 38, arrived on August 24, 1915, on the S.S. Vasilefs Constantinos.

Germanos, Troyanos, age 45, arrived on July 2, 1921, on the S.S. King Alexander.
 Note: Royalist Bishop who attempted to oust Bishop Alexander of Rodostolou.

Kaplanis, Chrysanthos, age 36, arrived on September 27, 1912, on the S.S. Macedonia.

Leloudas, Iakovos, age 45, arrived on May 30, 1907, on the S.S. Laura.

Leloudas, Iakovos, age 60, arrived on February 28, 1921, on the S.S. King Alexander.

Malahias, Joakim, age 38, arrived on August 1, 1923, on the S.S. Constantinople.

Marinakis, Polykarpos, age 27, arrived on September 27, 1909, on the S.S. Athinai.

Metaxakis, Meletios, age 46, arrived on August 22, 1918, on the S.S. Espagne.
 Note: Archbishop of Athens who later became Ecumenical Patriarch.

Papadopoulos, Joakim, age 32, arrived November 1, 1922, on the S.S. Madonna.
 Note: Following his ordination in New York, he took the last name of Papachristou.

Prousianos, Theodoros, age 33, arrived on September 25, 1902, on the S.S. Patricia.

Rodopoulos, Parthenios, age 34, arrived on November 12, 1906, on the S.S. Canopic.

Rodostolou, Alexander, age 43, arrived on August 22, 1918, on the S.S. Espagne.
 Note: Later became the first Archbishop of the Greek Orthodox Archdiocese.

Statheros, Constantinos, age 32, arrived on November 22, 1922, on the S.S. Saxonia.

Sideris, Nathanael, age 45, arrived on August 1, 1899, on the S.S. Patria.

Steamship Historical Society of America Collection, University of Baltimore.

Passenger steamship photographs and descriptions from pamphlets and reference books.

Directories and Yearbooks

AHEPA National Convention Books, Baltimore, Maryland, 1932 and 1946.

Baltimore City College, The Green Bag, Baltimore, 1906.
 Note: Reference and photograph of Professor Aristogeiton Soho on p. 6.

Baltimore City Directory, John W. Woods, 1877-1884.

Baltimore City Directory, Sheriff and Taylor, 1885-1887.

Baltimore City Directory, R. L. Polk and Company, 1888-1930.

GAPA 20th National Convention Book, Baltimore, Maryland, 1958.

Greek Orthodox Archdiocese, New York, New York: Yearbooks 1981, 1983, 1984, and 1998.

Greek Orthodox Church "Evangelismos," Baltimore, Maryland.
> Twenty-Fifth Anniversary of the Greek Orthodox Community "Evangelismos," 1936.
> Dedication Memorial Book, 1938.
> Fortieth Anniversary Celebration Book, 1946.
> Fiftieth Anniversary Souvenir Book, 1956.

Greek Orthodox Cathedral of the Annunciation, Baltimore, Maryland.
> Seventy-Fifth Anniversary Album, 1981.

Karpathian Educational Progressive Association of America, 25th Anniversary Souvenir Book,
> Supreme Lodge, Baltimore, Maryland, 1953.

Laconian Association "Lycourgos, Inc.," Twenty-First Anniversary Booklet
> of the Laconian Association, Baltimore, Maryland, May 1947.

Laconian Federation of the United States and Canada, Inc., Seventh National Convention
> Booklet, Baltimore, Maryland, June 1954.

Rhodian Society of America "Apollon," 22nd Annual Convention Souvenir Book,
> Baltimore, Maryland, July 1949.

St. Nicholas Greek Orthodox Church, Baltimore, Maryland.
> Souvenir Memorial Album, 1953-1958.
> Twenty-Fifth Anniversary Commemorative Album, 1978.

United Chios Societies of America, Seventh Annual Convention Souvenir Book,
> Baltimore, Maryland, July 1947.

Pamphlets, Brochures, Articles, and Internet Sources

Athenagoras, Ecumenical Patriarch. Historical brochure (not dated).
> *Note: See 1910 graduation photograph from the Theological School in Halki on p. 74.*

Critikos, Peter J. "A Social-Economic Study of Greeks in the United States."
> Baltimore, Maryland, January 1973.

Critikos, Peter J. "The Greeks in Greater Baltimore." Ethnic Heritage and Horizons: An
> Expanding Awareness. Ethnic Affairs Committee of Baltimore County, Maryland, 1980.

Ellis Island History. Internet source located at www.ellisisland.org.

"Elpis" Ladies Society of Baltimore, Maryland, Charter Record, January 1929.

Flezanis, Katherine. "The Greek Immigrant." Baltimore, Maryland, 1976.

GAPA. Junior Order Second Annual Dance Booklet, January 24, 1937.

George, Theodore J. "Baltimore's Hellenic University Club Spearheads Drive For Modern Greek."
> *National Herald*, October 25, 1959.

George, Theodore J. "Brief History of the Hellenic University Club" (undated manuscript).

Greek Orthodox Archdiocese of America – www.goarch.org.

Greek Orthodox Community "Evangelismos." House of God – Gate of Heaven. Brochure to
> promote the Education Building project, Baltimore, Maryland, 1959.

Greek Orthodox Community "Evangelismos." Baltimore, Maryland.
     Ninth Annual Ball Souvenir Booklet, 1931.
     15th Annual Ball Souvenir Booklet, 1937.
     18th Annual Ball Souvenir Booklet, 1940.
     20th Annual Ball Souvenir Booklet, 1942.

Greek Orthodox Community "Evangelismos." Financial Statements, June 30, 1942,
     compiled by Felix J. Christ, Public Accountant and Auditor.

Greek Orthodox Cathedral of the Annunciation, Baltimore, Maryland.
     70th Anniversary Luncheon Brochure, March 1976.
     75th Anniversary Commemorative Luncheon Brochures, March & November 1981.
     Patriarchal Doxology and Luncheon Brochures, October 1997.
     Centennial Grand Banquet Program Booklet, March 2006.

Greek Orthodox Metropolis of New Jersey – www.nj.goarch.org.

Greek War Relief Association. Brochure and correspondence from Campaign Headquarters at
     the Greek Center, Cathedral and Preston Streets, 1947.

Karavedas, Dionysios. Memoir (unpublished manuscript), Baltimore, April 12, 1979.

Konstant, Katheryn N. "A Brief History of the Greek Orthodox Community Schools." Fortieth
     Anniversary Celebration Book of the Annunciation Cathedral, Baltimore, Maryland, 1946.

Konstant, Niketas A. "A Synopsis of the History of the Greek Orthodox Community of Baltimore."
     Dedication Memorial Book of the Annunciation Cathedral, Baltimore, Maryland, 1938.

Konstant, Niketas A. "A Synopsis of the History of the Greek Orthodox Community of Baltimore."
     Fortieth Anniversary Celebration Book of the Annunciation Cathedral, Baltimore, Maryland, 1946.

Konstant, Niketas A. "Our Community – The Past." Fiftieth Anniversary Souvenir Book of the
     Annunciation Cathedral, Baltimore, Maryland, 1956.

Konstant, Niketas A. and Theodorides, Athanasios P. "The Community Progress." 18th Annual Ball of the
     Greek Orthodox Community "Evangelismos," Baltimore, Maryland, 1940 (in Greek).

Kytherian Brotherhood. Souvenir Program of the Second Annual Ball, 1935.

Laconian Association. Souvenir Program Booklet, Annual Ball, 1937.

Laconian Association. Souvenir Program Booklet, Annual Ball, 1939.

Leep, Georgia Vasilakos. Memoir (unpublished manuscript), January 1956.

Monos, Dimitri I. "Why Greeks Moved to Highlandtown" (unpublished manuscript), Baltimore, 1979.

National Herald, Weekly Greek-American Newspaper, Long Island City, New York.

Nicozisin, The Rev. George. "The Transfer of the Priest: Dimensions and Ramifications."
     Brookline, Massachusetts, May 29, 1980.

Orthodox Christian Laity - www.ocl.org.

Orthodox Church of America - www.oca.org. "Historical Perspective: Orthodoxy in
     Seattle." *The Orthodox Vision*, Spring 2004. Article written in 1985 on the occasion of
     the 90th Anniversary of the Saint Spiridon Orthodox Cathedral in Seattle, Washington,
     providing historical reference to Reverend Michael Andreades. (*See p. 82.*)

Orthodox Observer – miscellaneous newspaper editions.

Orthodox Research Institute – www.orthodoxresearchinstitute.org.

Panos, Louis G. "Our Community – The Present." Fiftieth Anniversary Souvenir Book of the
    Annunciation Cathedral, Baltimore, Maryland, 1956.

Pappas, Theodora N. "Greek Youth." Evangelismos Church Bulletin, Baltimore, Maryland, 1946.

Phillips, Steven. "Paths in the Wilderness: The Struggle of Greek Orthodoxy in America."
    Greek Accent, Vol. 5, No. 1, page 28, July-August 1984.

Poletis, Theodora Pappas. "The Greek Orthodox Churches in the State of Maryland."
    Baltimore, Maryland, 1981.

Prevas, Nicholas M. "Tracing 90 Years of Progress."
    Annunciation Cathedral, Baltimore, Maryland, 1996.

Prevas, Nicholas M. "90th Anniversary of the Greek Section at Woodlawn Cemetery."
    Annunciation Cathedral, Baltimore, Maryland, 2002.

Prevas, Nicholas M. "A Memorial Tribute to The Very Rev. Constantine M. Monios."
    Annunciation Cathedral, Baltimore, Maryland, 2002.

Prevas, Nicholas M. "A Memorial Tribute to The Rev. George P. Gallos."
    Annunciation Cathedral, Baltimore, Maryland, 2005.

Saint Demetrios Greek Orthodox Church. "Meeting the Challenge" Brochure, 1983.

Saint Demetrios Greek Orthodox Church. Consecration Brochure, October 1995.

Saint Nicholas Greek Orthodox Church. The Voice, Official Bulletins published
    June 1955, January-February 1956, and April 1956.

Saint Spiridon Orthodox Cathedral of Seattle, Washington. Parish History on-line at
    www.saintspiridon.org/history.html, providing historical reference to
    Reverend Michael Andreades. (*See p. 82.*)

Saloutos, Theodore. "The Greek Orthodox Church in the United States and its Assimilation."
    Reprinted from International Migration Review, Vol. 7, No. 4, Winter 1973. Published by
    the Center for Migration Studies of New York, Inc., Staten Island, New York.

Sons of Pericles. Plato Chapter No. 80, Second Annual Ball Booklet, 1935.

Tangires, Georgia. "Choir History." Baltimore, Maryland, 1981.

Vickrey, Charles V. Near East Relief – Review for 1922 (Annual Report to Congress),
    Near East Relief National Headquarters, New York, 1923.

Author's Note: A wealth of information pertaining to the history of the Annunciation Cathedral came from parishioners and friends of the Greek Orthodox community of Baltimore who experienced many of the events chronicled in this volume. Over the years, countless people graciously shared their recollections dealing with parish history which added a human element to the researched documentation. During these valuable interviews, many photographs were either donated or loaned for possible inclusion. The individuals or organizations that provided the images used in this publication are gratefully acknowledged and credited in the next section of this book.

Photo Credits

Page	Description of Image	From the Collection of...

Introduction

xxiv	Document from the Holy Synod, 1907	Helen Douropoulos Dracos
1	The *S.S. Sofia Hohenberg* of the Austro-Americana Line	Steamship Historical Society of America Collection, University of Baltimore
1	The Great Hall at Ellis Island, 1909	Canoutas, *Greek-American Guide*, 1909
2	The Rev. Constantine Douropoulos	Cathedral Archives
2	Passenger list – Douropoulos family, 1907	National Archives, Washington, D.C.
2	Great Fire of Baltimore, 1904	The Maryland Historical Society
3	Prevas ancestors in Greece, 1900	Katherine Moisakos Tsimas
3	Immigrants aboard a steamship	Ellis Island Immigration Museum
4	Lexington Market scene, 1910	The Maryland Historical Society
5	Market Stall Receipts	Baltimore City Archives
5	Baltimore City Directory, 1878	Enoch Pratt Central Library
5	Constantina and Sotirios Nifakos	Marie Rose Memphis
6	Professor Aristo Soho	Baltimore City College Archives
6	Sempeles Brothers Confectionery	Vasiliki G. Sempeles
6	Christos Sempeles	Vasiliki G. Sempeles
7	Epaminondas Asimakes, 1899	James P. Asimakes
7	Asimakes Military Discharge, 1906	James P. Asimakes
7	Anastasios Coroneos	Kotakis, *The Greeks in America*, 1908
8	Annie Martens	Leo W. Vulgaris
8	John L. Voulgaris	Kotakis, *The Greeks in America*, 1908
8	Evangelos Vasilakos	Kotakis, *The Greeks in America*, 1908
8	The *S.S. Amsterdam* passenger steamship	Peabody Museum of Salem, Massachusetts
9	Death Certificate – Evanthia Konstant, 1899	Maryland State Archives
9	George Konstant and family, 1905	Mary Konstant Thomas
10	Birth Certificate – Katherine Stavrakos, 1897	Maryland State Archives
10	The Very Rev. Nathanael Sideris	Kotakis, *The Greeks in America*, 1908
10	The Rev. Theodoros Prousianos	Kotakis, *The Greeks in America*, 1908
11	Margarita Coroneos and grandchildren	Catherine Cavacos Capsanes
11	*The Greeks in America* (sample pages), 1908	Chrysoula Carman Ponticas
12	"Atlantis" National Daily Greek Newspaper article published on March 22, 1906	*Fortieth Anniversary Celebration Book*, Greek Orthodox Church "Evangelismos," 1946

1906 – 1915

13	Baltimore City Hall, 1906	The Maryland Historical Society
13	The Very Rev. Joakim Alexopoulos	Canoutas, *Hellenism in America*, 1918
14	Peter and Olga Skalchunes and family, 1909	Stella Poulos Rasp
14	Patriarch Joakim III	Canoutas, *Greek-American Guide*, 1909
15	The Rev. Constantine Douropoulos	Helen Douropoulos Dracos
16	Historical Memorandum, 1908	*Dedication Memorial Book*, 1938
17	Constantine Diamond	Kotakis, *The Greeks in America*, 1908
17	George Sempeles	Kotakis, *The Greeks in America*, 1908
17	Elias and Anastasia Karangelen and family	Efstratios N. Karangelen
18	Certificate of Incorporation, June 4, 1909	Land Records of Baltimore City
18	Constantine Diamond	Kotakis, *The Greeks in America*, 1908
18	Theodore Doukas	Vasiliki Bristow

1916 – 1925

1936 – 1945

1956 – 1965

145	50th Anniversary Dance, 1956	Cathedral Archives
146	50th Anniversary Bazaar, 1956	Cathedral Archives
146	Golden Anniversary Commemorative Pin	Mr. and Mrs. Constantine G. Konstant
147	Bishop Ezekiel at 50th Anniversary Liturgy	Cathedral Archives
147	Rev. George and Presbytera Gallos	John and Katherine Padousis
147	Rev. John and Presbytera Gerotheou	Cathedral Archives
148	Sunday School teachers, 1956	Cathedral Archives
149	Acolytes and Priests, 1956	Cathedral Archives
150	Greek Independence Day Proclamation	Cathedral Archives
150	Presentation to Archbishop Michael	Cathedral Archives
151	Ladies' Tea Guild Fashion Show, 1958	Women's Guild of Annunciation
151	The Annunciation Church Choir, 1958	Presbytera Anna G. Gallos
152-153	Sunday School students and teachers, 1956	Cathedral Archives
154	Alex Zades with students, 1958	Cathedral Archives
154	Parish Councils of 1958 and 1959	Cathedral Archives
155	Education Building brochure, 1959	Cathedral Archives
156	Groundbreaking Ceremony, 1959	Paul Jordan Photography
157	AHEPA donation to parish officials, 1959	Cathedral Archives
157	Paul G. Stamas	Cathedral Archives
157	Education Building, Preston Street, 1960	Cathedral Archives
158	Archbishop Iakovos	Greek Orthodox Archdiocese
158	Cornerstone-Laying, February 1960	Cathedral Archives
159	"Greek Primate to Dedicate Church Center," *The Evening Sun*, May 11, 1961	Original newspaper from the Cathedral Archives
160	GOYA gathering with Father Gallos	Cathedral Archives
161	Annunciation's Senior Choir, 1959	Cathedral Archives
161	Testimonial for Gus Triandos, 1959	Paul Jordan Photography
162	Pappas and Zambounis Wedding, 1961	Mr. and Mrs. Harry P. Pappas
163	Rev. George Gallos at Resurrection Services	Cathedral Archives
163	Annunciation's Junior Choir, 1962	Presbytera Anna G. Gallos
164	Volunteers working in the new kitchen	Lanny Miyamoto Photography
165	Exterior renovations, 1964-65	*Annunciation Herald* / Cathedral Archives
165	Basketball game in parish gymnasium	Paul Jordan Photography
166	Rev. George P. Gallos at the new altar screen	Ellis Malashuk Photography
167	Tea Guild Fashion Show clipping, 1965	Hrysoula Klicos
167	7th Annual Fashion Show program book	Hrysoula Klicos
167	The Rev. Anastasios Voultsos	Paul Jordan Photography
168	Interior renovations, 1964-65	*Annunciation Herald* / Cathedral Archives
168	Peter G. Angelos	Cathedral Archives
169	Article from *The Baltimore Sun*, 1965	Georgia Topal Tangires
170	The Rev. Emmanuel E. Bouyoucas	Cathedral Archives

1966 – 1975

171	Cardinal Shehan and Archbishop Iakovos	Cathedral Archives
172	Icon of the Annunciation (altar screen)	James Keefe Photography
172	Fathers Bouyoucas and Voultsos	Paul Jordan Photography
173	Markulis and Rosemary Wedding, 1966	Mr. and Mrs. Basil G. Markulis
174	Crucifixion of Christ (balcony stained glass)	James Keefe Photography
174	Holy Week, 1967 (newspaper image)	*The Evening Sun* / Cathedral Archives

1986 – 1995

1996 – 2006

Page	Description of Image	From the Collection of...
364	Anthony N. Raptis	Cathedral Archives
364	Niketas A. Konstant	Cathedral Archives
364	John G. Lambros	Cathedral Archives
364	Constantine G. Mesologites	Cathedral Archives
364	George J. Karangelen	Cathedral Archives
365	Constantine J. Pecunes	Cathedral Archives
365	Nicholas L. Karangelen	Cathedral Archives
365	Michael Nicolaides	Cathedral Archives
365	Peter S. Sfekas	Cathedral Archives
365	Nicholas Manos	Cathedral Archives
365	Dionysios Karavedas	Cathedral Archives
365	James P. Karukas	Cathedral Archives
365	Nicholas B. Pergantis	Cathedral Archives
365	George C. Mesologites	Cathedral Archives
365	Anthony J. Xintas	Cathedral Archives
365	Sam Malas	Cathedral Archives
365	C. G. Paris	Cathedral Archives
365	Evan Alevizatos Chriss	Cathedral Archives
365	Paul G. Stamas	Cathedral Archives
365	Jack P. Pillas	Cathedral Archives
365	Peter M. Panopoulos	Cathedral Archives
366	Nicholas S. Morekas	Cathedral Archives
366	James N. Markakis	Cathedral Archives
366	Harry J. Anderson	Cathedral Archives
366	George H. Pappas	Cathedral Archives
366	Charles T. Pavlos	Cathedral Archives
366	Charles G. Pefinis	Cathedral Archives
366	Alex E. Zades	Cathedral Archives
366	Aristides W. Canelos	Cathedral Archives
366	Nicholas J. Kiladis	Cathedral Archives
366	Nicholas C. Lykos	Cathedral Archives
366	Anthony J. Cavas	Cathedral Archives
366	Edward F. Jackovitz	Cathedral Archives
366	Harry P. Pappas	Cathedral Archives
366	August A. Krometis	Cathedral Archives
366	Dr. Thomas Gleason	Cathedral Archives
366	Marinos Svolos	Cathedral Archives
367	George Spanos	George Spanos
367	Constantine Courpas	Cathedral Archives
367	Loretta S. Prevas	Cathedral Archives
367	Larry Burgan	Cathedral Archives
367	Charles Constantine	Cathedral Archives
367	Thomas Marudas	Thomas Marudas
367	Basil M. Pappas	Basil M. Pappas
367	Paul Agathoklis	Paul Agathoklis
367	Gary T. Padussis	Cathedral Archives
367	Michael A. Bouloubassis	Michael A. Bouloubassis
367	Evangelos D. Sidou	Evangelos D. Sidou
367	Georgeann N. Morekas	Georgeann N. Morekas

Name Index

Niktas, Stefanos G.
248, 279, 301

Nixon, Vice President Richard
161

Noplos, Dimitri
210, 264, 266

Noplos, Gregory
210, 264, 266

Noplos, Katrina
210, 262, 263, 264, 266

Noplos, Presbytera Alice
210, 264, 266

Noplos, Rev. Louis J.
210, 213, 216, 218, 220, 222, 224-228, 230, 231,
237, 238, 240, 242-244, 250, 255, 256, 258, 259,
264, 266, 273, 279, 284, 298, 301, 318, 321, 350

Nopulos, Pamela
370

O O'Malley, Mayor Martin
324, 334

Odell, Rev. Mark
194

Oldknow, Dina Skouras
240

Orfanos, Helen
102

Orfanoyianni, Eleni
69

P Padussis, Anthony
140, 143

Padussis, Donna
290, 325, 334

Padussis, Dr. Stephen K.
194, 196, 202, 216, 255, 283

Padussis, Gary T.
248, 257, 258, 264, 280, 282, 283, 288, 290, 304,
319, 320, 325, 326, 334, 367

Padussis, Helen K.
159, 216, 238, 370

Padussis, Theodore
93, 382

Pagonis, Anthony
64

Pakas, Litsa
240

Pamfilis Family
53

Pamfilis, Ann
70, 101, 102

Pamfilis, Betty
81

Pamfilis, Lemonia
70, 103

Pamfilis, Manuel
70

Pamfilis, Stylianos M.
45, 46, 49, 59, 60, 68, 70, 364

Pamfilis, Virginia
70, 101, 102

Panagakos, George
62

Panagakos, George P.
195, 202

Panageotou, Christina
262

Panaggio, Pat
231

Panagiotopoulos, Christos
280, 283, 292

Panagiotopoulos, Yanni
329

Panayiotopoulos, Athanasios
68, 143

Panayiotopoulos, Charles
62

Panopoulos, James M.
149

Panopoulos, Mrs. James (Eva)
148

Panopoulos, Mrs. Peter (Christine)
148

Panopoulos, Peter M.
148, 154, 161, 365

Panos Family
53

Panos, Aphrodite S.
159, 238, 303, 370

Panos, Athanasios
28

Panos, Gus A.
108

Panos, John G.
53, 62, 64, 101

Panos, Louis G.
141, 143, 298

Panos, Nicholas
28

Panos, Patricia T.
65

Panos, Stephanie
205

Panselinos, Effie
251

Panselinos, Martha
265, 285

Panteleakis, Nick
285

Panteleimon, Metropolitan
117

Pantelides, Elaine
179

Pantelides, Gabriel
179, 180

Papachristou, Athan
108

Papachristou, Dimitrios
88, 359

Papachristou, Euripides
140

Papachristou (Pappas), John
359

Papachristou, Maria
88, 359

Papachristou, Themistocles
88, 359

Papachristou, Very Rev. Joakim D.
79, 85-88, 90, 92, 93, 95, 100, 101, 104-107, 111, 112, 115-121, 123-131, 133, 134, 142, 143, 239, 320, 322, 349, 356-362, 373, 382, 393, 395

Papaconstantinou, Rev. Theodoros
7

Papadopoulos, Archimandrite Gerasimos
353

Papadopoulos, Christos
357

Papadopoulos, Deacon Joakim
357, 358

Papadopoulos, Deacon Panteleimon
300

Papadopoulos, Dimitrios
357

Papadopoulos, Giordanis
294

Papadopoulos, Maria Valassis
357

Papadopoulos, Nicholas
32, 116

Papadopoulos, Vasiliki N.
127

Papaioannou, Philimon
67

Papaioannou, Rev. and Bishop George
233, 251, 279, 280, 306, 345

Papaliou, Helen
81

Papaminas, Andrew A.
136, 180

Papaminas, Pat
114

Papanikolaou, Byron
354

Papapavlos, Harriet
69

Papapavlos, Reverend
75

Papapavlos, Theodore
111

Papastamatiou, George
221, 222, 229

Papathanou, Basil
108

Papathomaides, Ann
65, 81

Papavasiliou, Georgia
132

Papoulias, Ambassador George
216

Papoulias, Karolos
227

Pappas Family
53

Pappas, Alexander
278, 323

Pappas, Alexander H.
83, 145

Pappas, Amanda
218

Pappas, Anastazia (Nancy)
290, 370

Pappas, Anna Z.
162, 177, 203, 204, 212, 216, 224, 229, 231, 238, 258, 264, 274, 283, 315, 319, 320, 325, 333, 334, 370

Pappas, Basil M.
243, 248, 256, 290, 367

Pappas, Chrysanthe A.
142, 238, 369, 370

Pappas, Chrysanthy N.
115, 119, 122, 135

Pappas, Fi
370

Pappas, Frank G.
177

Pappas, George
92, 98

Pappas, George F.
305

Pappas, George H.
83, 171, 204, 366

Pappas, Harry G.
27, 31, 51, 53, 59, 91, 92, 198, 203, 204, 364

Pappas, Harry P.
162, 177, 178, 198, 204, 209, 251, 325, 366

Pappas, James N.
215, 290, 292, 310, 314, 320, 331

Pappas, Julia
81

Pappas, Kalliope H.
31, 81, 88, 198, 203, 204, 368

Pappas, Kalliope K.
81, 95, 97

Pappas, Linda
290

Pappas, Michael
84

Pappas, Presbytera Mary
242

Pappas, Rev. Angelo C.
230, 242

Epilogue

There was a growing sense of anticipation among the steamship passengers. The two-week journey across the Atlantic Ocean was nearly over. One can only imagine the overwhelming emotions experienced by Reverend Constantine Douropoulos when the Statue of Liberty finally appeared on the horizon—a magnificent symbol of hope in the New World. Father Douropoulos was traveling with his wife, Alexandra, and their five young daughters. He must have wondered how his family would adapt to their new life in America. Among the priest's possessions was an important document bearing the official seal of the King of Greece. This letter, signed by his superiors at the Holy Synod of Athens, authorized his assignment to a city thousands of miles from his homeland province of Arcadia, Greece.

Over one hundred years have passed since that historic day in 1907 when a pioneering Orthodox clergyman arrived in New York upon the request for a full-time priest from the newly established "Evangelismos" Greek Orthodox Church in Baltimore, Maryland. While the story of the Douropoulos family is significant to the history of Baltimore, it is merely one of thousands of immigrant stories. For each entry on every passenger list of all the ships that arrived, a story filled with hopes, dreams, and sorrows would no doubt unfold. The Greek immigrant experience is filled with hardships, struggles, and great aspirations. The year 1907 was, in fact, a peak year of immigration when over 45,000 Greeks passed through the gates at Ellis Island. Lured from their impoverished villages by the fabled "gold in the streets," the desire of the Greek people to improve their financial status was foremost on their agenda.

With America also serving as a symbol of religious freedom, immigrant groups immediately sought to perpetuate their religious beliefs and traditions in the United States. For decades, members of that immigrant generation fondly reminisced about life in their ancestral villages and related many of their early experiences in America to an attentive audience of children, grandchildren, and great-grandchildren. Vivid recollections told at family gatherings sparked the interest of succeeding generations of Greek-Americans. As a result, in Greek communities across this country, people have developed a special pride for their Orthodox religion and ethnic heritage.

As a tribute to that pioneering immigrant generation, this volume concludes with a magnificent photograph of the Annunciation Church community picnic of 1924. It shows an impressive gathering of members and supporters of the church, over 300 in number, at an event held during the second decade of parish history. The story of the Greek Orthodox Cathedral of the Annunciation is rich with human presence and dedication. A significant number of the Greeks who reached Baltimore made the decision to remain almost immediately. This was to be their country, and they placed firm foundations of family, home, and church. The spring of 1906 brought them into an ecclesiastical experience when they established the first Greek Orthodox house of worship in this city and state. For 100 years, the Annunciation community has stood as a beacon of the Eastern Orthodox faith in Maryland with an array of parish ministries that will undoubtedly flourish well into the next century and beyond.

The "Evangelismos" (Annunciation) community picnic on Sunday, August 17, 1924,
was held at Miller's Park with over 300 people in attendance. The Rev. Symeon Emmanuel,
who served the parish from March 1924 through September 1925, is standing third from the left.

The large banner translates as "Excursion (Outing) of the Greek Community of Baltimore."
Parish council minutes, dated September 3, 1924, document that this highly successful
event resulted in a net profit of over $500—an outstanding amount for that era.

This historic image was captured for posterity by the photography studio of "Cronhardt and Monios."
Raymond N. Cronhardt and Peter Monios operated their business from 226 Park Avenue. Note: A few
attendees are shown displaying an apparently significant edition of the Greek language newspaper, *O Kosmos*.

Proudly reflecting on our past, we continue to be inspired by those pioneering
Greek immigrants whose struggles and sacrifices laid the strong foundation of
faith for the Annunciation Greek Orthodox Cathedral community of today.